VENONA

ALSO BY NIGEL WEST

Spy! (*with Richard Deacon*)
MI5: British Security Service Operations 1909–45
MI6: British Secret Intelligence Service Operations 1909–45
A Matter of Trust: MI5 1945–72
Unreliable Witness: Espionage Myths of World War II
The Branch: A History of the Meteropolitan Police Special Branch
GARBO (*with Juan Pujol*)
GCHQ: The Secret Wireless War
The Friends: Britain's Postwar Secret Intelligence Operations
Molehunt
Games of Intelligence
Seven Spies Who Changed the World
Secret War: The Story of SOE
The Faber Book of Espionage
The Illegals
The Faber Book of Treachery
The Secret War for the Falklands
Counterfeit Spies
The Crown Jewels:
The British Secrets Exposed by the KGB's Archives (*with Oleg Tsarev*)

Fiction
The Blue List
Cuban Bluff
Murder in the Commons
Murder in the Lords

VENONA

The Greatest Secret of
The Cold War

NIGEL WEST

HarperCollins*Publishers*

In Memoriam

Cecil Phillips
1925–1998

HarperCollins*Publishers*
77–85 Fulham Palace Road,
Hammersmith, London W6 8JB

Published by HarperCollins*Publishers* 1999
1 3 5 7 9 8 6 4 2

Copyright © Westintel Research Ltd 1999

The Author asserts the moral right to
be identified as the author of this work

A catalogue record for this book is
available from the British Library

ISBN 0 00 257000 9

Set in Postscript Linotype Meridien
with Castellar display by
Rowland Phototypesetting Ltd,
Bury St Edmunds, Suffolk

Printed and bound in Great Britain by
Caledonian International Book Manufacturing Ltd, Glasgow

All rights reserved. No part of this publication may be
reproduced, stored in a retrieval system, or transmitted,
in any form or by any means, electronic, mechanical,
photocopying, recording or otherwise, without the prior
permission of the publishers.

Contents

	ACKNOWLEDGEMENTS	vii
	AUTHOR'S NOTE	ix
	ABBREVIATIONS	xi
	INTRODUCTION	xiii
I	Breakthrough	1
II	Compromised	39
III	The GRU's London Network	52
IV	The Canberra VENONA	95
V	The Cambridge Ring	121
VI	Operation ENORMOZ	141
VII	The Émigrés	198
VIII	British Security Coordination	216
IX	CLEVER GIRL	223
X	SIMA	236
XI	The HUT	248
XII	The Silvermaster Group	289
XIII	The RAIDER	317
	POSTSCRIPT	327
	APPENDICES	337
	I OSS Personnel Indentified in VENONA as CPUSA Members	339
	II Cryptonyms in 1940–41 London's GRU Traffic	340
	III The GRU *Rezidentura* in London	347
	IV The VENONA Releases	348
	GLOSSARY OF SOVIET COVERNAMES	353
	GLOSSARY OF SOVIET CRYPTONYMS	365
	NOTES	369
	BIBLIOGRAPHY	371
	INDEX	373

Acknowledgements

My thanks are due to the many intelligence professionals who made this book possible. I owe particular gratitude to Meredith Gardner, Cecil Phillips, Robert Louis Benson, Bob Lamphere, Hayden Peake, Stefan Burgland and some others who prefer to remain anonymous; also to Peter Tosic for his translating skills, and Stefan Backlund for his knowledge of STELLA POLARIS.

All the photographs are from my own collection, except those of Ivor Montagu and J.B.S. Haldane (*Hulton Getty*).

Author's Note

Some of the VENONA texts have been edited to make them more easily readable, although care has been taken not to lose any of the intended sense. Where the original translator has expressed a doubt about a particular word, his best guess has been included, and any footnoted identification of a covername or cryptonym has been inserted into the text in square brackets.

Most of the texts contain gaps, which fall into two categories. 'Groups unrecovered' means that, theoretically, they could still be read, although they have defeated cryptographers thus far. Where there are only one or two 'unrecovered' groups, the most likely explanation is a transmission garble in the original version; longer groups are probably as the consequence of obscurity or the use of arcane language. 'Groups unrecoverable' is quite different: it means that the groups are 'unpaired' with other messages, and therefore offer absolutely no possibility of future solution.

Small capitals, such as GREENS, generally indicate a codename, although in some texts they have been used to show that in the original text each letter was spelled individually.

Abbreviations

AFSA	Armed Forces Security Agency
AI-4	Air Intelligence liaison at Bletchley Park
ASIO	Australian Security Intelligence Organization
BCRA	Bureau Centrale de Renseignement et d'Action, Free French Intelligence Service
BSC	British Security Coordination
CAZAB	Canadian, American, New Zealand, Austrian and British counter-intelligence liaison
CIA	Central Intelligence Agency
CIAA	Coordinator of Inter-American Affairs
CIC	Counter-intelligence Corps
CPA	Communist Party of Australia
CPGB	Communist Party of Great Britain
CPUSA	Communist Party of the USA
DST	Direction de la Surveillance du Territoire, French Security Service
FAECT	Federation of Architects, Engineers, Chemists and Technicians
FBI	American Federal Bureau of Investigation
FRA	Forsvarets Radioanstalt, Swedish National Defence Radio Institute
GCCS	Government Code and Cypher School
GCHQ	British Government Communications Headquarters
GRU	Soviet Military Intelligence Service
KDP	German Communist Party
KGB	Soviet Intelligence Service
MI5	British Security Service
MI6	British Secret Intelligence Service
NKVD	Soviet Intelligence Service
NSA	National Security Agency

OGPU	Soviet Intelligence Service
OKW	German High Command
OSS	Office of Strategic Services, USA
PWE	Political Warfare Executive
SDECE	French Intelligence Service
SHAEF	Supreme Headquarters Allied Expeditionary Force
SIS	British Secret Intelligence Service
SIS	Signals Intelligence Service, USA
SOE	Special Operations Executive
SSA	Signals Security Agency, USA
TICOM	Target Identification Committee
UNRRA	United Nations Relief and Rehabilitation Administration
YCL	Young Communist League

Introduction

VENONA is the arbitrarily-chosen codeword given in 1961 to the greatest secret of the Cold War. It represents a collection of nearly three thousand partly decrypted Soviet secret messages sent to and from Moscow between 1940 and 1948, and, as an authentic glimpse into the clandestine activities of the KGB (the Soviet Intelligence Service) and the GRU (the Soviet Military Intelligence Service), was more highly prized than any other similar asset. VENONA was limited in nature, representing only a tiny fraction of the traffic exchanged between individual diplomatic missions abroad and what was referred to as 'the Centre'. Nevertheless, cryptographers in England and the USA continued to study the material until 1980, thirty-seven years after the US Army's Signal Security Agency began work on what was then termed 'the Russian problem'. In the end 2,900 individual messages were translated but, judging from their serial numbers, this was only a small proportion of the total number of Soviet communications, amounting to just under half of the NKVD's New York–Moscow circuit in 1944, 15 per cent of the 1943 traffic (about 200 out of 1,300), and only 23 of the estimated 1,300 telegrams sent in 1942, which represents only 1.8 per cent of the total. As for the Naval GRU, half was recovered from the 1943 Washington–Moscow channel, but none for any other year. In 1940, for instance, the New York GRU is calculated to have sent 992 messages to Moscow, with 335 from the NKVD (Soviet Intelligence Service, 1934–43). Although the VENONA material was recovered from more than a dozen geographical locations, ranging from Bogota to Montreal and Prague, the most illuminating traffic comes from the North American, British and Australian circuits.

VENONA was rightly regarded by the very few counter-intelligence experts indoctrinated into the programme as the holy grail, a vast database of incredibly secret information which provided clues to the identities of thousands of Soviet spies across the globe. Thousands of cryptographic hours and millions of dollars were devoted to accessing an espionage motherlode which proved to be the catalyst for hundreds of investigations, some successful, many less so. When combined with other intelligence information, known as collateral, the bare bones of a VENONA text could be enhanced by the use of footnotes. Often the collateral took the form of surveillance records, and it was physical observation that helped the FBI to work out the senior personalities operating under legal cover in Washington DC, San Francisco and elsewhere. For instance, it was noted that one of the doormen at the Soviet consulate, who was known to participate in counter-surveillance operations, showed unusual deference to a particular, relatively junior, vice-consul, Stepan Apreysan. Apreysan was in fact the local NKVD *rezident* – a figure of greater status than the consul-general himself – and his wife Aleksandra was also a senior NKVD officer, codenamed ZOYA.

As a direct consequence of hints gleaned from the often fragmented texts, Julius and Ethel Rosenberg died in the electric chair, the accusation that Alger Hiss and Harry Dexter White were NKVD agents was confirmed, Klaus Fuchs was imprisoned, Donald Maclean defected and an Australian diplomat fled to Czechoslovakia.

The work on VENONA was considered so secret that the CIA was told of its existence only in 1952. Each time a significant new word was decrypted in a text, or additional collateral had been acquired, the individual text would be recirculated to the handful of security officials who had been allowed to learn about what amounted to the most important codebreaking exercise since ULTRA. While testimony from a handful of Soviet defectors, such as Walter Krivitsky, Victor Kravchenko, Igor Gouzenko and Vladimir Petrov, added flesh to VENONA's bones, more collateral came from disaffected members of the Soviet apparatus in the United States. Whittaker Chambers, Hede Massing and Elizabeth Bentley achieved considerable notoriety for their denunciations of former comrades, and their Congressional evidence was seized on by politicians of all persuasions. The Left condemned an unprincipled witch-hunt of loyal civil servants, the Right demanded a purge of traitors who had penetrated deep into the administration. Alger Hiss proclaimed his innocence and Laurance Duggan committed suicide, but it is VENONA that offers a glimpse of the unvarnished truth.

When word eventually emerged of the existence of a cryptographic goldmine, pressure was applied on the American authorities to

Introduction

release the data that had an historic value, for instance the material that demonstrated the guilt of the Rosenbergs, or implicated Alger Hiss. Until the collapse of the Soviet Bloc, this seemed unlikely, but in 1995 the decision was taken to declassify the entire collection. While this was anathema to some of those who had toiled over VENONA for decades, and had sworn to go to their graves without revealing anything of their work, there were actually few practical reasons for continuing the ban on publication beyond the general principle, often espoused by insiders, that anything said publicly about cryptanalytical methods is damaging. However, with the end of the Cold War there was no necessity to fear the KGB, so the National Security Agency collaborated with the CIA to make public what none had dared hope would ever be seen outside the most closely-guarded government vaults.

The VENONA documents offer a breathtaking insight into Soviet clandestine activities over a period of eight years. Only the final texts have been released, so it is impossible to trace how a particular text developed, perhaps from a few meaningless words into a comprehensible message. If the final versions had been available from the outset, history would have been quite different: the Soviets would have made much slower progress in constructing an atomic bomb and the more notorious spies such as Guy Burgess, Kim Philby and Anthony Blunt would have been rendered impotent many years earlier. The only restriction now placed on release concerns ongoing investigations and the provisions of the US Privacy Act which protects private citizens not previously identified with espionage or active roles in the Communist Party from unwelcome disclosures from official files. This has led to deletions, with sensitive names being blacked out in the American releases. Similarly, the British government demanded some redactions, although the method adopted is more difficult to identify; inexplicable gaps appear in both the VENONA texts and the accompanying footnotes. Whereas the American policy appears to have provided a measure of protection to the living, being those suspected Soviet sources who were never positively identified or confronted with the allegations, their British partners seem to have adopted political embarrassment as their principal criterion for eliminating sensitive names. The only other deliberate excision in the declassified documents is the consistent removal throughout of all references to the first date of circulation. Each

VENONA text is marked with the last, and therefore most recent, distribution, but it is impossible to determine precisely when the first break in a particular message was achieved, or to chart the subsequent progress of the cryptographers.

Nevertheless, the astonishing story of VENONA remains one of the last untold chapters in the history of the Cold War, and goes far to explain many of the mysteries of the postwar era in which spies and counter-spies participated in a conflict largely unseen by anybody except those with the most cosmic of security clearances.

I

Breakthrough

CABLE 906 purported to be a routine circular in seven parts and, as it had come off the wireless circuit linking Tokyo to Berlin and Helsinki, it underwent the usual Allied scrutiny to see if it betrayed any information of strategic significance. Dated 6 October 1942, cable 906 was one of a mass of enciphered communications between Japan and Europe intercepted by Allied radio operators at the Vint Hill Farms Station, outside Warrenton, Virginia, and passed to the staff of thirty-five cryptographers and translators in the Japanese Military Attaché section at Arlington Hall Station (both stations were part of the Signals Security Agency). Although superficially innocuous, in that it appeared to contain nothing directly relevant to the Nazi war effort, it was to have an impact that lasted nearly forty years.

The interception and decryption of Japanese diplomatic traffic by the American Army Cipher Bureau, designated MI-8, dated back to 1919, but its funding was withdrawn at the end of October 1929 by Secretary of State Henry L. Stimson. On his appointment to office, the State Department had informed Stimson that its Black Chamber, located in New York under the commercial cover of the Code Compilation Company Inc, had been secretly reading foreign diplomatic telegrams. Stimson ended the practice forthwith on ethical grounds but, despite his ban, the US Army's team of five cryptanalysts continued to work on what was termed 'the Japanese problem' through the newly created Signals Intelligence Service (SIS) based at the Munitions Building in Washington DC, in parallel with the US Navy's Communications Security section designated OP-20-G. By 1935, after five years of toil, the SIS had achieved considerable success against RED, the 'Type A' cipher machine used by Japanese naval attachés to encrypt messages which were handed over to commercial carriers for onward transmission to Tokyo. As the Berlin–Tokyo Axis began to take shape, the huge volume of Japanese Foreign Ministry telegrams placed an increasing strain on the very limited resources of the Signals Intelligence Service, which boasted a staff of just seven, and an arrangement was made with OP-20-G to share the burden, with SIS handling traffic on even calendar days, and the Navy dealing with the odd days. This collaboration worked well, with SIS doubling its staff to fourteen, until March 1939 when the flow of decrypts suddenly ceased with the unexpected introduction by the Japanese of a more sophisticated replacement unit, the 'Type B', codenamed PURPLE.

The PURPLE cipher generated by the 'Type B' resisted the decoders until 25 September 1940 when the first complete text succumbed and was distributed to the very limited group indoctrinated into the highly classified programme. The breakthrough occurred after twenty months of pure cryptanalysis by a team established by William Friedman, who promptly underwent a nervous collapse. Friedman's subordinate, Frank B. Rowlett, and other cryptanalysts had been able to reconstruct the PURPLE cipher, and thereby develop a replica 'Type B' machine, by exploiting two flaws in Japanese procedures. The first was a common error, known as the stereotype, which consisted of the stilted diplomatic language which convention dictated should begin and end individual telegrams. The predictable repetition of the phrase 'I have the honour to inform Your Excellency' allowed the experts to glimpse the construction of particular messages. The second was the Japanese habit of reproducing word for word the contents of American State Department communiqués. Since the cryptanalysts worked with copies of the original texts, they had little difficulty in retracing the process by which the Japanese had transformed the original words, or plaintext, into cipher. Once Rowlett had grasped the principles upon which PURPLE was based, Lieutenant Leo Rosen was able to build an electro-magnetic device constructed from telephone exchange relays that duplicated the original machine, and by January 1941 a model had been delivered to OP-20-G in Washington DC, and another had been donated to the British Government Communications Headquarters (GCHQ) at Bletchley Park which had hitherto concentrated on the Japanese Navy's hand ciphers.

The Allied window into the Japanese military attaché circuits provided an invaluable source of intelligence, but it was the 906 cable addressed to Colonel Hayashi in Berlin and Major Hirose in Helsinki,

Breakthrough

dated October 1942 and translated early the following year, which proved to be a milestone. The message, written in the solved Japanese military attaché's cipher, disclosed the results of a lengthy Japanese study of Soviet diplomatic and commercial traffic based on material exchanged between the Soviet embassies and consulates in Japan and Manchuria, and the Foreign Ministry in Kuibyshev. The Japanese had been interested in Soviet ciphers for years, dating back at least to 1921, when the Polish Deuxième Bureau had seconded one of its experts, Captain Kowalewski, who was himself of Russian origin, to modernize Tokyo's cryptographic procedures.[1]

An American trawl through previous military attaché telegrams revealed that the first reports on Soviet cryptographic systems had been transmitted to Tokyo on 1 July 1941 from Berlin, Stockholm, Helsinki and Budapest, and evidently since then the Japanese had focused on the Moscow–Vladivostock link, as well as covering the diplomatic missions located at Seoul (Korea), Hakodate (Japan) and Dairen (China). According to the Japanese military attachés, progress on the Soviet project had depended upon help provided in Helsinki by the Finnish authorities.

On 30 November 1939 Stalin, on the spurious pretext of a purported military threat to Leningrad, had ordered twenty-six divisions of the Red Army to invade Finland in what was intended to be a short war of liberation. Although heavily outnumbered, the Finns fought the Soviets to a standstill. The Winter War lasted just 105 days, and left the Russians in occupation of much of the Karelian isthmus, leaving the rest of the country intact. The Finns, exhausted by war, had clearly taken the strategic decision to cooperate with the Japanese, presumably in the hope of drawing Stalin's attention to the Far East. One part of the collaboration was the exchange of cryptographic data, some of which had been gleaned from material recovered in the ruins of the Soviet consulate at the port of Liinahamari in Petsamo, in the extreme north of Finland. The Soviet 104th and 52nd Divisions had occupied Petsamo since the December 1939 offensive, but on 22 June 1941 the consulate had been overrun by Finnish troops before NKVD staff could completely destroy their codebooks. The isolated building, which also housed the British, German and Swedish consulates, overlooked the deep, ice-free harbour which was a valuable Finnish asset at the end of the narrow Petsamo corridor, providing valuable access to the Barents Sea.[2]

3

The recovered 'Petsamo documents', four partially burnt diplomatic codebooks, had encouraged the Finns, who had established a listening post at Otaniemi, just to the west of Helsinki, to monitor Soviet and American diplomatic traffic. They attempted to read some Soviet messages, and the results, shared with the Japanese, enabled Tokyo to break some messages from Harbin in China written in an emergency system. The four codebooks were a diplomatic codebook designated Kod-26; the NKVD *Pobeda* (Victory) code; one for use by the GRU; and one for use by the Naval GRU. Studied in conjunction with medium-grade military crypto items recovered from the battlefield, which included at least one NKVD Border Guards' codebook, the material allowed the Finnish analysts to understand how the Soviets adapted military terminology in their systems, built code-tables and relied on a very straightforward mathematical formula to encode emergency signals. The Finns placed a heavy emphasis on cryptography, and Field Marshal Mannerheim's crucial victory against the Soviet motorized 44th and 163rd Divisions at Suomussalmi, a turning-point in the Winter War, had been largely due to advance knowledge of the enemy's strategy gleaned from intercepted signals.

The collaboration between Finland and Japan was not as extraordinary as it may perhaps sound more than fifty years later. Although not a formal member of the Axis, and technically neutral for the first two years of the war, Finland participated in the assault on the Soviet Union the following year. Britain finally declared war on Finland on 6 December 1941, so by the time the 906 circular was intercepted, the Helsinki authorities had developed a strong relationship with the Axis countries (Germany, Italy, Japan). The fact that an NKVD Border Guards' codebook had fallen into Japanese hands, and had been passed to the Germans, was soon reported to Moscow by Harro Schulze-Boysen, an Air Ministry official in Berlin and GRU spy. His wife, Libertas, was having an affair with another member of his network, Horst Heilmann, who was a military intelligence (Abwehr) cryptographer. Most likely, Heilmann came across the Soviet codebook during the course of his work and alerted Schulze-Boysen, who relayed the news to his controller. However Moscow heard of it, there was nothing that could be done to retrieve the situation, and the Finns, the Germans and the Japanese continued to concentrate on the 'Russian military message problem' for the rest of the war.

Breakthrough

At the end of hostilities, on 17 September 1944, the Finns feared that, as had happened in Romania, the country would be occupied by the Soviets. A group of nearly 800 intelligence officers and their families, led by the Chief of Military Intelligence, Colonel Aladár Paasonen, and the head of the Signals Intelligence (Sigint) section, Colonel Reino Hallamaa, participated in Operation STELLA POLARIS, an extraordinary undertaking that remains both controversial and politically significant in Helsinki to this day.

Paasonen, still regarded as the father of Finnish cryptography, was a brilliant linguist who had been taught most European languages by his Hungarian mother and had studied Soviet cipher systems in Germany, Poland and the Baltic. Although it was Paasonen who had made the first purchases of intercept equipment in Italy in the 1920s, the principal figure in STELLA POLARIS was Hallamaa, who was convinced that Finland was about to become a Soviet surrogate. To some extent he was proved correct, for the Communist Party, together with the Social Democrats, held the majority in the first postwar government and the Security Police fell into its hands. As well as achieving considerable success with Soviet ciphers, Paasonen's department had recruited and run dozens of Soviet sources and he knew that both they and their case officers would be doomed if the NKVD got its hands on his files. In addition, Paasonen ran a commando battalion, designated ErP4, which operated behind Soviet lines and whose membership was also at considerable risk. Accordingly, with the tacit approval of the Finnish President, Field Marshal Gustaf Mannerheim, and his military Chief of Staff, General Erik Heinrichs, Hallamaa had invited his Swedish counterpart, Major Carl Petersén, the Director of Defence Staff's intelligence branch known as the C-Bureau, to open negotiations in June 1944 at his villa at Soukka, just outside Helsinki. His objective was to gain Swedish consent to his plan to re-establish his entire organization in Sweden from where it would continue operations against the Soviets. For their part, the Swedes knew that if Finland fell to the Soviets, their own territory would then become the front line, and few doubted that Stalin's ambitions included the whole of Scandinavia. Petersén was also aware that, as well as possessing useful assets across the Soviet frontier, the Finnish codebreakers had accomplished far more than the Swedish Sigint branch, known as the Swedish National Defence Radio Institute (FRA), then headed by Commander Torgil Thorén.

Relations between the FRA, which had been created in 1942, and the Finns, had been sufficiently close to allow Thorén to second one of his subordinates, Captain Åke Rossby, to Helsinki during part of the Russian–Finnish war, and he was again chosen to negotiate with Hallamaa. However, Thorén himself was kept deliberately isolated from the STELLA POLARIS plans because he had become distrustful of the Finns following an incident earlier in the war when the Finnish military attaché in Stockholm, Colonel Stewen, tipped off the Abwehr to the success the Swedes had achieved in intercepting and decrypting teletype traffic on the German Oslo–Berlin landline which happened to pass through the capital's telegraph exchange.

The extent to which the talks conducted by Hallamaa, Petersén and Rossby were officially authorized remains a matter of speculation, with both governments insisting, probably to assuage Moscow, that they were an unauthorized private venture. Nevertheless, Mannerheim and Heinrichs knew of the scheme, as did the Chief of the Swedish Defence Staff, Major-General C. A. Ehrensvärd. Whatever the truth, and it is still politically delicate, Hallamaa assigned two subordinates, Lieutenant-Captain Heikki Paulio and Lieutenant Veikko Virkkunen, to plan STELLA POLARIS, and they completed the preparations by the end of August 1944. A secret meeting was held by Hallamaa at his headquarters at Mikkeli to brief the heads of his five intelligence units – Lieutenant-Commander Pekka Visa, his brother Captain Paavo Visa, and Captains Mauri Hartikainen, Aarre Tunkelo and Bror Erkki Sten Pale – who were instructed to gather their equipment and families at the ports of Närpiö (near Kaskinen) and Uusikaupunki, ready to embark on the *Lokki* and two other coastal steamers for the voyage to Sweden. To ensure a proper reception, Virkkunen was transferred to the Finnish legation in Stockholm as assistant military attaché with instructions to represent the C-Bureau and make contact with his Axis counterparts, the Japanese General Makato Onodera, and the Abwehr's Büro Wagner. Elsewhere, the other two STELLA POLARIS components were put into action: Colonel Jussi Sovio led the ErP4 commandos to Liminka, conveniently close to the Swedish frontier; and ErP4 vehicles, trailers packed with Sigint equipment, were moved to Torneo, with orders to drive over the border to Haparanda at a moment's notice.

The first group of intelligence personnel left Närpiö for Härnösand on 20 September 1944 aboard the *Lokki*, the *Maininki* and the *Georg*; the others sailed for Gävle on the *Osmo* the next day. Upon arrival most of the 'refugees' were accommodated at a displaced persons' camp while their archives and equipment were taken by ship in more than 700 crates to a secret Swedish army store in a cave outside Härnösand, and then moved, not to the FRA's headquarters on the island of Lövön, but to a separate FRA facility in Stockholm at Karlaplan 4. Finally, the cipher documents were moved to the cellars of the Hotel Aston where, over a period, they were photographed by Pale and put on to microfiche using equipment supplied by the Finnish press attaché Heikki Brotherus. The film was then sent to Colonel Uljas Käkönen in Helsinki for processing, and when Pale finally left Stockholm in March 1945 he was carrying 900 metres of undeveloped film which was later returned to his C-Bureau successor in Stockholm, Lieutenant Pentti Hartikainen.

In November 1944, once the 'Stellists' were safely established in Sweden, a delegation of senior Finnish officers, led by the Chief of Staff and including Lieutenant-General Harald Öhquist, the Chief of Military Finance Colonel Runar Bäckström, Colonel Martin Stewen, the Finnish military attaché, Colonel Hans von Essen, Major Emil Lautkari and Captain Erkki Sten Pale, arrived in Stockholm to negotiate the sale of all the crypto equipment to the FRA director, Commander Torgil Thorén, for 252,875 Crowns. The deal, which was completed on 10 January 1945 in Stockholm's Grand Hotel, included the boxes of Soviet ciphers and codes, was backdated to 1 July 1944, the day before the armistice, and the name of a Swedish manufacturer was placed on the actual bill of sale, together with that of another service officer, Colonel Johan Ståhlström. According to General Öhquist, the Soviet material was crucial to the sale, which the Swedes would not conclude without it, and a separate annexe was completed which gave the Swedes control over the archival material for fifty years. This was signed by the general on behalf of the Finnish Defence Minister, General Rudolf Walden, but the exact nature of the 'property owned by the Finnish Defence Forces' sold was not specified, so as to ensure that the transaction was a strictly private one between Finnish officials and Swedish individuals.

Altogether, 100 boxes of Soviet cryptographic material was transferred by Captain Pale in March 1945 to a mansion run by the FRA, and Major Emil Lautkari delivered the other archives to an FRA flat. In addition, Lautkari supervised the construction by the Stellist refugees of a radio facility at Lidingö, outside Stockholm, which was used to open a radio channel with Colonel Paasonen in Helsinki. There Colonel Uljas Käkönen and Lieutenant Tauno Kylmänoja developed what amounted to a 'stay-behind' network in anticipation of a Soviet takeover. Another line of communication was maintained with the military radio station at Rauhanniemi, in the extreme east of the country, through the Finnish legation in Stockholm where Lieutenant Pentti Hartikainen and a secretary, Anneli Martola, had access to the diplomatic bag. According to a British Secret Intelligence Service report from the local station commander, Rex Bosley, 'all the "Stellists" in Sweden received a regular weekly salary in kronor and those who worked in Pale's bureau received a monthly salary varying from 400 to 1,000 kronor'.[3]

Fifty years later, the precise fate of the STELLA POLARIS archives remains a mystery. The Swedes insisted that twenty-nine boxes of the files, which were later traced to the manor house of Rottnerös, owned by an industrialist, Major Svente Påhlson, and 136 cases traced to Hörningsholm, the ancestral home of a royal equerry, Count Carl Bonde, were removed and burnt in November 1960. Both men were respected figures with considerable interests in Finland and appear to have acted in a semi-official capacity, storing the STELLA POLARIS files with the deniable knowledge of the Swedish authorities. Major Påhlson, whose estate included a large pulpmill, was a former director of the Defence Staff's security section, and he held strong views about the need for Scandinavian unity. His death in 1959, and the reluctance of his son to be further involved in keeping the files in the basement, may have prompted their destruction, which was carried out at an incineration plant at Löfsta by Captain Pehr Swartz, acting on instructions of the Swedish Commander-in-Chief, Lieutenant-General C. A. Ehrensvärd.

Doubt also surrounds what happened to the money paid for the Soviet material, although Colonel Hallamaa is known to have joined French intelligence with Paasonen after the war, and to have bought a substantial estate at Churriana in Spain, where he died in August 1979. The affair became public knowledge in November 1946 when an embarrassed Finnish government issued an official but highly disingenuous communiqué, explaining the entire episode, which Rex Bosley relayed to London:

Breakthrough

In the summer of 1944 the Finnish High Command asked the Swedish military authorities whether certain wireless equipment and personnel could be transferred to Sweden in the event of a military occupation of Finland. It was at the outset made clear by the Swedes that the establishment of a Finnish intelligence unit in Sweden could in no circumstances be permitted, but that there would be no objection in principle to the transfer of equipment and personnel, though the latter would be liable to internment if still in military service. The matter was dropped for the time being, but shortly before the Finnish armistice, the Finns expressed a desire to ship equipment and personnel to Sweden. Authority was given for their reception at Härnösand and Gävle, where they arrived in considerably larger numbers than the Swedes had contemplated, including women and children. They were treated as ordinary refugees, for such persons as had held military rank were already demobilised, and the majority had already returned to Finland. As regards the equipment, part of this was sold by the Finnish State to the Swedish State and negotiations in respect thereof were carried out by duly authorised representatives on either side. Payment had been made to a properly accredited Finnish authority and such equipment as was not purchased was returned to Finland. A number of packing cases containing archives had arrived with the equipment; these were not taken over by the Swedish authorities, but deposited with private individuals by an authorised Finnish representative.[4]

This version was far from the full story, which the Finnish Security Police learned only as some of the Stellists returned to Helsinki at the end of the war and were arrested. Erkki Pale underwent twenty months' imprisonment and interrogation, and was eventually confronted with a carbon copy of the STELLA POLARIS sale contract. As well as being infuriated by the circumvention, the Finnish Communists suspected, wrongly as it turned out, that the almost defunct German intelligence service had played a role in the affair, a claim made initially in the Communist *Ny Dag*. Certainly the Germans had trained and equipped a resistance network in Finland in early 1945 in anticipation of the widely expected Soviet occupation, but the members of the 'Buro Cellarius' had been rounded up in 1946. Named after a certain Captain Cellarius, it had been led by a prominent Nazi, Major Alarich Bross, who had evacuated his Sonderkommando Nord to Swinemünde in Germany, and ran a radio station at Pitäjänmäki, managed by his subordinate Thoralf Kyrre. Even after the Finnish armistice Bross continued to infiltrate saboteurs across the Baltic by plane and by U-boat, and it was only after the organization had been broken up that the Security Police were satisfied that the Sonderkommando Nord had not masterminded STELLA POLARIS, although suspicion remained that the millions of roubles accumulated by the Buro Cellarius to finance an anti-Soviet guerrilla organization and which subsequently disappeared, may have been used to pay for STELLA POLARIS.

Until the Finnish documents fell into American hands in 1945 there was some uncertainty about how the Finnish cryptographers had achieved their success with the Soviet code, but the work described in the 906 circular, and parallel analysis of a further two dozen Soviet military systems which had been in the Helsinki–Tokyo military attaché exchange, encouraged the SIS's successor, the Signals Security Agency (SSA) to do the same. The Japanese military attaché messages made it clear that the Finns had solved some military systems and reconstructed the codes involved, although the only help in regard to Soviet diplomatic and trade traffic was a method of distinguishing between the two, and there were some references to the Soviet emergency diplomatic systems which had been solved by the Japanese. When GCHQ made the STELLA POLARIS material available in 1946, the breadth of the Finnish work could be clearly understood by the SSA.

Based at what had been SIS's wartime headquarters at Arlington Hall Station in northern Virginia, formerly the financially troubled Arlington Junior College for Girls, the SSA had inherited a large quantity of prewar Soviet intercepts which had baffled the analysts, and in June 1942 had agreed with the US Navy and the FBI to take responsibility for dealing with diplomatic problems. Certainly the SSA had no shortage of raw material on which to work, for as well as acquiring the prewar collection of Soviet intercepts, the agency had immediate access to all the current Soviet telegrams on the

Breakthrough

New York–Moscow–Washington DC circuits which were sent by commercial carriers. Couriers from the embassy, consulate and trade missions made daily deliveries to Western Union, and by law the company was obliged to copy each telegram and supply it upon request to the US Office of Censorship, then headed by General Corderman who, in 1943, commanded Arlington Hall. Thus the SSA, which was to employ 7,000 men and (mainly) women at Arlington Hall, created an archive of thousands of enciphered texts each of which consisted of varying quantities of five-figure groups. Apart from the recipient's cable address in Moscow, and the identity of the paying originator, there was absolutely nothing to give a clue to the content of the messages.

News of the Japanese–Finnish exchanges inspired Colonel Carter W. Clarke, Chief of the Military Intelligence Special Branch, to direct Arlington Hall to create a new unit to start work on the accumulated collection of Soviet intercepts. Examination started on 1 February 1943 when a recently hired local schoolteacher of home economics, Gene Grabeel, who was one of a large number of civilians newly brought in as support staff, began the task of sorting the telegrams into categories based on the distinct groups identified by the Finns. Grabeel and her team, headed by Lieutenant Leonard M. Zubko, who had been at Arlington for several months working on the Japanese military attaché system, soon established from the Moscow cable address that more than half the texts were designated 'Trade', and had originated with the Soviet trade organization known as Amtorg, and with the Purchasing Commission. These messages were designated colours, RED, GREEN and LAVENDER, and the remaining categories were later found to be cipher systems employed by the NKVD, the People's Commissariat for Foreign Affairs, the GRU and Naval GRU. While the Foreign Ministry traffic was easily recognizable from the fact that it was used by every Soviet embassy and consulate, the GRU and Naval GRU were not identified until 1946, after the defection of the GRU cipher clerk Igor Gouzenko, and the NKVD material had to wait until 1948 for absolute proof of its affiliation, although its espionage content had been recognized by the American cryptanalyst Meredith Gardner two years earlier. However, progress under Zubko, a Slavic linguist, was slow and the project was restarted by Captain Ferdinand Coudert, a son of one of the famous Coudert Frères international lawyers who had lived in Russia. Unfortunately,

Coudert had no cryptanalytical skills and he was replaced in November 1943 by Captain William B. S. Smith, a shrewd cryptanalyst who targeted the Russian diplomatic problem and set the scene for Oliver Kirby to take over in 1946.

Having completed the long and hard process known as 'discrimination', the SSA set about the task of searching for clues and rebuilding the Soviet trade codebooks, the first stage of the Soviet encipherment procedure for all the diplomatic systems. Each organization possessed one or more codebooks that transformed frequently-used words, phrases, syllables, numbers and punctuation marks into four-digit numbers. These were then transformed by adding them to key numbers taken from one-time codepads bearing sixty random five-digit numbers on each page. Only the sender and the receiver had copies of the cipherpad and as long as each sheet was used only once and then destroyed, the code would be unbreakable.

Words that did not appear in the codebook were dealt with by using a 'spell/endspell' arrangement, so the text 'Meet ROSA at Central Post Office' would be transformed into:

Meet	(SPELL)	R	O	S	A	(ENDSPELL)	at	Central	Post Office
3219	7454	66	44	72	01	99	0297	1371	5437

On the basis that the codebook contained a codegroup for the words 'meet', 'at', 'Central' and 'Post Office', but no codegroup for ROSA, the message would be constructed by building the word ROSA. The codegroup 7454 means 'begin spelling' and the numbers 66, 44, 72, 01 are taken from a two-digit spelltable. The two-digit group 99 (endspell) instructs the cipher clerks to return to the normal code. The resulting text is then grouped in units of five in preparation for the addition of the key from the one-time pad (OTP). These five-digit groups would then be altered or 'reciphered' by the arithmetical addition (using the Fibonacci system which does not carry over numbers) of the appropriate five-figure 'additive' groups selected from the current one-time pad. Provided the recipient possessed the relevant pad and codebook, returning the cipher into plaintext was straightforward, though there were two additional complications. Whereas the chosen language was, of course, Russian, using the Cyrillic alphabet, a 'spell-code' was employed for those occasional awkward words or phrases that did not translate easily from the

Breakthrough

Cyrillic and Latin alphabets. The other complexity, particularly characteristic of the NKVD and GRU traffic, was the appearance of a kind of intelligence jargon. Local counter-intelligence agencies were known as GREENS, the Communist Party as CORPORATION, and the GRU as NEIGHBOURS, etc. Thus, for the uninitiated, even a plaintext version of a ciphered telegram might have little obvious meaning. While the word GREENS appeared in the Russian codebook against the appropriate codegroup, there was nothing on paper to indicate what the GREENS were. That knowledge could be deduced only after studying the context of many messages referring to GREENS, or alternatively seeking the help of someone privy to the system's secrets.

Beyond this private language of the NKVD and GRU, the system's intrinsic integrity against almost any kind of code-clerk error lay in the double level of security offered by the codebooks and the one-time pads. Even though each message contained an 'indicator' to tell the authorized recipient which page number had been selected, there was no chance of anyone else reconstructing the OTPs unless they had access to the manufacturing process. In the trade traffic, the indicator that told the cipher clerk which OTP page to use was the last two digits of the first five-figure group; and in one distinctive series of diplomatic telegrams, in a system designated ZDJ and later called JADE (the colour code of the codebook), the subtraction of the penultimate group from the last group was always 22222. Quite rightly, Moscow enjoyed complete confidence in this arrangement for, when managed properly, it meant that the acquisition of one organization's codebook would not compromise the messages sent using another's. Furthermore, because each page of the OTP was only employed once, the danger of potentially dangerous duplication was avoided. Finding repetition is at the heart of all successful cryptanalytical attacks, and the OTPs eliminated that risk, at least in theory. To protect the OTPs themselves from tampering or photography, they were distributed to designated cipher-clerks in special pouches, and kept under constant armed guard.

Although the Finns had enjoyed the huge advantage of access to what were to become known as the Petsamo documents, the SSA staff had none to begin with, and, in the absence of any original plaintexts, were obliged to use classic cryptanalytical techniques to develop the codebook. Much of this was accomplished by Meredith

Gardner, a linguist rather than a cryptanalyst, who exploited the unbelievable but nevertheless undeniable fact that the Soviets had compromised the integrity of their own systems by reusing the one-time pads.

Under normal circumstances the numbers printed on OTPs would be generated randomly, and single sheets, each unique, would be bound into books and used consecutively. However, eight months after Gene Grabeel had started her discrimination work, one of the Arlington Hall cryptographers, Lieutenant Richard Hallock, a Signals Corps reservist who had been an archaeologist at the University of Chicago and had been assigned to the project, realized that many of the sheets used in different systems had been duplicated, and once the beginning of a page had been spotted, the rest of it could be predicted. It was to be another six or eight months before he, with Mary Jo Dunning, Dr Burton Phillips and Genevieve Feinstein, could begin to extract the underlying numerical codegroups at the message beginnings in a few highly stereotyped texts – long shipping messages divided into parts for transmission. Following Hallock's discovery, prolonged study of JADE by Cecil Phillips and Genevieve Feinstein revealed an astonishing fact: the JADE material had been enciphered using precisely the same OTPs as the trade traffic.

Exactly what prompted this grotesque breach of security has never been explained, but the blunder took place in late 1942, at a time when the Soviet administration was under intense pressure following the Nazi invasion. The answer may lie in precisely how the Soviets generated their random numbers, for it is a cryptographic principle that it is almost impossible truly to replicate the random selection of numbers (a room full of people typing digits will eventually succumb to the rules of 'psychological random'). Interest in this was heightened when T. A. (Tom) Wagoner, while attempting to solve German diplomatic one-time pads, copies of which had been illicitly acquired from a courier's bag, made an astonishing discovery. Extended cryptographic analysis showed that the sheets of five-figure numbers were far from random, and eventually a pattern emerged which suggested that each page had been printed by a machine, with a single carbon copy, and stamped separately with a page number. Once this had been realized, the GCHQ liaison officer, Brigadier John Tiltman, recognized the distinctive process of a single, commercially-available Lorenz machine. This breakthrough had enabled the

Breakthrough

cryptographers to re-create their own versions of the one-time pads. Buoyed by this remarkable achievement, attention was turned to the Soviet OTPs, and two suggestions have been made about how they were developed. One witness has described a room full of women calling out numbers, while the defector Igor Gouzenko recalled a mechanical device, not unlike a lottery machine, in which numbered balls rolled into a frame. However, the best evidence came from Vladimir Petrov who had actually worked in the room which printed the Soviet ciphers. He remembered a machine with a flashing blue light, attached by cable to an inner sanctum to which he never had access. Such a device did exist in the West, turning electrical impulses generated on a filament into random numbers, and a lengthy but ultimately fruitless search was made by GCHQ in case a patent had been registered.

Whichever system had been adopted by the Russians, it had clearly proved impractical in the hectic atmosphere of the Wehrmacht's advance towards Moscow, and as an expedient some 70,000 pages were duplicated and then inserted, often in different order, into one-time pads for distribution to cipher clerks who doubtless never realized the fundamental flaw that had accidentally been introduced into the system. Altogether 35,000 duplicates were found, about half the estimated total, probably representing the total production of between three and six months. The earliest use was traced to May 1942, and the majority were used between July 1942 and July 1943. Hallock's discovery of the duplicate pages, which continued to appear in Soviet traffic until June 1948, allowed his colleagues to make impressive progress on the texts, of which there were an abundance between 1942 and 1944, a period of dramatic escalation in the volume of Soviet cable traffic overseas. In retrospect, the most plausible explanation for the error is human failure. Someone, somewhere in the manufacturing chain, simply doubled the output of OTPs by running off extra copies of pages that were never intended to be duplicated. This astonishing act of negligence served to undermine the intrinsic security of the OTPs and ultimately allowed British and American cryptographers to achieve what theoretically should have been impossible. Prolonged study by a team led by Cecil Phillips and including Frank Lewis, Genevieve Feinstein, Lucille Campbell and Frank Wanat, demonstrated that hundreds of OTPs used to recipher trade messages had been used for the same purpose by the NKVD.

Originally a private secretary in the civil service, and trained as a professional musician, Frank Lewis had been sent to Arlington Hall by the US Army in 1938 and subsequently had become the leading expert on Japanese army ciphers. He spent much of the war as Colonel Solomon Kullback's top civilian in the Japanese Section, which then consisted of some 2,000 people working three shifts, seven days a week. He undertook several tours with GCHQ in England, was at Bletchley Park when the war ended, and in his spare time compiled crossword puzzles for *The Nation* magazine.

In late 1943 Lewis produced a method of aligning page numbers that exposed several hundred more duplicates in the trade traffic; Frank Wanat, a Navy chief from the Naval Security Group, spotted similar characteristics in the Havana–Moscow traffic; and Lucille Campbell had been alongside Cecil Phillips when in November 1944 he noticed an excess of the number 6 in the first group of NKVD messages. These were vital faults that made the banal trade traffic so crucial, and the NKVD texts so vulnerable.

Lewis's discovery was not without its drama, for he had only been working in the section for a fortnight when he and Lieutenant Karl Elmquist exploited Hallock's lead. Together they found that further duplications could be traced both forwards and backwards if the original seven 'hits' in the messages were aligned page by page in sending order. This meant that the duplicate pages had been only partially reshuffled, and suggested tremendous possibilities, depending upon the scale of duplication. Unfortunately no one remembered to inform Colonel Rowlett of what had been achieved, and he learned of it only through a chance encounter with Kullback in the men's room, resulting in a series of administrative changes, and a permanent ban on Lewis and Elmquist entering the Diplomatic Section.

The first stage of the cryptographic attack was to establish the extent of the Russian error, and this was achieved by Hallock who transferred on to IBM punchcards the first five groups from 10,000 trade messages, on the basis that the first few words of any telegraphic message, regardless of origin, are likely to be stereotypic, probably containing the words 'to' and 'from', and perhaps a date and a potentially predictable serial number. Much of this work was supervised by Mary Jo Dunning, who had been hired by Arlington Hall in 1938 as an IBM key punch operator, and who was to become an impressive cryptographer, acting in tandem with Genevieve Feinstein. The cards were sorted automatically by an IBM machine and the comparison revealed seven matching pairs of trade messages, with at least two of the five-figure groups identical. If the OTP numbers had been genuinely random, the odds of finding seven such matches were calculated to be about 1,000 million to one. To find seven meant that the Soviets had indeed blundered. A tiny crack could now be exploited and much of 1944 was spent recovering codegroups from the paired trade messages. By the autumn this slow process had revealed that three different codes had been used in the trade messages at the same time, two being a five-digit code, the other being a four-digit code. Hallock and his colleagues made good progress on the trade texts, to the point that they were able to predict opening phrases and acquire tentative codegroups which were stored in the indexed key banks of IBM punchcards.

In late October, Cecil Phillips, who had studied chemistry at college and who had been posted to Arlington Hall in June 1943 because he 'knew what cryptography meant and passed the IQ test', became entranced with VENONA's possibilities. Initially he had been posted to Lieutenant William Haslep's section of nearly fifty people concentrating on Japanese Navy weather messages, but this work had become superfluous when an enemy codebook had been recovered intact by US Marines on a Pacific island, and on 1 May 1944 he had been assigned to the Soviet ambassadorial system, ZDA, hoping to find duplicate key pages that had been found in the trade messages. He also studied JADE with Lucille Campbell and noticed there were 'too many sixes' in the first group of ZDJ messages, or rather a disproportionate occurrence of that digit which appeared twice as often as would have been expected, a phenomenon that suggested it was not accidental. Further analysis by the section's chief cryptographer, Genevieve Feinstein, led to a full-scale comparison between the first groups in the JADE traffic and the trade data. They were found to be identical, and when Burton Phillips and Katie McDonald delved further they found several hundred duplicate keys in the New York JADE traffic and the Washington trade messages.

Hitherto it had been believed that JADE and its predecessors, DDE and JDF, were consular in nature, mainly because of their heavy use in New York, where the Soviet consulate general was located, and the fact that they were hardly used in Washington until 1943.

This mistaken belief led to greater resources being devoted to the Soviet diplomatic system, JDA, but in 1945 Katie McDonald, helped by Marie Meyer, a University of Chicago linguist, and Alice Joys, a student of Russian, identified the codegroups for months, punctuation and numbers from 1 to 100. This achievement coincided with the end of the war in the Far East which allowed members of the Japanese Army Section to be deployed against the Russian problem, and meant that more clerical staff became available to give support to the cryptographers.

Having had the duplicates 'dug out' by dozens of young women, among them Gene Grabeel and Katie McDonald, Gardner concentrated on the Soviet spellcode employed to encipher English words. Gardner, who had already worked on the trade traffic designated GREEN, tried to identify propositions and conjunctions first, followed by other common terms, including spelling syllables, and started to assign Russian meanings to the numeric codegroups. This, effectively, was reconstructing by analysis a Soviet codebook, and after much effort he found a message from New York in the JADE series dated 18 May 1944 which was entirely in English, and therefore had been enciphered with the spellcode:

> Your No. 2106, second paragraph:
> 'If election were held today R [President Roosevelt] would probably obtain slender majority of popular vote but lose election due heavy concentration his vote in South where his big majorities count no more in final result than would simple 51 percent.'

Although the groups containing the signature were unrecovered, Gardner had spotted that the codegroup for 't-i-o-n' had been repeated three times in quick succession, and this enabled him to read the rest, the answer to a request from Moscow for clarification of telegram number 2106. The content was obviously political – explaining how the President could lose in the Electoral College despite heavy Democratic support in the South – and not consular, and the use of English suggested a quote from an American political source. This was proof that JADE was diplomatic in nature, and might be broken to reveal evidence of espionage.

The value of Gardner's work really became apparent when, on 31 July 1946, he began to read a message sent to the head of the

Breakthrough

NKVD's foreign intelligence branch, Lieutenant-General Pavel M. Fitin, codenamed VIKTOR, in Moscow on 10 August 1944, from the New York *rezident*, Stepan Apresyan, codenamed MAY, on the subject of coding procedures in Mexico.

> No. 1142
> Your No. 3502
> 1. In accordance with a decision of the HOUSE [Comintern] SISKIN and KARLOS [Christian Cananova] before departure from TYRE [New York] were instructed in the use of a reciphered code which they were to [46 groups unrecoverable] alphabet and in addition SISKIN was to write in English and KARLOS in Spanish. We cannot establish whether the pads for the codes were sent home since they were entered under the heading 'SISKIN's Business' and 'KARLOS's Business' [4 groups unrecovered] there are no inventories. From TYRE no enciphered letters were sent by [or to] SISKIN and KARLOS. Both codes ended up in STOCK's [Mikhail. A. Shalyapin] hands.
> 2. For correspondence with ARTHUR a book in the Spanish language 'Una Excursion a Los Indios Ranqueles' was used as a code.
> 3. For correspondence with ALEKSANDR the books 'My Sister Eileen' and 'Defense Will Not Win War' were used as codes.
> 4. For correspondence with MARGO [Margarita Neklen] the book 'Opera' which was sent to you in accordance with your instructions, was used.
> 5. For correspondence with HARRY [Jacob Epstein], JUAN [Juan Gaytan] and ANITA books were used whose titles were not kept since they were destroyed after the departure of LUKA [Pavel Klarin] to the COUNTRYSIDE [Mexico].
> 6. In a sample cipher square TWAIN [Semyon Semyonov] trained [34 groups unrecoverable] ... ZUL, PAUL which were destroyed and for STAFFMAN which we are dispatching to you by the next regular post.

This was a hugely significant text because it was patently an espionage message, probably NKVD, and proved beyond doubt that it was really possible to read important intelligence communications; hitherto there had been a strong suspicion that the JADE collection of encrypted intercepts were consular telegrams of no intelligence interest whatsoever. This text mentioned numerous NKVD assets by their codenames, of whom Semyon Sam' Semyonov (TWAIN) and Pavel Klarin (LUKA) were very familiar to the FBI as members of the New York *rezidentura*, while Mikhail Shalyapin (STOCK) was listed officially as a humble clerk. ARTHUR, ALEKSANDR, ANITA, PAUL and STAFFMAN could not be identified, but by May 1972, when the text was reissued for the last time, collateral evidence had named KARLOS as Christian Cananova Subercaseaux, JUAN as Juan Gaytan Gody, MARGO as Margarita Neklen Hansberger de Paul and HARRY as Jacob Epstein. It subsequently emerged that the 10 August message was but one in a series, with references to KARLOS appearing in nine other VENONA signals, in a time span between May 1943 and December 1944.

On 13 December 1946 a further major breakthrough was made with another telegram from Apresyan in New York, dated 25 July 1944. It was apparently based on a conversation between one of his *rezidentura*'s staff, codenamed SUK, and BEAR, a leading figure in the Republican Party, concerning Thomas Dewey's (KULAK) chances in the November presidential elections. SUK's unidentified source correctly forecast that President Roosevelt (codenamed CAPTAIN) would be re-elected handsomely.

> To VIKTOR
> On 9th July SUK had a confidential chat with BEAR who expressed his opinion on a number of questions connected with the election campaign. While regarding KULAK [Dewey] as 'a rising star' who 'would probably become president' sooner or later, BEAR at the time expressed his conviction that CAPTAIN [President Roosevelt] would get 'a huge majority' in the elections. As the chat took place before the convention, advise whether to telegraph more.

While the content of this VENONA was not of any great significance, it was a complete text. Gardner's third success, however, accomplished on 20 December 1946, had the very widest implications, for it helpfully contained plenty of non-Russian names that required to be spelt out in full, using a spelltable to encode English letters, and proved the extent of Soviet interest in and knowledge of the wartime Manhattan Project two years earlier, in December 1944:

Breakthrough

Conclusion of Telegram No. 940
Enumerates the following scientists who are working on the problem – Hans BETHE, Niels BOHR, Enrico FERMI, John NEWMAN, Bruno ROSSI, George KISTIAKOWSKI, Emilio SEGRE, G. I. TAYLOR, William PENNEY, Arthur COMPTON, Ernest LAWRENCE, Harold UREY, Hans STANARN, Edward TELLER, Percy BRIDGEMAN, Werner EISENBERG, STRASSENMAN [7 groups unrecoverable] our country addressed himself to NAPOLI and the latter, not wanting to listen to him, sent him to BECK [Sergei Kurnakov] as military commentator on the paper. On attempting to visit HELMSMAN [Earl Browder] he was not admitted to him by the latter's secretary. ANTON

The fact that these seventeen physicists were developing an atomic weapon was one of the biggest secrets of the war in December 1944, so the accurate list demonstrated the scale of the leak. Dr George Kistiakowsky was the chief of the explosives division at Los Alamos; the American chemist Harold Urey headed the uranium production centre in New Jersey; Lawrence directed uranium production at Berkeley by the electro-magnetic method; Segrè was Fermi's protégé from Italy; Bethe directed the theoretical division at Los Alamos, where Bohr joined him after his escape from Denmark, and where the Hungarians Edward Teller and John von Neumann were working on an implosion trigger; Rossi, a close friend of Fermi's, had pioneered cosmic ray research; Percy Bridgeman was the Harvard expert on the measurement of high pressures; Sir Geoffrey Taylor was the Cambridge-educated meteorologist and leading British specialist on explosive hydrodynamics; Professor Compton was in charge of the Argonne Laboratories in Chicago, and Oak Ridge, Tennessee, where uranium was refined by the spectographic method; Hans Stanarn was, presumably, the Swiss physicist Hans Staub. Quite apart from the personalities involved, the sites where the Manhattan Project was undertaken were also considered top secret. Apart from the question of how the Soviets had acquired these names, the only real conundrum was the inclusion of Werner Heisenberg, who was at the time leading the Nazis' atomic research programme in Germany, and Fritz Strassman, the chemist who had first identified transuranic elements and first split the nucleus of the atom. Neither was ever at

Los Alamos, but doubtless their names had circulated among those working in the USA as likely competitors.

Evidently the report, signed by the Amtorg engineer Leonid R. Kvasnikov (codenamed ANTON), who had been based in New York between March 1943 and October 1945, indicated that his source had approached Nichola Napoli, the manager of a Soviet film distributor, for help, but she had been embarrassed and had sent him to Sergei N. Kurnakov (BECK). Instead he had called on the CPUSA's General-Secretary, Earl Browder, who had refused to see him, doubtless anxious not to be so obviously compromised by espionage.

The unrecovered groups in ANTON's message were tantalizing, but the clues were followed up by additional work on the preceding telegram which referred to a source codenamed MLAD, who was discovered to be Dr Theodore Hall, the Harvard-educated physicist. This disclosure alone was sufficient to justify the most searching investigation into breaches of security at Los Alamos, but VENONA was to reveal much, much more about a joint GRU/NKVD operation codenamed ENORMOZ (see Chapter VI).

Meredith Gardner's extraordinary success in 1946 in decoding some of the JADE messages, which had been stripped of their additive encipherment by Katie McDonald and her staff, raised the thorny question of how the 'product' should be handled. Clearly it was much too sensitive to be distributed in the way wartime Japanese decrypts had been circulated, and the only immediate consumer was the US Army's G-2 branch. Accordingly, arrangements were made for Gardner to make occasional reports on his progress to G-2, and there is a record of a brief 'Special Report No. 1' which the AFSA's Chief, Colonel Hayes, passed to Colonel Forney at G-2, but banned any further distribution. When the G-2 deputy chief, Colonel Carter Clarke, read this report, he called in the FBI.

Although the discovery of the duplication of the pages of the one-time pads looked like a breakthrough, there was a limit to the cryptographic success that it implied, and this was recognized at the outset by Hallock, Feinstein and the rest of the cryptographic team, including Meredith Gardner. Almost an obsessive, and certainly an eccentric, Gardner was undoubtedly a linguistic genius, speaking several languages fluently as well as reading some Sanskrit. He had been teaching German at Akron College in Ohio until the outbreak of war when the college dropped the subject. He then took a job at Arlington Hall, teaching himself Japanese in just three months and thereafter concentrating on Tokyo's signal traffic. As one of the SSA team assigned to the Russian problem, he knew that progress would be very slow without the aid of a 'crib' or shortcut, and this was the issue he raised with the FBI's liaison officer, special Agent Robert J. Lamphere.

Originally from Mullan, Idaho, Lamphere had gained a law degree before joining the Bureau in 1941. After seven months in Birmingham, Alabama, he was posted to the New York Field Office chasing draft dodgers, and in late 1944 was switched to the Soviet counter-espionage section which was then considered a dead-end assignment because of the long hours devoted to fruitless physical surveillance. Apart from information from the rare defector, such as Victor Kravchenko, who could identify some of the leading personalities within the local Soviet community, the FBI had precious little information about the scale of Russian spying and relied upon maintaining a covert watch on the principal suspects, mainly Soviet consular staff and their contacts. The fact that Walter Krivitsky, the GRU defector who fled from France in 1938, had died in mysterious circumstances in a locked hotel room in Washington DC in 1941 illustrated the dangers of becoming a Soviet turncoat. Whether his death was suicide or murder was not wholly relevant. Either way, the pressure of living with Stalin's anger was too great to contemplate, which accounted for the paucity of professionals willing to switch sides. Even when, as happened in August 1941, the senior NKVD illegal in North America was arrested, he admitted nothing and simply waited to be released in exchange for some Americans detained in Moscow. Gaik Ovakimian had been implicated in numerous illicit activities since his arrival in the United States in 1933, but the Armenian could be charged only with the relatively trivial offence of failing to register as a foreign agent. He was deported within two months, in exchange for a group of Americans held in Moscow. However, convinced that the Soviet Trade Delegation, Purchasing Commission and consulate were supplying cover for those supervising NKVD and GRU networks, the FBI recruited a burglar to arrange several surreptitious entries and over a period of weeks to photograph hundreds of Soviet files. Although their significance was not realized until Meredith Gardner asked Lamphere if the FBI had access to any original Soviet plaintexts, the documents did not provide any important cryptographic cribs. In about September 1947 another FBI Special Agent, S. Wesley Reynolds, was asked to compile a list of Soviet codenames that the Bureau had encountered, in the hope that they might appear in the texts. Reynolds had been the first person in the FBI to learn of BRIDE (an earlier name for VENONA), having been told by Carter Clarke in August or September 1947, and he confided in Lamphere early the following year. The Reynolds list amounted to some 200 names gleaned from technical surveillance, informants and defector testimony, but only a few of the covernames appeared in the traffic. However, for those that did, it represented useful collateral, and in October 1948 Wesley Reynolds recommended that Lamphere be appointed as a permanent link with the Bureau to exploit further leads. He remained working on VENONA until his resignation in 1955, with Reynolds being appointed the NSA's first Chief of Security.

The issue of the FBI's 'black bag' jobs, the illicit entries which were mounted against target Eastern Bloc diplomatic premises, remains extremely sensitive, even after the demise of the Cold War, and very little has been published about this intriguing aspect of US counter-intelligence activities, although Lamphere himself has referred to the theft of Amtorg messages in his memoirs, and a VENONA text from New York dated 25 July 1944 complains about the FBI entering Soviet property masquerading as certification engineers inspecting lift shafts:

> Yesterday two fellows came to see SHAH [Konstantin Chabanov] at the PLANT [consulate-general] and said that in the capacity of representatives of the City Housing Department they were to inspect the PLANT building and the neighbouring house. In reply to SHAH's question about the purpose of the inspection the fellows said that they were not obliged to call. SHAH managed to show them out but they hinted roughly that they might come back with people who would ensure them access. GRANDFATHER [Evgeni Kiselev] [3 groups unrecovered] [8 groups unrecoverable] plausible excuse the necessity of checking the lift mechanism is very bad. GRANDFATHER came to an agreement that he would send our architect to the Housing Department and he would

inform them about the lifts. With this the incident was closed, but it is difficult to doubt that the fellows represent the HUT [OSS]. BORIS [Aleksandr Saprygin] has no special instructions on the circumstances in which he is to destroy the ciphers without reference to anyone and when it is permissible to use weapons. Please give some guidance.

Within the FBI's Intelligence Division it is common knowledge that such operations were conducted throughout the 1960s, often over a weekend when the relevant building was more vulnerable, and a special laboratory was set up to photograph codebooks without disturbing the pages, and sophisticated techniques were adopted to reproduce Soviet seals which had been broken. Apart from Lamphere's mention of illicit access to the Soviet trade data, which has been acknowledged by the KGB but denied officially by the US government, there is a well-documented case of a Czech cipher-clerk, Frantisek Tisler, codenamed ARAGO, who routinely allowed FBI Special Ops teams into the embassy coderoom over a period of two years until his defection in 1958. However, those tackling the VENONA problem are emphatic that the only time they ever attempted to match texts was when Gouzenko supplied some originals, and on that occasion none matched.

Until September 1945, in the absence of any cribs, the American interest in Soviet ciphers had been pursued in an almost academic environment, but the dramatic defection of Igor Gouzenko in Canada was proof once again that it is by no means the most senior ranks that possess the greatest knowledge. Gouzenko was but a tiny cog in the GRU's worldwide espionage machine, being the cipher-clerk in the Soviet embassy in Ottawa. Nevertheless, his application for asylum for himself, his wife and their daughter, accompanied by the promise of a batch of 109 original GRU telegrams extracted from the *referentura*'s files, brought the GRU and the NKVD close to global paralysis and inflicted irreversible damage to Soviet prestige. Under cross-examination by the Royal Commission on Soviet Espionage in 1946, Gouzenko was the first wartime Soviet to describe the GRU's cipher procedures, explaining how he had worked alone in a tiny room with a barred and shuttered window on the second floor, entered through a steel double door, receiving telegrams through a small hatch from his colleague Aleksashkin:

> Colonel Zabotin wrote out the telegram in Russian and I coded that telegram, making a draft copy first, and then typed it out on Canadian Pacific or Canadian National telegram forms, which went to Aleksashkin for despatch to the telegraph company. Colonel Zabotin's original telegram or document was placed in the bag, in the sealed bag, and handed to Aleksashkin.

Even his superior, the GRU *Rezident* Nikolai Zabotin, was forbidden to enter the secret cipher room until Gouzenko had completed the first of the three-part coding procedure, which turned the text, handwritten on special blue paper, into cipher groups. Once transmitted, the original would be sent to Moscow together with bulky items, such as photos of secret documents by couriers using Soviet cargo ships that sailed from North American ports two or three times a week, a hazardous sea journey that in wartime sometimes took up to five months. When Gouzenko communicated with his superior, Colonel Baltenko, who was the GRU's Director of Special Communications, he adopted the cryptonym CLARK.

Although he subsequently claimed a political motive, asserting that he was disenchanted with the regime, the catalyst for Gouzenko's dramatic departure had been a minor administrative blunder which had resulted in his recall to headquarters. Fearful of the consequences, and anyway reluctant to swap a life of relative comfort in Canada for one of hardship and shortages in Moscow, Gouzenko had taken the precaution of marking some of the most sensitive papers in the *referentura*'s cipher room. When, on the night of 5 September, he made his move, he grabbed the preselected files, stuffed them into his clothes and left the building undetected.

Gouzenko's contribution to the VENONA programme was threefold: there were the documents themselves, comprising original plaintexts; there were pages extracted from the GRU *rezident*'s daily diary; and then there was his personal knowledge of the GRU's cipher procedures. Unfortunately, none of the plaintexts matched any of the material in the VENONA collection which contained only some of Ottawa's NKVD traffic, to which Gouzenko had never enjoyed access. The clerk also described the GRU's emergency cipher system, and although this was considered at the time to have potential, it was never found to have been used apart from the 1940–41

Breakthrough

London traffic, when the GRU apparently ran out of OTPs. Some years later a single VENONA, dated 25 January 1945, was found to have a reference to Gouzenko (codenamed CLARK), who evidently had made a mistake in the encipherment of a previous cable:

> In our No. 18 I transmitted the figure text of another party's cipher telegram. To ensure there is no difficulty [3 groups unrecovered] 18, here are the first and last groups of the figure text: 74389 and 48817. The figure text begins with the hundredth group of telegram No. 18. [2 groups unrecovered] telegrams [3 groups unrecovered] pad 1471, although in [3 groups unrecovered] pad 68 [2 digits unidentified]. In order to keep the sequence after using pad 1471 please [1 group unrecovered] to pad 68 [2 digits unidentified].

Meredith Gardner spent much of 1946 concentrating on the NKVD 1944 traffic, and by 1947 had begun to supply Reynolds with the first decrypts. At Eastcote, GCHQ's grim compound in West London, Cecil Phillips spent six months from June 1946 working in parallel on the same problem with GCHQ's expert, Philip Howse, who had prepared a briefing for Brigadier Tiltman and Major John Cheadle on some of the Australian (Canberra) traffic, but he was unable to get anyone's attention, chiefly because the material was believed to be consular, with no hint of NKVD involvement. It was only after the discovery of three truckloads of Soviet wartime bills of lading, found in a Department of Commerce warehouse by G-2's John Larkin, that the management was persuaded that a comparative analysis proved that the traffic was not commercial and deserved more Anglo-American resources, including the use of IBM punchcard-sorters to recover texts. The objective was to use the stereotypic cargo lists to strip away the unwanted cryptographic data and rebuild the sixty-group key pages which could simultaneously be used against the NKVD traffic. Where the same key had been used more than once, a phenomenon known as 'depth', there was a real opportunity to start the last stage of a multi-part decryption attack.

In the years that followed, formal translations became standard as British and American personnel were 'integrated' into each other's VENONA team. British linguists augmented Meredith Gardner and took over much of the translation effort and codebook building, both at Arlington Hall and at GCHQ. These arrangements had started with the secondment to Eastcote for five years of an outstanding American cryptanalyst, Joan Malone, to help begin work at GCHQ on the project then codenamed BRIDE. A brilliant 'depth reader', she was known as 'Sneezy' because of her chronic hayfever, and she collaborated with a small cell, led by Wilfred Bodsworth, who had been one of the first to study the Enigma machine ciphers in 1937. Having read Spanish at Cambridge, Bodsworth taught himself exemplary Russian while studying VENONA and was greatly respected as a linguist and cryptographer by his subordinates who referred to him as 'Snow White' because of his white hair. Always cheerful and charming, Bodsworth inspired his staff who were all strongly motivated by what was then perceived as a Communist threat. Malone's initial task had been to help GCHQ set up a small unit within the Russian Trade Section to work on the pairs of matched messages.

While at Eastcote, Malone, who was to spend years liaising with the CIA on VENONA, met and married Captain Harold Callaghan, then staff officer to Colonel Clough, the Chief US Liaison Officer to GCHQ. By the end of 1950 the BRIDE cell at Eastcote consisted of Bodsworth, Joan Malone, a retired colonel, 'Happy' Plumber, who acted as a typist and two others: 'Audrey West', an Italian linguist known as 'Bashful' who spoke good Russian and had worked during the war at GCHQ's Middle East base at Heliopolis, Egypt, and a young Englishman, 'Jeffrey Northbury', known as 'Doc'.

'Doc' was to concentrate on VENONA until 1966, and continued as a consultant until 1969 when he was appointed head of the Joint Technical Language Service, a government unit supplying linguists to Whitehall. Although he had read Modern History at Oxford, he had been sent on the Russian course at Cambridge by the Intelligence Corps, where he had been talent-spotted by Dr (later Professor Dame) Elizabeth Hall. Originally taught French by his bilingual mother, 'Doc' had been posted to Paris to perfect his Russian, based at the British embassy but living among the émigré White Russian community and meeting, among many others, Prince Felix Yusupev, the man credited with killing Rasputin. At that time GCHQ was hesitant to rely on expatriate language skills and anxious to encourage the talented children of born Britons to take up useful foreign languages, and once 'Doc' had perfected his command of Russian he was posted to Eastcote, where he was to develop a gift for cryptanalysis. Although many others were deployed against the trade and diplomatic component, the principal target remained the NKVD traffic, to which only a very few had any access. Those who focused on the very tedious trade material, for example, were sometimes told about how they had been able to help the main attack, but the work was highly compartmentalized, with the staff briefed on the trade problem being known as 'Q', or possessing a 'Q' clearance. Even Hugh Alexander, the former British chess champion who had made a vital contribution to breaking the Enigma ciphers, and who was then head of GCHQ's Cryptanalytic Division, was never fully aware, or wanted to be aware, of what progress was being made on BRIDE. There were, however, a few lapses. On one memorable occasion GCHQ's Tom Moss, who spent months concentrating on the trade traffic, was told unofficially that the arrest of Klaus Fuchs had been a direct consequence of a BRIDE breakthrough, but such indiscretions were rare.

The numbers working on BRIDE, the first at Eastcote and then from 1953 onwards at GCHQ's Benhall site at Cheltenham, constituted a mere handful compared to the numbers deployed in the United States, although even there the overall figure never exceeded 125, including ten to fifteen who concentrated on NKVD traffic. The overwhelming majority were women. The transatlantic exchange between GCHQ and Arlington Hall soon became institutionalized, particularly when Philip Howse, who had been assigned to Arlington in a general liaison capacity, was shown that messages in the Canberra–Moscow channel revealed the need for a British input into BRIDE. He was integrated into the JADE team to assist Meredith Gardner and the other cryptanalysts. In addition to looking after British interests in the Canberra traffic, Howse later focused much of his time on the leakage attributed to HOMER at the British embassy, and in May 1947 became a full-time member of the BRIDE project.

From the first break into the NKVD text in November 1944, through until 1953, all the NKVD messages were sent in two codebooks. The first had been studied by Meredith Gardner, who produced his translations in 1946, and was found to have been in use from November 1943 until early 1946. Its replacement was still in use in June 1948 when the last exploitable Canberra signals were transmitted. Work undertaken by Cecil Phillips in 1948 on the pre-

November 1943 NKVD traffic showed that short stretches of additive key had been used by code-clerks to avoid starting a whole new page, and this obviously was an approved procedure used by both senders and recipients, but attempts to reconstruct the codegroups at that time were unsuccessful and that part of the project was set aside.

Just when it looked as though further work on the NKVD's 1942-43 traffic would be worthless, Dr Samuel P. Chew made a crucial cryptographic breakthrough that opened up more texts to attack. Chew was able to convert the short stretches of code-clerk re-use into codegroups that matched the partially burnt Petsamo codebook. Chew's success occurred at the end of 1953 and allowed the cryptanalysts to search for duplicate key pages among pre-November 1943 NKVD messages by applying the Petsamo codebook, or what was left of it. This had been recovered at the end of the war by the Target Identification Committee (TICOM), a highly secret Anglo-American organization of Target Reporting officers based at Bletchley Park, which had been set up to exploit captured enemy cryptographic personnel and material in the hope that they could be used against the Japanese. Initially TICOM's creation had been little more than a flight of optimism, for the prevailing attitude was that the Nazis would methodically destroy anything of use to the Allies, and this view was confirmed in January 1945 when a Wehrmacht sigint unit was found in Leopoldsburg, Belgium, totally destroyed. The local Special Liaison Unit which searched what remained of the base reported that the fleeing Germans had even left a note of welcome for the arriving troops, written in English.

News of any interesting seizure by Allied troops was passed to TICOM headquarters, based in the Paris office of the senior SHAEF signals officer, Colonel Bicher, who had prepared ambitious plans to despatch teams to take control of enemy sites, and had even drawn up a contingency scheme to drop commandos into the path of the Russians to deny them access to vital crypto equipment. One such installation, at Burgscheidungen, ten miles north-west of Freyburg in Saxony, was discovered in April 1945 by the US 100th Infantry Division, and TICOM 6, consisting of Colonel Paul Neff of the US Army Signals Security Agency, Geoffrey Evans from Bletchley Park, and William Bundy, later the US Assistant Secretary of State, was quickly moved in a convoy of trucks from Paris, through

Verdun, to Magdeburg to take control of the castle. The TICOM senior staff operated under covernames, with Evans adopting the pseudonym 'Edwards', and Bundy calling himself 'Brown'. What they found stored at the ancient schloss was to have a dramatic impact on VENONA by opening pre-November 1943 NKVD messages to successful cryptanalytical attack.

The magnificent estate commands a strategic position overlooking the Unstutt river, surrounded by vineyards, and there has been a castle on the site since at least 1043. It has been in the hands of the von der Schulenburg family since 1721. When American troops entered the district they found it largely untouched by the war, with Leipzig to the north taking the brunt of Allied bombing. The nearest strategic target was a cement works a few kilometres away, but otherwise the tiny hamlet of Burgscheidungen, approached by a single bridge, had escaped the war. The castle had been used briefly as a draft office for the selection of military personnel. Apart from the local *volksturm* (home guard), the only sign of activity in the village in April 1945 was from the Polish prisoners who tended the estate under the benevolent supervision of the Graf von der Schulenburg who continued to live in the most habitable part of the castle. Although members of his family had been implicated in the 20 July plot to assassinate Hitler, the Graf himself had been left alone to run the estate and look after his five daughters.[5]

What made Burgscheidungen of interest to TICOM 6 had been the recent arrival at the castle of a group of Reich Foreign Ministry officials bearing the entire records of the *Balkanabteilung* cryptographic unit that had been dedicated to 'solving the Russian problem', which meant the interception and decryption of Soviet signals. When the men arrived in January 1945, from their former base at Hirschberg, near Breslau, they took over half the accommodation for their documents but lived in complete isolation from the village and the Graf, behind the closed gates of the splendid keep which to this day bears the family's coat-of-arms. As Allied troops moved closer, the *Balkanabteilung* carried some of their files to a railway wagon for evacuation, but it was to remain in the station until the Americans took possession. Of greatest anxiety to TICOM was the need to debrief the two dozen civilian members of the captured German unit before Russian troops arrived to occupy the area.

Arriving on 12 April, Paul Neff had no difficulty pacifying the Graf and, with the assistance of the TICOM group of about fourteen men, supported by a German expatriate staff sergeant, and guarded by Belgian troops, supervised the removal to England by air from the nearby airfield at Kolleda of what was believed to be the Nazi Foreign Ministry entire Balkan cryptographic archive. On 3 May the male members of the Balkan unit were flown to England, and Neff then eliminated all traces of what the castle had been used for during the past twelve months, blowing up all the remaining tabulating machines and typewriters to prevent them from falling into Russian hands. (The Soviets arrived on 23 June.) Much of the village was evacuated, with the civilian cryptographers transferred to an interrogation centre at Frankfurt, while the documents underwent assessment. Before leaving, the Graf, who had been classified as a non-Nazi and appointed mayor of the village, allowed TICOM 6 to celebrate the end of the war by holding a party in the schloss's impressive panelled ballroom on the first floor, and arranged for the furniture and the grand piano to be uncovered for the occasion.

Initially it was believed that the German unit had been concentrating on US diplomatic traffic exchanged between Berne and Washington DC, and it was only much later that the Russian codebook was discovered. The Graf von der Schulenburg, who took his daughters to Hesse to escape the Russian advance, died in 1951 without ever being aware of what had been hidden in his castle.

On 21 May, another TICOM team, led by Howard Campaigne, was taken by some German PoWs to a hiding place in a basement under an OKW (Wehrmacht High Command) communications centre at Rosenheim, near the Austrian frontier, where German technicians had intercepted Soviet military wireless traffic. The TICOM men were shown a still operational, fully-equipped intercept facility, complete with a machine for demodulating teletype signals, which they promptly dismantled and shipped to Bletchley. Altogether seven and a half tons of hardware were carried to England in a convoy of captured German trucks escorted by Selmer Norland and his British counterpart, Edward Rushworth.

One item in Neff's haul was the Finnish cryptographic collection, proof that the Finns had shared the Petsamo Kod-26 diplomatic codebook with the Nazis as well as the Japanese, and this material, used in conjunction with some other documents found in Schleswig by Lieutenant Oliver Kirby, also of Arlington Hall, enabled more progress to be made by the NSA from 1954 onwards. Kirby, who had worked on Enigma at Bletchley Park, headed the Russian Section between 1946 and 1952.

In addition, the cryptographers had access to 1,500 pages of Soviet coding material, comprising one military and three diplomatic codes, apparently bought from a Finnish refugee intelligence officer in Sweden in November 1944. Although not directly relevant to the VENONA texts, these codebooks were useful as linguistic models, allowing the cryptographers to develop an understanding of how the Soviets wrote their messages.

At that time the Office of Strategic Services station in Stockholm was headed by Wilho Tikander, a lawyer of Finnish origin from Chicago, and his staff included Calvin Hoover, an economist from Duke University who used his position in OSS's secret intelligence branch to collect information on the Soviets. Having spent five years in Moscow, Hoover was antagonistic towards Stalin and masterminded several important acquisitions, including the Red Army's complete order-of-battle, the register of the Red Banner Fleet, and the Petsamo codebooks. This latter purchase was to prove highly controversial for although General William Donovan, head of OSS, approved of it, the State Department did not. When the Assistant Secretary of State, Edward Stettinius, discovered that his ban had been ignored, he protested to the White House. Donovan had reported his coup to the President on 11 December, describing the material as the key to both military and NKVD codes, but word of it reached Stettinius four days later. The result was that the OSS liaison officer in Moscow, General John Deane, informed his Soviet counterpart, General Pavel Fitin, on 9 January 1945, that OSS wanted to return some 1,500 NKVD papers and associated material, and by 15 February they had been delivered to Andrei Gromyko, then Soviet Ambassador in Washington DC.

It is not known precisely what this OSS codebook really was or whether it was copied before it was returned to the Soviets, but the angry exchanges between Donovan, the State Department and the White House are well documented. However, it is equally clear that Arlington Hall relied on the TICOM material rather than on anything provided by OSS, and a summary of what the Finns had accomplished, dated 17 December 1946, indicates that they had worked on Soviet military, police, diplomatic and trade ciphers. It also mentions a four-digit NKVD code, which may be a reference to the *Pobeda* (Victory) code known to have been used between 1941 and October 1943 when a new system, designated 075-B, was introduced. The switch was disclosed in a VENONA text dated 31 October 1943, from Grigori Kheifets in San Francisco to Moscow, in which the *rezident* acknowledged receipt of copy No. 27, the new codebook, the B in the title being an abbreviation of *Bezopasnost* (Security), and undertaking to destroy the old *Pobeda* version.

Even if Donovan uncharacteristically failed to retain a copy of the Petsamo codebook, it is certain that others were acquired from the Finnish Stellists who had settled in Sweden, several of whom subsequently emigrated to the United States, Colonels Paasonen and Hallamaa among them. In addition, a copy was retained by the Swedish National Defence Radio Institute, another by the French, apparently sold by Paasonen who spoke the language and for a while lived in France, and yet another was bought by the Japanese military attaché, Lieutenant-General Makoto Onodera.[6] At least one original, bought for 100,000 Crowns, wound up at GCHQ, where the Stellists' material was known as SOURCE 267, and special measures were taken to preserve the crumbling pages which were turning to ash at the edges; a senior BRIDE cryptanalyst recalls handling a Soviet codebook with a bullet hole through the middle. A list of items sold by the Stellists, retrieved in Sweden, mentions a 'five digit from 1941' sold to the British for 100,000 Crowns, a 'strip-code' purchased by the Americans, and a code used by Soviet armoured formations bought by OSS *and* the Japanese.

Work on VENONA within the Armed Forces Security Agency (AFSA) was considered exceptionally secret, and it was not until Frank Rowlett transferred to the CIA in 1952 that the counter-intelligence staff became actively involved following up leads. The delay in indoctrinating the CIA, considered by some to be controversial, was primarily because the texts were regarded as the FBI's, but also because the messages showed that OSS, the CIA's forerunner, had been thoroughly penetrated. By the time the AFSA had been transformed into the National Security Agency (NSA) in November 1952, the CIA's Bill Harvey had grasped BRIDE's significance and a specialist unit, initially designated 'Staff D' and then later known as 'Division D', was assigned the task of exploiting cryptographic sources. In 1960 Carlton Swift, a physicist by training who had worked in OSS before running the CIA's Baghdad station, and who then moved to London as Frank Wisner's deputy, took over from Rowlett and built a compartmented office of 500 officers, of whom just eight were employed to run black bag (illicit entry) operations around the world. D was chiefly preoccupied with distributing 'Comint' from around half a dozen different sources, with VENONA being just one, but the staff also acted as a research arm for the NSA, attempting to fill in the gaps of partially decrypted VENONA texts. Other 'close support' teams undertook some bizarre missions, ranging from sonic research on printwheels used in Soviet embassy coderooms, to despatching cats, pigeons and even rats into target premises carrying miniaturized listening equipment. The fact that the CIA even contemplated such operations demonstrates the organization's commitment to developing clandestine methods of enhancing Comint collection, an effort that had justified itself as VENONA gave new insights into past Soviet activities. Eventually it was the legendary molehunter Jim Angleton who attempted to widen the collateral research and brought in selected counter-intelligence experts from the Royal Canadian Mounted Police (RCMP) Security Service, the Australian Security Intelligence Organization (ASIO) and the New Zealand Security Intelligence Service to form CAZAB and provide VENONA with global support. Eventually CAZAB became the basis of VENONA exploitation, with individual officers from the five countries cleared to handle the material and develop it by sharing collateral, particularly that provided by defectors, and holding annual conferences to discuss progress.

By October 1980, when work on the Stockholm VENONA had drawn to a close, with 750,000 messages examined and 2 million pages of key scrutinized for duplicates, a comprehensive order-of-battle for the NKVD had been reconstructed by the Anglo-American counter-intelligence analysts, listing twenty-four case officers in the US, of whom the FBI estimated only five could speak good English. In 1942–43 the New York *rezidentura* was ruled by the unpopular and bombastic Major-General Vasili M. Zarubin (MAXIM) who operated from January 1942 under the *nom-de-guerre* Zubilin with the rank of third (later second) secretary, and was married to the shrewd Elizaveta (VARDO) who held the rank of colonel. Originally from Bukovina in Romania, Elizaveta had a degree in philology, and spoke several languages, including French, German, English and her native

Romanian. According to her declassified KGB file, she had been recalled from Germany in April 1941 to cultivate the wife of a senior German diplomat in Moscow, and later successfully ran a code-clerk in the German Foreign Ministry.

Zubilin, who had been a banker in Moscow before he joined the NKVD, had worked under diplomatic cover at the Soviet embassy in China, and was believed to have been implicated in the massacre in 1939 of thousands of Polish officers at Kozielsk in the Katyn woods. In late 1943 Zubilin was replaced by Stepan Apresyan (MAY), and was transferred to Washington DC, where he initiated direct communications with Moscow, eliminating the necessity of relaying them via New York. The Zarubins stayed in Washington only briefly because, as a result of a false allegation made by Vasili's secretary, Colonel Mironov, the *rezident* and his wife were recalled to Moscow at the end of August 1944 to face a lengthy investigation. In March 1943 Leonid R. Kvasnikov (ANTON) was sent to New York to establish a separate *rezidentura* on behalf of the 8th Department and concentrate on collecting information about the Anglo-American atomic bomb programme, which he accomplished until his hasty withdrawal in October 1945.

In September 1944 Anatoli Gorsky (VADIM), who was listed officially at the Soviet embassy as Anatoli Gromov, was appointed *rezident* in Washington DC, a post he held until December the following year when he was transferred to Buenos Aires; and in March 1945 Apresyan was posted to San Francisco, a *rezidentura* which had been opened in December 1941 by Grigori M. Kheiffets (CHARON), with a sub-*rezidentura* based in Los Angeles. Kheiffets was recalled in January 1945 and replaced by Grigori P. Kasparov (GIFT). Apresyan's replacement in New York was Pavel Fedosimov (STEPAN). Together these Soviet handlers ran more than 200 spies, of whom 115 were identified as US citizens, and a further 100 remained undetected.

From the American perspective, VENONA offered a fascinating insight into the way the Soviets ran their intelligence operations, but while it had an interesting historical significance, there was always a doubt about the practicality of devoting so many resources to what some perceived as an exercise that was unlikely to uncover further active Soviet networks. This unusual view gained greater circulation after the announcement of the first Soviet nuclear test, prompting the suggestion that as the secrets of the Manhattan Project had been

Breakthrough

stolen, there was nothing further to be betrayed. The Americans took a rather more sanguine line than the British on the dangers of hostile penetration of the government bureaucracy, and in 1954 reduced their commitment to BRIDE, a reflection of the difficulty of keeping people working on the same challenging problem for years on end. Certainly the loss of Oliver Kirby and Cecil Phillips was a setback, as was the resignation from the FBI of Bob Lamphere in July 1955. In contrast, GCHQ remained convinced there was plenty of scope for progress, and this turned out to be true when, in 1957, the naval attaché channel between Washington and Moscow succumbed. GCHQ was also always conscious of the KGB and GRU spies mentioned in the early London traffic, and was particularly concerned about the possibility of a traitor inside GCHQ itself.

The cause of this long-term anxiety, which was fully justified, centred on a single VENONA text dated May 1941 but broken in 1962, that quite clearly was a raw ULTRA intercept from Bletchley Park, listing the railway stations across the Ukraine that the German armoured divisions intended to utilize in the forthcoming BARBAROSSA offensive. The certainty that there was a spy inside or close to Bletchley Park in May 1941 was traumatic for two reasons. First, the most obvious candidate for a traitor at Bletchley was John Cairncross, who became an espionage suspect in 1951 and was the subject of a lengthy Security Service investigation. While he was eventually to confess to having passed his NKVD contacts thousands of ULTRA decrypts, he had not arrived at Bletchley for a further year. So who had betrayed it? And secondly, had that person received promotion to a position where he (or she) could influence GCHQ's recruitment and arrange for another spy to be inserted? When the BRIDE team realized the implications, Nigel de Grey, one of the century's great cryptographers, who had solved German problems in the First World War, gathered the staff in the Eastcote lounge and delivered a chilling lecture on the probability of a Soviet spy at large in the building.

This conundrum was eventually resolved when in April 1964 Anthony Blunt named Leo Long as his source in MI-14, the German order-of-battle section in the War Office which was on the distribution list for ULTRA. Long had extracted the Russian railway decrypt and had handed it to his Soviet contact, an admission that relieved GCHQ from the spectre of penetration dating back to May 1941.

Both Kim Philby and Anthony Blunt knew about GCHQ's work on BRIDE, but there was very little that either could do to prevent the progress made jointly at Eastcote and Arlington Hall. With his more direct access, particularly while he was SIS's liaison officer in Washington DC from 1949 onwards, Philby could monitor events and keep his fellow-conspirators informed, but it was too late for the Soviets to repair their flawed cipher systems. In fact, there is some evidence that the NKVD learned as early as 1944 that BRIDE had been initiated, for in April that year a directive was suddenly circulated to all *rezidents* which was intended to enhance the system's security. Unusually, the change was notified by message, not in a couriered instruction as might have been expected, and became operational at very short notice, on 1 May. In the event, it achieved exactly the reverse of its intention. The new arrangement eliminated the identification in clear of the relevant one-time pad's page number, known as the 'indicator', and substituted a procedure in which the first five-digit group of the page was used in clear, to become the indicator, leaving the recipherment to begin with the *second* group on the page. This supposed improvement only changed the starting-point by one group, and actually made the task of the cryptanalyst easier as it dispensed with the time-consuming necessity of matching page numbers to particular sections of sixty numeric groups. Instead, the attack could be concentrated on comparing the new indicators on vulnerable JADE diplomatic texts to those already thought to have been duplicated.

Why this change was made, and on whose instructions, has never been determined, but it is likely that the NKVD senior management ordered a tightening-up of procedures, having been alerted that Arlington Hall had commenced operations in earnest. The tip probably came from a mole on the staff, William Weisband, but although his information was entirely accurate, the NKVD failed to take the root and branch counter-measures the situation really demanded. Instead, the supposed improvement was nothing more than a cosmetic exercise which was to allow the British and American cryptanalysts, when Cecil Phillips solved the problem in November 1944, even greater success.

II

Compromised

WILLIAM WEISBAND was never charged with espionage, and remains largely unknown to the general public. He is hardly mentioned in the dozens of books written about Soviet intelligence operations, yet as a spy he was infinitely more significant than most of those who have gained notoriety as traitors. In the opinion of two senior VENONA experts at the NSA, he and Donald Maclean get equal top billing as the most important of all the Soviet spies identified in the traffic.

Born in Odessa in 1908 (although his passport showed him to have been born in Alexandria), Volodya Weisband had been taken by his parents Isadore and Sarah to the United States in 1924 with his elder brothers Mark and Harold. He became a naturalized citizen in 1938. Isadore had left Odessa first, reaching Egypt via Turkey; his wife followed five years later with Volodya. A jeweller by trade, Isadore eventually owned three shops in New York City, while his wife had run a restaurant in Alexandria after the family had been reunited.

Fluent in Russian, Volodya adopted the name William and attended the American University in Washington DC, also working at the Statler Hotel in New York. He was drafted into the US Army in 1942 and commissioned as a second Lieutenant in April 1943. He then served with the Signals Security Agency in North Africa and Italy, and briefly acted as a liaison officer with the Red Navy in Naples. His Signal Corps commander in Italy, Colonel Harold Hayes, returned to Arlington Hall in mid-1944 as Chief of Production, and when he discovered the shortage of fluent interpreters in the Russian Section he arranged for Weisband to be posted home in October 1944. Weisband started work early in 1945 as a linguist in the Russian Section where he had constant contact with Meredith Gardner and the other AFSA cryptographers attempting to solve the Soviet ciphers. His role was that of an advisor, finding the right word or phrase for the cryptographers, and he was thus able to act as a 'floor-walker', roaming the section and offering advice about Russian idioms. His colleagues recalled that he had taken particular interest in the progress made on the list of atomic scientists that had so excited the BRIDE analysts, and demonstrated VENONA's counter-intelligence potential. Indeed, on one occasion Meredith Gardner recalls him looking over his shoulder as he worked on the names. Although Weisband had no direct official contact with the team handling VENONA, his sideline of selling jewellery to the Arlington Hall staff had given him considerable freedom of movement, visiting restricted areas, gossiping with the typists and showing them his wares which included several good pieces from the jewellery store, Harry Winston, inherited from his brother Harold who had run the family business after Mark's death in the war.[2] The gregarious Weisband had been popular with the Arlington Hall staff, and he is recalled as the owner of an unusual electrical item, a wire recorder, which in 1948, in the days before tape recorders, was quite a novelty. On one occasion he took the recorder to a party and recorded the voices of some of the AFSA staff, behaviour which was then considered to be slightly odd. The staff accepted that his subsequent suspension from duty was the result of a disagreement over tax with the Internal Revenue Service, and he was lent money by more than one sympathizer who thought he had been a victim of a McCarthyite witch-hunt.

Weisband also ingratiated himself with the senior ranks at Arlington Hall, and was close with Colonel Hayes, with whom he had served in North Africa and Italy. He also cultivated Major Maurice Klein, who was later to be appointed Chief of Personnel. The two men often socialized together, sometimes driving up to New York for the weekend, and when in 1949 Weisband married Klein's secretary, Klein acted as best man for the bride.

Mabel Woody, twenty years Weisband's junior, had been recruited into the ASA at Walnut, a small settlement just west of Marshall, the County seat, and had joined Arlington Hall early in 1943. Naturally her marriage to Weisband meant she too was dismissed, and although she was never accused of having aided his espionage, she has resolutely refused to discuss the issue.

Weisband's role as a Soviet spy was not directly disclosed by a

VENONA text. A message from Pavel Klarin in New York, dated 23 June 1943, about the travel movements of LINK, is thought to be the only significant reference to him, although it was not fully translated until 1979:

> The last 4 weeks LINK has spent [1 group unrecovered] school [4 groups unrecovered] ARLINGTON, VIRGINIA where he underwent a course of instruction in Italian. At the moment he has been given leave until the 27th of June [12 groups unrecovered] the ISLAND [England]. By his calculations he will leave the COUNTRY [America] in the first half of July and will arrive on the ISLAND at the end of July. We are setting up the following arrangements with LINK: The password for [1 group unrecovered] contact in any place in Russian or in English: our man: 'Hullo Bill. Greetings from Gregori.' He: '[7 groups unrecovered] on the West Coast.' Starting from 24 July LINK will wait for our man in LONDON on Sundays on the [1 group unrecovered] at the entrance to Leicester galleries, Leicester Square and on Wednesdays [2 groups unrecovered] on the [1 group unrecovered] east corner of Orchard and Wigmore [43 groups unrecoverable] Rush the telephone number and your instructions before [1 group unrecovered] June.

Coincidentally, Weisband was known to have studied Italian at Arlington Hall in June 1944, before leaving by ship for London on 17 July, where he arrived ten days later. That, combined with Weisband's first name, and his knowledge of Russian, is strong circumstantial evidence that LINK was indeed Weisband, and he was suspended from the AFSA on grounds of his suspected disloyalty. Certainly Klarin was a senior NKVD officer, for, after his tour of duty at the consulate in New York he was transferred to Mexico City as *rezident*. He had arrived in New York on the *Queen Mary* in April 1939 – supposedly a graduate of the Don State University and an expert in Ukrainian agrarian economics from Kharkov – to head the agricultural section in the Soviet pavilion at the World's Fair. Although he had been seconded to Amtorg, and was due to leave the country within a month of the World's Fair ending, he acquired formal diplomatic status in March 1940, and was to stay until the end of 1944.

Weisband, who died of a heart attack at the wheel of his car in Washington DC in May 1967, was never charged with espionage, even though a former girlfriend in New York volunteered the information to the FBI that he had used her to empty dead letter drops for him. Instead, he was convicted of contempt in November 1950 and sentenced to a year's imprisonment for having failed to turn up for a grand jury inquiry in his CPUSA membership. The clue that led the FBI to him came not from VENONA, but from Jones Orin York, a Soviet spy who did appear in several VENONAs, codenamed NEEDLE. Based in Berkeley, California, York was a pilot and aeronautical engine designer for the Douglas Aircraft Corporation who had been recruited by the NKVD in 1935 when his plant had been visited by a delegation from the Soviet Government Purchasing Commission. The FBI was put on to York by Amadeo Sabatini, codenamed NICK, a Spanish Civil War veteran who, coincidentally, had served alongside Morris Cohen (see p.163).

The first reference to NEEDLE occurred in a text dated 31 October 1943 from Grigori Kheiffets, the *rezident* in San Francisco:

> NEEDLE has handed over 5 films of material on the 'XP-58' and the new motors for it. [3 groups unrecovered] will be sent by the next post. NICK [Amadeo Sabatini] has received the impression that NEEDLE at present is doing all he can to [1 group unrecovered] our [1 group unrecovered] and to pass on to us the most essential material. NEEDLE considers that all material on [17 groups unrecovered] nevertheless complains of difficulties. NEEDLE is in desperate need of funds for buying a house and his [3 groups unrecovered] 800 dollars. [1 group unrecovered] giving of this sum.

Kheiffets's request to pay York was not approved instantly, for the *rezidentura*'s tight accounts were the subject of his next message to Moscow that included mention of York:

> At the 1st November according to the accounts there are 1,800 dollars left. By the end of the year 3,000 will be required. In addition to the expenses in accordance with the estimate we request 250–300 dollars for Christmas presents and in accordance with my No. 247 800 dollars for NEEDLE. Therefore please remit 1,200 for expenses up to the end of

the year in accordance with the estimate and an additional 1,100 dollars if you sanction the payment to NEEDLE and the expenditure on Christmas presents. Please let me know your decision regarding the presents urgently.

The last VENONA, dated 6 September 1944, was addressed to Moscow from Stepan Apresyan in New York;

Your number 3986. According to information of DOUGLAS [Joseph Katz] NICK [Amadeo Sabatini] is in excellent spirits and very much wishes to continue work, however [2 groups unrecovered] maximum caution will be required. In DOUGLAS's opinion he should not continue to work in the West, it would be better to transfer NICK to another place. NEEDLE [Jones O. York] of course he is not meeting pending a check by us to see whether surveillance of NEEDLE is still going on. As NICK has ceased meeting NEEDLE there is no fixed arrangement for them to meet [8 groups unrecovered] NICK in order to give him the task of seeking out NEEDLE. It is not known whether NEEDLE is living at the old address. However, as the results of the check on NEEDLE are not known we consider it inadvisable to entrust this matter to NICK. He has appealed for pecuniary assistance [1 group unrecovered]. He earns 150 dollars a month. He still has on hand 500 passed on by our man.

When interviewed by the FBI in 1950, York had confessed to having been paid to photograph dozens of classified aircraft plans, and identified Stanislav Shumovsky, ostensibly a technical expert from the Hydro-Aerodynamics Institute of Moscow, as the person who had cultivated him and then in 1936 passed him to a contact named Brooks. In January 1938 Brooks introduced York to 'Werner', but they lost touch a year later, and it was not until February 1940 that Werner reappeared to make arrangements for a rendezvous in Los Angeles with 'Bill Villesbend'. This third handler, who demonstrated a knowledge of Arabic, gave him $250 to buy a Contax camera in September 1941, and for the next year they held regular meetings in the Hollywood area at which York supplied details of aeroplane specifications from the Northrop Aircraft Company plant at Hawthorne, California. Towards the end of 1942 'Bill' was replaced by another controller, but York claimed not to have had any further contact with the Soviets after this individual had failed to attend an agreed meeting towards the end of 1943.

York gave evidence before a grand jury in August 1950, when he pointed out William Weisband to the FBI as the man he had known as 'Bill'. Weisband had been interviewed twice by FBI special agents in Washington DC during May 1950, and again in Los Angeles in August, but he always denied any involvement in espionage, although he declined to sign a formal statement, and served nine months of a year's sentence for contempt. When questioned again, in July 1953, he simply repeated his denials, and rejected an FBI suggestion that before the war he might have shared an apartment in New York with a Soviet spy named Kubarkin. Thereafter he was the subject of intermittent FBI surveillance at his home in Arlington, where he operated as an insurance agent, collecting subscriptions door to door in a poor, predominantly black, community. After his death his widow Mabel, a part-time teacher for children with special needs, struggled to bring up her own children, before marrying a Federal Aviation Authority official in the late 1970s.

The degree to which Weisband compromised the VENONA project remains unknown, for the main evidence of a Soviet reaction is the indicator change of 1 May 1944, at a time when Weisband was out of the country, having been based in North Africa since mid-1943. However, it is clear from those that recall his visits to the conference room that Kim Philby took an interest in what was being achieved at Arlington Hall. Indeed, some of his colleagues recalled, after his defection in 1964, that the Russian 'BJ', or 'Black Jumbo' diplomatic traffic, which had been routinely read by GCHQ, stopped unexpectedly in 1941, soon after Philby had been indoctrinated into the source when he joined SIS's Section V. Nevertheless, there is no reference in Philby's autobiography, *My Silent War*, that the source of the FBI's information, which led to a long search for a leak in the wartime British embassy in Washington DC codenamed HOMER, was VENONA:

> Joint Anglo-American investigation of Soviet intelligence activity in the United States had yielded a strong suggestion that there had been a leakage from the British Embassy in Washington during the years 1944–45, and

another from the atomic energy establishment in Los Alamos. I had no ideas about Los Alamos. But a swift check of the Foreign Office list left me in little doubt about the identity of the source in the British Embassy. My anxiety was tempered by relief, since I had been nagged for some months by a question put to me by my Soviet contact in Istanbul. He had asked me if I had any means of discovering what the British were doing in the case under investigation by the FBI – a case involving the British Embassy in Washington. At the time of asking there was nothing I could have done.

Philby served in Turkey as SIS head of station in Istanbul from January 1947 to September 1949, and arrived in the United States to take up his liaison post in Washington in October 1949. Thus the Centre had learned about the embassy investigation prior to Philby's departure from Istanbul, and the most obvious conclusion is that the tip had come from Weisband. Equally clear is the fact that Weisband had no knowledge of how the FBI was pursuing the VENONA leads, and the KGB were either partly or wholly reliant on Philby for help. This in turn implies that the KGB had failed to penetrate the other Allied security agencies that had been indoctrinated into the secret, a view confirmed by Philby's official briefing into the background of the leak given by Maurice Oldfield, head of counterintelligence at SIS, in London before his departure. This news Philby relayed to his local handler, Yuri Modin, who, according to Philby, 'after checking with headquarters ... was left in no doubt that information from the FBI and my own referred to one and the same case'. In Modin's slightly confused version of this episode, he claims that

> an American cipher expert from the Army Security Agency (later the National Security Agency) William Weisband, had just informed SIS that a brilliant analyst in his service named Meredith Gardner was attempting to decode telegraphic messages sent to the Lubyanka during the war by various KGB posts around the world. This caused a ripple of alarm at the Centre. We had no idea what the Americans might uncover, and this information hung over us like a sword of Damocles.[1]

Of course Weisband had no contact with SIS, and his news must have gone to Moscow and then been filtered back to Modin, but certainly Philby monitored the FBI's progress thereafter, and was able to keep his contacts informed of impending moves against Fuchs, and later Maclean. On the British side just three embassy officials knew of the investigation: Philby's predecessor Peter Dwyer, who was about to retire from SIS and settle in Canada, his MI5 counterpart, Geoffrey Paterson, and the embassy's security officer, Sir Robert Mackenzie. Although Philby attempted to warn Fuchs of the net closing in on him, the message was delayed and the scientist was interrogated and then arrested. In the HOMER case Philby saw the FBI documents building up against Maclean, and was able to alert the diplomat in sufficient time for him to escape to France.

Nor was treachery confined to the British and Americans. One of the most significant breakthroughs in the FBI's pursuit of Russian espionage came in the form of an anonymous letter addressed to J. Edgar Hoover and mailed to the organization's headquarters in Washington DC from a postbox close to the Soviet embassy. Typed on a Cyrillic typewriter, the author demonstrated a close knowledge of the NKVD's local operations and denounced Vasili Zarubin (Zubilin) as the *rezident*, and a war criminal implicated in the Katyn massacre of Polish officers in 1939. Bizarrely, the anonymous correspondent claimed that Zubilin was supplying information to the Japanese, and asserted that his wife Elizaveta, described as the NKVD's director of political espionage, supervising agents who had penetrated the State Department, was in touch with the Nazis through the Hollywood film producer Boris Morros. Although Morros was to approach the FBI in June 1947, having spotted the surveillance, and became a useful double agent, this was the first news that he was in touch with the NKVD.

Also identified in the letter were Pavel Klarin, in New York ('has a vast network of agents among Russian émigrés'), Grigori Kheiffets in San Francisco ('deals with political and military intelligence on the west coast'), and seven other significant figures: Leonid Kvasnikov ('Zubilin's assistant for technical intelligence, through [Semyon] Semyonov – who also works in Amtorg'), Andrei Shevchenko ('agent for the Purchasing Commission in Buffalo. Deals with the same as Semyonov'), Lukianov ('Zubilin's assistant for naval intelligence'), Pavlov (Zubilin's assistant in Canada'), Lev Tarasov ('Zubilin's assistant for Mexico'), and Dolgov ('Zubilin's assistant in Washington').

The last to be denounced was Colonel Markov, alias Mironov, who apparently had also participated in the Polish massacres. This final addition was especially piquant because he was later to be named as the author of the letter by Pavel Sudoplatov, who revealed that Markov had sent a similar letter to Stalin. His allegations against Zubilin had been investigated, found to be groundless and had resulted in his arrest for slander. However, at his trial Mironov was found to be schizophrenic, so he was discharged from the NKVD in 1944 on psychiatric grounds.

As a direct consequence of the Markov letter, the FBI targeted those named for intensive surveillance, and later Don Jardine of the FBI's intelligence division was to recruit two double agents who worked against Andrei I. Shevchenko, codenamed ARSENIJ, at the Bell Aircraft Corporation. Shevchenko, a graduate of Moscow's Aviation Institute, arrived in the USA in June 1942 to supervise the purchase of Bell P-39 Aircobra fighters, and began commuting between the Amtorg office in New York and Bell's plant on Niagara Falls Boulevard, Buffalo. His first recruits, whom he started to cultivate in October 1942, were Leona Franey, a clerk in the Bell library, and her husband Joseph J. Franey who was a repairman in the Hooker Electrochemical Company. While Franey's firm had a classified Manhattan Project contract, his wife (codenamed ZERO, then ERIC) had access to secret plans for the P-59 jet. Under the FBI's supervision the husband and wife team kept Shevchenko supplied with batches of photographs for which he paid $250 apiece. In addition, the FBI had a third double agent deployed against Shevchenko, a Bell Aircraft engineer named Loren G. Haas. Employed by Bell to train Russian pilots and technicians, he had been recruited by Shevchenko to supply classified data, and the Soviet continued to maintain contact with him when he moved to Philadelphia to work for the Westinghouse Electric Corporation. As with the Franeys, every delivery of microfilmed documents was prepared by the FBI which monitored his movements and eavesdropped on his lengthy drinking sessions with Haas, during which the increasingly maudlin Russian engineer would speculate about the size of bonus he would earn, and the need for scientists to share information, irrespective of their nationalities.

Jardine collected sufficient evidence to arrest Shevchenko, who was believed to be a GRU officer, but the State and Justice Departments refused to sanction the move, and soon afterwards Jardine left the FBI for a private law practice. As for the others, the claims made were certainly accurate in that they were Zubilin's direct subordinates, and most appeared in VENONA traffic, Semyon Semyonov as TWAIN, Leonid Kvasnikov as ANTON, Lev Tarasov as YURI (his real name being Lev Vasilevsky). As for Lukianov, there was little about his operational role, but plenty concerning his domestic circumstances, and more than enough in this text from Stepan Apresyan in New York dated 20 November 1944 to identify positively him as AKIM:

> A few days ago AKIM [Sergei G. Lukianov] had a severe heart attack which [20 groups unrecovered] the consultant's report is bad: Severe nervous overstrain which has produced a fall in cardiac activity, a severe lowering of blood pressure and attacks of vertigo. The doctor considers a two months' rest with treatment the absolute minimum necessary to avoid complications. In connection with this incident we may remark that a similar attack has already occurred in another town while AKIM was there on business. AKIM already suffers from a stomach complaint. We emphasize that the vague reaction of the Centre to AKIM's repeated requests and proposals for filling personnel vacancies in the Fifth Line and in general for improving the work, the absence of profound appreciation of his work so far, which is evidently to be explained by an inadequate conception of the colossal difficulties of his work, have always been hard for AKIM to bear and have undoubtedly helped to pave the way for his illness, bearing in mind the enormous pressure at which he works. To restore his health, which is in real danger, I urgently plead that he be granted two weeks' leave within the next few days. Furthermore I consider it essential that there should be sent a thorough-going appreciation of his work from the moment of his arrival in the COUNTRY [America], not merely enumerating his mistakes and failures but also [32 groups unrecoverable] neither the strength nor the health to cope with his difficult sector number 114. We

have received the statement in a special telegram and will give some practical consideration on what is involved in the changes scheduled.

On the following day Apresyan was again in touch with Moscow over Lukianov:

> In a chat with our worker AKIM's wife raised the question of the possibility of her departure for the [Soviet] Union, giving as her reason the fact that she had been specially fated: a brother had been killed, a second brother had been wounded three times and his whereabouts were unknown. For more than a year she has been unsuccessfully requesting that her mother [1 group unrecovered] (her mother lives with her brother's widow) and has been sending her a parcel every month but the mother during all this time has received only one parcel. The mother is old and unable to work and her own source of livelihood is the money which AKIM remits. Bearing in mind also the state of AKIM's health, which is having a very adverse effect on her, I urgently request [visit] her mother and the wife in MOSCOW and try to improve their living conditions. To recall AKIM's wife home without him I consider impermissible for understandable reasons. Please also take steps to see that letters arrive regularly as for a year past only one letter has been received.

This correspondence ended on 8 December with Apresyan's final directive, referring to a telegram missing in the VENONA series: 'Your number 131. Please pay AKIM's mother 200 a month and his wife's mother – CHUPIKOVA – 300, in all 500 roubles. Written authority by post.'

Clearly Lukianov recovered, for he received the following from Moscow, addressed personally, on 12 May 1945:

> The COMBINE [Ministry of Foreign Trade] is issuing instructions about appointing you to VANCOUVER in the post of Senior Inspector and representative of the Commercial Attaché. MAK is being appointed to your place. Draw up a report on the work you have carried out, explain the essentials of investigations in process, plans [50 groups unrecovered]

Lukianov's departure from the USA may not have been connected with Markov's letter, but there was to be an unprecedented exodus at the time of the withdrawal of Klarin, Kheiffets and the Zubilins at the end of August 1944. This may have been prompted by the unexpected arrival in the USA of two inspectors, Mikhail Milsky and Grigori Kossarev, who masqueraded as diplomatic couriers and toured Mexico and California before they left at the end of July 1944, following a fortnight in Ottawa. In reality, according to the defector Igor Gouzenko, this pair were actually a senior NKVD representative and General Solomon R. Milstein, the GRU's deputy chief, with responsibility for the GRU's North American operations, who together had conducted a critical review of Soviet espionage in the region. Their arrival in New York in April 1944 was timely, for the following day Viktor Kravchenko made his very public defection from the Purchasing Commission and published his criticism of the regime. Their visit certainly came after Markov's anonymous disclosures, and the heightened level of FBI surveillance, and was unlikely to have been coincidental. Most likely they were on a mission to reassess the joint GRU-NKVD penetration of the Manhattan Project, codenamed ENORMOZ. Whatever their purpose, which they did not confide to Gouzenko, their route, taking in Mexico, California and Canada, gave them an opportunity to evaluate ENORMOZ's principal targets in the USA, at Los Alamos, Berkeley, Chicago, Colombia, Hanford and Oak Ridge, and the two main Canadian sites, at Chalk River and the uranium production centre at Port Radium on the Great Bear Lake.³

The visitors' verdict had been unfavourable, for dramatic changes took place not long after the inspection had been completed, and it was followed a year later by another visit from Kossarev, this time accompanied by Sergei Fomichev of the GRU. Whereas the first inspection reportedly had been damning, and had condemned the *rezidentura*s for 'lack of vigilance', the second had expressed complete satisfaction with the performance of Colonel Nikolai Zabotin, who was awarded the Order of the Red Banner in August 1945, and his NKVD counterpart, Vitali G. Pavlov. Ironically, within the year, while Zaroubin was wholly innocent and attempting to recover his reputation, Zabotin and Pavlov would see their entire organization destroyed by Gouzenko. It had been Moscow's decision to withdraw Gouzenko, delayed until September 1945 but recommended by the inspectors, that proved the catalyst for his defection. The consequences were devastating for all concerned, with Allan Nunn May convicted of espionage, and twenty-three others arrested. As for Zabotin, a graduate of the Krasin Artillery School, he was recalled to Moscow in December 1945 and was not seen again after he boarded the *Alexander Suvorov* in New York shortly before it sailed. According to Vladimir Petrov, Zabotin shouldered the blame for the loss of his cipher-clerk and was sentenced to ten years' hard labour.

VENONA's value as a counter-espionage instrument was quite exceptional, although it rarely provided the FBI with all the answers. It shed unprecedented light on Soviet clandestine operations, helped identify undercover intelligence personnel, served to corroborate the testimony of defectors, informers and double agents, and occasionally provided the damning evidence required to confirm existing suspicions. The additional ingredient of undiscovered traitors within the camps of both protagonists added a further dimension to the conflict, with Weisband and Philby learning some of VENONA's secrets, while Colonel Markov was attempting anonymously to expose the entire Washington *rezidentura*.

To some extent VENONA can be characterized as part of a complex cerebral game relevant only to the participants, chiefly intelligence professionals pitting their wits against each other, but although the texts gave a tremendous advantage to the home team defending their turf, the real significance of the material extended far beyond covert skirmishes in New York and Washington DC.

III

The GRU's London Network

AT THE BEGINNING of the war the KGB's legal *rezident* in London, albeit in an acting capacity, was Anatoli V. Gorsky, alias 'Anatoli Gromov', who had succeeded Grigori B. Grafpen in 1938. In February 1940 Gorsky was withdrawn by the Centre because of NKVD chief Lavrenti Beria's belief that the local apparatus had suffered hostile penetration. Beria's fear proved to have no foundation and Gorsky returned under diplomatic cover in December 1940 with the status of full *rezident*. At that time the embassy was relatively small, with just five diplomats, plus the ambassador, and three trade representatives.

In contrast, the Soviet military intelligence apparatus in London was extensive throughout the war, and was headed by the military attaché, Colonel Ivan Sklyarov, who was appointed in October 1940. Like the NKVD in Moscow, which operated entirely independently, the GRU maintained a completely separate organization, and was headed between July 1941 and July 1942 by Major-General Aleksandr P. Panfilov, usually referred to by his subordinates as the DIREKTOR. Formerly the commander of the 2nd Mechanized Brigade in Manchuria, he was transferred to command the 316 Rifle Division in 1942 and was replaced by General Leonid Ilyichov, who was executed in a purge in April 1943. Most of the GRU VENONAS are addressed either to the DIREKTOR, or to the ADMINISTRATOR, believed to be the chief of the GRU's First (Western Europe) Department, Colonel Fedor F. Kuznetsov, formerly Commissar of the 60th Army, who succeeded Ilyichov as DIREKTOR. While the KGB has opened some of its archives to historians, the GRU appears to remain almost untouched by the changes that have swept through Eastern Europe, and none of its files has been declassified. However, there can be little doubt that, particularly during the NKVD's suspension of activities in London during 1940, the GRU's local *rezidentura* must have taken on a greater responsibility.

There has been little external information about the GRU's activities in London, for instance from the evidence of defectors, but the VENONA intercepts clearly identify several GRU officers, and show that upon the arrival of Sklyarov in October 1940 (his first intercept was dated 11 October 1940) two separate *rezidentura*s were created. In a signal dated 7 June 1941, apparently in response to a financial appeal, nine GRU officers made four-year loans to the state out of their salaries. Listed were Colonel Sklyarov, his secretary, Simon Kremer (who had been in London since 1937 and remained until 1946), and his chauffeur Nikolai M. Timofeev, who was in London between September 1939 and June 1943; Major Anatoli Lebedev (the assistant military attaché army, April 1941 to November 1943) and his secretary, Ivan M. Kozlov, who arrived in April 1941 and left in November 1945; Major Boris Shvetsov (assistant military attaché air, from October 1940 to his death in an air accident in April 1942); Nikolai V. Aptekar, a chauffeur who had driven first the naval attaché, between March and November 1937, and later the air attaché Ivan Cherny, and left in April 1944; Boris Dikiy, listed in January 1940 as Cherny's secretary, and later promoted to assistant air attaché; Fedor I. Moskvichev, the military attaché's clerk between December 1939 and January 1943.

In addition to these nine, two VENONAs refer to a staff member codenamed MIM, who has been tentatively identified as Mikhail I. Mikhailov working as an attaché at the Soviet consulate in Rosary Gardens between December 1939 and July 1943. Other references to MARK, DICK, NIK and KLARK suggest they too were the GRU *rezident*'s subordinates, doubtless his staff listed above. The texts signed BARCh (and later ALEXANDER) have been identified as originating with Simon Kremer, and BRION has been identified as Boris Shvetsov. There is also a reference to Colonel Grigori P. Pugachev, a member of the Soviet Military Mission who arrived in England in July 1941.

Before the VENONA texts were released to the public in July 1995, very little had been understood about the GRU's wartime operations in England, but it was known that at least three different networks had been active. Of the three, the first to be uncovered by MI5 was an organization built by Oliver C. Green, a printer by trade and veteran CPGB member from Birmingham who had been wounded in the Spanish Civil War. After his return to London he was based in Edgware and contributed to a history of the British Battalion of the International Brigade. He came to the Security Service's attention in 1941 when he was arrested by the police for using forged petrol coupons. A search of his home revealed a Leica camera, a collection of classified documents and other espionage paraphernalia, including an intelligence circular that was traced to a soldier, a Communist named Elliott stationed at Smedley's Hydro, Matlock. Under interrogation Green admitted that he routinely travelled the country by car to collect information from his sources, most of whom had fought in Spain; among them were a seaman, a pilot and several factory workers. It had been Green's illicit use of a private vehicle that had attracted the attention of the police, and because of his willingness to cooperate with MI5, no mention was made of his espionage when he was charged with offences connected with petrol coupons.

The GRU's second network in England had involved the remarkable Ursula Kuczynsky who had arrived in Oxford in January 1941, via Lisbon and Gibraltar, as a refugee from Switzerland, with the benefit of a British passport supplied by her new husband, Leon (Len) Beurton. Ursula was an experienced GRU illegal of Polish origin who had been recruited in Shanghai by the legendary Richard Sorge in 1932, and had moved to Lausanne where she had met and married Len, a veteran of the International Brigade in Spain. However, as the Swiss police closed in on the GRU network to which she had been assigned, she was ordered to England, where the rest of her family were living. Her father, Professor Robert Kuczynsky, who had fled to London from Berlin in 1933, was then lecturing at Oxford, and her brother Jurgen, also an academic and an economist, was a leading figure among the anti-Nazi refugees living in Britain.

When her husband was called up by the Coldstream Guards, Ursula established herself as an illegal in a rented house in north Oxford, and in 1943 played a key role in helping Klaus Fuchs to re-establish contact with the Soviets. Although Ursula today maintains that she was in direct communication with Moscow by radio, it is clear from the VENONA from BRION (believed to be Boris Shvetsov) dated 31 July 1941 that she had met IRIS (see below) the previous day to discuss wireless schedules and her finances.

Ursula says in *Sonia's Report* that before leaving Geneva she had been given instructions on how to make contact with her local controller, and she had held a rendezvous with him in a street near Hyde Park not far from Marble Arch:

> The first meeting in a new country is always exciting. Will someone be there? What sort of work will Centre want me to do? Will I be capable of carrying it out? What if no-one turns up? One or two dates had already passed, as I had not foreseen the delay in Portugal, nor the weeks at sea. My partner would probably also be pleased to make contact at last. I waited long beyond the appointed hour but no one came. I waited the next evening – in vain. And again a fortnight later. I do not recall how often I travelled to London and how many times I walked up and down that street. The area had been badly chosen. It was a favourite haunt of prostitutes, who did not appreciate my frequent appearance. I felt increasingly uneasy. Had there been a misunderstanding about the arrangements? Had I confused the location? I was not allowed to go to the Soviet Embassy, and anyway I would never have done so. When I went to the London meeting place in May, I had all but given up hope. A man approached me, not the first in this accursed street, but this time he was the one I wanted. He greeted me with the codewords I was waiting for, and I glided down the street and along two or more as if on wings to a place where we were to talk. The Soviet comrade Sergei (my cover-name for him) brought me greetings from the Centre and congratulations on my arrival. He also handed me enough money to allay all my financial worries. A car accident had delayed his appearance.

Ursula has never disclosed, and probably never knew, Sergei's true identity, concealed in the VENONA traffic by the codename IRIS, which in Russian means either the flower or toffee. IRIS appears only twice in the VENONA texts, the first being fragments of a report dated 1 August 1940 giving an account of IRIS's recent visit to Liverpool describing Blenheim bombers at an airfield. Several French warships in port had been noted, and the military nature of the observations, coinciding with other VENONA traffic, strongly suggests that IRIS was a staff member of the GRU's *rezidentura*. Since, according to Ursula, 'the "Sergeis" changed two or three times' while she was in England, it is not possible to identify him.

Although there is doubt about the identity of her contacts, Ursula was a skilled agent who organized her own network. She supplied political gossip gleaned from her father, who was acquainted with several senior Labour politicians, and was on good terms with the British ambassador to Moscow, Sir Stafford Cripps. She also acquired military documents.

> After I had succeeded in making some military contacts, I received material that could not be sent by radio. At one of these meetings Sergei gave me a little parcel measuring only about eight by six inches. It contained a small transmitter. Although I was as unenthusiastic as ever about theory, I became attached to the reliable, handy and technically superior instrument. I dismantled my own transmitter, which was six times the size, and hid the parts for emergency use. Altogether I transmitted from England for five or six years.

Among those who supplied information to Ursula were her brother Jurgen, who went to work for the Office of the Strategic Bombing Survey in London as an economist, and Erich Henschke who acted as an intermediary with Joseph Gould, an OSS officer assigned to the task of recruiting Germans willing to be parachuted back into Germany. Gould worked for OSS's Labor Division and through Jurgen met a group of suitable candidates, all members of the Free Germany Committee, and all Communists judged reliable by the Centre. Kuczynsky made the introductions while Henschke, another lifelong Communist who had fought in Spain, reported to Ursula on the progress each made in his OSS training course. Gould was apparently completely unaware of how he had been manipulated.

> Erich Henschke withdrew temporarily from party work in order to devote himself fully to his task of co-operating with the OSS and passing on material to me. He supplied me with photos and biographies of a number of comrades. After I had relayed these to Centre and received their

agreement; the names were proposed to the OSS. The comrades knew that this had been approved by the Soviet Union.

In addition, Ursula recruited two Britons, an RAF officer she called 'James', who was a welder by trade, and a radio operator, 'Tom', who were both ideologically motivated to spy:

> James belonged to the technical branch of the Air Force and had access to some of the newest developments in aeroplane construction. He got hold of exact data for us, weights and dimensions, load-carrying capacity, special characteristics, and even contrived to let me have blueprints of machines that had not yet flown. I remember a new invention, a small mechanical device, of which he gave me the original. As parts like this were all numbered and kept under lock and key, its disappearance caused an uproar.
>
> Tom was a fitter in a car plant. He did whatever was required of him without hesitation or fuss. He was tactful, witty and sensitive. He was reliable, too, and, when the work demanded it, he could be hard. You could always depend on Tom. In order to teach him Morse either Len or I had to visit him at his house or he would come to us. Tom, likewise, refused to accept any money. He wanted to have more time for learning and found a job that did not demand a full working day (he became a bill-sticker).
>
> In the period between his arrival in England in the late summer of 1942 and his brief induction in October 1943 into the RAF (before his transfer into the 1st Armoured Battalion of the Coldstream Guards) Len was also actively recruiting agents for Ursula to handle. One was a specialist in seaborne tank landing. Apart from information on tank-landing operations, he supplied us with an important instrument that was used for submarine radar. At that time radar was quite new and Centre was very interested in it. Usually we buried such treasures until the next meeting with Sergei, but, if they seemed exceptionally important, we could ask for an emergency meeting. Len also had contact with a chemist who gave him information.

The Beurton husband-and-wife team was obliged to suspend joint operations while Len served with his regiment. He was not demobbed until February 1947. While operating alone, Ursula was disconnected by the Centre from 'the summer or autumn 1946', probably as a consequence of information given to MI5 by GRU defector Allan Foote, with whom she had worked in Switzerland. Foote had defected in early August 1947 and his detailed account of his activities as a GRU wireless operator resulted in a visit to Ursula and Len by MI5 the following month. The encounter was unproductive, and although she made efforts to re-establish contact, they were ignored until January 1949 when she hand-delivered a letter to the Soviet embassy in Prague. This acted as the catalyst for a renewed link via a dead-drop in the Oxfordshire countryside. Evidently MI5 never connected her with Klaus Fuchs, who was arrested in February 1950, but unwilling to take any risks she left for Berlin the day before his trial, with Len following some months later. As for Ursula's agents, the RAF officer named James reportedly died of leukemia, and the wireless operator Tom was deliberately disconnected nine months after contact had been lost with the Centre, so as to avoid compromising him. This was a wise move, for once Fuchs had begun his fourteen years' imprisonment in February 1950 he underwent a lengthy interrogation at Wormwood Scrubs prison. He identified ALEXANDER, his first Soviet contact, from MI5's collection of diplomatic passport photos as Simon Kremer, whom he had met on 8 August 1941, having attended a rendezvous in London that had been facilitated by his Communist friend, Jurgen Kuczinsky. According to Fuchs's testimony, he had held four meetings with Kremer before being passed on to Ursula the following year. She arranged meetings near Banbury, which was conveniently midway between her home in Oxford and his in Birmingham. Fuchs, of course, never learned Ursula's true identity, and had no suspicion that she was in fact Jurgen's sister. Ursula continued to run Fuchs until December 1943 when the physicist was transferred from Birmingham to the United States. Before he left, Ursula gave him precise instructions on the recognition signals for his next rendezvous, which was to take place on Saturday 5 February 1944 at a street corner on the lower east side in New York. This was the last time Ursula met Fuchs, until they were reunited in Dresden after his release from prison, and it was only then that the scientist realized that his GRU contact in Banbury had been Jurgen Kuczinsky's sister.

The third GRU network known about prior to VENONA was run by a concert pianist, Ernest D. Weiss, who had been in England since May 1932 and had supervised two CPGB members, an Air Ministry official named Major Wilfred Vernon and an Irishman, Frederick Meredith. The pair knew Weiss as 'Alfred Lock', so when they were charged with breaches of the Official Secrets Act in August 1937, he escaped arrest and remained at liberty to handle several other GRU sources. After the war he identified five of them: a German refugee, Hans Lubszynski, who had worked for Telefunken; Dr Heinz Kallman, a physicist from Berlin employed by EMI to develop television; André Labarthe, who had worked for the French Ministry of Air until 1938; Professor Marcel Prenant, a biologist, formerly of the Sorbonne; and Jacques Soustelle, later to be head of General de Gaulle's Free French intelligence service.

Of this latter group, André Labarthe appears frequently in the VENONA traffic under the codename JEROME, and until September 1940 he held the post of director-general of French Armament and Scientific Research at de Gaulle's headquarters. He was easy to identify because, in a telegram dated 24 August 1940, he was described as having recently 'had a talk with CHURCHILL's private secretary. The latter stated that during the last three weeks morale had risen considerably in the ranks of the National Coalition Government partly as a result of the success of the RAF but mainly because of SASHA's [United States'] promise of support'. A simple check with (Sir) Jock Colville, who had fulfilled that role, would have enabled MI5 to put a name to the cryptonym. Labarthe's secretary, Alta Lecoutre, designated MARTHA, was married to Stanislas Szymonczyk, and had been Pierre Cot's mistress. Cot was Minister of Air in the governments of Edouard Daladier, Albert Saurrant and Leon Blum, and had also been a Soviet source.

Certainly the task of identifying the people behind the codenames was easier in some cases than in others. WRITER, for instance, was revealed on 15 August 1940 to have been serving aboard the *Malines* when it steamed 'into Rotterdam with the task of preparing for the evacuation of the Consulate'; he later mentioned that at Dunkirk his ship had rescued 750 seamen from the destroyers *Wakeful* and *Grafton*, which MI5 easily established had been sunk by E-boats on

30 and 29 May 1940, respectively. Similarly, THERAPUTIST had access to 'documentary material on the training of fighter pilots' (on 3 October 1940), 'on the officer career structure in the Air Force and on the methods of retraining Air Force cadres' (7 September 1940); he was stationed close to Swansea on the night of the Luftwaffe raid on the Shell refinery, and 'from his aerodrome alone 250 stretchers were sent there'; previously he had demonstrated a detailed knowledge of the RAF stations at Prestwich, Manston and Leuchars (24 August 1940); and had been stationed at an unnamed airfield holding 150 aircraft, guarded by 150 Dutch troops, which had been attacked in the week preceding 14 August in a raid in which two hangars and eight aircraft were destroyed. Helpfully, STANLEY is described on 22 July 1940 as 'a very cautious man. He himself is non-party and originates from the Canadian working-class elite'. He was also 'looking for work on an agricultural farm near the MUSIC [radio] so as to obtain deferment of his call-up to the Army and to regain his health'. As for BAUER, he is clearly named as a certain Lieutenant Hein of the Czech Army, stationed at Malpas, near Wrexham, who had attempted to recruit an officer, name unknown, who was considered 'of interest as an informant and talent-spotter'.

Another identified GRU ring centred on Douglas Springhall, a member of the CPGB's Central Committee since 1932 who had attended the 1924 Communist International in Moscow, and had formerly been the Commissar of the British Battalion of the International Brigade in Spain. In June 1943 'Dave' Springhall was arrested on the evidence of Olive Sheehan, a Customs and Excise clerk on temporary secondment to the Air Ministry, and he was convicted of having received classified papers from Captain Ormond Uren, a Highland Light Infantry officer attached to SOE's Hungarian Section. Both Uren and Springhall were sentenced to long terms of imprisonment, but nobody at the embassy was implicated although, as David Clark, MI5's Russian counter-espionage expert noted at the time, it was probably not a coincidence that a member of the Soviet military attaché's staff named Graur, who previously had been implicated in an espionage case in Sweden, left the country four days after Springhall's arrest. The investigation into Uren by MI5's F2a section had been prompted by the discovery in Springhall's notebook of the name of an Edinburgh Communist, Helen Grierson, through whom he apparently met an important source. Clark had travelled to Scotland, befriended Grierson, and pretended to know Springhall's contact. Impressed by Clark's encyclopedic knowledge of CPGB personalities, Grierson had let slip Uren's name.

The most intriguing, unresolved issue centres on the X GROUP, a GRU network headed by INTELLIGENSIA with help from the Honourable Ivor Montagu, codenamed NOBILITY. Hitherto completely unsuspected, this spy-ring operated in London undetected, and it was not until GCHQ began reading some of the London GRU traffic in the mid-1960s that the breathtaking scale of the organization, and the social status of its membership, was understood. Montagu was the third son of Lord Swaythling, and he was an ardent CPGB member who was to become the Party's president. Born in 1904, educated at Westminster and King's College, Cambridge, he had studied zoology at the Royal College of Science and was well known in artistic circles. A friend of the Russian director Eisenstein, he was particularly interested in the cinema, as an editor, writer, director, producer and critic. One of his great successes was the screenplay, co-authored with Walter Meade, of *Scott of the Antarctic*, starring John Mills, which was released in 1948. As well as being a Communist, Montagu was also extraordinarily rich, having a huge inheritance from his great-grandfather, the first Baron Swaythling who was one of the founders of Shell Oil. Predictably, there is no clue to his clandestine role in his autobiography. *The Youngest Son*, published in 1970, which was intended to be the first of several volumes, and gives an account of his life only until 1927. Nevertheless, his visit to Leningrad, Moscow and Tblisi in 1925 had a profound impact on his political consciousness:

> When I came back from the USSR, though deeply impressed, above all, by the sense of comradeship there and, in the current cant phrase, the evidence of the wind of change, I still did not join the Communist Party of Great Britain. I still did not know enough about Communism or Marxism. I admired both Lenin and Trotsky, and could not understand the issues between the Soviet Party and Trotsky which were then reaching the surface. I did join the scientists' trade union (the National Union, now the Association, of Scientific Workers) as soon as it was formed and, as a trade unionist, the Minority Movement. I

consorted with Communists and found among them the only political friends of like approach.

Montagu was also the author of *The Traitor Class*, published in 1940, and of many political pamphlets. After the war he headed the Soviet front organization, the World Council of Peace. He was also on the editorial board of *Labour Monthly*, with Rojani Palme Dutt and another leading figure in the CPGB, Robin Page Arnot. His elder brother Ewan was a barrister who during the war worked in the Naval Intelligence Division and represented the Admiralty on the XX Committee which supervised MI5's double agent operations. In 1953 he wrote *The Man Who Never Was*, an account of the celebrated wartime strategic deception which involved planting a corpse on the Spanish coast intended to mislead the Germans. Clearly he was oblivious to his brother's espionage on behalf of the Russians. Ivor eventually settled on the island of Rousay in the Orkneys where he died in November 1984. It is fair to say that none of the family realized that Ivor had been engaged in espionage, and the revelation will come as a shock to them.

Even though there are only six VENONA texts referring to Montagu, his importance to the GRU can be seen from the fact that Simon Kremer used him as a conduit to the X GROUP, apparently because, as he reported on 6 September 1940, 'INTELLIGENSIA lives in the provinces and it is difficult to contact him'. He was also trusted sufficiently to handle other agents, as is suggested by Colonel Sklyarov's fragmented signal of 12 August 1941 in which he stated that NOBILITY was undergoing training 'so that he can organise BARON's very onerous task'. Given BARON's key position (see pp.65ff), the GRU's willingness to let Montagu supervise him is highly significant.

Montagu was a useful observer ('NOBILITY has reported that the British have brought six destroyers in the THAMES and are evacuating EASTBOURNE', signalled Kremer on 17 September 1940) and his access to military sites was facilitated by his status as a newspaper correspondent. As a staff writer for the *Daily Worker*, where he worked for more than ten years, he was shown around the site in Denham occupied by 339th Battery of the 26th Searchlight Regiment of the 1st Anti-Aircraft Division in October 1940, and was able to give Colonel Sklyarov a detailed account of what he had seen.

In a regiment there are four batteries, each of four troops. A troop consists of two detachments. Each detachment constitutes a self-contained unit with an establishment of 12–13 men, one searchlight, one sound locator, one diesel generator and one Lewis gun. In all there are 350 men and 24 searchlights in a battery. The officers [1 group unrecovered] territorial troops; they received a special type [1 group unrecovered] beginning of the war. A detachment occupies a site 25 metres in diameter. The distance between detachments is 2.5–9 kilometres. The searchlights are automatically directed onto the targets by means of the data from the sound locator. The searchlight beams are effective up to a height of 5,000 metres. Detachments are linked to battery and battery is linked to regiment and to Sector Operations Room from which information about the enemy is sometimes received. The battery commander stated that during the last fortnight two SAUSAGE-DEALERS [Germans] had been shot down by gunfire.

As well as making these rather routine observations that were of value to the Soviets, and presumably their German allies, Montagu also acted as a link for other CPGB (CORPORATION) members anxious to convey classified information to the Soviets. On 20 December 1940 Colonel Sklyarov reported:

> Through NOBILITY the X GROUP has passed material [12 groups unrecovered] received from a member of the CORPORATION who has been working on technical work in intelligence departments [40 groups unrecovered]

Only on one occasion, on 16 October 1940, is there a clue to the kind of technical intelligence data Montagu had encountered. On that date Sklyarov signalled:

> NOBILITY has reported the following information on the SAUSAGE-DEALERS air-raid on FILTON 10 days ago. 30 SAUSAGE-DEALERS bombers and 30 fighters used a radio beam to fly from Northern France; they passed over PORTLAND straight to BRISTOL from where they turned on to the FILTON Aircraft Factory. All the bombs were dropped in a ring of smoke laid above the factory by one of the

SAUSAGE-DEALERS. Three shelters were destroyed by a direct hit, killing 81 people and injuring 300–500. The damage to production was slight. British fighters appeared after the raid.

Superficially this looks like a relatively straightforward account of a noteworthy Luftwaffe raid, perhaps the attack on Bristol that took place on 27 September, but the interesting item is the reference to a radio beam. At the time, at the height of the Blitz, the existence of the night navigation system codenamed KNICKEBEIN was a closely-guarded secret. The very first clue to KNICKEBEIN had been recorded at the RAF's PoW interrogation centre at Trent Park, Cockfosters, where two indiscreet Luftwaffe aircrew had been heard to discuss a new navigation device they called 'the X-Gerat'. Thereafter SIS and Air Intelligence had investigated the possibility, previously considered technically impossible, for radio signals to be used to guide bombers to their targets at night. The Germans were notoriously poor navigators after dusk, but their performance had steadily improved throughout the summer of 1940. SIS suspicion that the Luftwaffe had perfected an ingenious apparatus was confirmed in June by another talkative prisoner who explained that it had been developed at Rechlin, and obligingly drew a sketch of the transmitter tower. This breakthrough prompted the creation of the Night Interception Committee, a high-level gathering of scientists and RAF personnel keen to solve the puzzle of how the enemy's system worked. Close re-inspections of all the electrical equipment recovered from the Heinkel 111 that had been brought down near Edinburgh suggested that the receiving equipment was contained in what appeared to be a very standard, commercially available Lorenz blind-landing receiver. However, further examination revealed that the gadget had been modified and boasted an unusual sensitivity, of precisely the quality required for a long-range navigational aid. News of the interesting beams was reported to the Cabinet on 21 June, and the following month the RAF established a secret unit at Radlett in Hertfordshire, designated 80 Wing, to monitor the Lorenz transmitting frequencies, intercept the beams, and attempt to jam or even bend them. By August, the Telecommunications Research Establishment at Swanage had produced an effective counter-measure which transmitted an almost identical signal on the same frequency as the

German 'directional beacons' and these were placed in strategic sites so as to confuse the enemy pilots. While the beams were codenamed HEADACHES, the antidote was known appropriately as ASPIRIN. Thus, towards the end of the summer, stories had begun to circulate in both the RAF and the Luftwaffe that Air Intelligence had invented a method of bending the KNICKEBEIN beams. This, of course, was not strictly true, but as the counter-measures seemed effective, the RAF was particularly keen to keep a lid on what precisely had been accomplished so as to prevent the Germans from improving their equipment. Accordingly, Montagu's remarks about a radio beam, if they had become known to the boffins at 80 Wing, would have created much alarm. As it was, they now suggest an appalling breach of security.

Another key figure in the X GROUP was codenamed BARON, who can now be identified as Karel Sedlacek, then a senior member of the Czech intelligence service. Sedlacek had been hand-picked by the service's chief, General Frantisek Moravec, to work in southern Bohemia, and had spent a year in Prague becoming a skilled wireless operator until he was despatched to Zurich as 'Karl Zelsinger', the local correspondent for the Prague daily *Narodni Listy*, operating from the Czech consulate with the callsign KAZI. By the end of 1938 Sedlacek had cultivated a Swiss intelligence officer, Major Hans Hausamann, who directed a highly sophisticated network that stretched deep into Germany from his headquarters in the Villa Stutz, an innocuous-looking mansion at Kastanienbaum outside Lucerne, known as the Bureau Ha. Hausamann supplied Sedlacek with such an impressive quantity of information about German troop movements over the border that the latter moved from Zurich to Lucerne in order to be closer to the Bureau Ha. The data were relayed to London, whence Moravec fled in March 1939 just as his country was invaded. Among Hausamann's sources was Rudolf Roessler, codenamed LUCY, who was an anti-Nazi German refugee, and a publisher by trade, credited with impressive contacts inside Germany, and it was largely due to his efforts that General Moravec in London was able to keep President Eduard Beneš's Czech government-in-exile, and the British SIS, well informed about what was happening inside the Reich. However, exactly how Roessler, who in Switzerland printed and published numerous political pamphlets and articles, came to acquire such impressive sources has never been fully explained.

Moravec had enjoyed a particularly close relationship with the SIS, and it had been the local SIS station commander, Harold Gibson (designated 22500), who had arranged for Moravec's hasty exfiltration from Prague, together with his deputy, Major Emil Strankmueller, and ten of the senior staff, on a chartered Dutch airliner. The plane had flown to Amsterdam for refuelling before continuing the journey to London, where Moravec, listed on SIS's rolls as 22501, was installed by Gibson at the Victoria Hotel. Hours later, the Abwehr occupied Moravec's headquarters in Prague, only to find that the management and files had disappeared. Moravec was regarded by SIS as an especially welcome guest because of his access to 'A-54', a crucial source in the Abwehr named Paul Thummel who had volunteered to help the Czechs in February 1937. Thummel continued to supply Moravec with the Abwehr's secrets until his arrest in February 1942, thereby ensuring Moravec's exalted status with SIS.

Moravec's dramatic appearance in England did not go unnoticed by the Soviets, who probably spotted his picture in *The Times* on the morning following his arrival at Croydon Airport. Certainly the Soviet air attaché Ivan Cherny, established contact with him within a fortnight, and his invitation to dinner was accepted 'after consultation with my British friends. This contact was purely social and not a word was said about Intelligence matters'. According to Moravec's account, Cherny's interest in him waned, but 'when the USSR was attacked by the Nazis in 1941 the Soviet military attaché in London visited me at once and very politely, almost humbly, and asked me for information which would be of interest to his government. I consulted my British friends, who agreed on condition that I inform them of everything I gave to the Russians. Later that year there appeared in London another representative of Soviet intelligence. His name was Ivan A. Chichayev and was obviously an NKVD man.'

Moravec's reference to Chichayev is particularly interesting, partly because he was the *rezident* and head of the NKVD's declared liaison mission to SOE, and also because the KGB's General Pavel Sudoplatov has asserted that Moravec had been working for the NKVD: 'The head of Czech intelligence, Colonel Moravec, was a full-time KGB agent, recruited by our *rezident* in London, Chichayev. Among other items of intelligence, Moravec had reported that the British were interested in the processing of uranium ore and in shipping it from the Sudeten mountains in Czechoslovakia after the war. He had access to the minutes of the British-Czech talks on exploration for uranium.' In the light of Sudoplatov's disclosure, the question arises as to whether Moravec might have been BARON, but two factors mitigate against it. One is that BARON was emphatically a GRU source, not NKVD, and the second is that BARON was already operational in 1940, a period when the NKVD had virtually suspended their activities in England, whereas Chichayev did not arrive in London to take up his appointment as *rezident* in succession to Anatoli Gorsky until the following year.

The VENONA texts mention BARON on several occasions between March and August 1941, usually in the context of noting recent railway movements in Czechoslovakia, and on 17 May 1941 Boris Shvetsov (BRION) reported that BARON had held a meeting with DICK in London. Although there has been speculation that BARON was a British source based at Bletchley Park, with access to Enigma intercepts, it is more likely that he was indeed a senior figure within the Czech military intelligence service. This is indicated by a VENONA dated 3 April 1941 which indicates that BARON's data had been confirmed by an Enigma intercept. Far from suggesting that BARON himself was handling Enigma decrypts, which would be routine for an analyst or cryptographer at Bletchley, there is a strong indication of 'this delicate source's possible connection to Military Intelligence'.

> In reply to your telegram No. 3075
> This information originates solely from BARON, its provenance seems to be well known to you, the intercept bearing the designation ENIGMA. The information about the intention of the SAUSAGE-DEALERS [Germans] [13 groups unrecovered] on our part. What [4 groups unrecovered]. It is well known that [5 groups unrecovered], but [5 groups unrecovered] the government of the COLONY [Britain] and this delicate source's possible connection with Military Intelligence here we can take it that his information is fully deserving of attention and therefore I consider that it would be a profound error to take his [13 groups unrecovered] BARON's facts prove that [4 groups unrecovered] the COLONISTS [British] [6 groups unrecovered], that [5 groups unrecovered] [57 groups unrecoverable]

Naturally this text had a chilling effect on the GCHQ cryptanalysts who worked on it, for at the time the word 'Enigma' remained highly classified, and the context made clear that either BARON himself or his source had direct access to Enigma material at Bletchley Park. The implications of such a well-placed spy deep inside GCHQ as early as April 1941 were considered potentially devastating for the organization. That BARON too realized its significance seems to be apparent in a text dated 17 May 1941 from Sklyarov:

> To ADMINISTRATION. 17 May DICK had a meeting with BARON. 1. On the subject of handing over to us intercept [1 group unrecovered], BARON [16 groups unrecovered] declared that your answer to this question would determine all future work with him. As a matter of urgency send instructions by 19th May. 3. On the question of the reserve line of communication we suggest in a fortnight's time [36 groups unrecovered] [57 groups unrecoverable]

From postwar records it appears that Sedlacek worked for the British as well as the Swiss and the Russians, and the fact that he dried up as a source as soon as Rudolf Roessler was arrested in May 1944 supports the proposition that Sedlacek was heavily dependent upon him. A declassified CIA report on Sedlacek asserts that at one point in the war Sedlacek was operating with a British passport and using the name 'Charles Simpson', and a report dated 18 November 1945 from Philby to Moscow (translated by Yuri Modin on 7 February 1946, and declassified in April 1998) confirms that Sedlacek 'entered Switzerland on a British passport in the name of Simpson' and had been designated the code number 22505 by SIS. 'In the opinion of SIS', noted Philby, 'it is perfectly possible that he has worked at times for the Russians.' The significance, incidentally, of the number 22505 is that SIS agents recruited in Britain were assigned the country prefix of '22'. Accordingly, as well as having been run by the Swiss and the Soviets, Sedlacek had also worked for SIS.

After the war Sedlacek was promoted to lieutenant-colonel and appointed the Czech military attaché in Berne. He was recalled to Prague in early 1947 but retained his links with Switzerland, which resulted in Roessler being arrested on espionage charges in October 1945.

The GRU's London Network

Irrespective of BARON's identity, and judging by the content of his VENONA texts he was in a position to supply authentic intelligence from within the Reich with a delay of seven to ten days, the X GROUP enjoyed access to some impressive information. INTELLIGENSIA's first appearance in VENONA is 25 July 1940 when Kremer reports an initial meeting at which INTELLIGENSIA said 'that he had been detailed to organize work with me, but that he had not obtained a single contact'. This suggests that INTELLIGENSIA had little experience of clandestine work, but was the subject of some system of discipline which he allowed to direct him. The implication is that he is a faithful and trusted Party member, but the remainder of the text, which is really a well-informed political commentary on current events, is more sophisticated than might be expected from one of the cadres. Further evidence about INTELLIGENSIA is to be found in the 16 August 1940 text in which the author complains that 'we need a man of a different calibre and one who is bolder'. Combined with the observation that INTELLIGENSIA had 'not yet found the people in the military' and had failed to find a particular officer whose address he had been given, there is an impression of an academic without direct involvement with the military. This is reinforced on 6 September 1940 when Kremer reports that 'he does not deny the main point that for a month he has not been in touch with the British Army colonel picked out for work with us although the latter does come to LONDON. I have told the X GROUP via NOBILITY to give us someone else because of this.' INTELLIGENSIA's cultivation of the colonel eventually bore fruit, for he was recruited within the month and designated the codename RESERVIST, as Sklyarov reported on 18 October:

> BARCh [Simon Kremer] had a meeting today with one of the members of the X GROUP. This was an artillery colonel who had been in the British Expeditionary Force, but who at present is out of active service and doing a job at the Ministry of Supply because he was seriously wounded. He thinks he will be returning to service in the regular army in two months' time. RESERVIST has agreed to work with us. He has promised to bring to the next meeting in a fortnight's time his notes on the campaign in France and information on how the British Army is organized.

RESERVIST reports that the progress of reorganizing the army continues. The organizational structure of the Home Forces command, army corps, division. There are individual garrison districts which are directly subordinate to the C-in-C Home Forces, eg. the DOVER garrison which includes two infantry brigades and one tank division. The composition of an infantry battalion is: two infantry companies, one machine-gun company consisting of two heavy machine-gun platoons and one anti-tank defence platoon. A brigade consists of three battalions. East brigade deployed in a war zone has its own independent defence sectors and divisional reinforcements are placed under the command of brigades. Tanks are the main item of the work of the Ministry of Supply. The following are in mass production: 14-ton cruiser tanks and 25-ton ARMSTRONG-WOLSELEY MK-8's armed with one 37mm gun and two Browning machine-guns (it has been suggested that a machine-gun be tried on the turret for anti-aircraft fire). There were five tank divisions in the British Expeditionary Force in France; he does not know how many tank divisions there are now. 300 light tanks are expected to arrive from SASHA. A battalion of light tanks consists of three companies with 30 tanks per company. A battalion of 25-ton tanks is 40 strong. The different kind of organization can be explained by the shortage of officers.

In France the British had 25 and 36mm anti-tank guns. They proved to be too light against the German tanks and were replaced by 75mm French guns which were successful in action. The arming of units with 49mm anti-tank guns is now beginning. Anti-tank units are now being brought together into a brigade for training.

Artillery batteries are armed with 18 and 25-pounder guns. The LONDON air defence is now using new 6-inch guns as well as the 4.5 inch AA guns. They are experimenting with new 4.9-inch AA guns. He considers that the War Office is not making the slightest use of the experience of the French and the coastal defence is based on a network of blockhouses that are weak in design with no allowance made for the manoeuvrability or strong artillery and tank equipment of the SAUSAGE-DEALERS.

Close examination of this text reveals that it is not entirely accurate, as no 6-inch gun was ever used as anti-aircraft artillery, but the 6-pounder certainly was. Explanation probably lies in poor transliteration, of the type that is bound to occur, for example, when converting to or from metric measurements. For instance, the 25mm weapon referred to is undoubtedly the Hotchkiss, while the 36mm gun is most likely the ineffective 2-pounder, and the 14-ton cruiser tank is better known as the Matilda. So the question remains, who was RESERVIST? Based on the internal evidence, of a (possibly territorial) lieutenant-colonel wounded in France with the British Expeditionary Force (BEF) who subsequently worked at the Ministry of Supply, the spy cannot be identified conclusively. A large number of reserve officers and territorials were seconded to the Ministry of Supply in 1940. Of the three Royal Artillery lieutenant-colonels wounded while serving in the BEF, none was detached to the Ministry of Supply, making RESERVIST's true identity a mystery.

Extensive research into matching the VENONA codenames with authentic identities leaves numerous questions unanswered, and although MI5 achieved some success, other conundrums remain unresolved. One of the longest-standing mysteries centres on when Allan Nunn May, the experimental physicist arrested in London in the wake of Igor Gouzenko's defection, became a spy. Educated at Trinity Hall, Cambridge, where he gained his doctorate in 1936, May travelled to Leningrad in September that same year. Upon his return he joined the editorial board of *Scientific Worker*, the journal of the National Association of Scientific Workers, a union that was dominated by the CPGB. When war broke out, he was teaching at London University, and he remained there, apart from a short period in Bristol where he had been evacuated with the rest of his department, until April 1942 when he joined the Cavendish Laboratory in Cambridge to work on the TUBE ALLOYS (atomic bomb) project. It was during this eight-month period that May must have been of great potential importance to the Soviets, and the author Alan Moorehead, who was given partial access to some of MI5's investigation, later reported that 'there is no evidence that May was an active member of the Communist Party, or that during these eight months he was in contact with the Russian Intelligence Service'. Left unsaid, of course, is whether there was any evidence of May's inactive membership of the Party, or evidence of contact with the Soviets before April 1942.

Seven months later, in November 1942, May was invited to Montreal to work on the heavy-water pile at Chalk River, just outside Petawawa in Ontario, but even before he had arrived in Canada in January 1943 on a banana boat with Dr H. H. Halban and five other colleagues and their wives, he must have been in contact with the Soviets, for according to documents purloined by Gouzenko, Colonel Zabotin had been alerted to his imminent arrival, and had been supplied with a prearranged recognition protocol or password. In his oral evidence to the Royal Commission in 1946, the defector alleged that Nunn May had been a Communist Party member in England, 'a very valuable source' with whom the GRU had been obliged to break off contact, and that Moscow had urged Zabotin to re-establish contact with Nunn May in Montreal 'with the greatest care'.

During his interrogation in February 1946, May would admit only that 'about a year' earlier, in the spring of 1945, he had been contacted by an unnamed individual who called at his apartment on Swail Avenue in Montreal. According to Gouzenko's material, that person was Lieutenant Pavel N. Angelov, of the GRU *rezidentura*. Certainly May was paid $200 on 12 April 1945 by Angelov, but he admitted only to 'several' meetings with the Soviets, and his confession was limited to nothing more than what MI5 had learned from Gouzenko. However, this did include confirmation that he had passed on samples of Uranium 233 and U-235, which had been considered so important that the assistant military attaché, Colonel Motinov, carried it to Moscow by air. Unfortunately, the first document to refer to Nunn May, codenamed ALEK, was dated 9 July 1945, two and a half years after the scientist's arrival in Canada. If Gouzenko's recollection was correct, and he really did have personal knowledge of Angelov's contact with Nunn May, then this must have occurred after June 1943, when Gouzenko and Zabotin arrived in Ottawa from Moscow. On this timetable, the GRU had waited some six months before sending instructions to Zabotin, or to his predecessor Major Sokolov. Considering the importance attached by Moscow to cultivating sources with access to atomic secrets, this delay seems inexplicable. As Gouzenko said: 'everything pointed to the fact that he was long an ardent Communist before coming to Canada.' This was much the same as the Royal Commission's conclusion, that 'before coming to Canada, he was an ardent but secret Communist and already known to the authorities at Moscow'. However, although Gouzenko could not be exact about the precise date of Zabotin's first approach to Nunn May, he did place it as having happened 'several months before Hiroshima', which was bombed on 6 August 1945. Apparently Zabotin had been irritated to hear from Moscow that such a well-placed asset existed, and had been assigned a codename already, a sure sign that he was in harness. Gouzenko also claimed that Zabotin had rejected Moscow's advice to contact Nunn May through Sam Carr, the organizing secretary of the Canadian Communist Party, and instead had instructed Angelov to arrive unannounced at May's apartment and use the agreed password.[1]

Altogether Gouzenko supplied eight telegrams mentioning ALEK. All had originated in 1945, so there was no indication of just when Nunn May had been recruited by the GRU, and certainly no evidence that he had been in touch with the Soviets prior to his arrival in Canada. Accordingly, he was charged only with breaches of the Official Secrets Acts after 1 January 1945, and to these he pleaded guilty and was sentenced to ten years' imprisonment. Surprisingly, he declined to appeal the sentence and was sent to Wakefield prison in Yorkshire, steadfastly refusing to assist MI5. Nunn May's refusal to cooperate with the Security Service raised two problems: first, when did he first start to spy, and second, did he collaborate with anyone else?

The first issue is highly relevant to the unknown members of the GRU's networks in England. If Gouzenko's account was true, Nunn May had been in touch with the Soviets prior to January 1943. On the documentary evidence, it is clear that Zabotin had consulted Nunn May about whether his junior colleague Norman Veall, a Young Communist League member with whom Nunn May had worked at the Cavendish Laboratories, was suitable as a source for atomic data. Nunn May had warned the GRU off Veall, saying that Veall 'occupies a fairly low position and knows very little. He is inclined to be careless, as he began this conversation in the presence of his wife. He is pretty well known in the laboratory as a "Red".' The GRU then discovered that Veall had been compromised by a Party member in England who had given him a letter of recommendation addressed to the Canadian Communist Party, and had been arrested. This episode demonstrated that Zabotin trusted Nunn May sufficiently to seek his opinion about potential recruits, and suggests that the scientist enjoyed a status of some significance within the GRU.[2] Such a relationship could hardly have developed in the course of two or three meetings in early 1945, and could best be interpreted as compelling proof that Nunn May's link with the GRU was well established. There has been speculation that Nunn May, who was a contemporary and close friend of Donald Maclean at Trinity Hall, attended CPGB meetings while he was still at university, but there is no evidence to suggest that he was recruited by either the GRU or the NKVD at that time. Nevertheless, the Royal Commission heard plenty of testimony in private, and thus there may have been secret evidence to support the other contentious assertion that May had been contacted by the GRU 'not long after his arrival' in Canada. Certainly neither May nor Gouzenko said anything to support such a proposition.[3]

On the issue of whether Nunn May worked alone, MI5 was able only to retrace his steps and note that he had made four separate visits to Chicago in 1944, and spent longer at the Argonne Laboratory than any other British scientist. He had intended to spend a month at the Chicago Laboratory in 1945, but he had been refused access. He did make two visits to the Chalk River plant. His intense interest in the Argonne experiments had been reported to General Leslie Groves who had expressed concern to Professor (Sir) James Chadwick, the leader of the British contingent. Chadwick had given his personal assurance that he had known Nunn May since he had graduated from Trinity Hall, and considered him to be 'exceptionally reliable and close-mouthed'. This personal guarantee, which he was later to regret, was further to compromise Chadwick's own security clearance, which was suspended without explanation in January 1945. Chadwick was advised that he could not visit Canada to attend any classified scientific conferences, and was informed 'it would be most impolite to ignore' the ban.

At the time of May's arrest, when it was too early for the counter-intelligence authorities to realize the scale of the Soviet penetration of the Manhattan Project, it was believed that he alone had been responsible for compromising details of the research work undertaken at Hanford, Chicago, Oak Ridge and Los Alamos, even though he had no personal experience of most of those sites. It would be years before the full truth emerged, and long after Nunn May's release from prison in December 1952, but until then one of the principal suspects was the Polish physicist Joseph Rotblat who had been one of the first to seek permission to leave Los Alamos. According to US Military Intelligence, Rotblat had told a young woman in Santa Fe that he intended to return to England, join the RAF, and seize the first opportunity to bail out over Russia. His declared intention was to tell the Soviets everything about the Manhattan Project. When challenged, Rotblat admitted there was 'a grain of truth' within this 'load of rubbish' and he was quietly despatched to London late in 1944, not so much because of any alleged indiscretion, but primarily because his wife and family had remained in Poland, and he would therefore become vulnerable to coercion after the anticipated Soviet occupation of his homeland.

MI5's interest in May had led to a delay in rounding up the other GRU sources compromised in Gouzenko's documents, and the evidence against him was so compelling that a daring operation was mounted in the hope of learning more about his contacts. After his return to London on 17 September 1945 to take up his teaching post at King's College, London University, May had been placed under surveillance on the dates during the next month when, according to Gouzenko's material, he was to renew contact with his Soviet controller in London. The latter would introduce himself at eight in the evening with the identification protocol, 'What is the shortest way to the Strand?', which would be answered, 'Well, come along, I am going that way'. The reply would be: 'Best regards from Mikel.' When nobody materialized to meet May on 7, 17 and 27 October, MI5 opted to arrange for their agent Klop Ustinov to play the role of a GRU handler and attend the appointed rendezvous, outside the British Museum, on the same dates in the following months. Mysteriously, May failed to turn up, perhaps suggesting that the trap had been betrayed.

Even if INTELLIGENSIA was less than ideal as a conspirator, he did have good sources, as is demonstrated by the VENONA dated 2 October 1940, in which he noted that the X GROUP had reported to him that a girl working in a government establishment noticed in a document that the British had broken 'some Soviet code or other and apparently she noticed in the document the following words: "Soviet Embassy in Germany". I stated that this was a matter of exceptional importance and he should put to the group the question of developing this report further.'

Precisely which government department the source worked in is unclear, but his access is significant, as is his knowledge of technical matters, as shown by Sklyarov's VENONA of 11 October 1940 in which he notes: 'INTELLIGENSIA confirms that the British really do render delayed-action bombs safe by freezing the bombs' exploder mechanism.'

INTELLIGENSIA also had a source at the Air Ministry, and on 15 October gave an account of a conversation with him which serves to highlight his connection with Ivor Montagu:

> The shortage of trained night navigators is confirmed by the fact that the SAUSAGE-DEALERS have not used strong forces of aircraft in night air-raids on Britain. He stated that the British pilots who fly by night over Germany have an extra four months' training in addition to the usual six months' training. Apparently when there has been no anti-aircraft fire the SAUSAGE-DEALERS have been bombing from a height of up to 5,000 metres and at a speed of 290 kph, and from 6,000–7,000 metres at a speed of 400 kph when there has been no firing. He considers that the SAUSAGE-DEALERS proceed towards the target along a radio beam.

As well as emphasizing the KNICKEBEIN issue, mentioned in the following day's VENONA by Sklyarov (see p.64), attributed to NOBILITY, the text implies that INTELLIGENSIA may not have regular access to the Air Ministry. Accordingly, on the admittedly limited evidence available, it is possible to draw up a profile of a highly intelligent individual, perhaps an academic, living in the provinces and not entirely proficient at dealing with military personnel, who nevertheless occasionally mixes in circles which give him access to information about the enemy's radio beams and the measures taken to render detonators safe. In addition, he has strong Party connections. Given that the Soviets had relied heavily upon CPGB volunteers, including Percy Glading, Wilfred Vernon, Ivor Montagu, Wilfred Macartney and Douglas Springhall, it would not be surprising to know that the GRU had co-opted the author of *The Inequality of Man* and chairman of the editorial board of the *Daily Worker*, for which Springhall's wife worked.

Educated at Eton and New College, Oxford, Professor J. B. S. Haldane was known by MI5 to be a CPGB supporter of long standing, although he did not join the Party formally until 1942. Until MI5 studied VENONA, however, there had never been any suspicion that he had spied for the GRU. The embarrassment factor of this disclosure is such that the texts identifying Haldane as INTELLIGENSIA have been deleted by the British government from the declassified VENONA texts. As well as influencing several generations of British scientists, Haldane possessed one of the most remarkable scientific minds of his generation, and was exceptional in every sphere. During the First World War he served in the Black Watch, and was described by Field Marshal Haig as 'the bravest and the dirtiest officer in my army'. He was sent to France in January 1915, after four months of training, and was appointed his battalion's bombing officer, which required him to experiment with rather primitive trench mortars. As the regimental history notes, among his inventory of unusual weapons were 'stove-pipes almost as dangerous to their users as to the enemy'. Nevertheless, his men admired his gallantry under fire and his exploits in no man's land, even though his arrival in a particular sector of the front line inevitably heralded heavy enemy bombardment in return for his activities. As a nephew of Lord Haldane, then Lord Chancellor and later Secretary of State for War, he was able to advise about effective counter-measures for the clouds of chlorine deployed at Ypres in April 1915. He was joined at Hazebrouck by his father and Professor C. G. Douglas from Oxford, and together they worked in a small, improvised laboratory to develop methods of dealing with the mustard gas attacks. In April Haldane was wounded in the Festubert offensive and, after a period in hospital in Béthune, was evacuated and later posted to the Nigg bombing school as an instructor in the use of grenades. In March 1916 he was given an intelligence post in Edinburgh, and then in October transferred with the Second Black Watch to Mesopotamia. Here he was wounded again, this time by an accidental explosion on a temporary Royal Flying Corps aerodrome, and he was taken by hospital ship to India where he spent the remainder of the war lecturing Indian troops at the bombing school at Mhow in Central Provinces.

After the war Haldane took up a teaching post at University College, London, became active in the Association of Scientific Workers, and started to make regular contributions to the *Daily Worker*, establishing a reputation as a cantankerous, blunt-speaking but brilliant exponent of modern science. Memorably, in March 1939, he explained nuclear fission and reported: 'Nobody knows how large a lump of uranium is needed before it sets itself alight, so to say, but experiments are already under way in two British and one German laboratory to my knowledge, and doubtless in others in America, the Soviet Union and elsewhere.'

Haldane also fought during the Spanish Civil War, where the GRU defector Allan Foote recalled that for a short period he served with the Brigade as a private soldier, standing in a trench brandishing a tiny, snub-nosed revolver and shouting defiance at the advancing Franco infantry: 'Luckily for science, we managed to repel the rebel attack and the Professor was spared for his further contributions to world knowledge.'

Haldane made three visits to the Spanish Civil War and advised the defenders of Madrid on how to resist gas attacks and deal with Mills grenades. Unquestionably Haldane fits the bill of a trusted Marxist, a geneticist by trade, an academic unsuited to clandestine work, who lived outside London, at the Rothamsted Experimental Station in Harpenden, Hertfordshire. The journalist Douglas Hyde, an eye-witness at the *Daily Worker*'s editorial boards presided over by Haldane, described him as 'taking little part in the discussion and absent-mindedly doodling in Greek as the Dean of Canterbury held forth at length'. In fact, Haldane was far from an eccentric boffin, and his ideological commitment to the Party was total, to the extent of suppressing any adverse comments when Stalin began to interfere with scientific progress made in his field of genetics by persecuting his Soviet colleagues who happened to be his friends. Haldane's willingness to suspend his critical faculties on political grounds was exposed by his wife Charlotte Franken, who was also a Comintern agent. Born in London to German Jewish parents, Charlotte was a *Daily Express* journalist who first met the geneticist when she interviewed him at Cambridge in 1924. They were married two years later, and in 1928 they travelled to Moscow at the invitation of Professor Nicolai Vavilov, one of the world's leading plant geneticists. Although it is not known when Haldane was recruited as a spy, his wife became a member of the CPGB's underground in 1937, and her son Ronnie, by a previous marriage, became the youngest member of the British

Battalion of the International Brigade in Spain. She recalled:

> [I] had allowed my only child to volunteer, and he was fighting the Fascists on the outskirts of Madrid. I was doing my best to help him and his comrades and their dependants; I was speaking everywhere in aid of Spain; I was an active worker in a noble, just and lofty cause. The only nation in the whole world that was sponsoring the fight of the Spanish workers against Fascism was the Soviet Union; the Third International was putting to shame the timorous, almost traitorous inactivity of the Second International. I was proud to belong to the Party and the movement that was dedicated to freedom and liberty under the banners of Marx, Engels and Lenin.

Charlotte went to Spain twice on Party business and was also sent on a Comintern mission to China in 1938. Although a trusted underground agent she had 'never been officially and openly a member of the Communist Party, but one of those who nowadays are known as crypto-Communists. I was outwardly, as I had been for years, a member of the Labour Party'. However, she had operated 'under Party discipline'.

> I had been compelled to subordinate my judgment, on important or trivial matters, to that of my political superiors. I had to adjust even my most private personal relationships to their discipline. I had severed all my previous non-political contacts and friendships. Most of my non-political friends had dropped me. I became an intolerable bore, with my incessant propaganda and requests for help for the cause I served, either for money or for services.

Haldane's connection with Ivor Montagu dated back to Cambridge but their friendship developed through politics and the *Daily Worker*, as Montagu recalled:

> I lost sight of him for a time after leaving Cambridge, and ran into him again only after he started his *Daily Worker* contributions in the thirties. When I first knew him Haldane had not yet become a Marxist; he had seen the fallacies in what Marxists call 'mechanical materialism'

and been inclined to what they call 'God-building'. It was encountering Engels, whom he valued above Marx, that changed this attitude, and he found in dialectical materialism as outlined by Engels a view adequate to unify the disclosures of processes and reality achieved by science. The thirties, with their sense of gathering storm and the patent incompetence of the course followed by the statesmen, intensified his sense of social responsibility – as they did that of so many other intellectual workers in the most diverse fields. He asked himself how he might bring his special qualifications to participate in the fight against fascism and the coming war.[4]

In fact, Haldane's brilliant scientific brain was to be employed by the British government, initially as an expert on air-raid precautions, a subject that he had written about having studied the German aerial bombardment of Madrid. He used himself as a guinea pig, on one occasion arranging to be in a shelter that was subjected to detonations that came closer and closer. He was at the forefront of the 'deep shelter' campaign, intended to persuade the government to build sufficient underground accommodation to protect the urban population, a cause that became highly politically charged. His skill as a journalist attracted the attention of John Hilton, director of home publicity at the Ministry of Information, and Haldane's knowledge was used to support civilian morale through the distribution of several articles on semi-scientific subjects. He was also invited to investigate the *Thetis*, the submarine which had been lost with ninety-nine lives off Liverpool in June 1939, and this led to his interest in submarine escape techniques. Many of those who perished were civilian shipyard workers, and their union engaged Haldane at the public inquiry into the disaster to see how they had died. His conclusions, encapsulated in *Report on Effects of High Pressure, Carbon Dioxide and Cold*, was submitted in July 1940. Later he worked at the navy's secret underwater research establishment at Haslar near Gosport where he undertook much of the experimental work into the effects of carbon dioxide on divers, then a priority as the navy developed midget submarines. Once again, he tested many of his theories on himself instead of the volunteers offered by the Royal Navy, and recommended the employment of four assistants, Patrick

Duff, George Ives, Donald Renton and W. Alexander, all veterans of the International Brigade who had been turned down for military service with the Territorial Army on grounds of political unreliability.

The GRU's VENONA traffic between Moscow and London covers the period 3 March 1940 to 25 April 1942, and 1 September 1945 to 16 February 1947, but the second group is of a very routine nature, more concerned with political developments in Austria and the repatriation of Soviet citizens than espionage. Overall, the GRU *rezidentura* in London appears to have relied on a combination of individual agents, small rings like that of the X GROUP, based on the *Daily Worker*, items passed on by either the ambassador or the trade staff, and information volunteered by CPGB activists. This latter category is typified by the text sent to Moscow on 4 September 1940 which reported 'details received direct from the production line at the HENRY HUGHES works in LONDON have compromised an instrument for determining the distance through water between submarines and surface vessels. The principle is reflection. It is a so-called horizontal echo-sounder.' This clearly was a reference to the early sonar systems then being fitted to some destroyers and sub-hunters, a topic which was still highly classified. The principle of transmitting signals that echo off an underwater object to detect submarines was still experimental and revolutionary in that the Italians and Germans, then the leaders in submarine technology, relied upon passive hydrophones to search for targets. The deployment of sonar was very secret, as was another scientific breakthrough, the degaussing (demagnetizing) of surface vessels, reported to Moscow by DICK on 4 September 1940:

> One of our Trade Representatives has reported that the British are equipping ships with a special magnetic device against magnetic mines. The device is a special cable round the ship and a special magnetic installation in the ship for stopping the mines' magnetic action. The cost is about £1,000 in sterling. He reported that there is a large number of British ships in the GLASGOW area.

Like Asdic (the anti-submarine sonic detection system), degaussing was a technical achievement with considerable strategic implications, especially for an island so dependent on keeping the sea lanes open. The magnetic mine was considered to be a very effective weapon and at one point threatened to be the trump card immobilizing the Merchant Navy and strangling the nation's economy. The Soviet trade representative's account of the counter-measure is largely accurate, doubtless based on the then not uncommon sight of long electric cables, forming the coils, being manhandled about both warships and cargo vessels. Once again, the GRU had pulled off a considerable coup of scientific intelligence.

When the VENONA texts were studied in London they served as eloquent proof of the GRU's activities during and immediately after the war. The case against Klaus Fuchs had been based entirely on VENONA, and Donald Maclean would have experienced a similar interrogation based on intercept evidence if he had remained in England in May 1951. For the other spies identified by VENONA, the situation was more complicated. For a successful prosecution under the Official Secrets Acts, either the Crown would have to demonstrate that the accused had passed secrets to a foreign power, or the accused would have had to make a confession. The likelihood of either Professor Haldane or Ivor Montagu making any such admission was considered negligible, and as neither had enjoyed access to classified information for many years when the VENONA texts became available, the Security Service judged it expedient not to pursue their wartime espionage. Both were sophisticated, hardened Marxists and they could easily decline to be interviewed by MI5, although Charlotte Haldane, whom J. B. S. divorced in 1945, confirmed that at the outbreak of war her husband had been engaged on Party work so secret that even she had been excluded from it. Charlotte had left the Party after working in Russia between July and November 1941 as a war correspondent for the *Daily Sketch*, and she returned disillusioned with Stalin. She made a public announcement about her break from the CPGB and her husband, but remembered that in 1940 he had used his membership of an Air Raid Precautions Bureau as a cover for some unspecified clandestine activity:

> For some reason unknown to me, I was not invited to be a member of this Bureau, although it used to meet in my house. One afternoon, feeling slightly unwell, I was resting in the front sitting-room. The Bureau was meeting in the back sitting-room behind closed folding doors. I could not help overhearing its deliberations. At one point it was

clearly in a difficulty. Knowing the answer to the problem under discussion, I knocked at the door, asked if I might be allowed to speak, and gave the comrades the information they lacked. The only reward I received for my unsolicited help was a terrific wigging, afterwards, from my spouse, who accused me of 'eavesdropping' on a secret Party meeting.

Charlotte's departure from the Party obviously embarrassed Haldane, but she remained sufficiently loyal to him not to go further than merely hinting at his clandestine activities. In reality, she knew full well the depth of his commitment to the cause, and this is illustrated by a letter to the CPGB secretariat dated 7 April 1938, discovered after his death by his biographer, Ronald Clark, in which Haldane had sought Harry Pollitt's (the General Secretary) guidance over a collaboration with Charlotte on a book about air-raid precautions. As well as demonstrating Haldane's subservience to the Party (although apparently he was not yet openly a member), it indicates the nature of his relationship with Pollitt, and his willingness to deceive, suggesting that their book should be published by someone 'whose name would not immediately stamp it as Left-wing propaganda':

> In the first place, I am quite willing to undertake the work suggested in my wife's accompanying letter. This will imply a slight but not serious postponement of scientific and other work. It will, however, leave me no time during the next six weeks for the extra calls which according to Comrade Pollitt's letter of April 22nd may be necessary in the near future. However, I can certainly undertake the A.R.P. book if it is thought desirable.

For a scientist of Haldane's stature to be seeking Pollitt's consent to his choice of a jointly-authored book instead of a speaking tour of America is extraordinary. However, the proposed book was published by Victor Gollancz, and Haldane turned down the invitation to travel to the United States.

Although MI5 knew from VENONA in the mid-1960s that both Montagu and Haldane had been spies, it was hampered by the paramount desire to keep the existence of the cryptographic source a secret. While Fuchs, who was a somewhat naive scientist, might be entrapped into volunteering an incriminating statement, without prejudicing VENONA, the two ex-*Daily Worker* Communists were of quite a different order. Accordingly, there remains much uncertainty about the extent of their treachery, beyond what can be confirmed in VENONA. If, for instance, Haldane had been interrogated, MI5 would have pursued one intriguing connection between him and Klaus Fuchs. In 1940 Fuchs had been interned as an enemy alien and in July had been sent to a Camp L, near Quebec in Canada, where he was befriended by Hans Kahle, leader of the German Communist Party (KDP) who had fled to England to escape the Gestapo. A leader of the first International Brigade in Madrid in 1936, then of the ill-fated Edgar André Battalion which was decimated at Guadalajara in March 1937, and finally the commander of the XIth Brigade, Colonel Kahle was an extraordinary and eccentric figure whose carousing was particularly appreciated by Ernest Hemingway. The author of a history of the conflict, Colonel Kahle was politically active among refugees in Britain and was especially close to the KDP's London-based organizer, Jurgen Kuczynski. According to Jurgen's sister Ursula, Kahle was also an important source for the GRU:

> In England he worked, among other things, as a military correspondent of the magazines *Time* and *Fortune*, which belonged to the famous American Luce company. I do not know the background of this particular occupation, but in any case it was a fertile source of information. Centre agreed to my contact with Hans Kahle and so I began to see him, too, about twice a month. This resulted in some useful reports to the Centre, who frequently asked follow-up questions which gave us some idea of what was important to them. I enjoyed working with Hans Kahle.[5]

Before the First World War, Kahle had been a military cadet in Prussia, and later fought with the rank of lieutenant, only to be taken prisoner in France. After the war he had become a businessman in Mexico before returning to Germany in 1927 and joining the KDP the following year. Five years later, as the Nazis seized power, Kahle moved to Moscow, and then emigrated to Switzerland, then France, and finally England, where he arrived in 1939 and was befriended by Charlotte Haldane. She recalled:

Politically, we were of course of the same mind entirely, although occasionally I did wonder how so typical a member of the Herrenvolk could genuinely be a Communist. He would have made the ideal Nazi spy. But on no occasion did I have reason to doubt his integrity, not even on that shattering week-end in August, 1939, when we first learned of the Nazi–Soviet pact. For him, of course, as a German Communist, the shock was personally greater than for me. We dutifully spent the week-end working out the new Soviet line. No doubt we were slow in the uptake, politically weak, owing to our respective bourgeois backgrounds. But Party discipline and loyalty prevailed, probably because we were both convinced of the stupidity of Hitler and the Nazis, contrasted with the genius of Stalin, and the might of the Soviet Union.

Ursula's confirmation that Kahle was part of her GRU network is intriguing, for although there is no evidence that Kahle influenced Fuchs in Canada, or was even responsible for introducing him to Jurgen Kuczynski, there is a close connection between Kahle and the Haldanes. In the spring of 1940 Kahle was invited by Professor Haldane to join him in 'dangerous work to save the lives of British sailors', and on the understanding that he would not be asked to fight against his own country, the German worked for a few months before he was detained as an enemy alien.

Both Fuchs and Kahle were freed from their internment in Canada in January 1941, and upon their return Fuchs went to Edinburgh, where he was invited by the physicist (Sir) Rudolf Peierls to join the Manhattan Project. Kahle's release had been arranged by Haldane who had demanded to be freed to work with him at the Admiralty, and lent him and his pregnant wife Charlotte's flat in Hampstead. After the war Kahle moved to East Germany and before his death in 1952 was entrusted with the reorganization of the police, the *Volkspolizei*, in the Soviet sector, and was appointed police chief in Mecklenburg.

Haldane made an important contribution to the development of diving equipment, escape apparatus and midget submarines, at considerable cost to his own health, and played a key role in planning the attack on the *Tirpitz*. He also undertook some unspecified secret work for the air intelligence branch AI-4, the RAF unit liaising with Bletchley Park's air section which controlled the Y Service interception stations, and he acted as a scientific adviser on numerous other projects. Perhaps his least successful scheme involved a proposal to attach small magnets to millions of fish in the hope of destroying enemy minefields. The idea was abandoned as impractical on the grounds that the fish would not discriminate between Axis and Allied mines. While the latter project may not have interested Moscow, his connection with AI-4 would have been much appreciated.

After the war Haldane remained on the *Daily Worker*'s editorial board and wrote 'They Want to Sterilise the Poor', the last of some 300 articles, in August 1950. Three months later he announced his departure from the Party, having been obliged to resign from two government committees because his security clearance had been withdrawn. His membership of the physiology sub-committee of the Royal Navy Personnel Research Committee, sponsored by the Medical Research Council, required MI5's approval, and this was withheld because he had been compromised by VENONA, although this was never acknowledged publicly. In July 1957 Haldane moved to India with his second wife Dr Helen Spurway, renounced his British citizenship in protest at the Suez campaign, and died of cancer in December 1966.

MI5's dilemma about protecting VENONA can be seen from the way the Beurtons were handled. They received an unannounced visit from an MI5 officer, accompanied by a local Special Branch detective, in September 1947, and were encouraged to make a statement about their activities in Switzerland on the mistaken basis that neither had prejudiced British interests. At that time there was no VENONA material to be used against them, and the only evidence originated from their former comrade, the defector Allan Foote. Accordingly, it was not until after their departure for Berlin that it was realized that Ursula had acted as Fuchs's contact in Banbury. Quite when MI5 realized the blunder is unknown, as there is no way of discovering precisely when the relevant VENONA text, which connected SONIA to Fuchs, was decrypted. Certainly MI5 knew in August 1947 that Ursula Kuczynsky's GRU codename was SONIA, and Len's was JOHN, for Allan Foote had known them both well and had encrypted some of their messages. Indeed, his memoirs, *Handbook for Spies*, which was published in 1949 and written largely by his MI5 debriefer Courtney Young, describes how he was eventually entrusted with SONIA's true name:

> She told me that she was unfortunately not allowed to reveal her name to me nor to tell me for whom I would be working – for the moment. I could call her Sonia. She spoke English with a slight foreign accent and was, I should judge, a Russian or a Pole – certainly a Slav. When I was finally established in the network I learnt her name.

Curiously, because of the British laws of defamation, Foote was obliged to refer to Sonia as 'Maria Schultz', and Len as 'Bill Philips'. Nevertheless, Young knew exactly who she was, although in 1947 he had no idea that she was still active, and even less that Klaus Fuchs was haemorrhaging atomic secrets to Moscow. In fact, when the connection between Ursula and Fuchs was belatedly made, MI5 attempted to conceal their lapse. A distinguished war correspondent, Alan Moorehead, was granted unprecedented cooperation by MI5 when writing *The Traitors*, an account of the Fuchs, Nunn May and Bruno Pontecorvo cases. Jim Skardon, the MI5 interrogator who had extracted confessions from Fuchs and Nunn May, was assigned the task of assisting Moorehead with information from the Security Service files on the personal authority of the director-general, Sir Percy Sillitoe, who was concerned about criticism of his organization in the wake of the Burgess and Maclean defections. In referring to the contact Fuchs met at Banbury, Skardon inserted a deliberate falsehood into Moorehead's description of Fuchs's meetings with his new GRU contact:

> At the end of 1942 'Alexander' disappeared, and Fuchs was told that from then on he would be dealing with a new contact, a woman. In addition, the rendezvous was changed – no doubt to suit Fuchs' convenience – from London to Banbury. Banbury is a market town some forty miles from Birmingham. The new series of meetings began there in 1942, and continued at intervals of two or three months. On each occasion Fuchs took an afternoon train down from Birmingham during the weekend, and then walked out along a country road just outside the town. The woman waited for him there. She did not live at

Banbury; she came there specially for these meetings, then left by train, no doubt for London.

This, of course, was complete nonsense, for Skardon knew perfectly well by 1952 that Ursula had been Fuch's contact, and that she lived not in London but at The Firs, in Great Rollright, which was just nine miles from Banbury. The proposition that there were plenty of short, Slavic-looking, German-speaking pregnant women cycling around the Oxford countryside, accompanied by a little girl sitting in a wicker seat behind the saddle, at the height of the war, is quite ludicrous, yet Skardon, through Moorehead, clearly conceals the truth by speculating that she was really based in London, and that Banbury was more convenient for Fuchs than London. Skardon's motive for obfuscation is quite obvious, for he was the MI5 officer who had been sent to interview Ursula five years earlier. Far from realizing that she and her husband were both vital participants in Soviet espionage over many years, he had simply accepted her polite refusal to discuss her past, and by the time he realized the scale of his mistake, they had both fled abroad.

MI5 fared little better with the other spies identified in the London GRU VENONA. Several of the later breaks implicated André Labarthe (JEROME), and a series dating from 8 July 1940 indicated that he had been in the pay of the Soviets in GASTRONOMIA (France) for the past five years, in collaboration with his secretary, MARTHA. Among the many damning VENONA texts implicating them was one from Simon Kremer, dated 17 July 1940, which suggested that Labarthe was using his influence over de Gaulle to get Admiral Muselier appointed as head of the Free French air force.

> According to information from MARTHA and from the press, JEROME is successfully consolidating his position in the French group here. At the moment he is organizing French technical [1 group unrecovered] for the requirements of the British war industry. He has already been received by the Minister of Supply and has a letter of recommendation to another minister. The press writes about him favourably and puts him third in order after General de GAULLE. In spite of my tact, they were both somewhat surprised by the nature of my questions and assignments. Previously he provided only political intelligence, while she worked in the international

Trade Union movement. Comrade SHVERNIK apparently knows her through this work. I explained to them that they both had opportunities of helping us. She was formerly a member of the German CORPORATION [Communist Party] and though he is not a member of the Party, he is sympathetic towards us and he was in SPAIN.

He will continue with the General until he receives your instructions. If [1 group unrecovered] he will go where you instruct him to go. MARTHA declares that around JEROME and her husband a group of Frenchmen is forming who might agree to any sort of negotiations directed against Fascism. JEROME is taking steps to get an officer friend of his nominated to the post of Commander of the Air Force. In order to carry out your assignment JEROME will collect material under the pretence of writing a book on the subject of the defeat of GASTRONOMIA [France].

Last night MARTHA passed me some material on an invention by a French engineer for the improvement of bombing. This material is due to be handed over to the British. This morning the material was returned after being photographed. The material is in French and is accompanied by the appropriate drawings. Having formerly worked in the Ministere de l'Air, JEROME snapped up the material.

JEROME used to be paid according to the job in GASTRONOMIA. I confirmed that this would go on here as well. Apparently MARTHA did not get anything before, apart from occasional help from CACHIN. Since she will get very little as JEROME's secretary, I promised to give her financial support. Politically she is stronger than JEROME and influences him.

We came to an agreement that contact would be through MARTHA only. JEROME, incidentally, speaks English badly. Please give permission to make APTEKAR or MARK the contact with her.

With the NSA's consent, MI5 alerted Marcel Chalet, the deputy director of the French Direction de la Surveillance du Territoire (DST), to this incontrovertible evidence of espionage, and Labarthe was interviewed in 1965. He confessed, but because of the political implications, and the potential for pressure from his wartime cronies, the details were kept secret. He succumbed to a heart attack five years later, in 1970. As for the former Aviation Minister, Pierre Cot, the VENONA evidence against him was equally damning, for his movements to the United States in 1942 and later to Algiers in the autumn of 1943 could be followed through the intercepts. The first signal, from Vasili Zubilin in New York dated 26 June 1942, showed that contact had been established with the TASS correspondent, Vladimir Pravdin, but made no mention of his previous relationship with the GRU in Paris and London.

> Reference No. 230.
> Taking advantage of a speech by Pierre COT (see [2 groups unrecovered]) at a big gathering, SERGEI had a meeting with him [48 groups unrecovered], screening himself behind deceitful talk is trying to win the people's trust and to take on an important administrative post in WASHINGTON. [2 groups unrecovered] will be glad to meet SERGEI upon returning.

On 1 July 1942 the New York *rezidentura* reported the 'signing on of Pierre COT (henceforth DAEDALUS)', and subsequent texts, dating from a year later, referred to his active collaboration under that cryptonym. On 1 July 1943, Zubilin telegraphed Moscow about a report from DAEDALUS, but much of the text was unrecoverable, although a few fragments suggested that Cot was about to travel to Algiers, and was concentrating on political issues:

> [43 groups unrecoverable] elections. [44 groups unrecovered] I am ready in general to move to ALGIERS to study the situation, [15 groups unrecoverable] if there is [1 group unrecovered] use me in any sort of role in the future [1 group unrecovered] to begin the struggle with the Fascist [8 groups unrecovered] Anti-Fascist activity. [5 groups unrecovered] role in the setting up of the Popular Front, conducted during the war in SPAIN [55 groups unrecovered] BARBO. I personally did not see DAEDALUS and have had no opportunity to discuss his proposal. It is completely [30 groups unrecoverable] [1 group unrecovered] 10th July.
> I request your instructions as to the essentials of his proposals by that date.

The GRU's London Network

Moscow must have responded in the time demanded, for Pavel Klarin, operating under consular cover in New York, sent a long, two-part telegram on 8 July based on DAEDALUS's view of what he termed 'the Algiers Committee' and his perception of General de Gaulle's (codenamed RAS) ambition to mount a coup at the liberation, using the head of his intelligence bureau, André Dewavrin as the instrument.

> [46 groups unrecoverable] [2 groups unrecovered] PASSY's group has set up in FRANCE a secret organization with the task of seizing power after the war and forming a military dictatorship headed by RAS. (Part II) The group has established a monopoly of the business of illegal communications [36 groups unrecovered].

This account was not so far from the truth, for Dewavrin, who like many other senior figures in the Free French movement had adopted a Paris metro station as his nom-de-guerre, called himself Colonel Passy, and was an ardent Gaullist. His organization, the Bureau Centrale de Renseignement et d'Action (BCRA) had dominated the resistance scene in London and had eclipsed the Communists who initially had been better represented in occupied France. Judging by a highly fragmented text from Zubilin on 13 July 1943, Cot must have made a suggestion that caused some discussion in Moscow, and there is also a reference to a journey, perhaps the one Cot made later that year to Algiers. Later in the same month, on 22 July, Zubilin listed eight individuals who were to be checked 'through DAEDALUS', one of whom was identified only as BIBI, a covername that had occurred elsewhere three times, the others named being Commissaire Joseph Deprez of the French naval mission to the USA; Guy de la Tournelle, formerly the assistant director of the French military mission in Washington who had been transferred to Algiers in April 1943; and Raymond Treuil, formerly the commercial attaché in Montreal, but later the Director of Economic Relations in Algiers. From the context, it is likely that the list had been drawn up with a view to approaching each, but none cropped up again in VENONA so the issue remains unresolved. As for Cot himself, he did not reappear in a VENONA text until 12 October 1944 when Stepan Apresyan reported that Cot had made contact in

Algiers on 2 September. Cot had travelled to Russia in March 1944, and had remained there for five months, although the New York *rezidentura* may have been unsure of his whereabouts. Certainly Vladimir Pravdin had not been informed of Cot's movements, for Apresyan reported on 12 December 1944:

> SERGEI has repeatedly rung up DAEDALUS's wife and the woman who is living in her apartment says that she has left for Europe. When he rang earlier the answer was that she was out of town. The parcel and the letter have not been forwarded.

The extent to which Cot's wife knew about his clandestine activities is uncertain, although the VENONA from New York of 1 July 1942 have referred to her role in support of him:

> [46 groups unrecoverable] [1 group unrecovered] and how he carries out [2 groups unrecovered], [2 groups unrecovered] information about his wife, her [1 group unrecovered] of DAEDALUS. Report on how the training is progressing.

Pravdin failed to find Madame Cot in New York in December because she had sailed to Europe on 21 October to work for the United Nations Relief and Rehabilitation Administration, but the implication of the two references to her was that she had acted as an intermediary for her husband. At the very least it can be said that neither Pravdin nor Apresyan expressed any concern about possibly compromising her husband by contacting her, and this omission definitely suggests their confidence in her.

Cot was, of course, determined to exclude de Gaulle after the war, but he was never confronted with the VENONA material. After the Labarthe episode he was left alone, his long history of crypto-Communist support for Moscow's line being well known. He died in August 1977, his liaison with the Soviets widely suspected but never proved.

As for Vladimir Pravdin, there is VENONA evidence to show that he was an experienced case officer, well used to dealing with politicians and other valued sources, as was his wife Olga B. Pravdina. This is clear from a text from New York dated 22 July 1943, in which the *rezident* set out the arrangements for the TASS correspondent's departure the following autumn. He was to return in January 1944, and to leave the United States (with his wife) permanently in March 1946, but in the meantime elaborate arrangements had been made for other handlers to supervise his agents during his absence:

> Your No. 3155. Considering it inadvisable to transfer SERGEI's [Vladimir Pravdin] PROBATIONERS [agents] to cold storage in connection with his departure, I propose that: 1. GUARD, KOLO [Sava S. Kosanovic], 'CONTACT' and 'OFFICER' be handed over for technical liaison to [2 groups unrecovered] – KOLO will be under CONTACT. OFFICER [4 groups unrecovered] on operational tasks. KOLO, CONTACT and OFFICER know SERGEI's surname and [8 groups unrecovered]. 2. ' CRUCIAN' [Anton S. Ivancic] be handed over to ALEKSEI [Anatoli Yakovlev], 'YUR' to 'ARTEK' [Leonid D. Abramov] and 'OAK' for technical liaison – 'CLEMENS' [25 groups unrecovered] about BIBI' [7 groups unrecovered]. I feel that this is a better solution of the problem and consider it important that you should give your permission.

A Serb from Croatia, Kosanovic was a mild-mannered Yugoslav politician, the prewar secretary of the Independent Democratic Party who escaped from Yugoslavia in the king's entourage in April 1941. He was later to abandon his support for the royalist government-in-exile and switch his allegiance to the Communists, his reward being his appointment by Tito as his first ambassador to the USA. Although his political transformation is well documented, his involvement in espionage as KOLO on behalf of the Russians was never suspected. Anton Ivancic, who had arrived in the United States in December 1944, was to be elected president of the Yugoslav Seamen's Union in New York in early 1944. A virulent Communist, Ivancic was closely associated with the YSU's founder, Tomo Babin, who was later to be the merchant naval attaché in the postwar Yugoslav embassy in Washington. The implication of Zubilin's message was that these agents were too valuable to abandon while Pravdin was away. Some time later, on 9 October 1944, the *rezidentura*'s cipher-clerk, Aleksandr P. Saprygin, codenamed BORIS, complained that Pravdin had demanded that a signal addressed to General Fitin be transmitted without being seen by the *rezident*:

> SERGEI [Vladimir Pravdin] is insisting on sending a telegram addressed to you, the contents of which he does not want to show to MAY [Stepan Apresyan]. I have an instruction of MAY's, based on your instructions to the secret cipher office [1 group unrecovered], not to send any telegrams without authority. Please instruct me as soon as possible as to how I am to proceed in this and similar cases.

Such domestic housekeeping messages served to confirm the internal hierarchy within the local *rezidentura* and support the collateral evidence available from surveillance. This was particularly true in the United States where the FBI devoted considerable resources to monitoring Soviet activities, in complete contrast to the attitude in England which had allowed virtually all Russian premises to escape the attention of MI5's Watcher Service, then deployed against Fascist suspects.

Long after the war, some of MI5's security lapses were attributed to Anthony Blunt's malign influence within the counter-espionage division, where he had served as the director's personal assistant, but although it is true he conducted a review of the organization's surveillance targets in 1940, probably even he had little or no knowledge of the range of the GRU's very extensive network in London in 1940–41. Certainly the NKVD's own records indicate that its local *rezidentura* was suspended throughout most of 1940 so neither Blunt nor his fellow plotters were in a position to accept directions from Moscow. Blunt's duplicity became known only when he accepted an immunity from prosecution in April 1964 and made a confession, thus confirming suspicions that had been held since the defections of Burgess and Maclean in May 1951. His decision to cooperate with his MI5 interrogators coincided with the first breaks into the London GRU traffic, revealing the huge scale of Soviet espionage in Britain during the war which had gone almost completely undetected. For the molehunters the discovery was of far from academic interest for there was absolutely no likelihood of the Soviet's dismantling a successful apparat simply because the German war had come to an end. Indeed, Blunt's evidence was that his own network had grown even more important after the end of hostilities, thus leaving the molehunters with the challenge of pursuing every clue offered by VENONA.

IV

The Canberra VENONA

THE ARRIVAL in Sydney of the Director-General of MI5, Sir Percy Sillitoe, in February 1948, marked a significant milestone in the development of VENONA. Sillitoe carried with him a briefing paper which summarized the intelligence gleaned from VENONA intercepts dating back to August 1943, just five months after the Soviet Union had opened its first diplomatic mission in Australia. As the VENONA material had demonstrated to the few British and American analysts who had studied it, the new legation had contained a GRU *rezident*, Colonel Viktor S. Zaitsev,[1] operating under second secretary cover, and his NKVD counterpart, Semen I. Makarov (third, then first secretary). The evidence of their activities, as presented by Sillitoe, was intended to prove to his Australian hosts that a special organization was required to counter Soviet espionage. According to VENONA, from almost the moment they had arrived, the Soviets had emphasized the need to create illegal *rezidents*, and investigation of this threat would require considerable skill and commitment, of the kind the Australian government had never considered necessary, and of which it had had little experience. Hitherto, counter-subversion in Australia had been the responsibility of the Commonwealth Investigation Branch, with local Special Branches dealing with other related security issues. Extremism of the Left and Right had dogged the fringes of Australian politics, but there had never been evidence of external interference on the scale claimed by Sillitoe.

Publication of the report of the Royal Commission on Soviet Espionage in 1946 had sent a shockwave across the English-speaking world, but the Australian Labour administration had rejected proposals for a federal security agency. When eventually, in May 1948, the US State Department imposed a ban on sharing classified data with Australia, on the grounds that there was a complete absence of an acceptable local security apparatus, Canberra was obliged to reconsider. In fact the leaking of information alleged by Sillitoe was more like a haemorrhage, and a VENONA dated 16 March 1946 had provided proof that at least one highly sensitive British classified report had been copied and sent to Moscow. Doubtless others had too:

> As [6 groups unrecovered] to CLAUDE to get the document (the original) on 'Security of INDIA and the INDIAN Ocean' through his friends in the NOOK [Foreign Ministry]. Recently CLAUDE [6 groups unrecovered] copy of the documents (originals): 'Security of INDIA and the INDIAN Ocean', Copy No. 78, 14 pages, and 'Security in the Western MEDITERRANEAN and the Eastern ATLANTIC', copy No. 109, 10 pages. Both documents were prepared by the English Post-Hostilities Planning Staff [7 groups unrecovered] for the War Cabinet. The documents are dated 19 May 1945 and signed by three people: C. C. A. Allen; F. C. Curtis and P. Warburton. At the same time there is a note on the documents to the effect that their texts are final and that their circulation has been strictly limited. [2 groups unrecovered] there is an additional handwritten note to the effect that this copy of the documents is issued for the personal use of Colonel ROMKE. Appropriate operational maps are appended to the documents. The operation of handing over the documents was organized by CLAUDE in Canberra, where he recently arrived by car (one of the cars he uses to carry out his illegal work: the latter does not belong to the FRATERNAL [Communist Party]). The documents were handed over to us for 35 minutes. During this time we photographed them and returned them to CLAUDE.

The document that had been photographed was of immense significance and set out the future of British defence policy towards Spain and Italy, emphasizing the strategic value of the Azores, Sardinia and Sicily. As well as discussing the need to develop radar and air defence in the region, and to cooperate closely with France, Spain and the USA, the paper drafted by the Director of Post-Hostilities Plans, Brigadier Francis Curtis, effectively presaged the creation of the NATO alliance. For this to have fallen into Soviet hands at such an early stage was devastating, not to mention the likelihood that dozens of other sensitive items had gone the same way.

This VENONA was hard evidence of a particular classified document being compromised, and obviously was the cause of much embarrassment, although Sillitoe was discreet about the precise origin of his own information, implying that MI5 had acquired a highly-placed source in Moscow, leaving it to the partially indoctrinated to guess that the British had successfully recruited a superspy in the Kremlin. Either way, whatever the truth, there could be no doubt that a numbered, top secret paper had been removed by an individual codenamed CLAUDE, loaned to Semen Makarov at the Soviet legation for copying, and replaced before it could be missed. It was an appalling lapse in security, and apparently just one example of how the administration had been comprehensively penetrated.

The Australian government's relative naivety in matters of espionage was demonstrated in another VENONA, dated 1 June 1945, addressed to the Centre:

> The other day ZAITSEV visited MINTER, the American Chargé d'Affaires in CANBERRA, on consular business. The latter in the conversation with him under the guise of a joke began to speculate upon the representative of the 'mystical' Chief Political Directorate abroad. 'Only two countries in the world have a secret service abroad – Germany and Russia,' said MINTER. Of this, he thinks, all are convinced and here in CANBERRA all they had to do was to pin down who exactly on the staff of the Soviet Legation is the representative of the Chief Political Directorate. At first they supposed that ALEXANDROV was the said worker, but after his rapid departure it seems they became convinced that they had made a mistake and in the end apparently [1 group unrecovered] certain that SOLDATOV is the secret worker.

Whether this conversation really took place is not known, but it is entirely likely that both the Americans and the Australians would have been interested to identify the local NKVD *rezident*. The incorrect identification of Aleksandr M. Aleksandrov, who had worked at the legation with the rank of counsellor from May 1943 until his departure in April 1944, would have been an easy mistake to make without collateral information from technical coverage or the testimony of a knowledgeable defector. At that time no consideration had been given to eavesdropping on the legation, and none of the recent Soviet intelligence defectors, such as Walter Krivitsky in America, Igor Gouzenko in Canada or Ismail Akhmedov in Turkey, had flagged either Zaitsev or Makarov as intelligence professionals. Thus, until the advent of VENONA, the Australians had been obliged to rely on guesswork and, in their innocence, had harboured no suspicion of Soviet mischief.

The question of exploiting VENONA in Australia was difficult, for Sillitoe could confide only in Sir Frederick Shedden, who had served as Permanent Secretary at the Defence Department since 1937, and had been Secretary to the War Cabinet throughout hostilities. Together Shedden and Sillitoe briefed the Labour Prime Minister, Ben Chifley, on the existence of a high-level leak in his government, and it was agreed that the head of the Joint Intelligence Organization, Brigadier Frederick Chilton, should undertake a discreet investigation to see who might have passed the Curtis memorandum to CLAUDE. By the time Chifley had returned from a further meeting with Sillitoe in London in July, when the Prime Minister had visited his counterpart Clement Attlee in Downing Street, Chilton had narrowed the field of suspects to just four military members of the Joint Planning Committee, and to a single External Affairs official, but he was convinced of the need to create an Australian Security and Intelligence Organization (ASIO)) run on the British model. He agreed that an MI5 officer, Roger Hollis, should fly out to begin the necessary work the following month. At the time Hollis was director of MI5's counter-subversion branch, designated F Division, and had established an impressive reputation during the war monitoring the CPGB. Although he was dogged by poor health, having contracted tuberculosis in China before the war, he had written numerous papers on Communist activities and was his agency's expert on the Comintern. A dull bureaucrat by nature, he was respected in Whitehall as an exceptionally well-informed monitor of left-wing extremism.

Hollis stayed in Australia until September 1948 but made a second visit to Sydney the following year, accompanied by Robert Hemblys-Scales, who had recently completed a lengthy analysis of GRU operations, and by MI5's Japanese-speaking Far East expert, Courtney Young, who was to act as the first Security Liaison Officer to be

The Canberra VENONA

attached to the British High Commission in Canberra. By now Ben Chifley was persuaded of the scale of Soviet penetration, and he announced the creation of ASIO in March 1949, appointing a respected judge, (Sir) Geoffrey Reed, as its head, a post he was to hold for fifteen months. By skilful use of the Curtis memorandum, MI5 had cornered a reluctant Australian Labour government into reversing its policy on measures to protect internal security. The next task was to deal with the security suspects, which required great subtlety if VENONA itself was not to be prejudiced.

ASIO's first priority was to stem the flow of secrets to Russia, and a VENONA dated 1 September 1945 from Makarov, signed with his codename EFIM, illustrated how easy it had been for the *rezident* to operate in an environment that the NKVD had considered far from hostile:

> CLAUDE has communicated fairly detailed information received by him from BEN concerning the Australian Security Service. According to these data, there existed before the war a counter-intelligence department, the so-called Commonwealth Investigation Branch. [1 group unrecovered] during the war a Security Service of police and military [2 groups unrecovered] – although subordinate to EVATT as Minister of Justice. The director of the Federal Department of Security is [60 groups unrecoverable].
>
> By reason of this subordination the police have very big rights and powers. It deals also with the investigator of the FRATERNAL [Communist Party] and carries out counter-espionage work. It has qualified permanent staff workers, a better disciplinary set-up and secret [9 groups unrecovered] with the Security Service while the police [4 groups unrecovered] experience of the latter. The Federal police is comparatively unimportant. Both the above-mentioned services have departments in each state. The departments are subdivided into a number of sections. Thus, for example, in the state of New South Wales the Security Service Department consists of the following sections:
> 1. Investigation of the subversive activities of various organizations.

2. Investigation of anti-state activities of Germans [2 groups unrecovered] Indonesians.
3. Chinese Section.
4. [2 groups unrecovered] and Navy and [4 groups unrecovered]; the investigation of the diplomatic and consular corps is dealt with evidently by the Investigation Branch. Each operational worker has his own agency about which no one knows except him. There are both paid and unpaid agents. For the investigation of organizations agents are recruited within these organizations. Sometimes directors of sections carry out joint action on urgent questions of information. According to BEN's account the Security Service has no special [1 group unrecovered] surveillance but constant external surveillance. EVATT has a special worker in each state department whose job it is to carry out his special tasks. Thus in the State of New South Wales the Centre's deputy is Sergeant WILKE. Soon after the end of the war in the Pacific SIMPSON prepared an order [7 groups unrecovered] he did not succeed; as EVATT [2 groups unrecovered] about the service, said that they would still have need of it. Instead of liquidating it, it was decided to cut down its establishment. BEN has remained at work for the time being. He is considered there an expert on left-wing organizations, in particular on the FRATERNAL. Apart from the above-mentioned material, BEN handed over to CLAUDE a copy of information on a number of organizations which are being investigated:

1. Political Research Society Ltd., a reactionary organization set up by the Liberal Party to combat left-wing organizations.
2. The Australian Legion of Ex-Servicemen. The enormous influence of the first is emphasized by the FRATERNAL.
3. The Association of Greek Orthodox Christians – a reactionary organization uniting right-wing Greeks in Australia.

The documents are of operational value, as they give exact data on political personalities in these organizations. The Ministry of Home Security, which was set up for the duration of the war, was responsible for carrying out

> camouflage work, all defence [1 group unrecovered], guarding aerodromes and petroleum storage places, protecting the lives and property of the civilian population in wartime, blackout and other tasks. This is reported for your orientation; the materials we are sending by post.

This VENONA alone was enough for Hollis and Hemblys-Scales to identify two serious breaches of security: CLAUDE and BEN. CLAUDE was instantly identified as Walter (Wally) S. Clayton, a New Zealander with a long record of Communist activism, and his source BEN as Alfred T. Hughes, a police sergeant in the vice squad who had been attached to the security service during the war, and who was also known to be a leading left-winger. While Hughes had kept Clayton informed of what was happening within Australia's embryonic security apparatus, the former salesman and political hard-liner was revealed by VENONA to be the central figure in a very extensive, and hitherto undisturbed, Soviet espionage network based on the Communist Party of Australia (CPA) and its sympathizers. Clayton's precise role within the CPA was hard to fathom, but papers seized during a police raid on his office showed that he was a member of a shadowy entity known as the Control Commission, which enforced discipline and prevented ideological deviation within Party ranks. The close working relationship between Clayton and Hughes seemed, from a VENONA text dated 17 March 1945, to have been a quite recent development, considering that Clayton's identity had not been concealed with a cryptonym, and was to some degree a reflection of the ambition of the TASS correspondent, Fedor A. Nosov, codenamed TECHNICIAN, to play the hazardous game of penetrating the opponent's security apparatus.

> TECHNICIAN at the regular meeting on 15th March this year received from CLAYTON a reply to our indirect question on the possibility of using a worker of the counter-intelligence. In principle CLAYTON did not object to [2 groups unrecovered] TECHNICIAN with the said worker. He expressed the sole fear that this worker is being used by the police [6 groups unrecovered] insufficient preparation and tampering of him, in certain circumstances, may play [9 groups unrecovered]

> Alfred HUGHES, 45 years. Before the war served as a police con ... [54 groups unrecovered]

ASIO deduced from those VENONA texts that CLAUDE had quickly gained the trust of the *rezidentura*, for he was soon a major talent-spotter, recruiter and agent handler, and was supposedly ideologically motivated. This, of course, did not prevent Makarov from indulging in the common expedient of sealing the relationship with Clayton with money, as he reported to Moscow on 5 May 1945:

> At the regular meeting with CLAUDE on 4th May, the latter was given 15 pounds for the first time on the plausible pretext of compensating him for his personal efforts and the expenditure which he incurs when he meets people on assignments of ours. At first CLAUDE was somewhat taken aback and he declared that he didn't know how to proceed in such a situation, for he had always considered it his duty to help our country. As [2 groups unrecovered] quickly recovered himself, became noticeably more cheerful and expressed a desire to dine with him sometime.
>
> The money was handed over at the end of the conversation. CLAUDE was also told that the money was intended for him personally and no one should know of it.
>
> CLAUDE explained that he [missing verb] an assignment to BEN [2 groups unrecovered] he is working secretly on carrying out the latter. He promised also to give a reliable personal report on SISTER in the near future.

By early October, VENONA proved that Clayton had been inducted into the organization and put on the payroll, although Moscow had reservations about the quality of Makarov's supervision:

> 1. CLAUDE is a rather well-known figure; in view of this his activities in attracting new sources of information for us are dangerous. Recommend to CLAUDE not to burden himself with obtaining information of little importance to us, but to concentrate his attention on essential materials of an operational and intelligence nature.
> 2. Once more we remind you that information similar to that contained in your No. 73 should only be sent by post in view of its minor importance.

3. We draw your attention to the inadequacy of the translation and the style of the text to be transmitted by telegraph.
4. Pay all CLAUDE's operational expenses. Inform us by how much your next quarter's telegraph expenses will go up.

Later that same month, on 21 October, the Centre demanded caution and spelt out exactly how Nosov was to handle Clayton in the future:

> For specially important reasons, tell TECHNICIAN not to receive any documentary written materials from CLAUDE until special orders are received from us cancelling these instructions. Cut down meetings between TECHNICIAN and CLAUDE to one a month. Pass word to CLAUDE that during this period he should maintain only organizational liaison with BEN and the workers of the Australian NOOK [Foreign Ministry] and indoctrinate them in the direction which we require. Try to check to see whether TECHNICIAN is being watched. Help him to proceed with secrecy in this matter. If it should be noticed that he or our representatives are being made the subject of more intensive investigation, temporarily discontinue the liaisons of [20 groups unrecoverable]

As for the Curtis memorandum, which had been the instrument used by Sillitoe to make his case that Australia was vulnerable to Soviet espionage, the immediate suspect was Dr Ian Milner, a high-flying civil servant who had been the External Affairs representative on the Post Hostilities Planning Committee. According to the document records, he had requisitioned the relevant file twice, and had kept it for just over three months. Originally from New Zealand, Milner had been a Rhodes Scholar at New College, Oxford, had visited Leningrad and Moscow, and had studied at Columbia University, New York, and at the University of California at Berkeley. Openly a member of the CPA, he had become a lecturer in political science at Melbourne University in March 1940, and four years later had been accepted into the Department of External Affairs, then headed by Dr Herbert Evatt. The son of a respected headmaster, Frank Milner CMG, Ian had joined the Communist Party while at Oxford in 1934, where the leading lights of the local branch had been Tom Driberg, A. J. P. Taylor, Bernard Floud and Phillip Toynbee. Recent membership had included Claud Cockburn, Goronwy Rees and Graham Greene. Thus, by the time Hollis was considering Milner as a Soviet spy suspect, he had already accumulated a large Special Branch file which listed his anti-war activism, his appointment to the executive of the Australian Council for Civil Liberties, and his membership of the Australia Soviet Friendship League. There was never any doubt about his complicity. He had been mentioned by name in a fragmented VENONA text dated 29 September 1945, which was in itself inconclusive, but it had placed him in the company of James F. Hill, another External Affairs official who had been explicitly credited with supplying British Foreign Office documents:

> Apart from this, both at the first and second meeting MILNER and HILL told him many interesting things. In addition HILL gave him copies of several official telegrams from the British Foreign Office and also a copy of a most secret report of the Australian Department of External Affairs and the Institute of International Relations on the political and economic situation in South-East Europe. The report, addressed to EVATT, contains a [1 group unrecovered] secret information received from the British Foreign Office and also gives certain important conclusions on the current situation in BULGARIA, ROMANIA and GREECE.

Although the signature on this VENONA was unrecovered, and it remains one of only two VENONA texts referring to Milner, the evidence against both him and Hill was considered sufficiently conclusive. The other text, dated 6 October 1945 and sent in the name of General Pavel M. Fitin at Moscow Centre, contained instructions about the recruitment of new agents and, taken together with the heading, showing that the telegram was addressed to Makarov in direct response to his of 29 September, amounts to convincing proof that Makarov had taken the initiative for recruiting both Milner and Hill, and had accepted information from both without the proper authorization from the Centre. For this, Makarov had earned a rebuke:

> Send by the next post particulars required for clearing and detailed biographical descriptions for MILNER and HILL.

If possible do not take any steps in the way of bringing in new agents without a decision from us. As can be seen from your report about M and H, you automatically gave your consent to their employment without having informed us and are already receiving materials. Be careful in your work and more exacting both towards yourself and towards the agency as regards the quality of intelligence.

In spite of this compelling link with Makarov, Milner was never confronted with the allegation and was allowed to remain in External Affairs, having been detached to the United Nations secretariat in New York at the end of 1946. There he remained, with the rank of First Secretary, under intermittent surveillance by the FBI. Apart from one visit home in late 1949, when ASIO kept a watch on him, and a temporary secondment to UN duty in Seoul, he remained in the USA until his annual vacation in June 1950. Then he and his wife Margot took their leave in Switzerland, but unexpectedly travelled to Vienna, and early in July slipped over the Czech border, never to venture to the West again. Instead he took up a post teaching English literature at Charles University, and he remained in Prague until his death in May 1991.[2] There is good reason to suppose that his sudden decision to live behind the Iron Curtain was connected with what had happened very recently to his External Affairs colleague, James Hill.

Whereas Milner was mentioned in only two VENONA texts, Hill's name appeared in several others, and subsequently was ascribed the codename TOURIST. Indeed, one dated 5 May 1948 mentioned his sister's husband, Wilbur N. Christiansen, who apparently was also an active source for Makarov, codenamed MASTERCRAFTSMAN. Dr Christiansen was a radio astronomer at the Commonwealth Scientific and Industrial Research Organization where his work on radio physics was unclassified, and when, much later, he was interviewed by the Royal Commission, he denied ever having been a Communist, and was unable to explain how he might have acquired a Soviet codename.

There could be no question about Hill's involvement as one of Makarov's key sources, but he remained an official in the Department of External Affairs, first in the post-hostilities division working alongside Dr Milner, and then in London after his transfer to the

Australian High Commission with the rank of first secretary late in December 1949. His case illustrates the dilemma VENONA often posed those who knew its secret: how could a spy be prevented from inflicting further harm without tipping him off that he had come under suspicion. Although his brother Ted, a leading barrister, was a well-known Communist, Jim's CPA membership, which dated back to 1938, had lapsed, but he realized his connections had been investigated in the middle of June 1950 when he was visited at his office in the Aldwych by Jim Skardon, who gently invited him to follow the example of Allan Nunn May and Klaus Fuchs, and confess to having passed secrets to the Russians. Hill declined the offer and spluttered denials, but Skardon had succeeded in conveying the impression that the ubiquitous Security Service had accumulated a large file on the diplomat's illicit activities. That same evening Hill, thoroughly shaken by his alarming and unheralded encounter with MI5, recounted his experience to a group gathered at the home of the scientist Dr Eric Burhop. Among those present were Rojani Palme Dutt of the CPGB, and the Australian journalist and CPA activist Rupert Lockwood, who happened to be in London on his way back from a World Council of Peace meeting in Stockholm. It was very soon thereafter that Ian Milner sought permission in New York to go on his annual leave to Switzerland, and by the time he and his wife had fled into Czechoslovakia, Hill had been denied access to classified data and had been recalled to Canberra. In January 1951 he was transferred to the Legal Services Bureau of the Attorney-General's Department, and when it was made clear to him that his career would go no further, he retired into private practice in June 1953.

Undoubtedly Milner had been tipped off to Hill's confrontation with MI5's famed interrogator, and had drawn the necessary conclusions prompting his flight, but it is not clear who had acted as a conduit for the warning. Almost any of those present at the dinner held on the day of Skardon's interview could have passed on a message, as could Hill himself. Palme Dutt was a veteran Party member, and so was Lockwood, who came under suspicion four years later when he was identified as the author of a document removed from the KGB *rezident*'s safe by Vladimir Petrov as he defected in April 1954. As for Eric Burhop, who had worked on the Manhattan project at Berkeley, he had been the subject of a partly fragmented VENONA text dated 29 August 1945, which suggests that he too had been recommended by Clayton as being of interest to the Soviets as a potential source:

> CLAUDE at the end of a letter talks about a professor in MELBOURNE [6 groups unrecovered] physics Australian scientist – Eric BURHOP [42 groups unrecovered]
>
> BURHOP did not come to Australia and at the present time is in LONDON continuing scientific research. According to CLAUDE's words, VENONA was considered a prominent scientist in Australia. Furthermore the latter has been a member of the FRATERNAL [Communist Party] since 1937. On an assignment of the Party, he conducted great [1 word unrecovered] amongst scientific workers. [7 groups unrecovered] Note: CLAUDE has been given the task of collecting on BURHOP [6 groups unrecovered] his address, place of residence and work in America [25 groups unrecovered]

Wally Clayton's network may or may not have included Burhop, who appeared in only this one VENONA, but the intercepts proved that his organization extended even further into External Affairs, with three references to another diplomat, Ric Throssell, the son of a war hero, Hugo Throssell VC, and Katharine Prichard, a member of the CPA's Central Committee. The first VENONA concerning Throssell, from Makarov dated 30 September 1945, was unflattering.

> CLAUDE has reported that the Department of External Affairs has appointed THROSSELL – the son of a member of the FRATERNAL [Communist Party] the well-known authoress Katharine PRICHARD – as 3rd Secretary to the Australian Legation in MOSCOW. THROSSELL has only just passed out of the diplomatic school at the Australian Department of External Affairs. Even before he received the appointment, CLAUDE in a conversation with PRICHARD clearly hinted to her that from the point of view of the Party it would be better if he went to a post in Europe, for example in HOLLAND. PRICHARD, however, very much wanted her son to go to the Soviet Union and had her way.
>
> THROSSELL is described by CLAUDE as a person of limited intelligence. His relations with his mother are normal. His mother dotes on him.

Note: THROSSELL's appointment is rather strange in that EVATT is well aware who PRICHARD is. It may be possible abroad to establish clearly the significance of EVATT's move. CLAUDE has been given the task of discovering the real ulterior motive for THROSSELL's appointment and detailed information about his character.

This initial, unencouraging assessment was sent when Throssell was working in the post-hostilities division with Hill and Milner, and shortly before his departure to the legation in Moscow as a third secretary. Three years later, just before his appointment to Rio de Janeiro, Throssell appeared in two VENONAs, by which time he had achieved the codename FERRO. On 16 May Makarov was instructed by the Centre to

Hold the meeting with CLAUDE on 20 May and find out the following from him:
1. Among his old sources whose material he passed to us formerly, whom does CLAUDE recommend that we should take on, apart from PROFESSOR and TOURIST?
2. What opportunities have FERRO and GIRLFRIEND and does CLAUDE recommend that we should use them [74 groups unrecovered]

This directive was followed on 5 June 1948 by a longer questionnaire from Moscow, signed in the name of Fitin's successor, General Petr V. Fedotov, in which Throssell was mentioned again. A member of the Soviet Central Committee, Fedotov was very close to Beria and, according to the FBI's informant Boris Morros, was 'a softly-spoken intellectual, who had been Stalin's bodyguard at both Potsdam and Yalta'. For Throssell to come to Fedotov's personal attention was indeed significant:

1. At the next meeting with CLAUDE please ascertain:
(a) what positions SISTER and BEN occupy at present and whether they can be used for our work? (b) [2 groups unrecovered] GIRLFRIEND with the work and the possibility of using her in the future. (c) Where are FERRO and ARTISTE living? (d) Is it advisable to bring FERRO into our work in view of the fact that his mother is well known in the Commonwealth as an influential ACADEMICIAN [Party

member]? (e) How is it proposed to organize liaison between FERRO and MASTERCRAFTSMAN in view of the fact that they live in different town? (f) Will CLAUDE release ARTISTE from secretarial work if he is suitable for us?
2. Hurry up getting detailed character reports on all candidates recommended by CLAUDE. Ascertain what experience of working with people under illegal conditions [59 groups unrecoverable]

This VENONA casts some doubt on Throssell's status as one of Clayton's fully indoctrinated spies, and when he was interrogated by ASIO in March 1953 he denied ever having been a Communist (although his wife Dorothy had been between 1942 and 1944), or ever having met Clayton. ASIO remained dissatisfied and another, more hostile, interview was conducted in July 1954, but he remained adamant. Eventually the Royal Commission, which investigated Vladimir Petrov's assertion that Throssell had been a spy, but had been dormant since his return from Brazil in 1952, cleared Throssell of having consciously passed information to Clayton. Nevertheless, Throssell is discussed in the above VENONA in the same context as two other confirmed Soviet sources. The first was Herbert W. Tattersell, codenamed ARTISTE, an English migrant and veteran CPA member then working as a civil servant in the Department of Postwar Reconstruction, whose identity emerged only after Petrov's defection. A friend of Clayton's, he had probably not enjoyed access to classified information, but more likely had acted as his assistant. The second, however, was more important and was quickly identified as Frances Burnie, codenamed SISTER, a typist who had worked for Dr Evatt's secretary, Allan Dalziel, and who first had been the subject of a VENONA from Makarov on 25 April 1945:

CLAUDE has informed TECHNICIAN that Francisca BURNY who began to work 4 or 5 months ago at EVATT's as a secretary-typist, is an undercover member of the FRATERNAL [Communist Party]. Without giving details about BURNY, CLAUDE indicated that she is 22 years old, married and that he personally is connected with her through the FRATERNAL. Furthermore CLAUDE says that he is giving her detailed instructions on how to conduct herself while working in EVATT's outfit particularly emphasizing to her that she should

> be scrupulously careful in speaking about her work so that none of her friends, or even her relatives, with the exception of himself (CLAUDE) should know what she is doing and what materials pass through her hands. Note: Secretary-typist BURNY really does work at EVATT's. TECHNICIAN has seen her a number of times in the secretariat. At the next meeting with CLAUDE, TECHNICIAN will ask for detailed data about her and also will establish whether CLAUDE is receiving any materials through her and how.

Later, on 5 July 1945, Makarov had much more to report about Burnie:

> CLAUDE has given additional data about SISTER. In 1942 she took an active part in the work of the EUREKA youth organization (the local Young Communist League), and since 1943 has been a member of the FRATERNAL [Communist Party]. In 1943 SISTER was working as assistant secretary of the EUREKA organization. At this period the FRATERNAL had some doubts about her social past, environment and connections. The doubts were raised by the instability of her conduct. SISTER comes from the middle levels of the population. Her family was against her becoming a member of the FRATERNAL. Despite this, SISTER later of her own accord entered the FRATERNAL, but did not become an active member. In 1943 SISTER left her parents. She wanted to get away from family restrictions and be a bit nearer to the centre of the youth organization. While in the latter she appealed to CLAUDE to get her into a post in the FRATERNAL organization. Being at that time in an extremely poor state of health (advanced tuberculosis) she was advised to go back to her family and rest for about six months. Some months later she came back again and was told of a decision to find some sort of work [6 groups unrecovered]
>   ... X GLUCK who is a member of the FRATERNAL and that being married had had an exceptionally favourable influence upon her. She became steadier and more serious. Her husband at present is in the army in the Labour Corps, and is afraid that people might know about his being a member of the FRATERNAL.

While working as a journalist in AUSTRIA, he was a member of the Social-Democratic Party. He attempted to hide this fact saying that he was a member of the Austrian FRATERNAL. He apparently gives the impression of being a weak fellow and a typical social-democrat in his convictions and conduct. At one time he asked the Party to release him from the Labour Corps, but his request was refused. CLAUDE says that his connection with the Party is founded on a basis of emotion rather than of class. A good quality in SISTER as CLAUDE notes is that she is not talkative. However, he thinks that a lot of work will need to be put in on her in order to turn her into a worker we can be sure of. CLAUDE has begun to carry out work along these lines. He has already had a number of meetings with her. CLAUDE thinks SISTER is EVATT's secretaries' typist for secret correspondence. She sits in a separate room. At one of the meetings he brought CLAUDE some copies of some of secretary DALZIEL's letters to his minister EVATT in SAN FRANCISCO. The materials are of no great interest. However, there are some data on the increasing struggle between the Liberal Party (MENZIES) and the Labour people, and also on the growing squabble for power within the Labour Government, in view of which DALZIEL, giving vent to the opinion of some Labour Party members, advises him to hurry back to AUSTRALIA and make himself the power in the government. [6 groups unrecoverable] urgently put forward the necessary propaganda and agitation in opposition to the reactionary Liberal Party. CLAUDE warned me that for a start he refrained from accepting any documents from SISTER and instructed her on the lines that she should try to give interesting accounts herself from memory.

Frances Burnie, easily identified by the description and her marriage to Max Gluck, was a typist who had begun work for Allan Dalziel in Dr Evatt's office in Sydney in November 1944, and had been employed until 12 April 1945. She was eventually interviewed in 1953 by ASIO's regional director for New South Wales, Ron Richards, when she acted as a referee for a migrant's naturalization application. ASIO took the opportunity to interview her six times and, with the offer of immunity from prosecution, she admitted that she had passed documents to Clayton on about half a dozen occasions. In October 1954 she gave further testimony to the Royal Commission, and her evidence provided the essential link that could be made public by the authorities, connecting Clayton to Soviet espionage. However, she was far from candid, and deliberately limited her statements to avoid incriminating Clayton more than was absolutely necessary, so she denied she had ever been guided by Clayton, and insisted that she had found the job in Dr Evatt's office on her own initiative, answering a newspaper advertisement.

During the first months of ASIO's existence, inquiries prompted by the VENONA texts identified more than a dozen spies, and led ASIO to begin offensive operations, a programme which included the establishment of permanent observation posts, telephone interception, blanket physical surveillance cover on suspects and the installation of listening devices into premises occupied by confirmed intelligence adversaries. Under the guidance of Courtney Young, who was given an office in ASIO's secret headquarters building known as Agincourt in the centre of Sydney, a team was created to follow up the leads found in VENONA, although only Young himself and his successor, Derek Hamblen knew the true, cryptographic, nature of the source.

Some of the clues proved impossible to pursue, and ASIO simply filed the inconclusive codenames, which included SPIRITED, SANTO, GRANDSON and a woman referred to as GLORY. Other texts provided an insight into who was of interest to the Soviets, although their decision to conceal an identity with a codename was considered sinister by ASIO, so when Professor Sergei J. Paramonov, of the Australian Council for Scientific and Industrial Research, was designated SCORPION, on 30 May 1947, a very negative interpretation was drawn. One VENONA text in particular, dated 5 May 1945, was to be used thereafter as a vetting instrument. The telegram from Makarov listed eight members of the federal council of the Association of Scientific Workers of Australia who were Party members, an invaluable resource when screening applicants for scientific posts with access to classified papers, not to mention compiling a list of potential candidates for detention in the event of a conflict with the Soviet Union.

Young's team, directed by Robert F. B. Wake, a veteran Commonwealth Investigation Branch officer who had served in naval intelligence during the war, pursued every one of the local names, and traced more than a few that were not directly relevant to Australian security. One was Boris Lvovich, codenamed PALM, who was the French consul-general in Sydney. According to his biographical details, helpfully transmitted to Makarov on 29 August 1944, Lvovich had been born in Russia but had moved to France with his parents in 1917. He had joined the French Foreign Ministry before the war, and had been posted to Columbia where, in 1940, he had declared himself for de Gaulle and thereafter had represented the Free French. In 1942 he had been transferred to San Francisco as consul-general, and, after his recruitment in 1943, had been recalled to Algiers. Having been given details of the characteristically elaborate rendezvous arrangements and the recognition signals, Lvovich became a source of political intelligence for Makarov, although Moscow was to complain on 19 September 1945 that

> PALM's information does not present any interest for us. In future it should not be transmitted to us by telegraph. In sending his information, you clearly had an opportunity of showing us PALM's personality and the worth of his information. Limit meetings with him to one in 1–2 months.

With Young's encouragement, ASIO adopted an aggressive counter-intelligence approach and, having reconstructed the entire order-of-battle for the KGB and GRU *rezidentura*s, embarked on some ambitious operations. One of their principal targets was Fedor A. Nosov, the TASS correspondent in Sydney since March 1943, codenamed TECHNICIAN, who, according to VENONA dated 3 July 1945, had been put in direct contact with BEN (Detective Sergeant Alfred Hughes) and had photographed documents in his flat. ASIO assigned Ray Whitrod the task of renting the flat above Nosov and tapping his telephone, and the surveillance was to prove highly productive. Nosov merited the treatment because of his close connection with a Communist named Mark Younger, even though a VENONA text from Moscow dated 26 July 1945 judged that 'YOUNGER himself is of no direct interest to us. If, as you say, TECHNICIAN is meeting him and can get valuable information, presumably he is using [40 groups unrecoverable]'. Despite his Anglicized name, Younger was of Polish origin and was the Polish honorary consul in Sydney, and a frequent visitor to Nosov's apartment, as was

Dr Evatt's secretary, Allan Dalziel. All were placed under intensive surveillance to develop ASIO's knowledge of the VENONA's cryptonyms, and the overall effort was given a tremendous boost when a new arrival, Vladimir Petrov, came under their scrutiny.

When Petrov and his wife Evdokia landed in Sydney on 5 February 1950 from the liner *Orcades*, they were greeted on the quay by the embassy's second secretary and *rezident*, Valentin Sadovnikov, and the TASS correspondent Ivan Pakhomov. (Pakhomov was to succeed Sadovnikov briefly as *rezident*, based in Sydney, when the latter was recalled in April the following year.) The *rezidentura*'s strength had been depleted by the departure of Semen Makarov in June 1949, and Fedor Nosov was scheduled to leave in August 1950. As well as the two Russians standing on the dock, ASIO men were also watching the scene, having been tipped off by a passenger that neither Petrov nor his wife were the humble third secretary and code-clerk they purported to be. Indeed, ASIO's informant was correct, for both were professional intelligence officers, having already served together in Stockholm from March 1943 until October 1947. Nine years later, when the HASP material became available (see p.120), two 1945 VENONA intercepts from the Stockholm embassy, dated 16 July and 21 September, showed that Petrov, then codenamed SEAMAN, had been the personal cipher-clerk to two *rezident*s, first Mrs Yartseva, then Vasili F. Razin. However, their experience in Sweden had not prepared the Petrovs for the atmosphere of intrigue in Canberra.

Although some of the VENONA texts had given ASIO an indication of the turmoil that had gripped the Soviet embassy, only the members of the *rezidentura* knew the full story. ASIO had relied upon some fascinating signals of dissent and personal criticism, but had never appreciated the depth of the internal strife gripping the rather isolated Soviet colony in Canberra. Makarov had been reprimanded by the Centre several times, and the VENONA text from Moscow of 30 May 1946 had been proof of his unpopularity:

> We have received information which shows that lately you have begun to pay less attention to matters concerning the observation of security rules in the presence of members of the Soviet colony and without considering your position in the line of cover you frequently exceed your rights. In

particular the Soviet colony is struck by your unpunctuality in coming to work, unwarranted absence during working hours on journeys to distant towns without having as grounds for them such reasons as would be convincing to the other employees and so on. You make sharp remarks to colleagues who warn you about this. It has been stated that you do not always use information about individual members of the Soviet colony properly and thereby place people who give you the information in an awkward position. Within the colony guesses are made about the reason for your privileged position. In letting you know about this I am sure you will appreciate the shortcomings correctly, will take measures to remove them and will not use [word missing] to complicate your relations with your colleagues.

While Makarov may have been lax on security, and had to cope with hostility from his colleagues, his successor endured far worse. Sadovnikov managed to get a subordinate, Iya Griazanova, pregnant, and had been reported by another member of the staff for staying overnight drinking at the home of an Australian acquaintance in Sydney, in contravention of the *rezidentura*'s strict rules. The consequence was an adverse report to Moscow by Ambassador Lifanov, which in turn resulted in Sadovnikov being recalled home, together with his unamused wife, Elizaveta.

Neither of the Petrovs could cope with the gossip and backbiting at the embassy, which only escalated when Petrov was appointed acting *rezident* upon Pakhomov's departure at the end of 1951. Petrov fell out with Lifanov who, according to an embassy code-clerk named Prudnikov, had criticized him in a secret telegram, and his relationship with the new ambassador, Generalov, deteriorated even further when Evdokia rowed with his wife. Finally the Petrovs too were recalled to Moscow. The last straw proved to be a surprise inspection of Petrov's office safe, undertaken by the ambassador on 31 March 1954, accompanied by the first secretary Vislykh and his aide Christoborodov, who found papers that should have been kept more securely. Thus when Petrov's replacement, Evgeni Kovalenok, arrived by ship at Sydney on 3 April, Petrov accepted ASIO's offer to defect and took a briefcase of documents with him.

As well as liking life in Australia, and having invested in a farm,

Petrov was anxious about the reception he could expect in Moscow which, in recent weeks, had seen Beria arrested and executed, and a purge of all levels of the Centre. Neither Petrov had any children, so there was little to return home to, or so ASIO suggested, and he had no doubt that both ambassadors had submitted adverse reports on his performance. In fact, Petrov had long been cultivated by an ASIO agent, Dr Michael Bialoguski, whom he had met in July 1951, and his successful defection was the culmination of a long, painstaking ASIO operation codenamed CABIN. The unexpected bonus was Petrov's wife's decision a fortnight later to break free from her Soviet escorts at Darwin airport, while on her way home, and to join her husband.

The Petrov defections were a sensation, and a Royal Commission was appointed to take his evidence and examine the documents he had purloined from his safe in the embassy, but here ASIO was confronted with a dilemma. While Petrov's papers were interesting and even embarrassing, they were by themselves inconclusive and, in comparison to the VENONA intercepts, almost irrelevant. However, the secret of VENONA had to be maintained at all cost, so the Commission was briefed in private session about some of the VENONA material in order to establish a link between principal suspects, such as Jim Hill, Ian Milner and Wally Clayton, where there was a gap in the evidence. The problem arose in the Commission's conclusions, which could hardly condemn the spies without disclosing the evidence, or admit that Petrov had failed to deliver the proof required to bring criminal charges. The result was that Clayton denied ever having met either Hill or Milner, and admitted only that he had been shown some low-level papers by Frances Burnie. To cap it all, Clayton denied on oath that he had ever met any Soviets. This, of course, was a travesty, but both the British and the Americans insisted that VENONA was too important to be squandered on putting Clayton and his ring in prison. Accordingly, unlike its Canadian equivalent which resulted in no less than twenty-one prosecutions based on Igor Gouzenko's evidence, not a single charge was brought in Australia. Doubtless the outcome would have been rather different if ASIO had been permitted to reveal what had been achieved by the British and American cryptographers over the past decade, but this was never an option, so the Royal Commission confined itself to the various documents that Petrov had used as his 'meal-ticket'. These consisted of a short hand-written list of contacts, inherited from Pakhomov, that appeared to incriminate those named, and various other items, including a forty-page profile of leading Australian politicians and personalities containing some highly pejorative and controversial observations. Much to Rupert Lockwood's embarrassment, he was identified as the principal author of the notorious 'Document J' and he reluctantly conceded that he had visited the embassy to help compile it, claiming that he had simply acted as a professional journalist, assisting a foreign correspondent who had sought his help on what would now be called 'background'. Such behaviour, while reprehensible, amounted to neither espionage nor criminal conduct, and much the same was true of the others similarly tarnished.

Despite the disappointment of the Royal Commission, the Petrovs were nevertheless the most senior Soviet intelligence defectors to the West for two decades, and together they supplied a wealth of information to flesh out the bones already provided by VENONA. For instance, the Petrovs confirmed the composition of the *rezidentura* which, apart from himself and his wife, who had acted as his cipher-clerk, included the second secretary Filipp Kislytsin, who had arrived in 1952, having spent three years at the London *rezidentura*, the TASS correspondent Viktor Antonov, and an attaché from Latvia, Janis Plaitkais, who had arrived early in 1953 and had concentrated on monitoring the very substantial local émigré community. In addition, the *rezident* could rely on a few co-opted workers in the embassy, and these included the press attaché since 1951, Georgi Kharkovetz, and the commercial secretary since 1952, Nikolai Kovaliev (who was also the Party secretary). The Petrovs also gave valuable information about their previous posting in Stockholm, and revealed that the assumption that Boris N. Yartsev, codenamed KIN in VENONA, had been the NKVD *rezident* was incorrect. Actually he had been subordinate to his wife, who was the real *rezident*, a fact that did not emerge from scrutiny of the VENONA texts.

While they may not have had the same impact as Gouzenko, the Petrovs did achieve considerable political notoriety because the Left accused the government of Sir Robert Menzies of having made capital out of the defection, and having attempted to smear the Labour Opposition with disloyalty. When Dr Evatt, formerly the Minister for External Affairs, but now the leader of the Opposition, appeared before the Commission he denounced Petrov's papers as forgeries and accused him of conspiring to undermine the Labour Party. Tactically, his approach was a mistake as the documents were entirely authentic, but he did unite the Australian Left against what he claimed was a massive, politically-motivated plot. Dr Evatt, of course, had never been indoctrinated into the original VENONA-based inquiry, and therefore never realized that the accusations against Milner, Hill, Throssell and Clayton predated the Petrovs' arrival in the country.

Unlike Gouzenko, who revelled in publicity, and even appeared on television wearing a pillow-case over his head, the Petrovs relished the privacy of their ASIO safe-house and were employed as a pair of human encyclopaedias, filling out details of Soviet personnel whose names and codenames had appeared in the VENONA texts. Evdokia's decision to defect was especially fortuitous as she was a skilled cipher-clerk with a comprehensive knowledge of the NKVD's coding techniques. Naturally, neither Petrov was told about VENONA, but as astute intelligence officers they probably guessed during their numerous debriefings the purpose behind their interrogators' inordinate inquisitiveness about Soviet cipher methodology. Of course, by the time the Petrovs were available for detailed cross-examination, the GCHQ and NSA cryptanalysts had already reached certain conclusions, but the two NKVD code experts filled in the gaps and provided helpful confirmation: all the NKVD texts underwent a three-stage encipherment using the codebook to find regular codegroups, re-encipherment using the additive key from the one-time pad, and then final conversion by simple substitution from digits into letters for ease of transmission over commercial lines. As Gouzenko had explained, the recommended re-encipherment technique was to fold the OTP page under the code and make the addition without making the calculation in writing.

The Petrovs recalled the panic-stricken days of October 1941 when Evdokia's NKVD section, housed in the old Hotel Select overlooking the Lubianka in the centre of Moscow, was evacuated to Kuibyshev, while Vladimir's code unit stayed at the headquarters. This presumably was the moment when an unknown individual authorized the duplication of some OTP pages, the vital error that had made VENONA possible. The Petrovs were considered crucial witnesses because hitherto there had been only speculation about precisely what had really happened, the assumption being that pressure on the cipher channels caused by escalating diplomatic and Lend-Lease activity had threatened a shortage in OTPs. The NSA calculated that less than one per cent of the total traffic had involved key reuse, and by the end of the project, thirty-seven years and eight months later, the duplicates amounted to 25,000 pages. However, because of the difficulty in tracing the duplicates, and the need to have both messages, the cryptographers reckoned that they had found only about half of them. This meant some 70,000 OTP pages had been reused, but how, and why?

Because the diplomatic OTP pages bore different numbers, the duplicate pages must have been printed separately and then bound, with a page number stamped afterwards, a theory supported by examination of similar Soviet military codes captured by the Finns which bore digits printed in ten different typefaces, suggesting the use of some kind of typewriter or teletype machine. Since all other aspects of pad production, including cutting, binding, numbering, storage and distribution had been unaffected in the temporary period of duplication, the obvious conclusion was that the Soviets had suffered a temporary shortage in printing machines, forcing them to resort to carbon copies. On the basis that the estimated 70,000 sheets had been produced at a rate of 500 a day during an eight-hour day, this suggested the period of duplication lasted 140 days. Considering that this meant producing four key pages (three carbons to make the required two sets of cipher-decipher pads), such an exercise could easily have been undertaken by some form of mechanical typewriter. Having answered the 'how', the issue of 'why' remained a conundrum. The Soviets had introduced OTPs in 1930, long before their Western counterparts, and historically were extremely sensitive to cipher security. The lapse seemed baffling, but presumably the risk of inserting a relatively small number of duplicate pages into thousands of pads over a period of a few months must have seemed acceptably small.

The mystery deepened when the Petrovs confirmed there had been no recall of OTPs which, the NKVD had learned from William Weisband in early 1945, had been compromised by breaks into duplicate trade messages. This suggested that the decision to duplicate had been made at a very low level, and possibly there had been an internal cover-up.

Certainly the Petrovs would not have been told that their information would serve to end the cryptological work of VENONA. Henceforth cryptographers on both sides of the Atlantic were deployed on other tasks, leaving the partially broken VENONA texts as a tantalizing resource for counter-intelligence analysts.

That, of course, turned out not to be the case, because in 1959 the Swedish National Defence Radio Institute (Forsvarets Radioanstalt, FRA) revealed that it had retained copies of a vast quantity of the Stockholm–Moscow traffic, and negotiated with GCHQ to release its archive to the NSA via Cheltenham. This was the batch of intercepts codenamed HASP, and, bearing in mind that some of these texts had been encoded and signed by Petrov, there must have been a great temptation to confront him with them – if only to tax his memory by seeking clues to the missing, unrecovered groups. Elementary considerations of security, of course, would have mitigated against such a rash step, but the unexpected arrival of HASP meant that the entire VENONA project was put back into gear. In the view of some insiders, the real tragedy was that it was ever allowed to stall in the first place.

Certainly as far as the Canberra VENONA was concerned, always known within ASIO as 'the case', it had neutralized Wally Clayton's clandestine network, but had done little to educate the public or politicians to the true nature and scale of Soviet espionage in Australia. Clayton himself dropped from sight to become a fisherman in Nelson Bay, north of Sydney, where he remains, whil Ric Throssell moved to London to run the Commonwealth Foundation before returning to Sydney after forty years in the diplomatic service, to write *In A Wilderness of Mirrors* in 1992. Undoubtedly the greatest embarrassment to ASIO was Alfred Hughes, whose application to join ASIO had been rejected in 1951. He finally retired with the rank of detective sergeant in 1960, and died eighteen years later, his covert role as BEN, a Soviet mole, wholly unknown to the public.

V

The Cambridge Ring

ALTHOUGH it is now well understood that one of the triumphs of Soviet espionage was the successful recruitment of what was to become known as the Ring-of-Five at Cambridge – Anthony Blunt, Guy Burgess, John Cairncross, Donald Maclean and Kim Philby – five penetration agents who, most unusually, were apparently aware of the activities of the others, there was nothing in VENONA even to hint at the existence of such a network. That is not to say, of course, that VENONA did not contain evidence of high-level political penetration. Proof that someone with personal access to Winston Churchill was a Soviet spy was contained in a text from Iskhak Akhmerov, NKVD illegal *rezident* 1942–45, in New York, dated 29 May 1943, attributed to '19'.

> '19' reports that CAPTAIN [President Roosevelt] and BOAR [Winston Churchill], during conversations in the COUNTRY [USA], invited '19' to join them and DEPUTY [Vice-President Henry Wallace] openly told BOAR [10 groups unrecovered] second front against GERMANY this year. BOAR considers that, if a second front should prove unsuccessful, then this [3 groups unrecovered] harm to Russian interests and [6 groups unrecovered]. He considers it more advantageous and attractive to waken GERMANY by bombing and to sue this time for '[4 groups unrecovered] political crisis so that there may be no doubt that a second front next year will prove successful.' DEPUTY [14 groups unrecovered]. 19 thinks that CAPTAIN is not informing DEPUTY of important military decisions and that therefore DEPUTY may not have exact knowledge of [1 group unrecovered] with the opening of a second front against GERMANY and its postponement from this year to next year. 19 says that DEPUTY personally is an

ardent supporter of a second front at this time and considers postponement [15 groups unrecovered] can shed blood [13 groups unrecoverable] recently shipping between the USA and [40 groups unrecovered]. The COUNTRY hardly [9 groups unrecovered] insufficient reason for delaying a second front.

Discreet inquiries at the White House quickly established that Agent 19 was the Czech leader Eduard Beneš, long suspected of having been a Soviet source. However, by the time the connection had been made, Beneš had returned to Czechoslovakia at the end of the war, and had subsequently been removed from power.

The first clue to the existence of a highly-placed Soviet spy in the British Foreign Office came with the decryption of the New York–Moscow traffic in August 1944 which showed that the Washington DC *rezident*, Anatoli Gromov, had received consignments of classified data of a political nature from HOMER, a source in the British embassy. Eventually HOMER was to be linked to GOMER, GOMMER and simply 'G', and identified as Donald Maclean, who had been posted to the United States early in May 1944. However, the first relevant text was sent on 2/3 August from Stepan Apresyan in New York about British alternatives for the Allied plan codenamed ANVIL, the invasion of France's Mediterranean coast:

[149 groups unrecoverable] PART I The army [37 groups unrecovered] CAMBELL. The Committee is [2 groups unrecovered] on political and economic questions for drawing up instructions to EISENHOWER and WILSON [1 group unrecovered] treaties on civilian questions of the type already signed with Holland and Belgium and the treaty with [4 groups unrecovered] on the PO [4 groups unrecovered] Army of Liberation [20 groups unrecoverable] the Allies [1 group unrecovered] the European Advisory Commission in SIDON [London] will [8 groups unrecovered] in CARTHAGE [Washington DC] are taking part in the work of the Committee. Almost all the work is done by HOMER who is at present at all the sessions. In connection with this work HOMER obtains secret documents [6 groups unrecovered] The ISLANDERS [British] [13 groups unrecovered] The TRUST [Soviet embassy] in Carthage [12 groups

unrecoverable] work including the personal telegraphic correspondence of the BOAR [Winston Churchill] with CAPTAIN [President Roosevelt] [64 groups unrecoverable]
2. The LEAGUE [US Government] decided to force the ISLANDERS to alter the allocation of occupation zones in Germany in accordance with the existing plan of the European Advisory Commission. 6 weeks ago CAPTAIN informed BOAR that the COUNTRY [USA] wishes to detach minimal occupation forces [34 groups unrecoverable] would [2 groups unrecovered] involved in the complex political problems of European countries. BOAR replied that the ISLAND's vital interests lie in the North Sea, Belgium and Holland and therefore he was not in agreement with the stationing of occupation forces a long way from these areas. CAPTAIN did not agree with this argument. At this stage the ISLANDERS continue to assist on their plan.
3. In April Richard LAW passed to the ISLAND's Government a memorandum written by the War Office and the Foreign Office setting out the ISLAND's policy with respect to the use of the Army in south-west Europe. The document divides the aims to be pursued into 'inescapable' and 'desirable'. The inescapable aims include the occupation by the ISLAND of the Dodecanese to prevent a struggle for the possession of these islands among Turkey, Greece and Italy. The use in Greece of a large enough force of troops to organize relief, the despatch to Greece of military units to support the Greek Government, the basing in TRIESTE of adequate troops to control the Italo-Yugoslav frontier and maintain order there, [51 groups unrecoverable] ... ed Bulgaria, the despatch of adequate troops to Hungary to take part in the occupation, the despatch of troops to Albania to restore its independence which the British guaranteed [15 groups unrecovered] leading role [37 groups unrecoverable] weeks ago HOMER was entrusted with the decypherment of a confidential telegram from BOAR to CAPTAIN which said that WILSON and the other generals of the ISLAND were insisting strongly on a change in the plan to invade the South of France, suggesting instead an invasion through the Adriatic sea, TRIESTE and then north-eastwards. BOAR supported this

plan. From the contents of the telegram it is clear that BOAR will not succeed in overcoming the strong objection of CAPTAIN and the COUNTRY's generals. Yesterday HOMER learnt of a change in the plans [4 groups unrecovered] and ANVIL will be put into effect possibly in the middle of August. Commenting on this argument [15 groups unrecovered] the aims that are being pursued by each: the ISLAND – for strengthening of her influence in the Balkans; the COUNTRY – the desire for the minimum involvement in European politics. [7 groups unrecoverable] it is clear that the COUNTRY [72 groups unrecovered] [4 groups unrecovered] about him and STEPAN refused to pass the documents to him in view of [22 groups unrecovered]. Then he had convinced himself [39 groups unrecoverable]

In two weeks time on the agreement [38 groups unrecovered] [41 groups unrecoverable] insufficient indication was given [31 groups unrecovered]

This was followed on 10 August by a brief telegram from Apresyan in New York, referring to another text relayed from Maclean:

> Your No. 3608. HOMER's information was transmitted not in our words and without comments. It was transmitted in a condensed form word for word without any personal conclusions.

The next despatch from New York was a very short one dated 5 September 1944, revealing that the Prime Minister was to meet the President in Canada within the week. This text was the subject of sustained AFSA attack in 1947 and 1948, but initially it was not connected with the later traffic from Washington DC attributed to a spy referred to simply as 'G', for GOMER, which is HOMER in Russian.

> According to information from HOMER, CAPTAIN [Franklin Roosevelt] and BOAR [Winston Churchill] will meet about 9th September in QUEBEC to discuss matters connected with the impending occupation of GERMANY. A detailed account of HOMER's report will follow. [12 groups unrecoverable]

Two days later Apresyan sent a further report from Maclean regarding British policy on the postwar structure of Germany and on

The Cambridge Ring

the current situation in the Eastern Mediterranean, but the opening sentence, mentioning HOMER, was not solved until much later, in 1951:

> [3 groups unrecovered] HOMER's report of 2nd September (the verbatim quotations from the report are in inverted commas):
>
> 1. In connection with the Anglo-American economic talks HOMER points out that 'in the opinion of the majority of the members of the British Government the fate of England depends almost entirely on AMERICA. They consider that ENGLAND can remain a strong and prosperous power if she maintains the volume of her imports which she can do in two ways:
>
>   1. By getting supplies from AMERICA gratis by DECREE [Lend-Lease] or otherwise.
>   2. By restoring her exports to the required volume.
>
>   The immediate aim of the British Government consists in [12 groups unrecovered] will be delayed until the end of the war with JAPAN and also receiving permission [17 groups unrecovered] NABOB [Henry Morgenthau] to admit HEN-HARRIER [Cordell Hull] and others who concentrate on internal political difficulties. In negotiations with the LEAGUE [US Government] the British will advance the following arguments: [16 groups unrecovered] ENGLAND and eliminate her as an economic factor but this [39 groups unrecovered] ENGLAND, [70 groups unrecovered].'
>
> 2. 'The question as to whether the north-western and southern zones of GERMANY will be occupied respectively by the British or the Americans has not yet been decided and will be discussed by CAPTAIN and BOAR at their meeting which, as far as I know, will take place at QUEBEC about 9th September. Besides this no decision has been taken on two fundamental questions:
>
>   1. Is it desirable to attempt to maintain GERMANY on a moderately high level of economic stability and well-being or should the armies of occupation let her starve and go to pieces?

2. Is it desirable to help GERMANY to maintain a single administrative [2 groups unrecovered] or should the armies of occupation do all they can to split up GERMANY into separate states?

Citing the [Sir William] STRANG documents which you know of, HOMER emphasizes that the plans of the British, in large measure, are based on the opinion of the British Foreign Office. A sub-committee of post-hostilities planning of the British Chiefs of Staff issued a paper on 19th August, the authors of which [1 group unrecovered] the consideration from a military point of view of all the facts for and against the division of GERMANY into at least three states corresponding to the boundaries of the three zones of occupation and it is recommended that the Anglo-American armies of occupation should, as a first priority, [32 groups unrecoverable] divided GERMANY [25 groups unrecovered] undivided GERMANY would more probably get into [43 groups unrecovered] and ENGLAND [25 groups unrecoverable]

The Americans have created a special commission with the powers of a government department to examine policy relating to GERMANY. Among the questions which it is to discuss are

'Should GERMANY be helped (for instance by the American occupation forces) to maintain or restore order and economic stability?
Should GERMANY be split up into separate states?
How should HITLER, HIMMLER and the rest, be dealt with, if they should be caught?
Should the RUHR be internationalized?'

NABOB strongly opposes the first point and proposes letting economic ruin and chaos in GERMANY develop without restriction in order to show the Germans that wars are unprofitable. The assistant to the head of the ARSENAL [War Department], MCCLOY, points out that such a situation would be intolerable for the army of occupation, and that the responsibility for some minimum of order [4 groups unrecovered] and so forth – NABOB obtained CAPTAIN's consent to the use of yellow-seal dollars by American troops instead of military marks as had been previously agreed with the British and the Russians. The purpose of this is to turn the American military occupation forces into the economic masters of GERMANY. MCCLOY, LAWYER [Harry Dexter White], high officials in NABOB's establishment as well as the British, are opposed to this. The British and MCCLOY are trying to get CAPTAIN to revoke the decision. MCCLOY [4 groups unrecoverable] division of GERMANY averring that this attempt is doomed to failure. His views have some significance since he has direct access to CAPTAIN.

3. Under the influence of BOAR and [Sir Rex] LEEPER, the British intend to set up and keep in power in GREECE a government well-disposed towards ENGLAND and willing to help her and hostile to communism and Russian influence. Their tactics consist in supporting the King as much as possible but also in leaning on the so-called liberal elements which might take the King's place if the opposition to him becomes too strong. For military reasons the British were forced to support EAM and ELAS to a certain extent. In order to achieve their political ends the British intend to land a British division from Italy in GREECE to keep PAPANDREOU in power. As you know, this plan will be realized very soon. The LEAGUE regard the British intrigues in GREECE with some suspicion and HOMER hopes that we will take advantage of these circumstances to disrupt the plans of the British and all the more so since the HUT [OSS] still supports EAM and ELAS.

4. After Comrade STALIN had refused to allow American aircraft to land on our territory [9 groups unrecovered] personal message suggested to the CAPTAIN that he should agree to [30 groups unrecovered]

Thereafter, the HOMER traffic appeared to consist of entire British Foreign Office despatches. The first batch of three, sent on 29 March 1945, was a copy of a signal, designated No. 714 and dated 8 March from the British ambassador in Moscow, Sir Archie Clark Kerr, addressed to London, which was repeated to his counterpart in Washington DC, Lord Halifax, about the future of Poland. This, chronologically, was the first to be attacked by the AFSA cryptanalysts:

> To the 8th Department
> Material of HOMER [66 groups unrecoverable] His Majesty and the Government of the USSR, acting jointly or separately, – a document, a draft of which was sent in my telegram No. 698. If the Soviet Government has not yet reached some final decision in regard to the work of the Polish Commission (and I think they have not) there is some advantage in a written [7 groups unrecovered] meetings of the Commission [2 groups unrecovered] provide at least its full and careful consideration. I do not think that MOLOTOV, despite his stubbornness, has said his last word. I feel that we can still succeed in getting invitations issued to all or most of our nominees from POLAND, provided we are sufficiently firm [217 groups unrecoverable]

This was followed by signal 2535 of 16 March 1945, from the Foreign Secretary Anthony Eden to the Washington embassy, copied to Moscow.

> To the 8th Department
> Materials of HOMER. I am transmitting a telegram of the POOL [British Embassy in Washington] No. 2535 of 16 March this year to the POOL. Sent to WASHINGTON under No. 2535 of 16 March and repeated to MOSCOW.
> SECRET
> Reference telegrams from Moscow Nos. 823 and 824.
> 1. These telegrams arrived simultaneously with the President's messages to the Prime Minister (No. 718). The message shows that the President is still not inclined to support us in putting to the Russians all these questions, on which we consider it important to reach an agreement with them at this stage. From the Prime Minister's answer, transmitted in telegram No. 912, you can see that he is urging the President to reconsider his position in the light of the proposals now submitted by Sir A. Clark KERR, after consultation with Mr HARRIMAN.
> 2. As soon as possible please see Mr STETTINIUS and after that, if you can, the President and show them [2 groups unrecovered] to MOLOTOV, suggested by Sir A. Clark KERR and supplemented by my telegram No. 2537. You should

take part in the decision of these affairs. Use all arguments at your disposal to induce them to make a concerted effort with us on the basis of this draft. We are convinced that only on such a basis will it be possible to establish a foundation for the Commission's work. We believe that if we and the Americans together take a firm position, the Russians very likely will give way on some of the points.

3. If you do not succeed in persuading the President to accept Sir A. Clark KERR's draft as it stands, in my opinion you can induce him to send Mr HARRIMAN instructions covering at least the more important points put forth by us. (From the Prime Minister's message you will see that the point on which we cannot give way is the question of a truce.) If this were done, I should be ready to instruct Sir A. Clark KERR immediately to concert with Mr HARRIMAN in making a communication on similar lines. We fully realize the urgency of this question.

On 30 March Anatoli Gromov transmitted the Russian translation of the Foreign Office signal No. 1517, dated 7 March, from Lord Halifax to the Foreign Office, repeated to Moscow:

PART I
To the 8th Department
Materials of HOMER. I am transmitting a telegram of the NOOK [Foreign Office] No. 2212 of 8 March to the POOL [British Embassy in Washington].
Sent to Washington under No. 2212 of 8 March and repeated to Moscow, CASERTA and SAVING in Paris.
Supplementary to my telegram No. 1018 to MOSCOW.
1. The rapid deterioration in the situation in ROMANIA has already led us to support the demands of the US Government concerning the invocation of the Three [150 groups unrecoverable] objectives, enumerated in 'a–d' in the fourth paragraph of the Declaration. [2 groups unrecovered] assume that the word 'measures' includes the establishment of an appropriate organization along the lines, for example of the Polish Commission.
4. The second and wider interpretation is that the words 'joint responsibilities' in the third from the last paragraph of

the Declaration, should be taken to mean that no signatory government is permitted to take unilateral action as regards matters mentioned in the Declaration, in any liberated European State or in any former Axis Satellite in Europe.

PART II This interpretation is supported by reference to 'joint action' in the Preamble to [57 groups unrecoverable] require, 2 which presumably presuppose general agreement before joint assistance.

5. The first interpretation, set forth above, would naturally mean that any one government, according to the Declaration, could veto any action if it so desired. The interpretation of the Declaration would greatly impair the possibility of its use in situations such as that in ROMANIA.

6. The second alternative interpretation is the only one, which gives us the chance to use the Declaration to prevent arbitrary imposition of minority rule under Soviet encouragement in countries occupied by Russian troops.

7. Any [1 group unrecovered] arising from this interpretation can arouse serious objection. Insisting on such an interpretation we run the risk of a head-on collision with the Russians who certainly will refuse to accept any such restriction of their freedom of action.

8. Since the US Government is the author of the Declaration about liberated Europe, I [1 group unrecovered], without preliminary consultation and agreement with them [4 groups unrecovered] any definite view about the proper interpretation [117 groups unrecoverable]

Later the same day a further text was transmitted by Gromov from Washington DC, and although not directly attributed to HOMER, and lacking the familiar introduction – 'To the 8th department. Materials of HOMER' – was on a similar topic:

[75 groups unrecoverable] questions, though there are some major differences of tactics. This morning a member of my department discussed this question at some length in the State Department. Set forth below [46 groups unrecoverable] on this question and considers it essential to get a clear definition of the basis on which the Commission is to work.

The relevant paragraph of the Crimea communique should be taken for the definition of the functions of the Commission. It is essential that all three parties to the Commission constantly [2 groups unrecovered] purpose for which it was set up, namely: 'to consult with members of the present provisional government and with other Polish democratic leaders from Poland and from abroad with a view to reorganizing the present government ... on a broader democratic basis, with inclusion of democratic leaders from Poland and from Poles abroad.'
3. Invitation to Poles. The Commission must itself agree on lists of Poles who are to be invited for consultation. One cannot allow any outside organization to influence the composition of this list.
4. It is unnecessary to achieve a moratorium on political persecution in Poland. All Poles should now act in such a way as to create an atmosphere of freedom and independence, since only under such circumstances can [2 groups unrecovered] a representative government or conduct free elections (In this connection the State Department feels that the text of the draft note to MOLOTOV, set out in your telegram No. 2078, is too sharp and shows too great a distrust of Soviet intentions in POLAND; they entirely agree with those objectives which you set, but feel that we will gain nothing if we are too harsh at this stage; they are considering now the possibility of issuing instructions to HARRIMAN – to make a demarch on similar lines, but somewhat softened down in tone; at the present time, in their opinion, it is inadvisable to face MOLOTOV with a combined note on this subject).
5. Observers. The State Department learned with gratification that you for the moment do not intend to go ahead with your idea of sending [12 groups unrecoverable] Sir A. Clark KERR to press for full facilities for sending to POLAND a somewhat lower level technical commission. The aim of this commission will be to gather first-hand information about conditions now pertaining there in so far as they affect the question of appointing a government and the later elections.

On 31 March 1945 the Washington *rezidentura* sent a telegram addressed to the 8th Department described as 'Material from HOMER. I am transmitting telegram No. 2536 of 16th March from the NOOK [British Foreign Office] to the POOL [British embassy in Washington DC], classified SECRET', which was another copy of Lord Halifax's signal of 16 March.

In chronological terms, the first VENONA in the series which referred to HOMER was from Stepan Apresyan in New York on 28 June 1944, in which he described the logistics of the TASS correspondent Vladimir Pravdin's connection with the spy, inferring that the case had originated in London:

> Your No. 2712. SERGEI's [Vladimir Pravdin] meeting with HOMER took place on 25 June. HOMER did not hand anything over. The next meeting will take place on 30 July in TYRE [New York]. It has been made possible for HOMER to summon SERGEI in case of need. SIDON's [London] original instructions have been altered [34 groups unrecoverable] travel to TYRE where his wife is living with her mother while awaiting confinement. From there [2 groups unrecovered] with STEPAN [Pavel Fedosimov] [11 groups unrecovered] on the question of the postwar relations of the ISLAND [England] with the COUNTRY [America], France and Spain [16 groups unrecovered] on the ISLAND and material [8 groups unrecovered] on several questions touching the ISLAND's interests [6 groups unrecovered] our proposals that [20 groups unrecovered] HOMER [36 groups unrecovered] there.

The final version of this text was not circulated until 21 March 1973 so, like the other VENONA material, it is impossible to know how much of it was available when, but it is known that it was the reference to HOMER's pregnant wife which helped MI5 isolate the source of Donald Maclean, who had been First Secretary at the British embassy in Washington DC, and whose wife Melinda had stayed in New York at her mother's Park Avenue apartment until the birth of their son Fergus by Caesarean section on 22 September 1944. Maclean had sought and received special permission to make regular weekend visits to her in Manhattan, and at his mother-in-law's country home at South Egremont, Massachusetts. The final versions of the other VENONA texts were circulated in July and

The Cambridge Ring

October 1965, with a significant paragraph recovered in May 1960.

The main item, which could have been used to extract a confession from Maclean if he had not fled from his home in Kent hours before he was scheduled to be interrogated, in May 1951, concerned the government in Poland after the liberation:

> To the 8th Department
> Materials from HOMER. I am transmitting a cipher telegram, no. 95 of 8 March, from the ISLAND's [England] embassy in SMYRNA [Moscow] to the POOL [British Embassy in Washington]:
>
> Sent to the Foreign Office under no. 714 and repeated to WASHINGTON.
>
> 1. The US Ambassador showed me a telegram of 7 March, containing his recommendations to the State Department about the Polish Commission.
>
> 2. As a first step Mr HARRIMAN recommended one of the following two courses:
>
>> a) He and I, on instructions, should insist on the Commission accepting the principle that each of its members should have the right to name a reasonable number of individuals for consultation. This list at first should be small, but later, after preliminary consultations, it could be expanded.
>>
>> b) He and I should insist on MOLOTOV accepting in the first place two of our nominees from LONDON and two from POLAND. In return for this, we will allow MOLOTOV to invite one from each area and again reserving the right to expand the first list later, after preliminary consultations. Mr HARRIMAN wants to insist on inviting M. MIKOLAJCZCK and M. GRABSKI from LONDON, Professor KUTRZEBA and one of the strongest among our other candidates from POLAND. He agrees that MIKOLAJCZCK is the most important figure. Mr HARRIMAN, however, considers that a certain amount of pressure should be brought to bear upon MIKOLAJCZCK so that within the next 48 hours he will issue a statement accepting without reservation the CRIMEA decision, even though not necessarily approving of it.

5. Mr HARRIMAN suggests that possibly both of the above courses should be tried. In the event of their failure he put forward as a compromise a third course, inviting the Polish Provisional Government representatives first and listening to what they have to say, on condition that MOLOTOV agrees, in writing, that after hearing the Polish Provisional Government each member of the Commission shall have the right to invite any democratic leaders from Poland or abroad whom he considers useful for consultation. The names of the candidates would be submitted direct to the Commission who would discuss them but if after discussion and investigation the individual commissioner still wished to extend an invitation he would be free to do so.

Mr HARRIMAN concludes that without contemplating a breakdown now we should pursue no course on which we should not be willing to rest our case if MOLOTOV remains adamant.

When this particular VENONA series started to emerge in 1948 the British interest was immediately obvious, so the FBI's Washington field office consulted the two local British intelligence liaison officers at the embassy, Peter Dwyer from SIS and Dick Thistlethwaite who represented MI5 as the embassy's Security Liaison Officer, replacing Geoffrey Paterson. Both undertook to initiate an investigation in London into precisely who at the embassy four years earlier had been privy to the Foreign Office despatches quoted in the texts, but the inquiry seemed to take an interminably long time, and the FBI suspected the British of deliberate foot-dragging. Indeed, when Dwyer and Thistlethwaite were replaced the following year by Kim Philby and Geoffrey Paterson, little progress had been made. According to Philby's mischievous version of events, the official attitude was that any number of people could have had access to the telegrams, and that the task of tracing the clerical and cleaning staff, who were considered the most likely candidates, was unproductive. When Jeffrey Northbury joined the Eastcote BRIDE team in early 1950, his first priority was HOMER having been told by Wilfred Bodsworth in strict confidence that Klaus Fuchs had been identified by a decrypt, and this target was just as important. It was only when enough of Apresyan's message of 28 June 1944 succumbed to Bodsworth's prolonged cryptographic attack, on 30 March 1951, that it was transformed into a smoking gun with Donald Maclean the obvious suspect, and the urgent news was transmitted to MI5. Impressed by what Bodsworth had achieved, his American counterparts sent a congratulatory telegram: 'dazzled by your brilliance'.

Fortunately for Maclean, Philby was in a position in Washington DC to alert the Soviets to his imminent arrest and to convey a warning to him. Acting on Philby's tip Maclean, who was then head of the American Department, fled the country overnight, accompanied by his Foreign Office colleague Guy Burgess who, until the moment of his disappearance, had not come under suspicion. It was not until the defection of Vladimir Petrov in Australia three years later that MI5 realized that both men had been long-term moles, recruited at university to penetrate the highest reaches of Whitehall.

The only evidence in 1951 that Maclean could have been a member of a wider Soviet network was the unexpected defection of Burgess, and the undeniable fact that the diplomat had made his escape with only hours to spare, acting on a tip. Philby, of course, was immediately recalled to London for interrogation and dismissed from SIS, although he resolutely denied the accusation that he had played the role of the 'third man'. Certainly at that stage there was no evidence in VENONA to support the proposition of a wider spy ring inside the Foreign Office, but further cryptographic breaks into the NKVD's 1945 London traffic produced a single fragmented reference, dated 21 July 1945, to a source codenamed HICKS. Significantly, it was addressed to the 8th Department in Moscow, which set the spy apart from others with whom he was connected:

> Information from HICKS. 8th Department
> Herewith a telegram from the NOOK [Foreign Office], No. 22 of 2 July, addressed to the British Ambassador in WASHINGTON. The telegram was repeated to MOSCOW as No. 20: '1. When the Commission starts to consider the question as to which countries [812 groups missed]

That HICKS was part of a larger network became clear in the wake of the Gouzenko defection in Canada on 5 September, an event that had the profoundest impact on the Centre, as this message on 18 September addressed to BOB in London indicated:

> As I am thinking of relieving you of the burden of meetings with the valuable agent network thus ensuring that it is protected from compromise (this is because of STANLEY's information about the disruption of our work in CANADA, [3 groups unrecovered] and the intensification of counter-measures against us which is being carried out in the ISLAND [England], do you not consider that it would be advisable to transfer JOHNSON to BORIS's control and leave you only with STANLEY and HICKS?
>
> Report how BORIS is coping with the English language, how is he familiarizing himself with the conditions in the town, whether he is sufficiently careful, whether he can run JOHNSON with authority and so on. Until further notice do not, under any circumstances, increase the number of meetings with STANLEY, JOHNSON or HICKS.

According to the Petrovs, BOB was most likely Boris Krotov, a senior member of Konstantin Kutin's *rezidentura* who had been responsible for handling only the most important agents of the 3rd Department. He had arrived in London in August 1941 and had remained until March 1947 under third secretary cover at the consulate, and his aide, codenamed BORIS, was most likely a relatively junior newcomer who was quite inexperienced with only a limited grasp of English, a cause for some concern if he was to run JOHNSON, yet another member of the ring. As for STANLEY, he was undoubtedly one of the very few in London with a knowledge of the GRU cipher-clerk's defection in Ottawa less than a fortnight earlier, for a top priority message dated 17 September 1945, and transmitted at 2011 hours Moscow time, showed that he had been in touch already about the RCMP's coup:

> The Chiefs have given their consent to the confirmation of the accuracy of your telegram concerning STANLEY's data about the events in CANADA in the NEIGHBOURS [GRU] sphere of activity. STANLEY's information does correspond to the facts.

This interpretation, that STANLEY had alerted the Centre to Gouzenko's defection, is supported by the next VENONA fragment, dated, the following day:

The Cambridge Ring

[21 groups unrecovered] at the meeting last week with STANLEY he invited [8 groups unrecovered] everyday control [19 groups unrecoverable]

The Centre's alarm at the loss of Gouzenko was manifested most clearly in this directive from Moscow, dated 21 September and addressed to Krotov:

In view of the NEIGHBOURS [GRU] affair in CANADA and the circumstances which have arisen at your end as a result of this, transfer HICKS at the regular meeting to ADAM's control. Temporarily, until further notice, cut down meetings with HICKS to once a month. Urge HICKS to concentrate his attention on passing us material dealing only with large fundamental issues. As ADAM is by nature a rather phlegmatic person, encourage him to adopt a manner at meetings with HICKS which will impress the latter so that HICKS senses ADAM's authority. On JOHNSON's return from [2 groups unrecoverable] with him not oftener than once a month. The position remains the same for STANLEY also. If, however, you notice that, as a consequence of local circumstances, greater attention is being paid to you and to our workers by the COMPETITORS [MI5], you may break off contact temporarily with the sources. For the period of the lull in your work with the agents, try to create pretext [2 groups unrecovered] panic and cases of carelessness. Meet them more by neutral methods of contact, go to the theatres, cinemas, etc. Warn all our comrades to make a thorough check when going out to a meeting and, if surveillance is observed, not to try, under any circumstances, to evade the surveillance and meet the agent regardless. For such contingencies make use of check appointments. Come to an agreement on this with the sources. Verify once more the passwords, addresses and check appointments you have, so that, in case of loss of contact, the sources can be re-established without undue difficulty. We agree with your proposal about handing over JOHNSON [43 groups unrecoverable]

This important text introduced ADAM, later identified as the Soviet embassy's new young press attaché, Mikhail F. Shishkin, and gave a clue to JOHNSON, who had been overseas at the time of despatch. As if to emphasize the deepening crisis, Moscow sent two other short messages to Krotov on the same day, the first by the top priority wireless channel:

> Reference your telegram. In carrying out the meeting with STANLEY, be particularly cautious and careful to maintain secrecy. Do not have any documents with you and [8 groups unrecoverable]

Finally, Moscow sent this very short message which proved damning for Philby whose post is SIS's Iberian counter-intelligence branch had given him access to some Mexican files.

> Only in person [1 group unrecovered] STANLEY's material concerning our Mexican affairs reporting to me this material.

This brief telegram sealed Philby's fate for, as well as being the senior SIS officer consulted about the Gouzenko case, he had until recently worked in the Iberian counter-intelligence section that routinely dealt with Central American topics. That Gouzenko created chaos for both the NKVD and GRU is definite, but the level of havoc may have prompted a very short, unexplained VENONA text dated 19 September 1945, addressed to Krotov in London, which simply instructed 'Please expedite a reply to No. 6244 (re the conclusion about KIM)'. Was this Moscow's blunder, referring to Philby's nickname, and perhaps a measure of the panic that had gripped the Centre? Naturally MI5 considered the alternative explanations, that Kim was the name of a ship visiting Britain, or even an abbreviation for the Russian for Communist Youth International (Kommunsticheskli Internatsional Molodezhi), but those invited to speculate preferred to think the Soviet system had accidentally incriminated one of its star performers.

Although Philby was easily identified as STANLEY, this information was never part of the evidence used against him in Beirut when he was confronted by his SIS colleague Nicholas Elliott in January 1964 because, inexplicably, GCHQ had suspended its work on VENONA in 1954, apparently with MI5's consent on the grounds that the work was unproductive. The fact that the then Director of D Branch, Graham Mitchell, had authorized the suspension of the project was to count against him when he became the subject of a molehunt in 1962. Mitchell retired in September 1962 and work on VENONA was resumed, with the advantage of the computing facilities of the Atomic Weapons Research Establishment at Aldermaston – which at that time owned the most advanced data-processing equipment in Britain – that were far more sophisticated than anything GCHQ possessed. All the VENONA material was keyed on to magnetic tape and punchcards twice, to eliminate the possibility of operator error, and thereafter the breaks developed faster.

The certainty that STANLEY was Philby emerged only after his defection, although the information had been lurking in the texts for decades. As for HICKS, it was Guy Burgess who appeared the best candidate; the Foreign Office insider who had passed the Washington telegram to the Soviets in July 1945. With HOMER, HICKS and STANLEY exposed, MI5's attention centred on the remaining member of the ring, JOHNSON. When finally in April 1964 Anthony Blunt confessed to having been recruited as a mole at Cambridge, accepting an offer of immunity from prosecution, the link was confirmed. In September 1945, when the Centre mentioned JOHNSON's absence from London, Blunt had spent three weeks in Italy on a mission for MI5.

The remaining questions for MI5 arising out of VENONA concerned the other NKVD spies who appeared to be at liberty. A source codenamed LEAF had been active in 1941, according to two tiny fragments of texts dated 1 and 23 September, the latter reading: 'Material from LEAF [182 groups unrecoverable] in Bulgaria'. Then there was DAN, recently returned from a military appointment in Washington DC, according to a single text dated 15 September 1945:

> [74 groups unrecoverable] the FRATERNAL [Communist Party]. On returning from the Army to WASHINGTON at the beginning of 1945, again established contact with him on behalf of the FRATERNAL and came to an agreement to continue work on the collection of intelligence in the ISLAND [England]. However, did not disclose to DAN the importance of the intelligence, though it is quite likely that he suspects this. Arrangements for contact with DAN on the ISLAND [18 groups unrecoverable] DAN will go to
> the meetings and await our man for 10–15 minutes on the pavement immediately at the exit from Regents Park tube

station in Regent Street. DAN will have the magazine JOHN BULL in his hand. Our man is to approach first and, after greeting him, will say – 'Didn't I meet you at VICK's Restaurant at Connecticut Avenue?' To this DAN is to reply – 'Yes, VICK himself introduced you.' After this our man is to show DAN a small [19 groups unrecoverable] is to show an exact copy of this label. Then the two men will talk business. We recommend sending ALAN to contact DAN. Telegraph [2 groups unrecovered]

No progress was made by MI5 in its pursuit of DAN, although it was noted that the entrance to the Regents Park underground station was never located in Regent Street, which must have made the rendezvous tricky, but in the same week Krotov was directed by Moscow to avoid two further agents, JACK and ROSA: 'Your No. 1463. JACK and ROSA should not repeat not be met in public.'

So who were they? According to Peter Wright, who reviewed all the VENONA files in the 1970s in the hope of running to earth more Soviet spies, candidates included Victor and Tess Rothschild, who had both worked in the wartime Security Service, but as there was only this single short reference to the pair, MI5's investigation was doomed.[1]

For the few inside MI5 who were to privy to VENONA, the texts were to be the source of tremendous frustration because the incriminating information had come too late to be used against any of the spies. Maclean had fled before he could be challenged, taking Burgess with him. Philby too had narrowly escaped his interrogators by defecting from Beirut, and Blunt feigned cooperation to avoid prosecution. The mysteries of STANLEY, HICKS, HOMER and JOHNSON were eventually solved, but only when each was safe from the risk of arrest and imprisonment. For the molehunters dedicated to finding the traitors, the irritation of knowing that these spies had slipped from their grasp with such apparent ease was matched only by the certainty that others, including DAN, LEAF, JACK and ROSA, were still free, and probably still active.

VI

Operation ENORMOZ

THE DISCOVERY by Meredith Gardner in December 1946 of the list of seventeen atomic scientists was the first evidence that someone other than Allan Nunn May had been betraying details of the weapons development programme to the Soviets. Nunn May had been confronted in London with evidence that had originated with Igor Gouzenko, and in May 1946 had been sentenced to ten years' imprisonment. While his confession had described how he had passed a tiny sample of Uranium-235 to his contact in Canada, he had made no mention of a larger spy-ring that evidently had penetrated Los Alamos, with tentacles in the three university centres of atomic research: Berkeley, Chicago and Colombia in New York. In addition, the Manhattan Project was concentrated at a massive compound, covering an area of 16 miles by 7 miles, at Oak Ridge, Tennessee, which included accommodation for 13,000 people with buildings a mile long for Ernest Lawrence's electro-magnetic separation plants, and a 5,000-acre corner reserved for the gaseous diffusion unit, to provide bomb quality U-235. There was also a 670-square-mile reservation at Hanford in central Washington, 100 miles from the nearest habitation, where the fissionable material was developed. Bomb assembly and work on the trigger mechanism were based at Los Alamos which, though located on the remote forested site of a boys' school 35 miles north-west of Santa Fe, was regarded for administrative purposes as a branch of the Berkeley Radiation Laboratory.

. The central question was the extent to which the six separate, top secret, isolated sites had been penetrated, for someone had evidently identified the three top American physicists, all Nobel prizewinners, who had been selected to head different components of the bomb development programme: Arthur Compton at the University of Chicago dealing with chain reaction and plutonium production;

Ernest Lawrence at Berkeley using the cyclotron techniques to separate U-235; and Harold Urey at Colombia concentrating on the other U-235 separation methods, including 'heavy water'. Of particular concern was the fact that the list of scientists contained in telegram 940 of December 1944 (see p.21) was entirely accurate, whereas most of the senior physicists working in the Manhattan Project had been assigned noms-de-guerre to protect their identities. Thus the Dane Niels Bohr was 'Nicholas Baker', and Enrico Fermi was 'Henry Farmer', complete with full documentation to support the aliases. The news that this arrangement had been blown was doubly worrying.

Evidence in VENONA of a comprehensive haemorrhage of atomic secrets from the Manhattan Project centred on several suspects, including Dr Theodore Hall, who was implicated first in a text dated 12 November 1944 which described the young physicist's encounter with his Soviet contact, a former White Russian cavalry officer named Sergei N. Kurnakov who had emigrated to the USA, converted to Communism and then operated under journalistic cover for *Russian Voice* in New York:[1]

> BECK [Sergei Kurnakov] visited Theodore HALL, 19 years old, the son of a furrier. He is a graduate of Harvard University. As a talented physicist he was taken on for government work. He was a GYMNAST [member of the Young Communist League] and conducted work in the Steel Founders' Union. According to BECK's account, HALL has an exceptionally keen mind and a broad outlook, and is politically developed. At the present time HALL is in charge of a group at CAMP-2 (SANTA-FE) [Los Alamos]. HALL handed over to BECK a report about the CAMP and named the key personnel employed on ENORMOZ. He decided to do this on the advice of his colleague Saville SAKS, a GYMNAST living in TYRE [New York]. SAK's mother is a FELLOWCOUNTRYMAN [Communist] and works for RUSSIAN WAR RELIEF. With the aim of hastening a meeting with a competent person, HALL on the following day sent a copy of the report by SAKS to the PLANT [Soviet consulate]. ALEKSEI [Anatoli Yakovlev] received SAKS. HALL had to leave for CAMP-2 in two days' time. He was compelled to

make a decision quickly. Jointly with MAY [Stepan Apreysan] he gave BECK consent to feel out HALL, to assure him that everything was in order and to arrange liaison with him. HALL left his photograph and came to an understanding with BECK about a place for meeting him. BECK met SAKS [1 group garbled] our automobile. We consider it expedient to maintain liaison with HALL. [1 group unidentified] through SAKS and not to bring in anybody else. MAY has no objection to this. We shall send the details by post.

Nor was this the only material on Hall, for there were further VENONAs in 1945, including the following dated 23 January from New York which introduced OLD as Saville S. Sax, Hall's roommate at Harvard, and the hitherto unknown role of Bernard Schuster, a well-known figure in the Communist Party who evidently knew Sax. The telegram also revealed some tension between Sax's handler, Sergei N. Kurnakov, and Anatoli A. Yatskov, alias Yakovlev of the 8th (Economic) Directorate, who had replaced him and had been sent to New York to work under Leonid Kvasnikov, the principal coordinator of Operation ENORMOZ, who held the rank of *rezident*:

Your Nos. 316 and 121. The checking of OLD [Saville Sax] and YOUNG [Theodore Hall] we entrusted to ECHO [Bernard Schuster] a month ago, the result of the check we have not yet had. We are checking OLD's mother [Mrs Bluma Sax] also.

BECK [Sergei Kurnakov] is extremely displeased over the handing over of OLD to ALEKSEI [Anatoli Yakovlev]. He gives a favourable report of him. ALEKSEI has met OLD twice but cannot yet give a final judgment. YOUNG has been seen by no one except BECK. On the 8th January YOUNG sent a letter but never made arrangements for calling to a meeting. He has been called up into the army and left to work in the CAMP [Los Alamos]. OLD intends to renew his studies at Harvard University at the end of January.

Another VENONA, dated 26 May 1945 from Leonid Kvasnikov, ostensibly an engineer attached to Amtorg in New York between March 1943 and October 1945, showed the type of information Hall was disclosing.

Reference your 3367. YOUNG's material contains:

(a) A list of places where work on ENORMOZ is being carried out: 1. HANFORD, State of WASHINGTON, production of 49. 2. State of NEW JERSEY, production of 25 by the diffusion method. Director UREY. 3. BERKELEY, State of CALIFORNIA, production of 25 by the electro-magnetic method. Director LAWRENCE. 4. NEW CONSTRUCTION, administrative centre for ENORMOZ; also production of 25 by the spectographic method, Director COMPTON. 5. CHICAGO, ARGONNE Laboratories – nuclear research. At present work there has almost ceased. Director COMPTON. 6. The RESERVATION, the main practical research work on ENORMOZ. Director BILL OF EXCHANGE [Robert Oppenheimer]. 7. Camp [2 groups unrecovered] base in the area of CARLSBAD, State of NEW MEXICO, the place for the practical testing of the ENORMOZ bomb. 8. MONTREAL, CANADA – theoretical research.

(b) a brief description of the four methods of production of 25 – the diffusion, thermal diffusion, electro-magnetic and spectographic methods.

The material has not been fully worked over. We shall let you know the contents of the rest later.

In fact, Kvasnikov was the key figure overseeing ENORMOZ, and he communicated not to the local NKVD *rezident*, but direct to Moscow from a special substation in New York, designated 'XY' for scientific and technical intelligence. A graduate of the Institute of Chemical Engineering, he was rather better qualified to deal with details of nuclear physics than his immediate subordinates, Anatoli A. Yakovlev and Aleksandr S. Feklisov, who were not technically qualified.[2] The same could be said for Vladimir B. Barkovsky and Pavel D. Yerzin, who were undertaking similar duties in London for the 8th Department. Only Semyon M. Semyonov (codenamed TWAIN) was a scientist, having graduated from the Leningrad Institute of Chemical Engineering. He was then sent to the Massachusetts Institute of Technology in 1939 when he was posted to Amtorg. Thus the prime responsibility for ENORMOZ rested with Kvasnikov's XY *rezidentura* at Amtorg, which provided cover for both GRU and NKVD personnel.

Right J. Robert Oppenheimer was a strong candidate for the Soviet spy codenamed BILL OF EXCHANGE. The FBI discovered that, apart from his own Communist sympathies, his wife, brother and mistress were all CPUSA members.

Below Klaus Fuchs, codenamed CHARLES, was the first spy to be arrested on evidence supplied by VENONA. However, his interrogators never let him realise the source of their information and he was induced to confess.

Below right Judith Coplon, the NKVD spy in the Department of Justice, continued to maintain her innocence of espionage and denied having tipped off her Soviet contact to current FBI investigations. Compelling evidence from VENONA, identifying her as the source codenamed SIMA, was considered too secret to disclose to the prosecution.

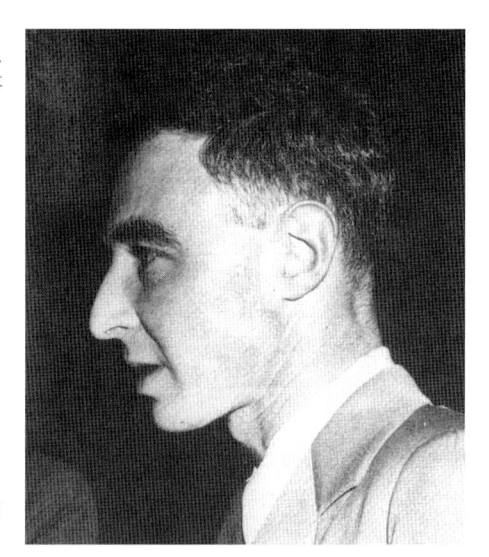

Kim Philby visited Arlington Hall and was briefed about the BRIDE project, but the crucial decrypts dated 1945 incriminating him as STANLEY were not broken until after his defection in January 1963.

Having been the subject of lengthy MI5 investigation, Donald Maclean was finally identified as the spy code-named HOMER at the end of April 1951. Two days later, he defected.

Julius Rosenberg, codenamed ANTENNA and then LIBERAL, was a key figure in the Soviet penetration of the Manhattan project and was executed, prompting a worldwide Communist-inspired campaign to protest his innocence.

Ethel Rosenberg acted as a courier in her husband's network and was shown by VENONA to be fully aware of the extent of his activities. Nevertheless, the FBI argued that her life should be spared.

Below Harry Gold was formally identified by Klaus Fuchs as his contact, and he then incriminated his sister, Ethel Rosenberg. Gold apeared in the VENONA traffic many times, first codenamed GOOSE, then ARNO.

Elizabeth Bentley and Alger Hiss (right) appear before a Congressional investigation. Hiss denied having been a Soviet spy, not realising that he appeared in the VENONA traffic as ALES. Few of Bentley's allegations of espionage were accepted at the time she confessed to the FBI in 1945, but VENONA revealed her to have been codenamed CLEVER GIRL and proved her charges to be true.

Right Captain Ferdinand Coudert restarted study of 'the Russian problem' and encouraged the cryptographers until his replacement in November 1943.

Below One of the TICOM teams at Bletchley Park before their deployment in Europe. Their task was to seize enemy cryptographic equipment before it could be destroyed. TICOM/3 discovered a secret cache of German Foreign Ministry archives at the Schloss Bergsheidegen near Leipzig.

Right Major William J. Bundy was a member of the TICOM/3 team that occupied the von der Schulenberg family home at Bergsheidegen and recovered a veritable treasure trove of crypto material, including a charred copy of the famous Soviet *Podjeba* codebook captured by the Finns and then passed to the Nazis.

Genevieve Feinstein and Frank Lewis (centre) were to devote years to what was euphemistically termed 'the Russian problem' and helped match thousands of duplicated cipher groups in Soviet one-time pads, making BRIDE a practical proposition.

Genevieve Feinstein receiving an award for her contribution to the BRIDE project. Her work was considered so secret that few at the National Security Agency knew what it involved.

David Greenglass, codenamed BUMBLEBEE and then CALIBRE in VENONA, provided vital information about the atomic bomb development programme at Los Alamos. He gave the FBI a confession without guessing that he had been compromised by VENONA.

Above The FBI's record of Vladimir Pravdin's passport photograph. Pravdin, codenamed SERGEI, operated under journalistic cover as the TASS correspondent in New York, and having been brought up in Paris he was well qualified to run several important French-speaking agents, including the former Minister of Air, Pierre Cot. His initial attempts to cultivate the *Nation*'s Washington editor, Isadore Stone, proved less successful.

Left Vassili M. Zarubin was a highly experienced NKVD officer before he was sent to New York as *rezident* in 1940, having served as an illegal in France and Germany. In 1943 he was transferred to Washington DC, using the surname Zubilin.

Outbuildings of Arlington Hall, Virginia, formerly a girls' school. The Armed Forces Security Agency turned the entire grounds into a top security compound, offering maximum protection to the BRIDE project.

General Cordern presents an award to Captain Coudert, who started the BRIDE project, and Bill Smith (right), who replaced him in November 1943 and supervised many of the breakthroughs before he was moved on in 1946.

Cecil Phillips in Paris while on attachment to GCHQ at Eastcote. Phillips was to become one of the key figures in the BRIDE programme, and was responsible for the breakthrough that enabled the duplicated Soviet one-time pads to be matched and decrypted.

The GRU defector Ismail Akhmedov recalls attending a conference at the NKVD's Lubianka headquarters in the late autumn of 1940 which had been called to apportion Amtorg cover:

> The NKVD insisted on 60 per cent of the technical intelligence agents in Amtorg on the grounds that they were responsible for economic as well as scientific intelligence. However, we did not really fare so badly. The gents allotted to the Red Navy in New York came only from GRU, and we had some of the wives of our operatives recruited, too. That left us with more than the minority of 40 per cent of the agents proposed by the NKVD.

Two months later, on 5 July 1945, Yakovlev was rebuked by Moscow for his performance in handling the atomic spies, citing some episode involving YOUNG:

> Your No. 613. The incident involving GRAUBER should be regarded as a compromise of YOUNG [Theodore Hall]. The cause of this is ALEKSEI's [Yakovlev] completely unsatisfactory work with the agents on ENORMOZ. His work with [9 groups unrecovered] for this reason we consider it of the utmost importance to ensure supervision so that the COUNTRY [America] [23 groups unrecoverable] we once more [3 groups unrecovered] attention to [2 groups unrecovered] our instructions. For the future [4 groups unrecovered]: immediately inform us by telegraph about each meeting with the agents of ENORMOZ. In the next post [3 groups unrecovered] on this same question to send the most precise reports on meetings [14 groups unrecovered] every meeting with permanent staff [14 groups unrecovered] from all these areas. You [18 groups unrecovered] to seek safe flats in the areas of the camps. This question you must [17 groups unrecovered] our workers on the development [35 groups unrecovered] GRAUBER case meetings of our operational worker with YOUNG you must [4 groups unrecovered].
> VIKTOR

As Kurnakov had described correctly, Hall was the son of a Russian furrier who had escaped the pogroms and settled in the Washington Heights district of New York. A brilliant student, he had been educated at the City College of New York and in 1940 had entered Queens College, having been turned down by Colombia University on the grounds of his youth. Two years later, aged sixteen, he transferred to Harvard to read physics and advanced mathematics, and came under the spell of his room-mate, the leftist Saville Sax whose Russian-born mother Bluma ran a Russia War Relief branch. In October 1943 Hall was interviewed for a post at Los Alamos, and in January 1944 began work on the Manhattan Project. However, during his first leave, in October 1944 he met Sax in New York and together they called at the Amtorg office at 238 West 28th Street where they met Sergei Kurnakov, then working under journalistic cover. Kurnakov arranged for Sax to act as a courier for Hall, and a rendezvous was arranged in Albuquerque for December 1944. At this meeting, which Hall later described, he received a Russian questionnaire and in exchange gave Sax a two-page account of the atomic bomb's implosion principle. At the end of the war Sax returned to Harvard, and he was replaced by Lona Cohen who maintained irregular contact with Hall until 16 March 1951, when Hall was visited at the Institute for Radiobiology and Biophysics at Chicago University by two FBI special agents. During a three-hour interview Hall denied any involvement with espionage, but refused the FBI permission to search his home. At a second interview, two days later, Hall declined to answer any further questions, and soon afterwards he took up a research post at Memorial Sloan-Kettering in New York. Sax, who was then driving a taxi in Chicago, was also interviewed by the FBI on 16 March, but denied espionage, claiming that his occasional visits to the Soviet Consulate in New York had been in connection with relatives still living in the Soviet Union, and his single trip to New Mexico had been taken after he had dropped out of Harvard, to consult his trusted friend Ted Hall about another university course. Sax denied ever having received a list of atomic scientists from Hall, and consented to a search of his home, which revealed nothing incriminating.

In 1953 Hall broke off all contact with the Soviets and eleven years later he was offered a twelve-month contract at the Cavendish Laboratory at Cambridge University. At the end of the year, instead of returning to the United States (by this time Sax was dead), Hall remained at the university, and he still lives in the town with his wife Joan. Taken together, the VENONA texts amount to as comprehensive an indictment of Hall's espionage as could be asked for, but the necessity to protect the source's integrity meant that Hall was allowed his liberty. All he is prepared to say now is that

> In 1944 I was nineteen years old – immature, inexperienced and not too sure of myself. I recognize that I could easily have been wrong in my judgement of what was necessary, and that I was indeed mistaken about some things, in particular my view of the nature of the Soviet state. The world has moved on since then, and certainly so have I.

The same, however, was not true of Klaus Fuchs, who was eventually identified as the source codenamed REST (and, after a change in cryptonyms in October 1944, CHARLES). The first clue that at least one other spy had penetrated the Manhattan Project appeared in a message from Leonid Kvasnikov, dated 9 February 1944:

> On 5th February a meeting took place between GOOSE and REST. Beforehand GOOSE was given a detailed briefing by us. REST greeted him pleasantly but was rather cautious at first, (1 group unrecovered] the discussion GOOSE satisfied himself that REST was aware of whom he was working with. REST arrived in the COUNTRY [America] in September as a member of the ISLAND [England] mission on ENORMOZ. According to him the work on ENORMOZ in the COUNTRY is being carried out under the direct control of the COUNTRY's army represented by General SOMERVELL and STIMSON: at the head of the group of ISLANDERS is a Labour Member of Parliament, Ben SMITH.
>
> The whole operation amounts to the working out of the process for the separation of isotypes of ENORMOZ. The work is proceeding in two directions: the electron method developed by LAWRENCE [71 groups unrecoverable] separation of isotopes by the combined method, using the diffusion method for preliminary and the electron method for final separation. The work [46 groups unrecovered] 18th February, we shall report the results.

The content of this telegram suggested that REST had arrived in the USA in September 1944, was sufficiently senior to know that

Ben Smith, the Minister for Supply resident in Washington DC, was overseeing the British contribution to the Manhattan Project, and that his technical knowledge was far from theoretical. On 8 May 1944 the New York *rezident* Stepan Apresyan described how REST had revealed a policy disagreement between the British and American scientists on the future of the weapons development programme:

> REST advises that the work of the Commission of the ISLANDERS [British] in the COUNTRY [America] is not meeting with success in view of the unwillingness of workers of the COUNTRY to share secrets with the ISLANDERS.
>
> It will be proposed to REST that he should either return to the ISLAND or work at the special laboratory-camp for study [35 groups unrecoverable] the work of REST from the two indicated.

The next month, on 15 June, Apresyan expanded on the crisis that had hit inter-allied relations on the Manhattan Project:

> [1 group unrecovered] received from REST the third part of Report 'SN – 12 Efferent Fluctuation in a Steam [37 groups unrecoverable] Diffusion Method – work his speciality. REST expressed doubt about the possibility of remaining in the COUNTRY [America] without arousing suspicion. According to what REST says, the ISLANDERS [British] and TOWNSMEN [Americans] have finally fallen out as a result of the delay in research work on diffusion. The TOWNSMEN have told the representatives of the ISLAND that construction of a plant in the ISLAND 'would be in direct contradiction to the spirit of the agreement on ENORMOZ signed together with the Atlantic Charter'. At present the ISLAND's director in CARTHAGE [Washington DC] is ascertaining the details of the transfer of work to the ISLAND. REST assumes he will have to leave in a month or six weeks.

This telegram was followed on 25 July 1944 by Apresyan's proposal to pay REST:

> Almost half a year of contact established with REST has demonstrated the value of his work for us. We consider it

necessary to pay him for this half year the due reward of 500 dollars. He fully deserves this sum. Telegraph consent.

However, the *rezident* never got the chance to pay REST, for neither his cut-out (intermediary), codenamed GOOSE, nor Anatoli Yakovlev (ALEKSEI) had managed to make contact, as Apresyan explained on 29 August 1944:

> In July when it became known that REST might be leaving for the ISLAND [Britain], instructions were given to ALEKSEI, and by the letter to GOOSE, to arrange a password for meeting with REST in case he was leaving. On 5 August REST did not appear at the meeting and GOOSE missed the next meeting. When he checked on REST's apartment GOOSE was informed that REST had left for the ISLAND. In order to re-check, I sent GOOSE to REST's sister, she and her husband the departure up to 20 September [67 groups unrecoverable] should check his arrival. I did not have
> time to hand over to REST the 500 dollars authorized by you.

Clearly, REST's disappearance had given Apresyan and Moscow some cause for concern, as is indicated by the next VENONA, dated 22 September 1944:

> GOOSE will travel to REST's sister on 26th September. The sister has not been traced by means of external surveillance; her whereabouts are unknown; she was to have returned after the 20th. We shall report the outcome of GOOSE's journey immediately.

A telegram from Moscow on 16 November 1944 showed that GOOSE (now referred to as ARNO) had discovered that REST (now CHARLES) had not gone to England, as anticipated, but had been transferred to Los Alamos:

> On ARNO's last visit to CHARLES's sister it became known that CHARLES has not left for the ISLAND [England] but is at CAMP No. 2 [Los Alamos]. He flew to Chicago and telephoned his sister. He named the state where the camp is and promised to come on leave for Christmas. He is taking steps to establish liaison with CHARLES while he is on leave.

The assumption that CHARLES has left for the ISLAND was due to [40 groups unrecoverable]

On 27 February 1945 Moscow asked the New York *rezidentura* for details of CHARLES's work:

Advise forthwith: exactly where and in what capacity CHARLES is working in the PRESERVE [Argonne Radiation Laboratory]; the object of his trip to CHICAGO and whom he met there; what has he been doing since August; why has the meeting with him been arranged only in June; why did he not have a discussion [2 groups unrecovered] and by what [4 groups unrecovered]. ARNO, CHARLES's sister (henceforth ANT); how [6 groups unrecovered] ARNO about CHARLES's arrival, how in detail their meeting went off; what materials were received from CHARLES.

On 31 March, Moscow noted CHARLES's value, referring specifically to the Manhattan Project's gaseous diffusion plant at Clinton, Tennessee:

We are sending herewith an evaluation on ENORMOZ. Referenced are materials from CHARLES about the FUNICULAR:
 a) 5/46 [groups unrecovered]
 b) 5/60 [6 groups unrecovered] – contains an interesting method of calculation, which will be used during the design.
 c) 5/62 technical data on the FUNICULAR and [12 groups unrecovered]
 d) 7/83 paragraph 1 – about the degree of separation of the membrane – offers substantial interest.
 e) 7/84 paragraph 1 – about tests of the membrane and information about the layout of the plant – is of interest. What is needed is [7 groups unrecovered] plan of the plant.
 f) 7/83 and 84 – on the theory of the stability of the FUNICULAR together with CHARLES's materials on this question received earlier they form a full and valuable place of information.
 2. YOUNG's [Theodore Hall] report about work [4 groups unrecovered]. [1 group unrecovered] great interest.

Operation ENORMOZ

Seen in their correct chronology, the VENONA material pointing to Fuchs as a spy is compelling, but at the time of the FBI's investigation, only fragments of these texts were available, although there was never any room for doubt that CHARLES was engaged on atomic research, for the reference to the PRESERVE on 27 February was repeated on 26 May 1945 by New York in YOUNG's list of nuclear energy establishments. Accordingly, the hunt was on for a spy who had been out of touch for some time, had met a contact codenamed ARNO, and had a sister codenamed ANT. At the FBI, Special Agents Robert Lamphere and Ernie Van Loon narrowed the search for the culprit to a scientist who had worked both in New York and Los Alamos, had travelled to Chicago, was scheduled to go to England and had a sister living somewhere in the United States.

As for the value of CHARLES's information, that became clear in a text from Moscow dated 10 April 1945:

> CHARLES's information under No. 2/57 on the atomic bomb (henceforth BALLOON) is of great value. Apart from the data on the atomic mass of the nuclear explosive and on the details of the explosive method of actuating BALLOON it contains information received for the first time from you about the electro-magnetic method of separation of ENORMOZ. We wish in addition to establish the following: 1. What kind of fission – by means of fast or slow neutrons – [35 groups unrecovered] [281 groups unrecoverable]

In this context ENORMOZ meant uranium, but the many other telegrams mentioning the codename suggested that it was also used as the title of the joint NKVD/GRU operation. However, the FBI was slow to grasp this crucial point, and had assumed, partly because of Soviet orthodoxy, but also because Klaus Fuchs's name had been found in the address book of Israel Halperin, that if he was a spy, he had been working for the GRU exclusively. Professor Halperin had been implicated by the defector Igor Gouzenko in Canada, and the connection between the mathematician and the physicist was far from clear, although Halperin had sent Fuchs magazines and newspapers while the latter had been interned as an enemy alien at Sherbrooke Camp outside Quebec for six months in 1940. The FBI considered the link between the veteran Communist Halperin, who had expressed much interest in uranium production at Chalk River, and the Manhattan Project scientist Fuchs to be rather too much of a coincidence, but that was precisely what eventually it turned out to be.

This unusual departure from conventional Soviet methodology, with a GRU asset handled by the NKVD, baffled Lamphere: 'The mention of Fuchs's name puzzled me, because the deciphered message told me that Fuchs's involvement – if it was Fuchs – was a KGB matter, and usually there was no crossover of GRU and KGB operations.'

By the time MI5 was ready to interview Fuchs, on the pretext of the security implications of his father who was then living in the Soviet zone of East Germany, the scientist had raised the issue with the security staff at Harwell on his own initiative. When Fuchs first mentioned the topic, the evidence against him accumulated from VENONA was considerable, and dated back to the original reference by Colonel Sklyarov to Simon Kremer's meeting with him in August 1941:

> On 8th August BARCh [Kremer] had a meeting with a former acquaintance, Doctor FUCHS who [1 group unidentified] that [10 groups unrecovered] in Birmingham [34 groups unrecovered] in three months time and then all the material will be sent to CANADA for the industrial production. [1 group unidentified] the fact that in GERMANY, in LEIPZIG [9 groups unrecovered] Professor HEISENBERG [34 groups unrecovered] 1000 tons of dynamite. Report when opportunity occurs. BRION

The fact that Klaus Fuchs had joined Birmingham University's atomic research team on 28 May 1941, and had studied in Leipzig under Werner Heisenberg, the Professor of Theoretical Physics between 1927 and 1941, dovetailed neatly with the fragments extracted from the GRU telegram. Similarly, the comment about a production process in Canada fitted with the Manhattan Project, as did the description of a thousand tons of dynamite, an easy way of explaining the potential of an atomic weapon to be uninitiated. What remained unexplained, and was to baffle the counter-intelligence experts, was the proposition that a GRU asset in 1941 could be handed over to the NKVD in 1944.

Investigation of Fuchs's travel in the United States, conducted by

Special Agent Ernie Van Loon, culminated in October 1949 when he showed that the scientist had made the visit to Chicago mentioned in VENONA, and to his sister and brother-in-law, Kristel and Robert Heineman, who lived in Cambridge, Massachusetts. Evidently Kristel was ANT, so all that remained was the identification of his cut-out, codenamed GOOSE and then ARNO, and this was eventually achieved when Fuchs, after his conviction, confirmed that surveillance footage, filmed secretly by the FBI, of Harry Gold showed the person whom he had known as 'Raymond' who had been his contact in New York. After Fuchs had acknowledged meeting Gold nine times, in New York, at Los Alamos and at Kristel's home, the Swiss-born chemist was interrogated and confessed to having received material from Fuchs. Gold made a lengthy confession in which he admitted having spied since 1935, initially supplying industrial information before graduating to atomic data, and he was sentenced to thirty years' imprisonment.

Undoubtedly, Gold was a figure of some importance in the ENORMOZ operation, as the New York *rezidentura* had observed in a text dated 13 December 1944:

> We consider it risky to concentrate all the contacts relating to ENORMOZ on ARNO [Harry Gold] alone. This is good in that it limits the circles of [2 groups unrecovered] but it is dangerous to disrupt [1 group unrecovered] work on ENORMOZ [45 groups unrecoverable]

Fuchs's own confession, delivered to Bob Lamphere and Hugh Clegg of the FBI in Wormwood Scrubs, where they were accompanied by MI5's Jim Skardon, appeared comprehensive, but he was anxious not to implicate Kristel who had by then undergone a nervous breakdown. He denied ever having passed secrets to Gold in her house, in contradiction to Gold's version, but although she was definitely ANT, there was no additional VENONA evidence to implicate her. As she and her husband had cooperated with the FBI, and had also identified Gold from photographs as a man who had visited them unexpectedly in an effort to make contact with Klaus, she featured no further in the FBI's inquiries.

Confirmation of Gold's espionage represented a considerable breakthrough, partly because he was no stranger to the FBI, having been called before a grand jury in 1947 looking into Elizabeth Bentley's allegations. Bentley had claimed that her lover, Jacob Golos, had received technical, but non-classified, information from Abraham Brothman, and when called as a witness he asserted that he had been introduced to Golos by another legitimate businessman, Harry Gold. A chemist by trade, Brothman had denied having done anything illegal, and he had escaped all charges, as had Gold, but four years later, a VENONA from Apresyan dated 1 October 1944 was to shed a different light on the relationship between Gold (GOOSE) and Brothman (CONSTRUCTOR).

> According to GOOSE's [Harry Gold] latest advice CONSTRUCTOR [Abraham Brothman] has stopped working at the Cheturgy Design Company where jointly with Henry GOLVINE and Art WEBER he was working on the production of BUNA-5. At the same time CONSTRUCTOR collaborated on the Aerosol problem (the work has partly been sent to you) with HENLIG. In both cases his partners cheated CONSTRUCTOR. They appropriated his work and chucked him out. Right now CONSTRUCTOR at his laboratory at 114 East 32nd Street with the help of the Grover Tank Company and the Bridgeport Brass Company has organized his own company and in the course of two or three weeks proposes to finish work on Aerosol and DDT and consolidate his position with these.
> According to GOOSE's advice he had known about the disagreements for three weeks or so but he considered them a temporary quarrel and did not [1 group unrecoverable] us [40 groups unrecoverable] sum of 100 dollars a month. Telegraph your decision. We shall advise in detail by post.

According to Gold, Brothman had also been involved in industrial espionage since 1935, but Gold's decision to go into partnership with him effectively ended their connection with the Soviets. Gold's principal contact had been Semyon Semyonov, but in September 1944 Anatoli Yakovlev took him over as a courier for Fuchs and discovered during a meeting held in New York in late 1946 that, contrary to instructions, Gold had kept in touch with Brothman. Furious, Yakovlev had berated Gold for maintaining contact with someone who had come under FBI surveillance, for it was clear that Brothman had been a marked man after he had been denounced as a Soviet source by Elizabeth Bentley. Discarded by Yakovlev, Gold saw no alternative to cooperating with the FBI, and giving evidence against Abe Brothman who received a prison sentence.

As well as supporting Bentley's testimony over Brothman, it was Gold who led the FBI to David Greenglass, who in turn exposed the extent of the Soviet operation ENORMOZ. In May 1945 Yakovlev had asked Gold to collect information from a source in Albuquerque when he next held a rendezvous with Fuchs in Santa Fe, and had given him the contact's name and address, together with 500 dollars and a recognition signal in the form of a torn cardboard boxtop which would match the part held by the spy. Under interrogation, five years later, Gold was able to pinpoint the address on a map of Albuquerque that he had visited in June 1945, and recall that his contact's wife had been named Ruth. Although he could not remember their surname, he knew that Ruth's husband was Jewish and was a young army technician. As for his information, it had consisted of several pages of handwritten notes and sketches. By the middle of June 1950 Bob Lamphere had traced David Greenglass, a soldier previously employed at Los Alamos and once suspected of having stolen a tiny sample of Uranium-235. Evidence of a spy at Los Alamos in 1944 codenamed CALIBRE had been revealed in a VENONA from Kvasnikov dated 14 November 1944:

> WASP has agreed to cooperate with us in drawing in BUMBLEBEE (henceforth CALIBRE – see your no. 5258) with a view to ENORMOZ. On summons from CALIBRE she is leaving on 22 November for the CAMP-2 [Los Alamos] area. CALIBRE will have a week's leave. Before WASP's departure LIBERAL will carry out two briefing meetings.

That CALIBRE enjoyed good access to Los Alamos was revealed in a telegram from Leonid Kvasnikov dated 16 December 1944 in which he reported the results of WASP's visit to CALIBRE, although there is still no clue that he is her husband:

> WASP has returned from a trip to see CALIBRE. CALIBRE expressed his readiness to help in throwing light on the work being carried out at CAMP-2 [Los Alamos] and stated that he had already given thought to this question earlier. CALIBRE said that the authorities of the camp were openly taking all

precautionary measures to prevent information about ENORMOZ falling into Russian hands. This is causing serious discontent among the progressive workers [17 groups unrecoverable] the middle of January CALIBRE will be in TYRE [New York]. LIBERAL referred to his ignorance of the problem, expresses the wish that our man should meet CALIBRE and interrogate him personally. He asserts that CALIBRE would be very glad of such a meeting. Do you consider such a meeting advisable? If not, I shall be obliged to draw up a questionnaire and pass it to LIBERAL. Report whether you have any questions of priority interest to us.

CALIBRE also reports: OPPENHEIM from California and KISTIAKOWSKI's (YOUNG's report mentioned the latter) are at present working at the Camp. The latter is doing research on the thermodynamic process. Advise whether you have information on these two professors.

Kvasnikov was to have more to say about CALIBRE on 8 January 1945, when he reported his appearance in New York:

CALIBRE has arrived in TYRE [New York] on leave. He has confirmed his agreement to help us. In addition to the information passed to us through WASP he has given us a hand-written plan of the layout of CAMP-2 and facts known to him about the work and the personnel. The basic task of the camp is to make the mechanism which is to serve as the detonator. Experimental work is being carried out on the construction of a tube of this kind and experiments are being tried with explosive – [13 groups unrecoverable] is still [17 groups unrecovered] gave you for [91 groups unrecovered] TYRE in six months' time [32 groups unrecoverable] LIBERAL to WASP [16 groups unrecovered]. Telegraph your opinion.

A check on Greenglass's service record by the FBI showed that he had taken some leave in December 1944 and had travelled to New York in January 1945, which fitted with CALIBRE's known movements. After prolonged interrogation, Greenglass admitted his complicity and implicated both his wife, Ruth, and his brother-in-

Operation ENORMOZ

law, Julius Rosenberg. In fact, their involvement had been set out very explicitly in a report from Apresyan dated 21 September 1944:

> Lately the development of new people has been in progress. LIBERAL [Julius Rosenberg] recommended the wife of his wife's brother, Ruth GREENGLASS, with a safe flat in view. She is 21 years old, a TOWNSWOMAN [American], a GYMNAST [member of the Young Communist League] since 1942. She lives on STANTON Street. LIBERAL and his wife recommend her as an intelligent and clever girl. [15 groups unrecoverable] Ruth learned that her husband was called up by the army but he was not sent to the front. He is a mechanical engineer and is now working at the ENORMOZ plant in SANTA FE, New Mexico [45 groups unrecoverable] detain VOLOK who is working on a plant on ENORMOZ. He is a FELLOWCOUNTRYMAN [Communist]. Yesterday he learned that they dismissed him from his work. His active work in progressive organizations in the past was the cause of his dismissal.
>
> In the FELLOWCOUNTRYMAN line LIBERAL is in touch with CHESTER [Bernard Schuster]. They meet once a month for the payment of dues. CHESTER is interested in whether we are satisfied with the collaboration and whether there are not any misunderstandings. He does not inquire about specific items of work. In as much as CHESTER knows about the role of the LIBERAL group we beg consent to ask CHESTER through LIBERAL about leads from among people who are working on ENORMOZ and in other technical fields.

With David Greenglass identified as CALIBRE, the rest of the network fell into place, with Ruth, codenamed WASP, having recruited him for her brother-in-law, LIBERAL. Once Rosenberg had been named by Greenglass he was arrested by the FBI, but although he denied all knowledge of espionage, VENONA was to reveal a very different story.

Initially codenamed ANTENNA, Julius Rosenberg was at the heart of a massive spy-ring, and the FBI was to conclude that he had been a spy since his discharge from the Army Signal Corps. On 5 May 1944 Apresyan requested Moscow:

> Please carry out a check and sanction the recruitment of Alfred SARANT, a lead of ANTENNA [Julius Rosenberg]. He is 25 years old, a Greek, an American citizen and lives in TYRE [New York City]. He completed the engineering course at Cooper Union in 1940. He worked for two years in the Signal Corps laboratory at Fort MONMOUTH. He was discharged for past union activity. He has been working for two years at Western Electric [45 groups unrecoverable] entry into the FELLOWCOUNTRYMAN [Communist Party]. SARANT lives apart from his family. Answer without delay.

As well as drawing in members of his family, his neighbours and many of his oldest friends, in this case Al Sarant, Rosenberg was revealed to be his network's key figure, even to the point of handling his sub-agents' data himself, as was disclosed in a telegram to Moscow dated 22 May 1944. This showed that his productivity had increased during the year, and established a direct link with Anatoli Yakovlev at the Soviet consulate:

> The work of the KhU [Economic Directorate] connected with the receipt of bulky materials is attended by great risk particularly the secret materials which were coming in during 1943 and are coming in now. The danger has increased because of the periodic surveillance of the cadre workers and the increasing surveillance of the PLANT [Soviet Consulate] to which the materials are being brought for filming. It has become impossible to bring [18 groups unrecoverable] to film at ALEKSEI's [Anatoli Yakovlev] apartment to which a portable camera had been brought earlier. It is intended in the future to practise such filming only now and then. What is your opinion? We consider it necessary to organize the filming of ANTENNA's [Julius Rosenberg] PROBATIONER's [agents] materials by ANTENNA himself. Again the question of a camera for ALEKSEI has been raised. Exceptionally secret materials are conveyed in the original or in manuscript which is more dangerous than the presence of a camera at ALEKSEI's. It is incomprehensible why one cannot do this in the course of the next half year (your No. 2031). We assume that it is connected with conservation and not the danger of ALEKSEI's disclosure [34 groups unrecoverable]

Operation ENORMOZ

Apresyan subsequently addressed the problem of copying documents on 14 June 1944 by passing it to Leonid Kvasnikov, who headed the parallel *rezidentura* in New York on behalf of the 8th Department:

> Your No. 2542. ANTON's [Leonid Kvasnikov] apartment is needed for photographing the material of ANTENNA's [Julius Rosenberg] group.

Having established where the photography was to take place, Moscow was unable to supply the necessary equipment and on 11 July 1944 arranged for German cameras, which were the subject of a wartime trade ban in the USA, to be purchased in Mexico:

> Please give instructions to the COUNTRYSIDE [Mexico] to buy two cameras and send them to TYRE [New York] by the first post. You allowed one camera for ANTENNA [Julius Rosenberg]. The second is needed for the work of the OFFICE [*rezidentura*]. The cameras find their way to the COUNTRYSIDE from Germany and cost 200 dollars. There are no cameras in TYRE. Inform us of your instructions. With a view to reducing the time required for the receipt and handing back of RELAY's [Morton Sobell] materials we consider it would be a good thing to make it his job to photograph his own materials and bring to TYRE only undeveloped films. For this purpose we want to pass on to him INFORMER's [Joseph Katz] old camera. The camera [17 groups unrecoverable]

The NKVD's demand for good German cameras in New York was reflected in a VENONA text recovered from the Mexico City circuit, dated 30 September 1944, in which Moscow had directed:

> Buy up quickly, and send to WASHINGTON for VADIM [Anatoli Gromov] 10 'LEICA' cameras with a full set of lenses. Report their cost to the CENTRE.

This demand was subsequently followed up on 17 November by another from Kvasnikov for the necessary accessories:

> In connection with the plans for the photographing of material by LIBERAL [Julius Rosenberg] and then by LENS

[Michael Sidorovich], a shortage of cassettes is making itself felt. We cannot get them without a priority. Please order 100 cassettes for a Leica camera through the COUNTRYSIDE [Mexico] and send them to us without delay.

Study of the VENONA material on ANTENNA in June and July 1944 showed that Rosenberg was an effective recruiter. His friend Al Sarant had studied electrical engineering at Colombia University and between October 1942 and September 1946, and therefore at the time of the VENONA intercepts, was a radar expert working for Bell Telephone Laboratories in New York on highly classified computer systems for the B-29 bomber. That some of this data, relating to the AN/APQ-7 high resolution airborne radar developed by the Massachusetts Institute of Technology, was compromised by a spy codenamed HUGHES emerged unmistakably in part two of a long text dated 13 December 1944 from New York which also referred to LIBERAL (Julius Rosenberg), WASP (Ruth Greenglass), CALIBRE (David Greenglass), YOUNG (Theodore Hall), ARNO (Harry Gold) and METER (Joel Barr). Clearly the burden of running these agents was becoming too much for one man, and on 5 December 1944 Apresyan warned about overworking Rosenberg:

> Expedite consent to the joint filming of their materials by both METER [Joel Barr] and HUGHES [Alfred Sarant] (see our letter no. 8). LIBERAL [Julius Rosenberg] has on hand eight people plus the filming of materials. The state of LIBERAL's health is nothing splendid. We are afraid of putting LIBERAL out of action with overwork.

Accordingly, the *rezidentura* sought to introduce two additional handlers, Aleksandr Raev and Aleksandr Fomin:

> Further [14 groups unrecovered] Both are FELLOWCOUNTRYMEN [Communists]. Both are helping us and both meet LIBERAL [Julius Rosenberg] and ARNO [Harry Gold] [3 groups unrecovered] HUGHES [Alfred Sarant] handed over 17 authentic drawings related to the APQ-7 (postal despatch No. 9). He can be trusted. The transfer of HUGHES to LIGHT [Aleksandr Raev] is no way out of the situation. It will be necessary to put LIGHT in touch with CALISTRATUS [Aleksandr Feklisov] in order to bring

material for photography into the PLANT [Soviet Consulate]. I cannot carry material in and out of the PLANT late in the evening. I insist on bringing HUGHES and METER [Joel Barr] together, putting the latter in touch with CALISTRATUS or LIGHT and separating both from LIBERAL.

In TYRE [New York] [16 groups unrecoverable] round the clock. There are no major contradictions between letters 5 and 7 about LIBERAL. They complement each other. LIBERAL's shortcomings do not mean that he will be completely useless for photography. He is gradually getting used to photography.

In 1948 Sarant had taken a post at the Cornell nuclear physics laboratory, and when interviewed by the FBI at his home in Ithaca, New York, in 1950 he acknowledged having been a Communist and having known Julius through their union, the Federation of Architects, Engineers, Chemists and Technicians (FAECT). Sarant denied any involvement in espionage and claimed not to have seen the Rosenbergs since 1946, but when he realized he was under FBI surveillance in August 1950 he fled to Mexico and then turned up in Prague.

Morton Sobell, tentatively identified as the codename RELAY, behaved similarly. Although never formally a Party member, he had been one of Julius's classmates at the City College of New York, and had served in the US Navy before gaining an electrical engineering degree. In 1944 he was working on classified military contracts at the Reeves Instrument Company, but in June 1950, when the Rosenbergs were questioned, Morton, his wife Helen and their children had flown to Mexico. When traced by the FBI, they were returned by the Mexican police to the Texas border where Morton was arrested. The following year, protesting his innocence, he was sentenced to thirty years' imprisonment without parole.

The identification of Sobell as RELAY is controversial, and something he disputes vigorously, for there is considerable doubt about it, as is indicated in the footnotes to the two relevant VENONA texts. The first, dated 4 July 1944 from Stepan Apresyan, gives some strong clues to his identity:

> [73 groups unrecoverable] moveover FISHERMAN and NYNA will be handed over to RELAY who has been introduced to

CALISTRATUS [Aleksandr Fomin]. Concerning MASTERCRAFTSMAN [Charles B. Sheppard] see our No. 483. Your proposal to make RELAY group leader for FISHERMAN, MASTERCRAFTSMAN [4 groups unrecovered] is impracticable. RELAY is disabled and has an artificial leg. Frequent trips are difficult for him. He lives in the PHILADELPHIA area.

3. ARSENIJ [Andrei Shevchenko] – he will control [2 groups unrecovered], STAMP, SPLINE, CORK [William Pinsly], EMULSION, BROTHER. It goes without saying that he is in close touch with AUTHOR [Vladimir B. Morkovin]. We shall inform you of the possibilities of handing over ARSENIJ's people to EMULSION's control. TWAIN [Semyon M. Semyonov] controls the following PROBATIONERS [agents] [9 groups unrecovered], RELAY [17 groups unrecovered] MAXIM [Vasili Zubilin], BASS [Michael J. Burd], S-1 [Herman R. Jacobson] [25 groups unrecovered]

Sobell not unreasonably points out that he does not have an artificial leg, and lived in Queens, not Pennsylvania, and although much of this telegram resisted the cryptographers, the context is one of industrial espionage, not atomic secrets. Of the sources identified, all had connections with the aircraft industry. Charles B. Sheppard [MASTERCRAFTSMAN] was a radio engineer with the Hazeltine Electronics Corporation of Little Neck, Long Island; William Pinsly [CORK] worked for the Curtis-Wright Corporation at Williamsville, New York; Michael J. Burd [BASS] was employed by the Midland Export Corporation; Herman R. Jacobson (S-1) was the office manager at the Avery Manufacturing Company of New York. Of the Soviets, Semyon M. Semyonov [TWAIN] worked for Amtorg in New York, Vladimir B. Morkovin [AUTHOR], was a research aerodynamicist at the Bell Aircraft plant in Niagara Falls and Andrei I. Shevchenko [ARSENIJ] was an engineer representing the Soviet Purchasing Commission and Amtorg at Bell Aircraft in Buffalo. Certainly Sobell might have been considered suitable as a controller of this group, for he had joined the General Electric Company upon leaving the Navy Department in 1941, and was closely connected to classified defence contracts, but that is the only link. A CPUSA and FAECT activist, Sobell lived and worked at Schenectady between 1941 and

1947, when he joined Reeves Instruments in New York, and was a regular visitor to the Rosenberg home at the weekends.

The second VENONA text, dated a week later on 11 July, referred to a suggestion to Moscow that RELAY be allowed to photograph his own material and deliver the undeveloped films to New York (see above). In a routine administrative circular dated 2 September, the New York *rezidentura* notified Moscow that RELAY's codename had been changed to SERB, which was to appear in just one text, on 11 January 1945, from Leonid Kvasnikov (ANTON):

> SERB has been advised that VOLUNTEER has died at the front in Europe. The last meeting with LESLEY [Lona Cohen] was had by TWAIN [Semyon Semyonov] about six months ago. Do you consider it desirable to establish liaison with LESLEY to render her assistance and activate her in the future as a go-between [1 group unrecovered] special conspirative apartment?

VOLUNTEER has never been identified positively; he is thought to have been Morris Cohen, and LESLEY is believed to have been his wife Lona, but there is no collateral to sustain Sobell as RELAY/SERB, the one-legged man from Pennsylvania, so the supposedly tenuous identification remains highly doubtful, and a rare example of the counter-intelligence sleuths naming the wrong suspect. As for Lona Cohen, who was later to achieve notoriety in England under the alias Helen Kroger (and be sentenced in 1961 to twenty years' imprisonment), she had been recruited as a courier by her husband Morris, a veteran of the Mackenzie-Papineau Battalion of the International Brigade who had attended a special NKVD spy school in Barcelona during the Spanish Civil War. Formerly a waiter, journalist and college football coach, Cohen had joined the CPUSA in December 1935 but had been talent-spotted in Spain, allegedly by Alexander Orlov, who supervised his training as a clandestine wireless operator. After his return to New York, Morris married Lona, then a factory worker and union activist, and she most likely acted as a courier for Theodore Hall twice while he was at Los Alamos, and perhaps afterwards. According to Pavel Sudoplatov, 'when Morris was drafted into the US Army in July 1942, Anatoli Yatskov, aka Yakovlev, used Lona as a courier to pick up information. Lona's trips to New Mexico were explained as visits to a sanatorium for a tuberculosis cure.' As friends of the Rosenbergs, Morris and Lona suddenly disappeared from their New York apartment as soon as Julius was arrested.

Also implicated in the 1944 ANTENNA traffic was Joseph Katz, codenamed INFORMER, and Michael Sidorovich (LENS). Katz was one of those denounced to the FBI in 1945 by Elizabeth Bentley, who had known him as 'Jack', and he was also named as a contact by Harry Gold. According to a very short VENONA text from New York dated 22 July 1944, Katz had helped run the Spanish Civil War veteran Amadeo Sabatini in San Francisco, having been put in touch with him by the local *rezidentura* which Kasparov was later to head:

> INFORMER [Joseph Katz] can leave for the West for a meeting with NICK [Amadeo Sebatini]. We can ask GIFT [Grigori Kasparov] for the address. We await your [1 group unrecovered]

When the FBI researched Katz's background they discovered he had been born Joseph Hlat in Russia in 1912, and had changed his name legally in New York in 1928. He had acquired US citizenship when his father had naturalized in 1925, and he had married Bessie Bogorad in Los Angeles in 1936. Their daughter Paula Jo had been born in New York in January 1941, but when the FBI attempted to trace Katz in 1953 he had moved to Paris, and as soon as the DST expressed an interest in him he disappeared. Eventually he turned up in Haifa, where he was interviewed but denied any knowledge of espionage. Nevertheless, the FBI was able to link him directly to the chemist Thomas L. Black (codenamed BLACK and then PETER in a total of five VENONA texts) from whom he had obtained industrial secrets; Robert O. Menaker (CZECH in seven VENONA texts) and Floyd C. Miller, whom Katz had deployed to infiltrate the Trotskyite Socialist Workers Party; and Amadeo Sabatini (codenamed NICK), who was used with Irving J. Schuman to keep a watch on Walter Krivitsky.

The FBI had equally little success with Michael Sidorovich who, according to David Greenglass, was married to Anne Sidorovich, the woman who had acted as his courier before Harry Gold had taken on that role. Michael had served in the Abraham Lincoln Division of the International Brigade in Spain, and before moving to Cleveland had been the Rosenbergs' neighbour in Knickerbocker Village,

New York. Despite the FBI's persistent cross-examination, neither Sidorovich was willing to make an incriminating admission. As for evidence from VENONA, there were only two other fleeting references to LENS, the first from Kvasnikov dated 22 October 1944:

> Inquiring [36 groups unrecovered] [34 groups unrecoverable] was explained that he, as a specialist, received from the draft board an inquiry about where he is working and on what means he lives. [60 groups unrecoverable] ...' In view of poor health [24 groups unrecovered] LIBERAL. He worked there 5 months in 1942. Contact was discontinued because of [36 groups unrecovered] FELLOWCOUNTRYMEN. He was a volunteer in Spain. He lives in the western part of New York State, for the past three years has not carried on active political work. LIBERAL has known him since childhood, during the past 14 years has known him in political life. He characterizes him and his wife as devoted and reliable people. The wife by profession is a dressmaker and can open a shop in the city for cover. Let us know whether you consider LENS more suitable to go to YAKOV [William Perl]. A reply for communicating to LIBERAL is necessary before 23 October. At the meeting with LIBERAL, LENS expressed readiness to renew contact with us.

Later, on 20 December 1944, there was a further telegram from New York, describing the Sidorovichs' recent move to 'JAKOV's town', meaning Cleveland, where William Perl (YAKOV) was then living:

> LENS and his wife have left for YAKOV's town. At the end of December LIBERAL will go there and will put LENS in touch with YAKOV. Before making the move, LENS and his wife visited the town and took an apartment, the address of which we reported in letter No. 9. LENS sold his house and spent part of the money on the move. We gave him a once for all payment of 500: I consider that [24 groups unrecoverable]

The last name in the 1944 ANTENNA series was that of Max Elitcher, who was to be confirmed as a vital member of the Rosenberg network, although his recruitment was not signalled until a telegram from Apresyan dated 26 July 1944:

In July ANTENNA was sent by the firm for ten days to work in CARTHAGE [Washington DC]. There he visited his school friend Max ELITCHER, who works in the Bureau of Standards as head of the fire control section for warships (which mount guns) of over five-inch calibre. He has access to extremely valuable materials on guns. Five years ago Max ELITCHER graduated from the Electro-Technical Department of the City College of NEW YORK. He has a Master of Science degree. Since finishing college he has been working at the Bureau of Standards. He is a FELLOWCOUNTRYMAN [Communist]. He entered the FELLOWCOUNTRYMAN'S organization [Party] after finishing his studies.

By ANTENNA he is characterized as a loyal, reliable, level-headed and able man. Married, his wife is a FELLOWCOUNTRYMAN. She is a psychiatrist by profession, she works at the War Department.

Max ELITCHER is an excellent amateur photographer and has all the necessary equipment for taking photographs.

Please check ELITCHER and communicate your consent to his clearance.

A childhood friend of Morton Sobell, Elitcher had graduated as an electrical engineer from the City College of New York in 1938, where he had studied alongside Julius Rosenberg, and had joined the US Navy. In 1948 the Office of Naval Intelligence had investigated Elitcher as a possible Communist, prompting him to buy a house next to Sobell in Queens, New York, and join his friend at the Reeves Instrument Company. When the FBI interviewed him in July 1950 he admitted having been approached by both Sobell and the Rosenbergs, but denied having passed any classified documents to either. Instead he agreed to give evidence against them, and appeared as a prosecution witness at their trial in March 1951. Although the FBI had some doubts about the extent to which Elitcher had refused to help Morton and Julius, there was no further VENONA material to incriminate him, and the single text in which he was mentioned by Apresyan gave no indication that he had subsequently become an active member of the network. Thus his crime had been limited to knowing of their espionage and failing to report it.

On 2 September 1944 Moscow changed many of the cryptonyms

assigned to the New York *rezidentura* and listed a total of twenty-two names. Among them was ANTENNA who became LIBERAL. Another was GNOME, a member of the Rosenberg ring who was transformed into YAKOV, but on 14 September Apresyan was still referring to him as GNOME:

> Until recently GNOME was paid only the expenses connected with his coming to TYRE. Judging by an appraisal of the material received and the last [1 group garbled] sent to us GNOME deserves remuneration for material no less valuable than that given by the rest of the members of the LIBERAL group who were given a bonus by you. Please agree to paying him 500 dollars.

On 20 September Moscow gave Apresyan permission to pay GNOME:

> Your No. 736. We agree to paying GNOME five hundred dollars [12 groups unrecovered] September on trips to TYRE [New York] [2 groups unrecovered], and [211 groups unrecoverable].

So who was GNOME? The best candidate was another electrical engineer, William Perl, who had shared a room at Colombia University with Al Sarant, and had studied with Elitcher, Sobell and Julius Rosenberg at the City College of New York. An expert on supersonic flight and jet propulsion, he was working on a research project at the National Advisory Committee on Aeronatics, at Cleveland, Ohio, when he was interviewed by the FBI in July 1950. Perl denied knowing Sobell and Rosenberg, and it was for this lie that he was sentenced to five years' imprisonment on a perjury charge in 1950, but the FBI remained convinced that he had been responsible for the leakage of several classified files on the subject of advanced jet propulsion that David Greenglass mentioned as having reached Julius Rosenberg. In the absence of any other evidence, or the damning request for payment to GNOME in September 1944, Perl escaped any more serious consequences.

The huge extent of Rosenberg's reach, from papers dealing with wind turbulence to components of nuclear weapons, was increased in a VENONA dated 15 September 1945 concerning a source codenamed STAMP at the Republic Aviation Corporation factory who was supplying information to Andrei I. Shevchenko, the Soviet representative at the Bell Aircraft Corporation. Codenamed ARSENIJ, Shevchenko's illicit activities had been reported to the FBI by Loren Haas and Joseph and Leona Franey, three of his sources who agreed to act as double agents. In making a routine report on aircraft production and guided missiles, the New York *rezidentura* stated:

> LIBERAL [Julius Rosenberg] confirms that the output of robots [guided weapons] has begun and reports that robot launchers will apparently be mounted on aircraft carriers for action against JAPAN.

On 14 November 1944 a VENONA from Kvasnikov introduced yet another member of the Rosenberg ring, Joel Barr, codenamed METER:

> LIBERAL has safely carried through the contracting of HUGHES [Sarant]. HUGHES is a good friend of METER [Barr]. We propose to pair them off and get them to photograph their own materials having given a camera for this purpose. HUGHES is a good photographer, has a large darkroom and all the equipment but he does not have a Leica. LIBERAL will receive the films from METER for passing on. Direction of the PROBATIONERS [agents] will be continued through LIBERAL, this will ease the load on him. Details about the contracting are in letter No. 8.

Barr had much in common with others in Julius's network. He had studied electrical engineering with Sobell and Elitcher, graduating in 1938. He had worked alongside Al Sarant in the Army Signal Corps laboratory at Fort Monmouth until his discharge in 1942 because of his political activities on behalf of the Communist Party, and then had found a job as a radar specialist with Western Electric, designing systems for the B-29 bomber. In 1946 he had switched to Sperry Gyroscope, with a reference signed by Al Sarant, but left a year later when his security clearance had been declined. By the time the FBI linked him to the source codenamed METER, Barr was living in Finland, well beyond its reach, so the investigation into whether HUGHES ever spied remained inconclusive. Obviously the NKVD had cultivated him as one in November 1944, but apart from hearsay evidence from David Greenglass, there was nothing positive, and no further VENONA evidence apart from a single reference in the text dated 5 December 1944 (see p.160 above) which certainly implies that Barr and Sarant (METER and HUGHES) were highly productive.

There can be no doubt of either Rosenberg's industry or his ideological commitment, but Moscow was always keen to reward effort, and a telegram on 6 March 1945 refers to a financial inducement:

> [66 groups unrecovered] decision was made about awarding the sources as a bonus the following sums: to LIBERAL 1,000 dollars, NIL [58 groups unrecoverable] either the purchase of valuable gifts for the PROBATIONERS [agents] or payment to them of money on the basis of well thought out cover stories. [28 groups unrecovered]

As the FBI researched the interconnections between LIBERAL's organization, and started building the legal case against the Rosenbergs, doubt was expressed about the wisdom of charging Ethel, for the proof against her was contained in a VENONA text dated 27 November 1944 from Kvasnikov:

> Your 5356. Information on LIBERAL's wife. Surname that of her husband, first name ETHEL, 29 years old. Married five years. Finished secondary school. A FELLOWCOUNTRYMAN since 1938. Sufficiently well developed politically. Knows about her husband's work and the role of METER and NIL. In view of delicate health does not work. Is characterized positively and as a devoted person.

This text was of particular importance because the search for LIBERAL, formerly ANTENNA, and married to ETHEL had been underway since August 1947 when Meredith Gardner had identified the pair of spies in his first 'Special Analysis Report'. Cryptographically, the word ETHEL had been a special challenge, for Gardner had broken the spellcode for 'E' and 'L', but initially had been baffled by a single value for 'THE, for there is no definite article in Russian. However, he deduced that the NKVD must have anticipated enciphering masses of English text, and therefore had attributed a codegroup to THE, which is after all the most common word in the language.

The damning sentence about Ethel's knowledge of her husband's work was enough to persuade those with a knowledge of VENONA who had doubted her involvement that she had played a role in Julius's organization. After her arrest she proved rather more resilient than Julius, but the evidence which condemned her to the electric chair was strictly limited to what was admissible in court.

Once convictions had been obtained against Julius, Ethel, Harry Gold and the Greenglasses, the FBI concentrated on the various loose ends that remained unresolved at the end of a lengthy analysis of the confessions, the clues contained in Elizabeth Bentley's testimony and the evidence from VENONA. Principal among the mysteries were the identities of the sources in America codenamed QUANTUM, SMART, ERIE, HURON and PERS. The first of only two references to QUANTUM had occurred in one of the earliest ENORMOZ texts, a telegram dated 22–23 June 1943 which displayed considerable technical knowledge:

> Information from QUANTUM. Translated from the English. The basic idea for a method of separation of ENORMOZ consists in repeated [1 group unrecovered] distillation by sublimation (vaporization from a crystal state) and rapid condensation of vapours. With the specified components and degree of vaporization of chemically [1 group unrecovered] identical molecules (but different in mass) is inversely proportional to the square root of the mass and directly proportional to the partial vapour pressure sustained by a molecule without condensation. On the other hand the partial vapour pressure of such molecules, in accordance with quantum mechanics, is inversely proportional to the cube of the square root of the mass. Consequently the speeds at which two isotopic molecules [7 groups unrecovered] will be proportional to the square [19 groups unrecovered]

This message, which included a series of technical algebraic calculations, was followed on 27 August by the following fragment from New York which introduced another cryptonym, SOLID:

> About his affairs and [43 groups unrecovered] for SOLID and No. 534 of 22 June reported information from QUANTUM on ENORMOZ.

The question is, who was QUANTUM? Klaus Fuchs had worked on uranium separation, but he was still in England in June 1943, and did not meet Harry Gold until February 1944. This suggested there was another ENORMOZ spy, perhaps in touch with SOLID, and maybe based at either the Kellex plant or the Substitute Alloy Material (SAM) Laboratory at Colombia where the separation work was pioneered, but there was also SMART, ERIE and HURON who seemed to be connected to Harry Gold, according to a VENONA text from Apresyan dated 27 June 1944:

> Your No. 2700. [19 groups unrecovered] and canalization. Connected with us in the KhU Line [Economic Directorate] [1 group unrecovered] is SMART. We propose to transfer ERIE and HURON to him. We request your sanction. To transfer these PROBATIONERS [agents] to GOOSE [Harry Gold] [6 groups unrecovered] GOOSE. [14 groups unrecovered] receive constant [1 groups unidentified]. He is wondering why the monthly payment of 100 dollars was discontinued [15 groups unrecovered] with him.

This left the FBI speculating that SMART was a handler supervising other agents, but Harry Gold was unable to shed any light on their identities, and to have pressed him harder would have jeopardized VENONA. One possible clue to the identity of SMART, ERIE and HURON is to be found in a pair of administrative circulars, dated 2 September and 5 October 1944, in which Apresyan announced to Moscow a fairly comprehensive change in codenames.

> In accordance with our telegram no. 403 we are advising you of the new covernames: CAVALRYMAN – BECK [Sergei Kurnakov], THRUSH – AKHMED, CLEMENCE – LEE, ABRAM – CZECH [Jack Soble]. TULIP – KANT [Mark Zborowski], AIDA – KLO [Esther Trabach Rand], OSPREY – BLOCK, RELAY – SERB, ANTENNA – LIBERAL [Julius Rosenberg], GNOME – YAKOV [William Perl], SCOUT – METER [Joel Barr], TU ... – NIL, VOGEL – PERS, ODESSITE – GROWTH. All these covernames were selected by you with a view to economy of means. Among the new covernames introduced by you there were disadvantageous ones which we propose to replace as follows: STELLA – EMILYA, DONALD – PILOT [William Ludwig Ullman], LAWYER – RICHARD [Harry Dexter White], DOUGLAS – X [Joseph Katz], SHERWOOD –

> PRINCE [Laurance Duggan], [1 group unrecovered] T – ZONE, MIRANDA – ART [Helen Koral], SENOR – BERG. All these covernames are economical from the point of view of encoding. Please confirm. Continuation will follow later.

The continuation came a month later:

> Further to our 700. Herewith are changes in covernames: GOOSE – ARNO [Harry Gold], L – BEER, CONSTRUCTOR – EXPERT [Abraham Brothman], ERIE – [1 group unrecovered] HURON – ERNEST, BLACK – PETER [Thomas L. Black], EMULSION – SIGNAL, BROTHER – THOMAS, FIN – FERRO [Aleksandr N. Petroff], ZERO – ERIC [Leona O. Franey], SPLINE – NOISE [deleted], STAMP – ARMOUR [deleted], REST – CHARLES [Klaus Fuchs], SOLID – KINSMAN, EXPRESS MESSENGER – JEAN [Ricardo Setaro], PLUCKY – KURT, OSPREY – KEEN, JUPITER – ODD FELLOW, HUDSON – JOHN, FAKIR – ARNOLD, RAY – KARL [Ricardo Setaro], JEANETTE – CUPID, LONG – DAVIS, TALENT – HENRY [William M. Malisoff], OLA – JEANNE [Christina Krotkova]. Please confirm. Continuation later. No. 798.

While there may be a clue in the charge of HURON's codename to ERNEST, ERIE is more difficult as the unrecovered group is most likely either GEORGES or LEADER. Curiously, four days after this directive, Apresyan was still using HURON's original codename:

> [23 groups unrecovered] I request your consent in principle to the use for this purpose of BLACK [Thomas L. Black] who has no work at present. We will negotiate with BLACK upon receipt of your answer. RAY will be in liaison with BLACK should BLACK be transferred [16 groups unrecoverable] BLACK HURON [6 groups unrecovered]
>
> Reference your No. 563. We object to the transfer of MARGARITA to BLACK in view of the undesirability [22 groups unrecovered]
> 2. A report with all the technical details of the COUNTRY's [America] robots [guided weapons] and their [3 groups unrecovered] robots. The COUNTRY's robots are fitted with I-16 engines, information about which was sent to you. Also other reports.

Operation ENORMOZ

> We have received from METER [Joel Barr] a 730A valve, which is of particular interest. Technical details of this valve were sent in number 71 [7 groups unrecovered]. Confirm receipt of the materials by diplomatic post.

This appears to link HURON to Thomas Black, though not necessarily to RAY and MARGARITA, whose identities have been deleted in the VENONA footnotes. Equally tantalizing are the other unidentified codenames that simply do not appear in other VENONA texts. That, combined with the indication that there was a further continuation, gives an idea of the sheer volume of agents run by the New York *rezidentura* in 1944. For those sleuths convinced the NKVD sometimes hid a clue in the codename, attention focused on PERS, one of the most fascinating atomic spies, known initially as VOGEL, and referred to on 11 February 1944 in a very fragmented text from New York:

> Herewith a report from VOGEL on the work of ENORMOZ [163 groups unrecovered] 800 pounds for the neutralization of weak [305 groups unrecoverable]

On 16 June Pavel Fedosimov (Apreysan's successor) made another tantalizing reference to VOGEL in a telegram to Moscow.

> By the same post were despatched the secret plans of the layout of ENORMOZ plant received from VOGEL.

Apart from one routine administrative text, dated 2 September 1944, confirming that VOGEL was henceforth to be known as PERS, there was only one further text, dated 13 December 1944 from New York, which, though far from conclusive, confirmed his vantage-point inside ENORMOZ:

> [45 groups unrecovered] PERS. [7 groups unrecovered] Camp-1. Our proposal [24 groups unrecovered] not to give any more on ENORMOZ.
> 2. To leave WASP [Ruth Greenglass] and CALIBRE [David Greenglass] in contact with LIBERAL [Julius Rosenberg] until [3 groups unrecovered] work.
> 3. YOUNG [51 groups unrecoverable]

While PERS has been identified mistakenly as a spy codenamed PERCY, the footnotes show that PERS was considered an abbreviation for PERSIAN by the VENONA analysts.³ He has also been linked to PERSIUS, allegedly a crucial atomic source handled by illegals reporting to Anatoli Yatskov, although the two may be quite different persons. As to the identity of this important spy, who is believed to have been based at the huge purpose-built Oak Ridge site, there have been several candidates, but perhaps there is a clue in the codename VOGEL, which is German and not Russian, to his true identity. Among the German émigrés working on the Manhattan Project was (Sir) Rudolf Peierls, who virtually adopted Klaus Fuchs as a son. Peierls, who was himself born in Berlin and naturalized in February 1940, knew Fuchs 'had been politically active as a member of a socialist student group (which was essentially communist)' had brought him into the British research team, and had arranged his security clearance in May 1941. Fuchs lodged with Peierls and his wife in Birmingham, travelled to America with Peierls on the *Andes* in November 1943, and even went on a motoring holiday with them to Mexico in December 1945 when the British contingent completed its work at Los Alamos.

Peierls was to attract much attention from MI5 and the FBI, not least because he had married a Russian physicist, Eugenia Kannegiesser, whom he had met while on a visit to Odessa in the summer of 1930. They were married in Leningrad in March 1931, and to their surprise no obstacles were placed on her emigration or on her acquisition of German citizenship. This was unusual, considering the sensitive nature of her work and her family circumstances: her sister Nina was a biologist and her widowed mother had married a writer. Coincidentally, Peierls's older brother Alfred had also married a Russian, a woman who had been working for the Soviet Trade Delegation in Berlin where they met in a minor road accident. Alfred was an expert on electric condensers and, after he fled Germany in 1935, managed a condenser factory in London until he and his wife were interned on the Isle of Man as enemy aliens.

Initially Rudolf Peierls, with his strong Russian connections, was considered a likely suspect by MI5, especially as he had worked at Kellex upon his arrival in New York, before the British party moved to Los Alamos in August 1944, but the search in England for a leak was abandoned as soon as Fuchs confessed. Whatever the truth, the mystery of VOGEL/PERS remains unresolved, as does the true identity of another spy, codenamed TINA. According to an almost complete text from Moscow addressed to the London *rezidentura* and dated 16 September 1945, there was yet another source with access to ENORMOZ papers:

> We agree with your proposal about working with TINA. At the next meeting tell her that her documentary material on ENORMOZ is of great interest and represents a valuable contribution to the development of the work in this field. Telegraph [1 group unrecovered]. In the [1 group unrecovered] which have arisen, instruct her not to discuss her work with us with her husband and not to say anything to him about the nature of the documentary material which is being obtained by her.

Eugenia, who was known as Genia, was investigated as a promising candidate for TINA, in part because her remaining family in Leningrad was considered likely to make her vulnerable to pressure from the KGB. Certainly she matched TINA in that she was married to an ENORMOZ scientist, but she was not in England in September 1945, at the time of the message, which indicated that at least one meeting had already taken place with her. The FBI's inquiries culminated in the permanent removal of Peierls's security clearance by MI5 in 1957, and soon afterwards he resigned his consultancy post at the Atomic Energy Research Establishment at Harwell, but neither setback prevented him from receiving a knighthood in the 1968 New Year's honours.

The case officer Anatoli Yatskov, who maintained before his death in March 1993 that 'perhaps less than half' his network had been uncovered by the FBI, claimed that PERS was an abbreviation for PERSIUS, a source whom he believed to be alive in 1992, and whose identity required protection. Although PERS's identity remains a tantalizing enigma, the NSA's censorship suggests that HURON's real name was discovered, whereas very little seems to be known about either him or ERIE. Nevertheless, the codenames alone suggest a Chicago link, bearing in mind the NKVD preference for obscure connections between the sources and their cryptonyms. A strong candidate must be Clarence F. Hiskey, originally from Milwaukee, where the family name had been changed from Szczechowski. A first-rate physicist, he had achieved his doctorate in 1939 from the University of Wisconsin, where he had met his wife Marcia Sand, also a CPUSA activist, and was granted a reserve commission in the chemical warfare service. He was appointed director of research into rhenium at the University of Tennessee's laboratory at Knoxville, and in the autumn of 1941 took up a post teaching chemistry at Colombia University. The following year he joined Dr Harold Urey's SAM project concentrating on the gaseous diffusion method of separating Uranium-235 which was to be incorporated into the K-25 plant at Oak Ridge, Tennessee. This work was moved to the Metallurgical Laboratory at Chicago in May 1943, where Hiskey continued his union activism on behalf of FAECT and worked in a CPUSA educational front, the Abraham Lincoln School. His participation in atomic research was swiftly terminated in April 1944 after he had been compromised by an Amtorg official, Arthur A. Adams. Hiskey had played a key role in developing the U-235 separation plant at Oak Ridge, and had worked on the metallurgical project at the University of Chicago. Details of both were leaked to Adams. A Comintern agent of long-standing who had entered the country through Buffalo on a Canadian passport in May 1938, together with his wife Dorothea, Adams had acted as an intermediary for Pavel Mikhailov of the New York *rezidentura*, and had set up a business, Technological Laboratories, with a Canadian partner, which operated from the City offices of the Electronics Corporation of America and Keynote Recordings. His previous visas had been issued in 1927, when he had represented AMO, the first Soviet car manufacturer, and then in 1932, ostensibly on a mission to buy Curtiss-Wright aircraft. Badly crippled, apparently as a result of beatings inflicted in Russia in the turmoil of 1905, he had visited the USA on several occasions as a Soviet trade official, and was often seen at the Soviet consulate, but it was his interest in atomic scientists as a suspected GRU officer that led to intensive CIC surveillance.

Adams attempted to leave the country from Portland, Oregon, in February 1945 on a Soviet ship, but returned to spend a further year as a recluse in a New York hotel before finally disappearing without trace. A GRU defector, Colonel Ismail Akhmedov, testified in October 1953 that Adams was an

> illegal agent, or illegal *rezident*, correctly speaking, of the Fourth Section . . . He was head of the network, having his contact with legal network through cutout . . . Adams was

> born in some Scandinavian country, Sweden or Norway. He was an old Bolshevik working for the Comintern. He was a friend of Lenin and an engineer. He came to the United States several times during the late 1920s and '30s, ostensibly for business purposes. Now, somewhere in the late '30s, according to his file, he was sent illegally to the US ... He was sent through Canada by a false passport and when I was Chief of the Fourth Section Adams was operating in the United States, having contact with Amtorg foreign chief engineer Korovin.

Hiskey's link with Adams, with whom he was spotted on several occasions, was cut when the scientist was called up for military service, posted to the Quartermaster Corps and sent to a remote Arctic base near Mineral Springs in Alaska where he sorted winter underwear. During a posting to White Horse, in the Yukon, he was the subject of a clandestine search, and he was found to have 'had in his effects a personal notebook which contained notes that he had made while working on the atomic bomb project at Chicago, Illinois, relative to the development of several components of the bomb'.

After he protested about the waste of his talent, Hiskey was transferred to an army installation in Hawaii manufacturing soap for troops in the Pacific. He was discharged in May 1946 and began teaching analytical chemistry at the Brooklyn Polytechnic Institute in Brooklyn, New York. In 1950, having refused to testify about Adams before Congress, he was indicted for contempt, but the charge was dismissed in April 1951. Considering Hiskey's connection with Adams, and his own access to Manhattan Project secrets, he must be considered a likely candidate for HURON. Certainly his relationship with Adams was highly suspicious, as the FBI later discovered after the war from two witnesses, John H. Chapin and Edward T. Manning. Dr Chapin, who knew Hiskey as a colleague at Colombia, had studied chemistry at Cornell and the University of Illinois, and was recruited into the Manhattan Project from DuPont. When Hiskey was drafted he asked Chapin to meet Adams, and in September 1944 the two men discussed in Chicago how the scientist could help the Soviets. When Adams offered Chapin money for classified data, the chemist took fright and eventually reported the approach to the FBI.

Similarly, Manning, who worked as a technician on the metallurgical project at Colombia and Chicago, had been introduced to Adams by Hiskey but when they met in New York they must have been under surveillance for he was suspended. In January 1945 he was drafted into the army and had one final meeting with Adams who declared that it was still not too late for him to supply details from his former work. Manning angrily blamed Adams for wrecking his career, and later reported his encounter to the FBI. The combined testimony of Chapin, who later joined the M. W. Kellogg Company to work on a classified Air Corps contract, and Manning, appeared to confirm that Adams was an active Soviet spy, and to incriminate Hiskey.

Pavel Mikhailov's role in ENORMOZ remains unclear, although his interests appear, from a text addressed to Moscow dated 12 August 1943, to have extended into Canada. Judging from his instruction to the Ottawa *rezident*, Sergei Kudriavtsev:

> 1. FRED [Fred Rose], our man in LESOVIA (Canada), has been elected to the LESOVIAN parliament. His personal opportunities [1 group garbled] undoubtedly are improving, but warn LION [Sergei Kudriavtsev] about increasing caution to the maximum.
> 2. In SACRAMENTO, California, in Radiation Laboratories, large-scale experimental work is being conducted for the War Department. Working there is a progressive professor [deleted], whom one can approach through the CORPORANT [Communist] [Paul G.] PINSKY – one of the directors [24 groups unrecoverable]

The identity of the recruitment prospect, to be pitched by Paul Pinsky who was then the research director of the Congress of Industrial Organizations (CIO) in California, has been concealed, but clearly he would have become a spy suspect and must have been investigated by the FBI. As for Fred Rose MP, who had been born Fred Rosenberg to Russian parents in Lublin, Poland, he had been elected as a Communist in 1932, and his NKVD activities were to be exposed two years later by Igor Gouzenko. Both he and his mistress, Freda Linton, were vital links between the GRU *rezident*, Colonel Zabotin, and a large network which included Kay Willsher of the British High Commission. Freda Linton, who had been born Fritzie Lipchitz in Montreal of Polish parents, had recently worked for the Film Board

Operation ENORMOZ

of Canada, and apparently had acted as a go-between for Professor Boyer, an academic from McGill University who had researched the development of high explosive.

Equal concern has been manifested in the excisions made in the text from Moscow addressed to Leonid Kvasnikov dated 21 March 1945, although execution of the deletion has been less than effective. Whereas the VENONA title reads

> 1. HURON TO VISIT CHICAGO TO RE-ESTABLISH CONTACT WITH BILL OF EXCHANGE AND MEET [DELETED]
> 2. GOLDSMITH AND GREGORI BREIT WORKING ON ENORMOZ

it is clear that the published text does not contain the name Goldsmith. However, there is a single excision in the text, and this doubtless is the removal of Goldsmith's surname:

> 1. In our Nos. 5823 of 9 December 1944, 309 of 17 January 1945 and 606 of 1 February 1945 instructions were given to send HURON to CHICAGO to re-establish contact with BILL OF EXCHANGE. Carry these out as soon as possible. HURON should also make use of his stay in CHICAGO to renew his acquaintance with [deleted], who is known to you and who is taking part in the work on ENORMOZ.
> 2. [15 groups unrecovered] – the well-known physicist Gregory BREIT, an emigrant from RUSSIA. According to available information BREIT is taking part in the work of ENORMOZ
> 3. [4 groups unrecovered] 759 of 8 February 1945 [2 groups unrecovered] with [Norman F] RAMSEY.
> 4. By the next mail report on the carrying out of the instructions in our No. 416 of 25 January 1945 concerning the collection through PETER [Thomas L. Black] and the other agent network of information on the structure and activities of the Bureau of Standards.

This VENONA text is also significant for the mention of Thomas Black, a chemist employed by Organics in New York between 1944 and 1949, who reported to Joseph Katz. Its continuation (see below) also raises the question of ERNEST, and therefore HURON. The confusion over these two spies is compounded by the footnotes of a

VENONA from San Francisco dated 27 November 1945 in which ERNEST is incorrectly stated to have been 'known as ERIE' in a previous telegram from New York sent on 20 February 1945. In fact, of course, ERIE had become GEORGES in October 1944, just as HURON had been transformed into ERNEST:

> Part I. At the second meeting with VOLKOV [Andrei R. Orlov] [10 groups unrecovered] about the production of high octane gasoline which includes a diagram of the production process [18 groups unrecovered] [10 groups unrecovered] in the near future [32 groups unrecovered] the TOWNSMEN [Americans] [80 groups unrecovered] [49 groups unrecoverable]
>
> Part II. After this Professor SMYTH was forbidden to print [4 groups unrecovered] laboratory. ERNEST has [17 groups unrecovered]. In the book there is no information about the quantity of uranium being crushed but he confirms this information in conversations with the people connected with [6 groups unrecovered] at his place and can turn it over to us at any time. In the book there is a complete description of the process with a diagram and all necessary materials are enumerated. Two weeks ago ERNEST received a letter from D who said that he had not written because of lack of time. VOLKOV permitted ERNEST to meet the people with whom Professor SMYTH collaborated. Among them are the engineer Morris PERELMAN and Professor [67 groups unrecovered] dictionary.

Professor Henry D. Smyth's official history of the bomb project, *Atomic Energy for Military Purposes*, had been published some months before this text had been sent by an unknown member of the San Francisco *rezidentura*, but the latter did show that HURON/ERNEST had been run by Andrei Orlov, who operated under Soviet Government Purchasing Commission cover, and was connected with Morris Perelman, who worked at Los Alamos. As for the source 'D', it is likely that this is an abbreviation for his full codename which most probably appears in one of the unrecovered groups.

Although VENONA texts frequently referred to sources by the real names – the Soviets demonstrating their full confidence in the integrity of their cipher system – it seems unlikely from the context that

Operation ENORMOZ

Grigori Breit was a spy. Of Russian origin, as mentioned in the VENONA text, Breit had taught theoretical physics at Yale, lived in South Dakota and was the co-author of the Breit–Wigner formula. While at Los Alamos, Breit, who had lodged with Rudolf Peierls, held the title Director of Rapid Rupture, and had joined with Leo Szilard to argue against the openness advocated by Fermi. Appalled by the authorities' reluctance to impose greater security restrictions on their research, Breit resigned in 1943 and went to work on a US Navy project, where he was already well established by the date of Moscow's telegram to Kvasnikov dated 21 March. Fluent in Danish, Russian and German, Breit married a German in 1952 and in 1960 took up a teaching post in Copenhagen.

Since there is no mention in the published text of 'Goldsmith', or of anyone else working on ENORMOZ, it is safe to assume that this is the deletion made in connection with HURON, and perhaps is a reference to Hyman Goldsmith, a respected physicist trained at the City College of New York who worked at the Brookhaven Institute and moved to Chicago with Fermi. Goldsmith died in 1949, so he was never interviewed by the FBI, and there is no obvious explanation for the redaction of his name in the only VENONA text in which he is mentioned. BILL OF EXCHANGE had been identified previously as Dr J. Robert Oppenheimer, and his status as the leader of the Manhattan Project explains official American reticence, although doubts about his political reliability dated back to at least June 1954 when his security clearance had been suspended by the Atomic Energy Commission. Oppenheimer, who died in February 1967, was always a controversial figure, not least because his younger brother Frank, his sister-in-law Jackenette, his wife Kitty and his mistress Jean Tatlock (who committed suicide in January 1944) were all CPUSA members, although only Frank's name appears in a VENONA text, from VAVILOV in San Francisco dated 13 November 1945:

> Part I A trustworthy dock worker [Jerome Michael] CALLAGHAN has advised that his friend, the Communist Rudolph LAMBERT [43 groups unrecoverable] Nevada, Utah and Arizona.
> Concerning Uranium deposits [4 groups unrecovered] before the publication of the communication on [48 groups

unrecoverable] to us. Please advise whether we are interested in receiving further [8 groups unrecovered].

Supplementary to our no. 47 the brother of Robert OPPENHEIMER – Frank [1 group unrecovered] member of [9 groups unrecovered], took part in atomic research. One must [1 group unrecovered] that scholars who have taken part in these pursuits are under the surveillance of the American counter-intelligence.

Part II Robert OPPENHEIMER and the Ernst LAWRENCE mentioned in our number 435 (two of the chief scientific leaders on the atomic bomb) [53 groups unrecovered]. VAVILOV.

Evidently Rudolph C. Lambert, a senior member of the CPUSA's northern California district, had relayed some information about atomic research, but the message is too fragmented to understand the NKVD's interest in the Oppenheimer brothers. The precise nature of Robert Oppenheimer's relationship with the NKVD has long been a topic of intense interest. Although Robert was never formally a member of the Party, practically all his friends were, and, as he subsequently admitted, he 'probably joined every Communist front on the West Coast'. Frank, who joined the Radiation Laboratory in 1941 from Stanford University (and worked at both Oak Ridge and Los Alamos), had been a member of the CPUSA's Palo Alto branch since 1937, as was Robert's wife, Kitty. Her first husband, Joseph Dallet, was a CPUSA official who had fought in Spain as a member of the International Brigade, and the news of his death in 1937 had been broken to her in Paris by one of his comrades, Steve Nelson. Her second husband, whom she married in December 1938, was an English physician, Richard Harrison, who was interested in radiation and travelled with her to Pasadena where she took a graduate course in mycology and met Robert Oppenheimer. After eighteen months of marriage, Kitty divorced Harrison, and married Oppenheimer, and this was how the latter came into contact with Nelson, a senior CPUSA functionary and an NKVD courier for Oppenheimer's students Joseph W. Weinberg, Giovanni Rossi Lomanitz and David Bohm who worked at the Radiation Laboratory at Berkeley.

Originally from New York, Weinberg had graduated from the City College and become an active member of the Young Communist

League before moving to California. His wife Muriel, who had studied at the University of Wisconsin, was also a Party activist, and CPUSA literature mailed to Radiation Laboratory scientists was traced to her. In March 1943 FBI surveillance on Steve Nelson's home and telephone identified Weinberg as a late-night visitor who wanted to copy a formula written in the handwriting of another scientist. This had been followed soon afterwards by a covert rendezvous in a park between Nelson and a Soviet vice-consul, Piotr Ivanov, at which packages were seen to be exchanged, and then by Zubilin's visit to Nelson's home. In August Weinberg was watched by Counter-Intelligence Corps (CIC) agents George Rathman and Harold Zindle while he hosted a clandestine Party gathering at his apartment in Black Street, Berkeley, attended by Nelson and Lomanitz. Weinberg always denied his membership of the Party, his involvement in espionage and any knowledge of Steve Nelson, despite surveillance evidence showing Nelson's secretary, Bernadette Doyle, was a visitor to his home. He was indicted on four counts of contempt after he had pleaded the Fifth Amendment before the House Un-American Activities Committee (HUAC). The charges were dismissed in March 1953 on the grounds that Weinberg had exercised his constitutional right, but nevertheless he lost his post at the University of Minnesota's Department of Physics.

Weinberg was closely connected with another brilliant young physicist, Giovanni Rossi Lomanitz, originally from Bryan, Texas, who was an openly declared member of the CPUSA and a union organizer for the Federation of Architects, Engineers, Chemists and Technicians (FAECT). He ran the CPUSA's Merriman branch, until it was dissolved by Nelson, and he specialized in recruiting atomic research staff into the union and the Party. According to Robert R. Davis, a technician, who confirmed his membership of the Party between January and April 1943, when he had been transferred from Berkeley to Los Alamos, it had been Lomanitz who had recruited both him and his wife into the CPUSA. Having pleaded the Fifth Amendment before Congress, Lomanitz was indicted on contempt charges in December 1949, and was acquitted in June 1951, as was Bohm who chose to move to São Paulo that same autumn, finally settling in England in 1957 where he was appointed Professor of Theoretical Physics at Birkbeck College, London University. Shortly after his death in October 1992 his biography, *Infinite Potential*, was published, documenting his lifetime commitment to Marxism and his paranoid fear of surveillance which caused him several mental breakdowns.

Between 1938 and early 1942 Oppenheimer was also in touch with another CPUSA official, Isaac Folkoff, and with Piotr Ivanov, the San Francisco *rezident* Grigori Kheiffets's subordinate, who was a suspected GRU officer. Another of Kheiffets's sources was Oppenheimer's friend the chemist Dr Martin Kamen, who was monitored by the FBI when the Soviets pumped him for details of the American stockpile of uranium in Chicago. Born in Canada to Russian immigrants, but educated in Chicago, Kamen had co-discovered Carbon-14 and had been credited with pioneering a method of using a cyclotron to make Iron-55. He had worked at Berkeley's Radiation Laboratory since 1936, and had been connected with several Communist front organizations, including the American–Soviet Science Society, the Joint Anti-Fascist Refugee Committee, the American League against War and Fascism, and Russian War Relief. On 2 July 1943 an FBI surveillance team attempted to eavesdrop on a dinner conversation in Berstein's Fish Grotto in San Francisco between the San Francisco *rezident*, Grigori Kheiffets, and another Soviet diplomat, Grigori Kasparov, during which Kamen was recorded mentioning Niels Bohr, atomic piles and Santa Fe. Because of background noise in the busy restaurant, the quality of the recording was poor, but it was sufficiently incriminating for Kamen's security clearance to be suspended ten days later, and he was transferred to a non-sensitive post in a shipyard. When he was later confronted with the FBI's evidence he insisted that he had met Kheiffets only twice, socially, and that the purpose of the dinner was simply to thank him for intervening on behalf of a Soviet official in Seattle whose leukaemia needed radiation treatment. Nevertheless, the FBI regarded Kamen with deep suspicion, and for a while he too experienced difficulties with the State Department in obtaining a US passport, although his reputation was fully restored in 1996 when he was awarded the prestigious Fermi Prize, worth $100,000, and the adulation of his peers. He now lives in Santa Barbara, California.

Kheiffets was an experienced intelligence officer who had acted as secretary to Lenin's widow, Nadezhda Krupskaya, had served as deputy *rezident* in Italy before the war, and, while working as an illegal in Germany, had achieved a diploma at the Jena Polytechnical Institute. He spoke fluent English, French and German and while in

Operation ENORMOZ

San Francisco conducted an affair with Louise Bransten, the wealthy former wife of Bruce Minton, about whom Elizabeth Bentley had said much, crediting him with being one of Jacob Golos's recruiters and a contributor to the CPUSA's journal *New Masses*. Although Kheiffets was both sophisticated and professional, he adopted the alias 'Mr Brown' to run unwittingly at least one double agent who reported to the FBI. The local field office never harboured any doubts about his dual role.

According to Pavel Sudoplatov, Kheiffets had targeted the leftist physicists Enrico Fermi and his pupil Bruno Pontecorvo for recruitment long before they joined the Manhattan project. As the NKVD's Director of Special Tasks in Moscow responsible for supervising Kheiffets, Sudoplatov should have been well placed to help identify the VENONA cryptonyms. He has suggested that MLAD was Bruno Pontecorvo, and claimed that Fermi and Oppenheimer were known as EDITOR and STAR respectively, but neither cryptonym appears in VENONA, which leaves the vexed question of how far Oppenheimer collaborated with the NKVD unresolved. Sudoplatov recalls that Elizaveta Zubilina, herself an experienced intelligence professional who had worked as an illegal in Turkey, had travelled to California to recruit sources inside the Manhattan Project, a mission for which she was ideally suited:

> She hardly appeared foreign in the United States. Her manner was so natural and sociable that she immediately made friends. Slim, with dark eyes, she had a classic Semitic beauty that attracted men, and she was one of the most successful agent recruiters, establishing her own illegal network of Jewish refugees from Poland, and recruiting one of Szilard's secretaries, who provided technical data. She spoke excellent English, German, French, Romanian and Hebrew. Usually she looked like a sophisticated, upper-class European, but she had the ability to change her appearance like a chameleon.

As well as establishing direct contact with Oppenheimer through his wife, Elizaveta cultivated another source close to his family. Her

> other mission was to check on the two Polish Jewish agents established on the West Coast as illegals by Eitingon

in the early 1930s. They had remained under deep cover for more than ten years. One of these agents was a dentist with a French medical degree that the OGPU had subsidized. His codename was Chess Player. The dentist's wife became a close friend of the Oppenheimer family, and they were our clandestine contacts with Oppenheimer and his friends, contacts that went undetected by the FBI.

Sudoplatov's memory of Oppenheimer is difficult to interpret, for on the one hand he insists that the scientist cooperated fully. 'In all, there were five classified reports made available by Oppenheimer describing the progress of work on the atomic bomb,' he recalls, noting that 'Oppenheimer, together with Fermi and Szilard, helped us place moles in Tennessee, Los Alamos, and Chicago as assistants in those three labs. In total there were four important sources of information who transmitted documents from the labs to the New York and Washington *rezidentura*s and to our illegal station, which was a drugstore in Santa Fe.' While this sounds conclusive, Sudoplatov explains that not all sources were necessarily conscious agents:

> The line between valuable connections and acquaintances, and confidential relations is very shaky. In traditional espionage terminology, there is a special term, *agenturnaya razvedka*, which means that the material is received through a network of agents or case officers acting under cover. Occasionally the most valuable information comes from a contact who is not an agent in the true sense – that is, working for and paid by us – but who is still regarded in the archives as an agent source of information. Our problem was that the atomic espionage business required new approaches; we used every potential method to penetrate into a unique area of activities that was intensely guarded by the American authorities.

So into which category did Oppenheimer fall? The question has to be asked because the physicist had reported Haakon Chevalier, then Professor of French at Berkeley, to the Manhattan Project's director of security in 1943. Chevalier pitched the idea to Oppenheimer that it was his moral duty to share technical data with the Russians. Born in America to French and Norwegian parents,

Chevalier was a scholar who had studied at the Leningrad Institute. When first introduced to Oppenheimer in late 1937, he had an established reputation as André Malraux's translator, and as the author of a study of Anatole France. Oppenheimer had refused Chevalier's proposal, which supposedly had been made at Steve Nelson's suggestion, later declaring it to be outright treason, but he waited ten months before reporting the incident.

This episode, which took place in Oppenheimer's kitchen, with just the two men present, also served to incriminate George C. Eltenton, a British-born chemical engineer who had visited Russia in 1930 and was then at Berkeley on behalf of the Shell Development Corporation. At his encounter with Oppenheimer, Chevalier had named Eltenton – well known as a union activist at the Radiation Laboratory – as his link to the Soviet consulate in San Francisco, but when interviewed by the FBI three years later, Eltenton denied any involvement with espionage. Later he returned to England. His wife Dolly, who was active in the Institute of Pacific Relations, had attempted to find a job with the American Russian Institute, and had made an approach for his support to Grigori Kheiffets, via an intermediary. Oppenheimer's version of precisely what had happened was to vary, whereas Chevalier protested to the FBI that he had not asked his friend to betray atomic secrets, but merely had described Eltenton's purported relationship with the Soviets, as a warning. Either way, Chevalier left the USA in November 1950 and took up a post as an interpreter with UNESCO in Paris, but continued to experience difficulty with the State Department over his American passport for many years. Curiously, despite the impact of Oppenheimer's allegation on his career, Chevalier remained friendly with him, and saw Robert and Kitty socially in Paris in December 1953.

Precisely when VENONA played a part in the Oppenheimer investigation is difficult to determine, but the FBI certainly considered him a possible suspect in the hunt for the accomplice who was believed to have collaborated with Klaus Fuchs. Based on the Fuchs interrogation conducted in London after his conviction, the FBI and the AEC realized that the spy had not acted alone, and Fuchs confirmed that the Russians had run an agent in Berkeley who had told them about electro-magnetic separation research in 1942, or even earlier. Could Oppenheimer have been the spy? The FBI certainly thought so, and compiled an impressive list of reasons for continuing their inquiries:

his commitment to the Party had been sufficiently strong to survive the two crises, the Molotov–Ribbentrop pact and the invasion of Finland, that tested the most hardened supporters; he recruited Communists into the Berkeley atomic project, and even brought in nontechnical CPUSA members to Los Alamos; his open financial support for the Party dried up only in May 1942, the month following his employment by the government, and his application for a security clearance. In addition, there was his contact with known NKVD agents, and his opposition to postwar weapons development which led to him calling for the Los Alamos laboratory to be disbanded. However, despite the weight of circumstantial evidence, and Oppenheimer's own lamentable performance while under cross-examination during his AEC security review, the case against him remained inconclusive, although VENONA seems to show that the Soviets were anxious to re-establish contact with him through HURON in the period between December 1944 and March 1945. The implication, of course, is that hitherto Oppenheimer had been in uninterrupted contact with the NKVD, and had been assigned BILL OF EXCHANGE as his codename. But is this enough to conclude he was a conscious source? Certainly Sudoplatov believed he was, and even alleged that Oppenheimer had been instrumental in obtaining Fuchs's transfer to Los Alamos, an intervention that he might not necessarily have been aware of. Slightly improbably, Sudoplatov suggests that, as the son of German immigrants, Oppenheimer expressed a preference for German refugees with a history of opposing fascism.

Accordingly, there seems some room for doubt about the degree to which Oppenheimer actively cooperated with the NKVD, although Sudoplatov is less ambiguous about others, and clearly identifies George Gamow as a source who had been coerced by Elizaveta Zubilina/Zarubina:

> [Elizaveta] approached Gamow through his wife, Rho, who was also a physicist. She and her husband were vulnerable because of their concern for relatives in the Soviet Union. Gamow taught physics at George Washington University in Washington DC, and instituted the annual Washington Conference on Theoretical Physics, which brought together the best physicists to discuss the latest developments at small meetings. We were able to take

advantage of the network of colleagues that Gamow had established. Using implied threats against Gamow's relatives in Moscow, Elizaveta Zarubina pressured him into cooperating with us. In exchange for safety and material support for his relatives, Gamow provided the names of left-wing scientists who might be recruited to supply secret information. On some occasions Gamow had essential data in his house for several days, in violation of security regulations. Scientists on the bomb project asked him for his comments on the data, which he then verbally repeated to our illegals by arrangement with Zarubina.

The disclosure that Gamow was a coerced spy was remarkable, for hitherto no suspicion had been attached to him, even though in his autobiography *My World Line* (1970) he mentions having served in a non-combat role as an artillery lieutenant-colonel in the Red Army. His distinguished scientific career had begun in his native Leningrad, and he had achieved recognition within the relatively small international community of nuclear physicists for his explanation of alpha decay, described by his friend Sir Rudolf Peierls as 'one of the early successes of quantum mechanics'. This comment naturally suggests a possible identity for the mysterious QUANTUM, although it is likely that Gamow would have communicated in his native language with his Soviet contact, and according to the VENONA dated 22–23 June 1944, QUANTUM's message had been translated from English. In any event, Gamow, who never visited Los Alamos, made no admission before his death from alcohol-related liver disease in August 1968.

The line of communication between the New York *rezidentura* and Los Alamos was via a system of couriers, among them Harry Gold and Lona Cohen, and this was the method adopted to exchange messages with Klaus Fuchs and Ted Hall, but what of the others? Sudoplatov reveals another parallel link to the Centre via Mexico. Apparently a veteran agent, Joseph Grigulevich, who had fought in the Spanish Civil War, had been assigned a support role in the assassination of Trotsky which required him to establish a commercial cover in New Mexico. Like his father, who ran a pharmacy in Argentina, Grigulevich was a chemist by profession, so he had opened a drugstore in Sante Fe. When he was recalled in 1941 he had transferred the ownership to one of his agents, and this had been the link to a

> mole who worked with Fermi and Pontecorvo. The mole in Tennessee was connected with the illegal station at the Sante Fe drugstore, from which material was sent by courier to Mexico. These unidentified young moles, along with the Los Alamos mole, were junior scientists or administrators who copied vital documents to which they were allowed access by Oppenheimer, Fermi, and Szilard, who were knowingly part of the scheme.

While the experimental physicist Bruno Pontecorvo was unquestionably a Communist, as were most members of his family, and he had demonstrated his political commitment most dramatically by his defection with his wife and children to Russia via Helsinki in September 1950, there is no evidence to show that he was in contact with the Soviets during the six years (1943–49) he spent working on the heavy-water pile at Chalk River, or afterwards during the year he was at Harwell. Sudoplatov alleges that Pontecorvo had been cultivated in Rome before the war by Grigori Kheiffets, and then contacted by Lev Vasilevsky, the Mexico City *rezident* working under diplomatic cover, in January 1943: 'At the end of January 1943 we received through Semyonov a full report on the first nuclear chain reaction from Bruno Pontecorvo, describing Enrico Fermi's experiment in Chicago on December 2, 1942.' Quite how Pontecorvo might have gained access to this highly classified breakthrough is unexplained, for at the time he was working for an oil survey company in Oklahoma, having arrived in the United States in August 1942. He was not invited to join the British contingent to the Manhattan Project in Montreal until after its arrival there in January 1943. Although Sudoplatov is emphatic that Vasilevsky 'was the first intelligence officer to approach Pontecorvo directly in 1943', there must be some doubt about the claim. Later purged because of his Jewish origins, Vasilevsky died in 1979, and Pontecorvo died at the Soviet nuclear research centre at Dubna, outside Moscow, in 1993.

Sudoplatov's proposition that Enrico Fermi, the Italian Nobel prizewinner who was responsible for the world's first controlled nuclear chain reaction, and the Hungarian Leo Szilard were spies is also hard to accept. So who was HURON, and did he succeed in making contact with Oppenheimer and 'Goldsmith'? An AFSA report dated 30 August 1947 mentions that the selection of the Great Lakes as covernames was no coincidence, and that 'ERIE gave the clue for the identification of HURON'. But who was he? If there is a connection between the two Great Lakes, Erie and Huron, and the true name, a strong possibility must be Dr Ernest Lawrence, the brilliant experimental physicist, of Norwegian stock, from a small prairie town in South Dakota, who had been educated at the universities of South Dakota, Minnesota, Chicago and Yale. HURON's codename was to change to ERNEST, and the St Lawrence River is the waterway connecting the two Canadian lakes.

These are just a few of the questions of historical importance thrown up by the New York channel of VENONA.

Although much attention has focused on the Soviet penetration of the Manhattan Project, with VENONA supplying the compelling proof of the scale of the success achieved by ENORMOZ, very little is known of the British dimension apart from Nunn May, Fuchs and Bruno Pontecorvo (to whom there is no discernible VENONA reference). TINA's identity remains a fascinating mystery. One leading contender, now dead, was an English physicist married to another scientist. The mother of two children, her identity has not been disclosed to protect their privacy.

Ethel and Julius Rosenberg died in the electric chair at Sing Sing prison in June 1953; Harry Gold was released from prison in May 1966, after serving fifteen years, and died six years later. Al Sarant became a senior research scientist, founding the Zelenograd microelectronics centre in Leningrad to develop computer systems for Soviet submarines, and died in Vladivostock in 1979. Joel Barr, who married in the Soviet Union but for twenty years failed to tell his Czech wife, Vera Bergova, or his four children of his past, adopted the identity of a South African, Josef V. Berg, but eventually returned to New York in 1992 on a Soviet passport, resumed his American citizenship and died in August 1998. Lona Cohen, who had been released from a prison sentence in England as part of a spy-swap in 1969, died in Moscow in 1993. Her husband Morris died in July 1995.

In retrospect it seems astonishing that the FBI was so slow to react to the threat to the Manhattan Project, but it must be remembered that the programme was so secret that not even J.

Edgar Hoover had any idea of its existence until 10 April 1943, when he first became aware of it – from the Soviets. This remarkable state of affairs came about through the FBI's clandestine surveillance on the home in Oakland, California, of Steve Nelson, the CPUSA functionary who supervised the East Bay branch which covered the Berkeley campus. Born in Chaglich, Yugoslavia, where he had been active in radical politics, Nelson had landed in New York illegally in June 1920, accompanied by his mother and two sisters, pretending to be Joseph Fleischinger, an American citizen who was actually married to his mother's sister. The impersonation was discovered and deportation proceedings were initiated, but then abandoned two years later, thus allowing him to become a naturalized American citizen in Detroit in November 1928. It was under his true name, Stephan Mesarosh, that in 1930 he had used Golos's firm World Tourists Inc. to travel to Moscow where he attended a course at the Lenin School between September 1931 and May 1933. After his graduation he had undertaken a secret mission in Central Europe, and was spotted in Shanghai where he was associated with William Ewart, a veteran Comintern agent. Nelson returned to the USA in 1933, having renewed his US passport in Austria in July, to organize CPUSA industrial branches in Pittsburgh, Chicago and Cleveland, and served as a political commissar in the Abraham Lincoln Brigade during the Spanish Civil War. In February 1937, while still in Spain, he obtained another US passport in the name of Joseph Fleischinger (even though he twice misspelled the surname on the application form).

It was during the course of a disjointed conversation with an unknown Russian (later identified as Vasili Zubilin) who had called at Nelson's home, that Special Agent William Branigan discovered that the NKVD *apparat* in East Bay was preoccupied with recruiting agents inside the Allied atomic weapon development project. From the transcript of the recording it was clear that Nelson was Zubilin's subordinate, and was acting as an intermediary, financing an extensive spy-ring. The FBI hastily organized surveillance on Nelson's mysterious Russian visitor, who was seen to board a train in San Francisco bound for New York. James R. Malley, then head of the Internal Security Squad at the New York Field Office, despatched three Special Agents, Warren R. Hearn, Kenneth R. Routon and Herman O. Bly, to join the train in Newark, and they maintained a watch at Penn Station while their target was met by an official Soviet diplomatic car and driven up Fifth Avenue to his apartment building. The three FBI men then returned to their office where they identified Zubilin from photographs and initiated a major espionage investigation designated COMINTERN APPARATUS. Until that moment, Hoover had no idea that the Manhattan Project even existed, and although Zubilin was to be placed under blanket surveillance thereafter, until his departure from New York on 28 August 1944, Hoover was unable to persuade the White House that the Soviets were engaged in wholesale espionage against their ally. As for Steve Nelson, he was convicted under the Smith Act in July 1952 of plotting to overthrow the US government, and sentenced to twenty years' imprisonment. The conviction was overturned on appeal in 1957, and he died in December 1993.

It was only after Zubilin's departure that his significance, and that of his wife, was recognized, largely through the evidence of Boris Morros, who had originally known Zubilin as Edward Herbert, 'a thick-set man with powerful shoulders. He had red hair and, despite the heavy accent ... spoke French, English and German fairly well'. However, it was his wife, a 'frail, pretty, middle-aged woman with an aristocratic manner' who often appeared to Morros to be in charge:

> I often heard of other Communist women talking of Elizabeth Zubilin as though she was a sort of Red Joan of Arc, a saint whose faith in the Soviet was pure and bottomless. They also had great respect for her intellect and judgment. Often I heard these wives of other spies say, while in the midst of a dispute over some matter of strategy, 'Well, what did she say about it?' or 'Let's ask Liza,' or 'Don't argue, Helen said so!' as though Madame Zubilin had the last word. She was generally acknowledged to be the real brain behind whatever shrewd moves her blustering husband made.

In retrospect it is amazing that the Zubilins could have fallen under suspicion in Moscow and been investigated as traitors who had sold out to the FBI, especially as their penetration of the Manhattan Project was so comprehensive. For its part, the FBI was slow to grasp the scale of Soviet espionage conducted on the West Coast, but much of the blame must be shared with the military authorities which were reluctant to share secrets with the FBI, or even tell J. Edgar Hoover the purpose of Los Alamos. By the time the FBI were ready to take Soviet espionage seriously, it was almost too late and some important suspects, such as Al Sarant and the Cohens, slipped away unimpeded. Nor was the FBI's investigation particularly sophisticated, for example relying on a young car thief who shared Rosenberg's prison cell for information. Clearly Rosenberg confided in Jerome Tartakow because, although initially sceptical of his value, the FBI was able to demonstrate that the surprisingly talkative spy had imparted information that Tartakow could not possibly have learnt elsewhere. On one occasion Tartakow reported that the two Los Alamos scientists whom Harry Gold had named to David Greenglass as potential recruits, Philip Morrison and Hans Bethe, had been in touch with Al Sarant after the war. Since both had worked with Fuchs, and also had seen him after the war, they too became the subjects of long but ultimately fruitless investigations. Like Fuchs, Bethe had lodged with Rudolf Peierls (before the war, in Manchester) but the FBI was far too late to pick up a trail, if indeed there was one to be found.

As for Morrison, who had been a member of the YCL at the age of eighteen before his full CPUSA membership in the Berkeley branch, he had joined the Metallurgical Laboratory in late 1942, and had remained in Chicago until 1944 when he had joined DuPont to work on the construction of new facilities at Hanford. However, instead of moving to Washington State he was assigned by military intelligence to a study of German atomic research. Once this had been completed, in late 1944, he was transferred to Los Alamos where he participated in the first bomb test before flying to the Pacific as a member of the weapons team. However, he failed to disclose his CPUSA membership until May 1953, when he was called to give evidence to the Senate Internal Security Subcommittee, and even at that late date was a leader of a CPUSA front, the American Peace Crusade. Crippled with polio, he achieved considerable academic prominence at the Massachusetts Institute of Technology and a Professor of Physics at Cornell University, where he now lives.

Evidence of the NKVD's willingness to approach CPUSA members associated with the Manhattan Project can be seen in the VENONA traffic relating to Norman F. Ramsey, a senior scientist who worked at Los Alamos between October 1943 and February 1946. On 4 May 1944 Stepan Apresyan advised Moscow that Bernard Schuster had made a special journey to Chicago to take over Ramsey's cultivation from Rose Olsen:

> In reply to No. 950, the object of ECHO's [Bernard Schuster] trips is as follows: OLSEN is district leader of the FRATERNAL [Communist Party] in Chicago. OLSEN's wife, who has been meeting RAMSAY, is also an active FELLOWCOUNTRYMAN [Communist] and met RAMSAY on the instructions of the organization. At our suggestion ECHO can get a letter from OLSEN with which one or other of our people will meet RAMSAY and thereafter will be able to strike up an acquaintance. Advise your consent to these measures.

By 18 September 1944, it appears from the end of a lengthy apologia from Apresyan that the recruitment had been completed:

> Your No. 4161. Your instructions concerning delays on our part in answering telegrams have been taken into account. The delays [1 group unrecovered] regular information about the work [1 group unrecovered] on KHU [Economic Directorate] were due to:
> 1. The impossibility of ANTON's [Leonid Kvasnikov] [4 groups unrecovered] the PLANT [Soviet consulate general] in view of surveillance on the PLANT and at times on ANTON himself.
> 2. At the beginning of the year the lack of time at moments of visiting the PLANT owing to the absence of the Master of the OFFICE [*rezident*].
> 3. The great pressure of work for the FACTORY [Amtorg].
>
> Despite the holding up of information at various moments of the work it cannot be said that there has been no information at all. In 1943 the information was regular. In 1944 also, but see letters 1, 5, and parts of others; all the questions put to us could not be answered as your letter no. 5 was received a few days before our letter no. 7 went off and letter no. 6 has not yet been received. We will try not to hold up answers to letters.
>
> By telegrams: Your number 2962 could not be carried out

because of surveillance on TWAIN [Semyon Semyonov]. [1 group unrecovered] BERG who was in liaison with SMART, was without liaison with us; this was evident from the [1 group unrecovered] on the occasion of handing over TWAIN's liaison. There has been a report on SEAMAN's absence (see also our number 701). Your no. 3554. The money was received by MAXIM [Vasili Zubilin]. ANTON has nothing to do with this matter. Your telegram no. 3338. Refer to our numbers 550 and 711. [28 groups unrecoverable] and passing on your directive was entrusted to ECHO [Bernard Schuster] The task was passed on through X [Joseph Katz]. The task is being protracted by reason of the subsequent absence from TYRE [New York] of X on a trip to the West, ECHO on leave, at present PHLOX [Rose Olsen] is absent, has left with her husband for RAMSAY's area. ECHO cannot meet PHLOX until her return in only about three weeks' time.

On 5 December 1944 Leonid Kvasnikov was providing Moscow with a further explanation about Ramsay:

Your No. 5673. DICK [Bernard Schuster] is directly in touch with PHLOX's [Rose Olsen] husband and not with PHLOX herself. The intention of sending the husband to see RAMSAY is explained by the possibility of avoiding a superfluous stage for transmitting instructions.

The VENONA texts leave little doubt about the overlap between the CPUSA underground cells and the NKVD's spy-rings. ENORMOZ was considered such a high priority that Moscow had authorized two radical departures from its usual methodology: the separation between GRU and NKVD operations, and the insulation of the Party from espionage. In reality, as has been seen, the NKVD regarded local Communist organizations, and the CPUSA in particular, as useful pools of talent from which it was expedient to recruit agents. At the very least they were a means of checking on a candidate's ideological reliability. Although Earl Browder tried to distance himself from illicit activity, he was often drawn in, and he certainly knew a great deal about the underground *apparat*. Only very gradually, and much too late, did the NKVD come to realize the extent to which the CPUSA had been infiltrated by the FBI. Indeed, by the end of the House Un-American Activities Committee hearings, it was often joked that the only CPUSA members who paid their dues on time were FBI informants working on government expenses, and the FBI suspected that several CPUSA branches were supported entirely by its own nominees.

Once VENONA had demonstrated that the importance given to ENORMOZ had ensured that almost every CPUSA member connected with the Manhattan Project had been the subject of an unambiguous recruitment pitch, the FBI became increasingly sceptical of those known Party members who subsequently denied ever having been approached. Into this category fell David Hawkins, who had been a member of the San Francisco, Palo Alto and Berkeley branches of the CPUSA between 1938 and March 1943, before his arrival at Los Alamos as an administrator in May 1943. A philosopher by training, Hawkins had written the first draft of the Manhattan Project's official history, for which he had required access to classified data. After the war he taught at the University of Colorado, and at the time of his testimony to the Senate Internal Security Subcommittee in May 1953 he had been teaching at Harvard.

It was VENONA more than any other single intelligence source that demonstrated the extent to which the Manhattan Project had been penetrated by the Soviets, but the most frustrating aspect was the continuing doubt about the precise identities of the traitors. Opinion at the time prevailing in leftist scientific circles perpetuated the dangerous proposition that atomic knowledge should be shared internationally, so there were more than a few physicists willing to convey the secrets of the bomb to Moscow. Of those referred to in the texts, none has openly declared his or her role or attempted to justify any actions, with just one exception: Ted Hall, now living in retirement in Cambridge, acknowledges that in his youth he acted in a way that, with the benefit of hindsight, he should not have, and although he accepts his identification as MLAD, he has never publicly admitted espionage. Accordingly, he remains, like Allan Nunn May who leads a reclusive life in Scotland, possibly the last of the agents that made ENORMOZ one of Stalin's greatest intelligence triumphs.

VII

The Émigrés

THE NKVD's preoccupation with émigrés is a significant feature of VENONA, doubtless because of the regime's paranoia about external threats. Of course, since the early days of the Cheka and the Russian civil war, Soviet intelligence had been preoccupied with the plots of expatriates, particularly where they were concentrated together in Paris and New York, but these communities also offered good opportunities for recruitment, with so many families having vulnerable relatives in the old country. The NKVD's interest in Russian expatriates, as shown through VENONA, concentrated mainly on three individuals, the first of whom, Victor Kravchenko, was perceived to be a threat to the regime.

Born in Ekaterinoslav in the Ukraine to a revolutionary activist in 1905, Kravchenko started his career as a miner before he joined the Party and attended the Technological Institute at Kharkov. Having received a diploma for the design of a pipe-rolling fabricator, he was sent to manage a steel factory in Nikopol. Here he experienced continuous surveillance by the omnipotent OGPU and, as he later claimed, he began to develop doubts about the regime that had originally emerged during Stalin's purges.

Following the evacuation of Moscow in August 1942 Kravchenko supervised the dismantling of his factory and its removal to a new, safer site in the Urals. Once completed, he was drafted into the Red Army and assigned to an engineering company which liaised closely with an NKVD demolition battalion. These duties lasted until November when, following treatment in Moscow for an infected jaw, he was transferred to Sovnarkom, the centralized bureaucracy that ran what was left of the Soviet manufacturing and heavy industry. In January 1943 Kravchenko was nominated to travel to the United States as a metallurgical specialist on behalf of the Ministry of Foreign Trade to help negotiate details of the Lend-Lease agreement. For six

The Émigrés

months he was investigated by the NKVD to ensure his suitability for the appointment, and when he had won approval he went by train to Vladivostock and thence to Vancouver by ship.

Canada, and then Washington DC, proved to be revelations for Kravchenko, who had been instructed by the NKVD to deny his Party membership if questioned by American officials while en route to join the Soviet Purchasing Commission on 16th Street. Although not coopted to assist the NKVD in espionage, during the seven months he was based at the Commission he acquired a comprehensive knowledge of the NKVD's local structure. At the end of March 1944, following official inspection visits to Pennsylvania and Chicago, he abandoned his rented room in Washington and took the train to New York where he surrendered to the federal authorities. Within a couple of days his 'resignation' was front-page news, but the Soviets responded by charging Kravchenko, who held the Red Army rank of captain, with military desertion.

Kravchenko gave evidence before the House Committee on Un-American Activities in 1947, soon after his book *I Chose Freedom*,[1] had been published. In it Kravchenko gave a harrowing account of police terror in the Soviet Union, and of the gulags. As soon as it was released it was denounced as a forgery by the Soviets and similar allegations were circulated in leftist journals in Europe, although Kravchenko admitted to having had only professional editorial help. Incensed by an article in the Paris weekly magazine *Les Lettres Français* entitled 'How Kravchenko Was Manufactured', which called him a traitor and a liar, the author brought a defamation suit in France. The Communist periodical's story claimed that Kravchenko had stolen papers from a safe in the Soviet embassy in Washington DC and had sold them to officials from the State Department. The correspondent credited with the story, an American named 'Sim Thomas', also asserted that he had been told that the US Office of Strategic Services had fabricated the entire book.

Kravchenko's litigation, which was concluded in March 1949, effectively proved that there was no 'Sim Thomas' and that the magazine publishers had no evidence to substantiate their libels. Although the court awarded Kravchenko barely enough to cover his costs, he capitalized on his experience by releasing *I Chose Justice*, an account of the trial, the following year.

Kravchenko was the subject of no fewer than ten VENONA texts, the NKVD being understandably anxious about the extent of his knowledge, his potential for damaging the organization, and the need to monitor his adoption by anti-Soviet groups. As it turned out, the NKVD were right to be worried on all three counts, but VENONA does demonstrate how successfully the activities of the defector, codenamed GNAT, were monitored. The first text, dated 1 May 1944 from Stepan Apresyan, revealed that Mark Zborowski, codenamed TULIP, had been assigned the task of getting close to Kravchenko:

> In spite of measures taken TULIP has not so far succeeded in making GNAT's acquaintance. One cannot insist strongly to [Lydia] ESTRINA and [David J.] DALLIN as this would arouse suspicion. In a day or so TULIP is meeting with DALLIN and ESTRINA. The latter promised to have a detailed chat on the GNAT affair after which the meeting will probably take place. In the last conversation ESTRINA declared that something serious is still expected, but what they are afraid of she did not say. We shall do everything possible to find out what she is talking about and measures have been taken accordingly.
>
> Comrade PETROV's [Lavrenti Beria] instructions were put into effect immediately upon receipt. Concerning measures against the STORE [Soviet Government Purchasing Commission] you should report to MAXIM [Vasili Zubilin] (particularly in relation to R. and M. As regards our [25 groups unrecoverable] as we waited for concrete results.

Although the full text is unavailable, it is possible to deduce that Zborowski, previously regarded as an anti-Soviet activist close to Trotsky, was an NKVD asset, as was Lydia Estrina, who was married to David J. Dallin, later the author of *Soviet Espionage*.[2] Although ostensibly anti-Soviet, Dallin's wife was better known as Lola Estrine, and had been close to Trotsky, and to Trotsky's son Leon Sedov. When the defector Alexander Orlov wrote to Trotsky warning that Zborowski was not to be trusted, Lydia had persuaded him that Orlov's letter was nothing more than a provocation. Later, it was the Dallins who sponsored Zborowski's arrival in the USA and found him a job and a place to live, even though he had played a key role in Sedov's murder in Paris, and had been responsible for alerting Moscow to the intention of Ignace Reiss, a highly experienced illegal,

The Émigrés

to defect. As a consequence, Reiss's bullet-riddled body had been found on a road outside Lausanne in September 1937.

Equally clear is Beria's personal interest in Kravchenko, presumably because the Purchasing Commission was such an important component of his apparatus, providing cover for dozens of NKVD and GRU personnel.

Two days after this text was sent from New York, Apresyan despatched a longer report to Beria in Moscow, in which he referred to the FBI as KhATA, a characteristically Ukrainian whitewashed thatched cottage of the kind lived in by peasants:

> 1. On our behalf under a plausible pretext OLA [Sara Veksler] visited CARTHAGE [Washington DC], met a fascist acquaintance of whom you know, [Aleksei A.] STUPENKOV (works at present guarding buildings of the DOCK [US Navy Department], who, when he had drunk quite a bit, told her the following: He had to do with the desertion of GNAT, whom he met four times, had got him drunk, and had carried on 'heart-to-heart talks'. GNAT said he had acted from 'ideological' considerations, 'he was fed up with what he had seen over the span of 20 years.' At the same time STUPENKOV acknowledged that a no less powerful motive was the desire of an easy, comfortable life and did not deny that this was just what had produced on GNAT an impression. STUPENKOV helped GNAT to make contact with the TOWNSMEN [Americans]. For this he met him in a club for military personnel located in the same building as the 'Associated Press', conducted GNAT to the doors of that agency, which at once got in contact with [Joseph] SHAPLEN. Thereafter SHAPLEN took the affair of GNAT into his own hands and GNAT went to TYRE [New York]. By what STUPENKOV said, SHAPLEN knows GNAT's whereabouts and continues to maintain direct contact with the latter. GNAT has been declaring that he does not doubt that 'they will liquidate' him. He has been trying to inflate the importance of what he has to tell and thus enable himself to have a quiet and comfortable life in the PERIPHERY [countryside] or the PROVINCES [Latin America]. The letter in 'The Times' was written by SHAPLEN.

The affair simmered down because the LEAGUE [US Government] did not want [31 groups unrecoverable] [Nikolai A.] SKRYAGIN. The last meeting between them was six months ago, after which contact was, apparently, broken off. According to STUPENKOV's story, he used to meet SKRYAGIN once a fortnight. The latter was interested in the newspaper 'ROSSIYA' and attempted through STUPENKOV to influence [editor Nikolai P.] RYBAKOV, apparently not imagining that STUPENKOV had for a long time been employed on the paper.

PART II The break with SKRYAGIN STUPENKOV explains as due to the fact that during their acquaintance he placed a [1 group unrecovered] article in 'ROSSIYA', which very much surprised SKRYAGIN and the latter put an end to the meetings. The meetings took place in SKRYAGIN's apartment. One day STUPENKOV met there twelve Soviet persons, among them GNAT. Recently they summoned STUPENKOV to the KhATA [FBI] and interrogated him about WASP [Ludmilla N. Alexeef] and her husband, a member of [Sergei] ZHAROV's chorus, [Paul I.] ALEKSEEV (WASP was trying unsuccessfully [2 groups unrecovered] NTSNP [National Labor Union of the New Generation]: OSIPOV [Prince Nikolai V. Orlov], CAVALRYMAN [Sergei N. Kurnakov].

2. In CARTHAGE OLA made the acquaintance of an American woman CUNNINGHAM of the well-known PEABODY family. The latter works on the secret reception of foreign radio transmissions including those from the USSR. The reception of transmissions from the USSR is the business of 5–6 persons, all TOWNSMEN [Americans]. There are no Russians. CUNNINGHAM is friendly with STUPENKOV. The Soviet citizen LOMONOSOV lives in her house. STUPENKOV sticks into his mailbox copies of the newspaper 'ROSSIYA' after cutting his own name off the paper. [9 groups unrecoverable] hopes to meet.

On a recent occasion, OLA became acquainted with SHAPLEN. She was given the task of cautiously endeavouring to enter into closer relations with the latter, verifying what STUPENKOV says, and, if the opportunity presents itself,

The Émigrés

finding out more detailed information on the GNAT affair. OLA is well acquainted with ESTRINA, who in the past more than once invited her to work in the 'Union of Russian Jews'. As a result of OLA's joining the RADIO STATION [Office of War Information] they have not met for a long time, but when occasion offers OLA may be able to resume their old acquaintance. We think OLA should arrange to associate with ESTRINA and SHAPLEN.

This VENONA caused some comment at Arlington Hall as Leora Cunningham worked on Russian police radio traffic at the US Navy's signals intelligence headquarters on Nebraska Avenue where Stupenkov, a former Czarist officer, had been a US Marine NCO assigned to guard duties.

On 9 May Apresyan addressed a further despatch to Beria in Moscow:

Your number 195. OLA [Sara Veksler] has reported that GNAT [Kravchenko] is living out of town. He sometimes comes into TYRE [New York City]. SHAPLEN and [Alexander] KERENSKY's right-hand man, [Vladimir] ZENZINOV, often go to see him. The latter told her that GNAT had used SHAPLEN [25 groups unrecovered] that the latter may introduce her to GNAT.

On 24 May Apresyan reported the latest news to Moscow, including the first reference in a VENONA text to Kravchenko's book:

TULIP [Mark Zborowski] had informed us: ESTRINA often sees GNAT [Victor Kravchenko], who is dictating his book to her. DALLIN and DON-LEVINE he consults privately. So far the biographical part of the book has been composed. GNAT is hurrying with the book, being afraid that he may not manage to finish it. GNAT was a member of the BUKHARIN opposition, but the book will not say so. GNAT's family with the exception of his wife was always anti-Soviet in temper. GNAT is well informed about the KRIVITSKY case.

Obviously Kravchenko had no idea that his innermost circle of friends and advisers, and even his secretary, were working for the

NKVD, but he must have known the danger he was running, for Walter Krivitsky was always fearful of assassination.

On 4 July Apresyan made a slight correction to an earlier telegram, the content of which is unknown, but it must have shed some light on another NKVD source close to Kravchenko, Sara Veksler, who had known Lydia Estrina in Germany before the war. Later Veksler married Herman Judey and worked in Washington DC for the Soviet Government Purchasing Commission.

> Your 2942. The person that sent GNAT [Victor Kravchenko] to [Lydia] ESTRINA and that is working in our establishments in CARTHAGE [Washington DC] was acquainted in BERLIN with ESTRINA, and not with GNAT. Evidently our telegram was worded imprecisely.

This correction appeared to identify OLA as Sara Veksler, and not, as had been thought previously, as Christina Krotkova, Kravchenko's typist and translator, although it is likely that both were supplying information about the defector.

On 10 August 1944 the New York *rezidentura* reported, in a much longer telegram concerning Trotsky, about Mark Zborowski: 'At present TULIP is being used by us on the GNAT case and is carrying out the work very DILIGENTLY.' On the same day Apresyan sent a second despatch:

> GNAT told TULIP that he had a friend in our firm, KARLOV, through whom he found out that his mistress NINA (he did not mention the surname), whose father and husband had been arrested, was a PROBATIONER [agent] of ours. After GNAT's first article in 'Cosmopolitan' GNAT broke with Don LEVIN because the latter signed the article as co-author. LEVIN in reply to this accused GNAT of commercialism and pettiness and said that the latter [3 groups unrecovered] questions of money and that he was duty bound as a citizen of the COUNTRY [America] to keep an eye on the behaviour of a type like GNAT and that the latter still had to give proof of his sincerity to the government of the COUNTRY. At this point GNAT decided to take [24 groups unrecoverable] Max EASTMAN.
>
> In a conversation with a certain Nadezhda Ivanovna MEDVEDEVA, OLA discovered that GNAT is living at the

The Émigrés

address 209 West 97th Street. ZENZINOV told OLA GNAT's book would be ready in a month's time. GNAT's first wife was said to have worked with us since she was threatened that her first husband – an agricultural expert, who had been accused of being a saboteur – would be persecuted. In SMYRNA [Moscow] GNAT began living with his second wife who also was said to have worked with us and to have been in ISTANBUL, in PARIS, in ITALY and in SWITZERLAND. In CARTHAGE [Washington DC] GNAT is said to have received a letter from her saying that the parents he had left behind had died and that she wanted to give up her work.

ESTRINA told TULIP [24 groups unrecoverable] Louis FISCHER. Details are being ascertained.

This fragmented text sowed the NKVD's interest in the editor and translator Max Eastman, and in Vladimir Zenzinov, then the editor of *Za Svoboda*, and finally in the author Louis Fischer.

Later that same month, on 23 August, Apresyan made a bizarre assertion regarding Kravchenko, which was attributed to an unknown source codenamed THRUSH, later AKHMED:

THRUSH advises: The KhATA [FBI] is supposed to have established that GNAT [Victor Kravchenko] is meeting secretly with a number of workers of the TRUST [Soviet Embassy] and STORE [Soviet Government Purchasing Commission]. In the BANK [State Department] there is supposed to exist the conviction that the business with GNAT is a put-up job with a special purpose. We will try to check this information and as far as possible get to know the facts.

The New York *rezidentura*'s concern for Zborowski, who apparently had become eligible for compulsory military service, is evident from this short message to Moscow, dated 23 September 1944:

No. 766. On the basis of the latest law of the COUNTRY [America] about drafting into the army TULIP [Mark Zborowski] has an opportunity to change his job [21 groups unrecoverable; 6 groups unrecovered]. Telegraph your position.

On 19 January 1945 Stepan Apresyan made his last VENONA despatch to Moscow about Kravchenko, disclosing Zborowski's new codename as KANT, and Christina Krotkova's as JEANNE:

> [16 groups unrecovered] [Vladimir] ZENZINOV [18 groups unrecovered] DALLIN and allegedly KERENSKY [21 groups unrecoverable] the last three weeks GNAT and [David] DALLIN have been in a great panic. GNAT has noticed that he is being intensively shadowed; moreover he and DALLIN have received warnings by telephone from some persons or other that CARTHAGE [Washington DC] is preparing to hand GNAT over to the HOUSE [Soviet embassy]. GNAT is alarmed by the incessant shadowing and is said to be hiring two bodyguards. DALLIN says that he supposes that it is not the 'GPU' which is having GNAT shadowed, preparing to do away with him. The work on GNAT is being carried out by KANT [Mark Zborowski] and JEANNE [Christina Krotkova]. KANT is acquainted with GNAT personally, but for the most part gets his information through a woman neighbour. JEANNE takes part in reading at ZENZINOV's and from him gets information about GNAT. KANT has been instructed to develop his acquaintance with GNAT to the point of friendship.

The disclosure concerning Mark Zborowski was a considerable shock to the FBI as he had been a respected figure within the White Russian émigré community and had been especially close to Leon Trotsky. A VENONA text from Moscow dated 5 April 1945 demonstrated that Zborowski's principal role was that of penetrating groups supporting Trotsky, a role he fulfilled with convincing enthusiasm:

> At the beginning of February this year KANT [Mark Zborowski] reported that [Jean Louis] VAN HEIJENOORT intended leaving for FRANCE to head the French Trotskyist organization. Report [1 group unrecovered]:
> 1. How are things going as regards VAN's departure?
> 2. By what route does VAN intend to travel to FRANCE?
> 3. From whom is he counting on receiving assistance during his trip?
> What is the extent of KANT's knowledge about the plan for VAN's trip? If VAN's trip remains realizable and can be

The Émigrés

decided upon definitely, get KANT to take up this question in real earnest so that he knows all the details of the preparation of the trip.

The FBI's surprise at Zborowski's duplicity was short-lived, for soon after Zborowski had been interviewed by a special agent, Jack Soble sent a nine-page letter to Moscow seeking Zborowski's immediate withdrawal on the grounds that he too might be incriminated. Soble explained that Zborowski had admitted to working for the NKVD in Europe, but had denied any espionage since arriving in the United States, a deception that was intended to protect his links to Soble, which had dated back many years. The FBI learned of the letter's contents because in May 1956 Soble had entrusted it to Boris Morros for delivery to Moscow, and he had routinely copied it to his FBI handler. Reinterviewed, Zborowski was later to confess to his espionage, admit to his part in several murders, and be sentenced to five years' imprisonment. After his release he lectured on sociology at Berkeley, and in 1969 wrote *People in Pain*. As for Kravchenko, he survived in New York until February 1966 when he was found shot dead in his apartment, apparently the victim of suicide.

The second defector in whom VENONA reveals the NKVD's interest is Alexander Barmine, whose real surname was Graf, and who defected from the Soviet embassy in Athens where he held the rank of Chargé d'Affaires in June 1937. He took the train to Paris where he went into hiding with the Greek woman who was to become his wife, and eventually emigrated to America in 1939.

A much-decorated political commissar during the First World War, Barmine left the Red Army in 1923 with the rank of brigadier general to take up the appointment of Consul General in Persia. Upon his return to Moscow he worked in the Department of Foreign Trade and in 1929 was director-general of imports in Paris and Rome. In 1932 he moved to Brussels and the following year headed an official delegation to Warsaw. He was then made president of the Auto-Moto-Export Trust, 'tangled deep in the red tape of Soviet bureaucratization', controlling the export of all Soviet cars and aircraft, and in December 1935 was sent as a diplomat to the Soviet legation in Athens with the rank of first secretary.

During a routine visit to Moscow in December 1936, in the midst of Stalin's notorious show trails, Barmine learned that many of his friends had been arrested, and by the time he returned to Athens more of his colleagues and superiors had disappeared in the purges. Fearful that his relationship with Mari Pavlides, the Greek architect who was his fiancée, would place him under suspicion, he resigned his post and fled to Paris. In 1938 he published his first book in London, *Memoirs of a Soviet Diplomat: Twenty Years in the Service of the USSR*.

Barmine joined the US Army during the war as a private soldier and was later commissioned and transferred to the Office of Strategic Services as a linguist. In 1944 he was dismissed for having written an article in *Reader's Digest* without first having submitted it for approval. He headed the Russian section of the Voice of America radio station for much of the postwar period and his autobiography, *One Who Survived: The Life Story of a Russian under the Soviets*, was published in 1945. The single VENONA reference to Barmine is contained in a telegram from Moscow to New York, dated 3 March 1945, coinciding with the book's release:

> [75 groups unrecoverable] title 'One Who Survived'. We are very interested in the content of the book, where the manuscript is, how many copies there are, who is the publisher, where it will be published, how one might prevent the publication of the book, whether it is possible to pinch the manuscript. Deal with the affair through the newspaper so that the desire to examine [4 groups unrecovered]. The apparatus must not know about their investigation. Telegraph a detailed reply urgently.

Clearly the Soviets were much embarrassed by the damaging disclosures made by Kravchenko and Barmine, but the Russian émigré community as often as not provided the NKVD with a plentiful supply of willing agents. One such 'volunteer' was the Russian-born Hollywood-based independent movie producer Boris Morros, whose name also appears in two VENONA texts, and who was the subject of FBI surveillance when Vasili Zubilin, the man believed to be the Soviet illegal *rezident* in New York, was spotted holding a clandestine meeting with him in March 1947. When interviewed, Morros admitted that he had been recruited by Zubilin in 1936, when he had known Zubilin not as a Soviet diplomat but as an Amtorg official named Edward J. Herbert. Morros explained that 'Herbert' had persuaded him to provide authentic Paramount Studios cover as a movie talent scout for Herbert so he could travel freely in Nazi Germany. In return, Boris Morros's two brothers, who had been in danger of being prosecuted, were freed by the Soviet authorities and his father had been allowed to emigrate, arriving in the USA from Moscow in January 1943. It was at a rendezvous soon after this that the FBI had first latched on to Boris.

According to Morros, Zubilin had operated in the USA as an illegal for several years before his official arrival in San Francisco with diplomatic status in December 1941. After his father's release, Boris had agreed to allow his independent movie production company to be used by Zubilin's organization, and it had been financed by Alfred Stern, a wealthy Soviet sympathizer from a Fargo, North Dakota, banking family. Educated at Harvard, Stern had first married the daughter of the Chicago merchant baron Julius Rosenwald, and reputedly had been paid $1 million to divorce her. His second wife, Martha Dodd, was the daughter of Roosevelt's ambassador in Berlin, and equally committed to the Party. Apart from supporting the CPUSA and Morros, Stern's only other interest was psychotherapy; he was head of the Chicago Psychoanalytical Institute. Boris Morros was also assigned a partner, Jack Soble, a Lithuanian by birth who had a degree in economics from Leipzig University and who operated in Germany under journalistic cover until he had been withdrawn to Moscow in 1940. His father had once owned a bristle factory near Chantilly, in France, and, according to Morros, Soble

> held the rank of colonel, at least he was permitted to travel as a Russian Army colonel while in Europe, which is not always the same thing. Later he told me that he had handled several millions of dollars while working as a secret agent in the Balkans, and in Spain during the Spanish Civil War. He also had worked as a newspaper reporter in Hitler's Germany, while pursuing his dangerous undercover recruiting activities in that police state.

Jane Foster, who later complained that she had lent Soble money which had never been repaid, remembered him as 'a good-looking bear of a man'.

Soble was allowed to leave Russia for Japan, just before the Second World War broke out, with his whole family: wife, child, father, mother, sister and two brothers. I can only suppose with hindsight that the reason for such an unusual favour was that he had promised to work for the Russian underground. He had then made his way to the United States and, after five years there, had taken out American citizenship.

Officially his occupation in America, while his naturalization application was being processed, was that of manager of the S & V Cafeteria in Manhattan, ostensibly run by his brother-in-law, Arnold Wolston. In reality Soble (codenamed ABRAM), his wife Myra and his brother Dr Robert A. Soble were key illegals, supervising a network of other agents in Europe. A VENONA text from Vassili Zubilin in New York dated 24 June 1943 showed Soble was receiving financial support from the *rezidentura*:

> In January of this year we received in the 'LAND' [Canada] from '[1 group unrecovered]' five thousand Canadian dollars of his own for the conveyance to TYRE [New York] by diplomatic post. The money was handed over to KLIM who sent us one thousand US dollars and promised to send on the rest later. Now KLIM says he is spending the money, told you about this and can give us no more. Since ABRAM [Jack Soble] needs the money please send urgently 3,900 Canadian dollars in order to settle with ABRAM.

Soon afterwards, on 6 July, Zubilin replied to what had evidently been a query from Moscow about Soble's money, which had been routed via KLIM in Canada to Mikhail A. Shalyapin, a clerk in the New York consulate, and one of the *rezident*'s subordinates:

> Your No. 2088. ABRAM had no liaison with our worker in the 'LAND' [Canada]. He handed over the money to STOCK [Mikhail Shalyapin] who [48 groups unrecoverable] [9 groups unrecovered]

A further related text, sent almost a year later, on 5 May 1944, revealed that Soble's business partner, Sam Appel, was not entirely honest, and that the NKVD had provided the original capital:

> In mail No. 2 we informed you that cover had been fixed up for ABRAM. He [2 groups unrecovered] directly to set up the cafeteria. For this we gave him the authorized advance of

The Émigrés

2,000. ABRAM's partner in the cafeteria, a certain APPEL, had several relatives in the business and ABRAM came to suspect that APPEL was stealing a valuable business from him. To improve control and expand the business, he decided to run the cafeteria himself. [42 groups unrecovered] APPEL [79 groups unrecovered] dollars. [9 groups unrecoverable]

The final VENONA reference to Soble is from Apresyan, dated 12 October 1944, which was largely unrecoverable:

[64 groups unrecoverable] ABRAM's [Jack Soble] personal responsibility. You have already been advised of our views of putting KANT [Mark Zborowski] in the hands of a worker of the OFFICE [*rezidentura*]

Among Soble's network were two ardent CPUSA members, George Zlatovski, a former US Army intelligence officer, and his wife Jane Foster. A naturalized US citizen originally from Kiev who had come to America with her parents as a child, Zlatovski had fought with the Abraham Lincoln Brigade during the Spanish Civil War and had served in the US Army in Austria until 1948. Jane Foster had joined OSS in December 1943 as an expert on Indonesia, having lived in Java for four years before the war, and was strongly suspected of having passed OSS secrets to her future husband while based in Salzburg in 1947. As we shall see, she made appearances in VENONA texts, codenamed SLANG (see Chapter XI).

The first VENONA reference to Morros was dated 27 December 1944, in which Stepan Apresyan identified him as FROST (which is 'morros' in Russian):

ALBERT [Iskhak Akhmerov] sent a confidential memorandum from LOUIS [Alfred K. Stern] which was handed over to ALBERT through FROST's wife. LOUIS is complaining about FROST and emphasizes that unless prompt drastic measures of reorganization are taken the whole business is doomed to failure. To the memorandum are attached a series of corroborating documents. Advise whether to telegraph the contents of the memorandum in more detail and what instructions to give ALBERT. Take into account that I am not abreast of the scheme.

2. FROST received a letter from SKRIB [unidentified] from ALASKA in which he says 'Ivory is cheap, if you want to take it I can get it.' In FROST's opinion this means that SKRIB is ready to work if we want. Telegraph instructions.

On 4 January 1945 Apresyan elaborated on the critique he had received from Stern about Morros:

> Further to No. 2. Here is the gist of the enclosure to LOUIS's [Alfred K. Stern] memorandum:
> 1. In 'Memoranda on Conversations' LOUIS sets out the reactions to FROST of various persons with whom he and FROST came in contact. Opinions agree that FROST is not running the business competently, that he makes many empty promises, that he does not listen to advice and that he over-estimates his capabilities.
> 2. In 'Summary Report' LOUIS reports about the various steps in the development of the company and FROST's mistakes which were connected with them. He considers it necessary soon to reorganize the company by setting up the following departments (in order of importance):
>> 1. Production. 2. Selection of music to publish, of the artists and gramophone recordings. 3. Promotion. 4. Distribution
>
> Except for FROST LOUIS considers that none of the present personnel is adequate to deal with the tasks which confront each of these departments. In his opinion FROST should concentrate his attention on the problems of the second department; LOUIS himself, not knowing the technology of production, undertakes to head distribution. For promoting the products, ability of high order is required. At present the company is failing to deal with the problem of production and this means that business is at a standstill. In this area is needed a specialist who could surround himself with experienced sound recorders, chemists and machine experts and who would know the market.
> PART II He and 4 qualified workers could solve the personnel problem. He [68 groups unrecoverable] 'Chronological Report for 1944' LOUIS describes the activities of the company.

The Émigrés

4 and 5. Magazine clippings and copies of postal and telegraphic correspondence on company business.

Dr Robert Soble also appeared in the VENONA traffic, codenamed ROMAN, and in the first occurrence, dated 9 July 1943, it seems he was acting as a talent-spotter for Pavel Klarin and his brother's network:

> In post No. 3 of this year we reported on an acquaintance of ROMAN, Professor [deleted]. According to ROMAN's information [deleted] is a Jew, active in public life, a rich man [20 groups unrecovered] contacts in medical and politico-social circles in the COUNTRY [USA] [30 groups unrecovered], drugs, etc. The end of the war. [55 groups unrecoverable] [deleted] [3 groups unrecovered] us help presumably he is in a position to help the advancement of people who are useful to us in government establishments which are of interest to us. He can be used for a cover for illegal [1 group unrecovered], [2 groups unrecovered] other countries, [1 group unrecovered], participation in our operational enterprises etc. [1 group unrecovered] T is a [1 group unrecovered] man for us please urgently check on him and sanction him being signed on.

Robert Soble may also have experienced difficulty with his handlers, judging by his message from New York dated 23 September 1944 which mentions his brother Jack, codenamed ABRAM:

> ROMAN who is in touch with SULLEN [Viktor Kirilov] refuses to go into [4 groups unrecovered] meeting with '[1 group unrecovered]' [33 groups unrecovered] meeting with NAZAR [Stepan N. Shundenko]. Concerning [4 groups unrecovered] U. We will advise further. Telegraph consent.

This was followed by the news that the United Nations Relief and Rehabilitation Administration (UNRRA), for whom Dr Soble worked, intended to post him abroad:

> 1. The SHELTER [UNRRA] is proposing to ROMAN [Robert Soble] to send him to EUROPE (presumably the Near East) on duty as a doctor. Put us in the picture about your opinion

of such personnel. We will advise in more detail on receipt of your reply.
2. In the line of the PLANT [Soviet consulate general] a certain PADVA (or PADUA) has applied to NAZAR [Stepan N. Shundenko] to help his wife to get in touch with LUKA's [Pavel Klarin] successor as she has interesting materials. However [1 group unrecovered] liaison with her [1 group garbled] [10 groups unrecovered]

A short VENONA text from Stepan Apresyan dated 19 December 1944 suggested that Robert Soble was receiving financial support amounting to nearly $300 a month, apparently supplied by Zoya Semenovna Myakotina, a typist based at the Soviet consulate general who was married to Mikhail Shalyapin:

> According to ROMAN's [Robert Soble] assertion his group did not receive maintenance for August amounting to 290. LINA [Zoya Semenovna Myakotina] [3 groups unrecovered] for this sum. Please get an explanation from her.

Soble's status as an important and trusted Soviet spy is confirmed by a VENONA text from Pravdin dated 25 May 1945 in which the New York *rezidentura* made arrangements for him to take over control of agents penetrating the Trotskyite Socialist Workers Party, including Robert Owen Menaker:

> Your No. 3396. On 29th May CZECH [Robert O. Menaker] will complete the transfer to ROMAN [Robert Soble] of the PROBATIONERS [agents] dealing with the POLECATS [Trotskyites] and RATS [Jews]. On 1st June in accordance with the understanding with VADIM [Anatoli Gromov], CZECH will be handed over by NAZAR [Stepan N. Shundenko] to VADIM in TYRE [Washington DC].

After a decade of continuous surveillance the FBI arrested the Sobles in 1957, together with Jack's successor as controller, Jacob Albam. Testimony from Morros, who revealed his role as a double agent in his memoirs *My Ten Years as a Counterspy*, released in 1959, ensured convictions for Albam and the Sobles, but the Zlatovskys resisted attempts to extradite them from France, while the others identified by Morros also remained out of reach. Albam was sen-

The Émigrés

tenced to five and a half years' imprisonment, which was subsequently reduced to five in exchange for his cooperation with the FBI.

Alfred and Martha Stern, both wealthy Soviet sympathizers, were indicted but moved to Mexico and then used Paraguayan passports to travel to Prague. Suffering from cancer, Dr Soble disappeared to Israel in 1962 when the Supreme Court rejected his appeal against a life sentence, and in September 1962 he committed suicide in London soon after he had been deported from Tel Aviv. His first attempt, on the plane to England, failed, but a second, when his plea for political asylum had been rejected by the British authorities, was successful.

Under interrogation Jack Soble admitted his espionage and as well as providing evidence against his brother Robert, he implicated Martha Stern, neé Dodd, whom he claimed had spied as a Soviet agent in her father's embassy when he had been the US Ambassador in Berlin for four years before the war. Soble, who was sentenced to seven years' imprisonment in September 1957, and later tried to commit suicide in the Lewisburg Federal Penitentiary, also identified one of his Soviet handlers in Paris as Pavel S. Kuznetsov, a KGB officer who had since been compromised in an espionage case which occurred in London in June 1952. The Sterns remained in Czechoslovakia until 1979 when they made a successful application to have their indictment quashed. As the principal prosecution witness, Boris Morros, had succumbed to cancer in January 1961 in New York, all charges against them in the USA were dropped. As usual, the fact that all concerned had been compromised by VENONA remained a tightly-guarded secret.

VIII

British Security Coordination

IF ANY single Soviet attitude is revealed by VENONA, it is the insatiable Soviet appetite for information about secret organizations, and the discovery of a hitherto unknown branch of the ubiquitous British intelligence was made a priority. Like the rest of VENONA, the exact chronology of breaks into the original text is difficult to reconstruct, but the evidence of interest in British Security Coordination (BSC) is undeniable.

BSC was created in 1941 as a legal cover for the Secret Intelligence Service, the Security Service, Special Operations Executive and the Political Warfare Executive.[1] Headed by the Canadian industrialist (Sir) William Stephenson, it offered a wartime umbrella under which British clandestine organizations could work in the Western hemisphere. Although liaison with the FBI was uneasy at the best of times, as J. Edgar Hoover strongly disapproved of foreign espionage conducted on American soil, BSC stretched from its headquarters in New York to Canada, Bermuda, the Caribbean and Latin America through a network of imperial censorship offices (to screen the mails), defence security officers (for MI5) and passport control officers (for SIS). The energetic, diminutive Stephenson had been appointed in 1941 by SIS's chief, Stewart Menzies, and although some accounts of his wartime role have exaggerated his importance, BSC constructed an impressive security apparatus in the Americas and waged an espionage and propaganda offensive against the Axis enemy. Among its many tasks was the recruitment of Yugoslav migrants in Canada who would be suitable for despatch back into their home country by SOE, and the creation of a propaganda branch to counter the pro-Nazi publicity of the German Bund in the United States.

As well as being intrigued by BSC, the NKVD was keen to learn about British attitudes to Tito. The first VENONA reference to a source codenamed UCN/9 occurred on 29 April 1943 in a telegram from Vasili Zubilin in New York which disclosed:

> The basic points of a memorandum on the Yugoslav Partisans and on MIHAILOVIC [Chetnik leader] which was received by UCN/9 from the HUT [OSS] [5 groups unrecovered].

There was nothing in this rather mundane text to hint that UCN/9 was a particularly sensitive source, although he was attributing his information, concerning Yugoslav guerrilla movements, to the US Office of Strategic Services. As for 'UCN/9', this was an NSA abbreviation for unknown covername, meaning that the cryptographers had been unable to solve the whole of the original cryptonym. However, the next VENONA from Zubilin, dated 19 May, was to help MI5 identify UCN/9, even if his exact NKVD codename had remained elusive:

> UCN/9 reports: The local head of the BAR [British Intelligence], STEPHENSON, has returned here with BOAR [Winston Churchill]. He told UCN/9 that the main reason for BOAR's journey here was a growing movement in the ISLAND [England] for opening a second front in EUROPE and further because of the mood in the ISLAND [3 groups unrecovered]. The COUNTRY [America] has promised to supply the ISLAND with maritime resources [82 groups unrecovered] the BAR and [65 groups unrecoverable] PARK LONDON W.11. Password for liaison: 'Greetings from Molly'. UCN/9 told SOUND [Jacob Golos] that if he remained in the ISLAND he would help there [1 group unidentified] [6 groups unrecovered]

Another telegram, dated 29 May 1943 and also from Zubilin, was more significant.

> I know about UCN/9's departure. SOUND [Jacob Golos] [72 groups unrecovered] of 'the BAR' [British Intelligence] STEPHENSON used [33 groups unrecovered] However the measures 'the BAR' took were unacceptable to the 'KhATA' [FBI] which objects to the BAR's subversive activity here. The BAR had to give up its agent network here to the KhATA. As a result [1 group unrecovered] work was shrivelled up and the Military Attaché in the COUNTRY

[America] is returning to SIDON [London]. The BAR's fate in the future is unknown. [11 groups unrecovered] in SIDON about the work there he said nothing [7 groups unrecovered] on the acquisition of political information about the COUNTRY. UCN/9 does not know whether he will be connected in this work with the Embassy or [52 groups unrecovered] former head of the British [70 groups unrecovered] he considers that 25 persons are being used. CRUCIAN [Anton Ivancic] [9 groups unrecovered] sources. If it will be necessary CRUCIAN [3 groups unrecovered], then [54 groups unrecovered] on the street for some reason or other contact does not take place [27 groups unrecovered] on the street with her were arranged for 6th and 13th June.

At first glance it could be deduced that UCN/9, presumably one of the agents recruited by Jacob Golos, had recently left New York, probably for London, and arrangements had been made to resume contact upon his arrival in June. However, on 21 June Pavel Klarin, the vice-consul in New York claimed:

The organization 'British Security Coordination' is not known to us. We have taken steps to find out what it is. We will report the result in the next few days. We know Aleksandr HALPERN. We presume that it is he who is meant. HALPERN has been reported on repeatedly by MARS [Vasili Sukhomlin], CAVALRYMAN [Sergei Kurnakov], OSIPOV [Prince Nikolai Orlov], UCN/9, SERES [Dr Ivan Subasic], KOLO [Sava S. Kosanovic] and an agent [12 groups unrecovered] see paragraph [4 groups unrecovered] 283 and 355 [53 groups unrecovered] KERENSKY was [1 group unrecovered] Council of Ministers [1 group unrecovered] October Revolution fled to England [11 groups unrecovered] his wife Salome [23 groups unrecovered] HALPERN is one of the heads of the British COMPETITORS [Intelligence] here who for cover [1 group unrecovered] have a number of official posts in the INSTITUTE [4 groups unrecovered] post of assistant to STEPHENSON head of the BAR and organizer of the British Consulate. He apparently has contacts with the Labour Party. He is described as an enemy of the USSR. He has been admitted [4 groups unrecovered] with the

INSTITUTE in CARTHAGE [Washington DC] and TYRE [New York]. He is conducting active work among Russian and all European [1 group unrecovered] He maintains contact with [1 group unrecovered] ER, the Social-Revolutionary Victor Chernov and [5 groups unrecovered] DUBOIS, the Hungarian 'UCN/41'. OTTO HA ... [60 groups unrecoverable] [24 groups unrecovered] is described as a person hostile to us. Please sanction [24 groups unrecovered]

Apart from the inexplicable contradiction between Zubilin's obvious knowledge of BSC and Klarin's apparent ignorance only a month later, the text suggests that Alexander Halpern, who was then head of the Minorities Branch of British Security Coordination, had been the subject of considerable NKVD interest. This, of course, was not surprising, considering that the elderly White Russian had been a member of the Duma before the Revolution, and had served as Kerensky's private secretary. However, the lack of internal communication is evident, for the very next day Zubilin revealed the existence of another Soviet source inside BSC.

HAVRE reports that 'British Security Coordination' is a British intelligence organization [13 groups unrecovered] with the BAR. (This is evidently UCN/9's go-between, whose name he did not give us). HALPERN is in fact concerned with this organization. He [16 groups unrecovered] HALPERN works chiefly on questions [2 groups unrecovered]
2. In connection with the processing of OFFICER [Jan Fierlinger] [1 group unrecovered] ER, I [3 groups unrecovered]

There was no clue to HAVRE's identity, although the deliberate excision of his name from the relevant VENONA footnote suggests that it is known to the FBI. Certainly OFFICER was identified as Captain Jan Fierlinger, then assigned to the Czech consulate in New York as an information officer, and in this context (and seven other VENONA texts) a definite Soviet spy run by Vladimir Pravdin. As for UCN/9, he evidently returned to New York later in 1943, for Zubilin reported on 2 September:

UCN/9 returned to the ISLAND [England] [141 groups unrecoverable] [25 groups unrecovered] SOUND [Jacob Golos]

> says that after his trip to the ISLAND, UCN/9 has become [6 groups unrecovered]. In his opinion [5 groups unrecovered] will be the ISLAND and the COUNTRY [America] will be its 'errand boy'. At the first meeting with SOUND UCN/9 talked not [14 groups unrecovered] meeting handed over to SOUND 3 documents [4 groups unrecovered] to you by postal despatch No. 8. SOUND [3 groups unrecovered] very carefully, trying to avoid serious clashes and is gradually drawing him into the work. UCN/9 asked SOUND to introduce him to HELMSMAN [Earl Browder] for a chat on [4 groups unrecovered]. Considering that such a [1 group unrecovered] will help [1 group unrecovered] the work of UCN/9, SOUND without our [1 group unrecovered] UCN/9 returned to the ISLAND [141 groups unrecoverable] [25 groups unrecovered] promised him that he would arrange a meeting.

The last of the seven VENONA texts to mention UCN/9 was dated 8 September and addressed to Moscow:

> UCN/9 reported that the 'OVERSEAS NEWS AGENCY' [5 groups unrecovered] LANDAU [7 groups unrecovered] with many of whom he is personally acquainted. On the instructions of the British, LANDAU left for the COUNTRYSIDE [Mexico] to meet SEAL [unidentified], who [66 groups unrecovered]

The Jacob Landau referred to was the director of the Overseas News Agency (ONA), a subsidiary of the Jewish Telegraph Agency he had founded in the First World War, supported by newspaper subscriptions and wealthy private backers, among them the merchant banker Felix Warburg. With branches in Jerusalem, Warsaw, Berlin and Paris, having moved its headquarters from London to New York early in the war, the ONA became a commercial front for BSC's political warfare branch, distributing BSC-inspired propaganda across the globe. An early, enthusiastic supporter of the British cause against the Axis, Landau was an effective BSC agent and did indeed spend much of October and November 1943 in Mexico City, where he held several meetings with the Soviet ambassador Konstantin A. Umansky, a diplomat known on the Mexico City and San Francisco channels by the codename REDAKTOR. Even though this particular text is far from complete, it is reasonably clear that UCN/9 was telling the Soviets about ONA's true status, and explaining Landau's mission for BSC to Mexico, a topic that must have been of considerable interest given Umansky's involvement.

Although neither this nor the previous six VENONA texts directly identified the spy, MI5 had little difficulty in putting a name to UCN/9, who had been denounced by Elizabeth Bentley as one of her lover Jacob Golos's agents. Cedric Belfrage was a well-known journalist who had joined BSC in December 1941, and his departure to London on 27 May 1943 neatly coincided with Zubilin's discussion of UCN/9's reference to the event two days later. There is a further clue to be spotted in UCN/9's recognition signal in London, concerning 'Molly', which happened to be the Christian name of Belfrage's wife, herself the author of a cookery book.

According to Elizabeth Bentley, Belfrage 'was an extremely odd character, and rather difficult to deal with. Although passionately devoted to the cause, he still considered himself a patriotic Britisher, and hence he would give us no information that showed up England's mistakes or tended to make her a laughing-stock. In addition, he was very nervous at what he was doing, and Yasha [Jacob Golos] had all he could do to keep him in line.'

> Cedric Belfrage had been a Party member in Britain and after coming to this country got in touch with V. J. Jerome, who in turn put Belfrage in contact with Yasha. For some time Cedric had been turning over to us extremely valuable information from the files of the British Intelligence Service, most of which I saw before it was relayed on to the Russians. I remember one large volume of instructions to agents of British Intelligence which Yasha thought so good that we kept a copy of it in the safe at World Tourists, reading it occasionally for hints on undercover work. It was a most thorough manual: it gave minute directions on how to conduct a surveillance and how to avoid being tailed, and it even had a section on 'breaking and entering which had been patriotically contributed by the burglars of Great Britain'. As I looked through it I realized why the British Intelligence had long been known as a very excellent one. Obviously they knew their business from A to Z.

According to Bentley, Belfrage's espionage had come to an abrupt conclusion in the autumn of 1943 when he was compromised inadvertently by Earl Browder. Apparently Golos had shown some of Belfrage's material to Browder who had used some of it as the basis of an article in *The Protestant,* a CPUSA-controlled publication. Terrified that SIS might trace the source of the leak, Belfrage had broken off contact with Golos. Significantly, VENONA contained no further references to a source codenamed UCN/9 after September 1943.

IX

CLEVER GIRL

WHILE THE FBI and MI5 pursued every lead that held even the slightest promise of identifying one of the VENONA cryptonyms, they were heavily dependent upon 'collateral' or external evidence to support their inquiries. Of that outside evidence, the very best was provided by Elizabeth Bentley in the autumn of 1945, almost simultaneously with the defection of Igor Gouzenko in Canada. However, while the Soviets became aware almost immediately of the cipher-clerk's disappearance (although no public statements were made for a further five months), they did not realize that Bentley had defected until they detected FBI surveillance on those she had identified as agents recruited or run by her charismatic lover, Jacob Golos.

A dedicated Marxist, a member of the CPUSA's Central Control Commission and once a friend of Lenin's, Golos's real name was Jacob Rasin, and he was well-known to the FBI, although some aspects of his extraordinary career remained concealed until after his death. He had been born into a well-off Jewish family in the Ukraine and had been imprisoned in Ekaterinoslav for his revolutionary activities, and in Siberia. He had escaped to China, found a ship to Japan, and was eventually reunited with his family in California in 1908. Later he acquired US citizenship and attended Columbia University's medical school. He did not graduate, but instead became a printer and chemist. After the Revolution he had returned to Russia, and managed a mine before joining the GPU (NKVD) which dispatched him to New York. There he had used the name Golos ('voice' in Russian) to publish articles in *Novy Mir*, New York's Communist Russian newspaper, and then had run World Tourists Inc., a travel agency set up in 1927 and funded by the CPUSA, which was to become the subject of an intensive FBI investigation that led to Earl Browder being imprisoned on passport fraud charges in 1940. Evidence seized in a Department of Justice raid on World

Tourists, in which Golos was the sole stockholder, proved that Browder had travelled abroad on forged documents, and while he served a prison term in the Atlanta Federal Penitentiary, Golos was cross-examined about his failure to register as a foreign agent. It was while he was working at World Tourists that he met and cultivated Bentley, a Vassar graduate who had drifted into Communism from the anti-fascist movement.

Originally from Rochester, New York, Elizabeth Bentley had joined the Columbia University branch of the CPUSA in March 1935 while completing her Master's degree in Italian and French. By then she had visited Europe three times, studied at the University of Florence on a scholarship and taken a summer course at the University of Perugia. After her graduation she worked briefly as a shop assistant at Macy's department store, at an Amtorg summer school for Russian children, for the New York City Home Relief Bureau, and on Governor Dewey's election campaign committee. She encountered Jacob Golos in October 1938, having been interviewed at the CPUSA headquarters by Ferruccio Marini, a senior Party functionary who was later to edit the Communist *Unita del Popolo* in Italy. Marini used his Party workname, 'F. Brown', and prepared Bentley for underground work on behalf of the Comintern against the fascists, by introducing her to Golos. Although married to Celia, a fellow student at Colombia, Golos had despatched her to Moscow, together with their son Milton in the mid-1930s, and since had lived with his mistress, Caroline Klein, in New York. His only remaining family member in America was his sister, who had married an American, Edward Emmett, and lived in the Bronx.

At first Bentley had thought Golos unimpressive, 'rather colorless and shabby – a little man in a battered brown hat, nondescript suit and well-worn brown shoes', but she was soon to realize that she had underestimated him:

> his mind was quick, keen, incisive. Also I revised my first impression on his appearance, which was decidedly not colorless. Although short of stature, he was powerfully built with a large head, very broad shoulders and strong square hands. His eyes were startlingly blue, his hair bright red, and I was intrigued by the fact that his mouth was very much like my mother's.

By the time he succumbed to heart failure in November 1943, Golos had trained Bentley as a skilful courier, become her lover, and bequeathed to her the role of controller for a network that was concentrated in Washington DC. Among his many agents were Nathan Gregory Silvermaster, a Russian emigrant working in the Farm Security Administration, his wife Helen (see Chapter XII), and several highly-placed sub-agents, including the Assistant Secretary of the Treasury, Harry Dexter White, and the White House counsellor Lauchlin B. Currie. Another key figure was Victor Perlo of the War Production Board, and Major Duncan Lee, an aide to General Donovan of the Office of Strategic Services (OSS). Most had strong CPUSA connections, as did Robert T. Miller, editor of the *Hemisphere*, a pro-Communist newsletter covering political developments in Latin America. Although well-known as a Party member, Miller was persuaded by Golos to sell the *Hemisphere* and take a job as head of the political research division in Washington DC for the Coordinator of Inter-American Affairs (CIAA), then headed by Nelson Rockefeller. When the CIAA was absorbed into the State Department, Miller remained on its staff, and the organization was known in the VENONA traffic by the codename CABARET. According to Bentley, the other Soviet spies in the CIAA were Joseph Gregg, who had fought in the Spanish Civil War, the journalist Bernard Redmont and William Z. Park.

Bentley was prompted to switch sides for a variety of motives, not all of which she subsequently set out in her memoirs, *Out of Bondage* (1951), an account of her love for Golos, her enchantment with the Party and finally her disaffection. Her critics suggested that when Louis Budenz, formerly the editor of the *Daily Worker*, publicly renounced Communism and left the CPUSA, she would have known that it would have been only a matter of time before the FBI called on her, so she took the initiative. Budenz had been close to Golos and had acted as an intermediary between Bentley and an OSS source, the Communist novelist Louis Adamic who worked as an adviser regarding his native Yugoslavia. Whatever her motives, she quickly followed Budenz to the FBI, making her initial tentative approach in New Haven in August 1945, and her value to the Bureau was to act as a human encyclopedia, putting names and faces to members of the network. After Golos's death she had been supervised by a man she knew as 'Jack', who turned out to be Joseph

Katz, and he had introduced her to 'Al' in early November 1944, whom she recognized from the FBI's collection of surveillance photographs as Anatoli Gromov, the *rezident* at the Soviet embassy in Washington DC who had taken up his post in September 1944. According to collateral from MI5 and defector information provided by Piotr Deriabin and Yuri Rastvorov, Gromov's real name was Gorsky, and he had served as acting *rezident* in London between 1938 and February 1940, and then as *rezident* from December 1940 to 1943 when he had been recalled to Moscow for reassignment, presumably following Donald Maclean to the United States. He was to remain in Washington DC until January 1946. He next turned up in Tokyo as head of the local Soviet Trade Delegation.

Early in 1945 Bentley had been eased out of the NKVD's network and she had resented the loss of her dual role of courier and controller. Her disaffection was complete by the time she approached the FBI again, this time in New York in October. The FBI initially suggested she try and rejoin the organization by re-establishing contact with Gromov. The first interview at which the topic of Soviet espionage was raised took place with Special Agent Edward J. Buckley on 7 November 1945, but she suspected that the FBI had been present when she had last met Gromov, on 17 October. A further meeting took place at Gugganti's restaurant in New York on 21 November 1945, under heavy FBI surveillance, but the wily *rezident* was unwilling to let her return. Frustrated in her attempt to become a double agent, she signed a lengthy statement, covering 113 pages, on 30 November, and was given the FBI codename GREGORY. Eventually she provided the FBI with enough information to fill nearly half a million pages in 175 volumes, and identified more than eighty Soviet espionage suspects, including twenty-seven in the administration, but was unaware that her knowledge was being used to develop the leads embedded in VENONA. Although she received a clandestine call to a rendezvous with Gromov in March 1946, at Bickford's restaurant, he failed to turn up, and she had no further contact with the Soviets.

Bentley herself appeared in several VENONA texts as CLEVER GIRL and then MYRNA, although, of course, she was never aware of her NKVD codenames. However, she came close to learning about CLEVER GIRL, thanks to a slip made by her first Soviet contact, an inexperienced handler whom she knew as 'John'. 'He was to know me only as Miss Wise (a translation of the Russian word *umnitsa*, which means, roughly, "smart gal"). For my part, I was to know nothing about him except his code name, which was John.' In fact UMNITSA was the cryptonym which concealed her true identity in the NKVD's secret communications, so the covername of 'Miss Wise' was an unusual and uncharacteristic breach of Soviet security. Initially Bentley was unimpressed by 'John', who made a poor impression as

> a thin, pale, blond young man of about my height, who was dressed in badly fitting clothes of obviously European make. Indubitably he had not been in this country very long. He had that half-starved look so characteristic of new Soviet arrivals, his English was so meager that I had difficulty in understanding him, and he displayed an astounding ignorance of American life. Indeed, I remember with some amusement his stubborn and unshakeable belief that American workers were so terrorized by the police that they had to carry revolvers to the polls on election day. Evidently, too, he had not been too well briefed on undercover work in the United States.

Later, Bentley was to identify John from the FBI's collection of surveillance film as Anatoli Yakovlev, who worked at the Soviet consulate in New York under the alias Yatskov. He was to develop into a shrewd operator, and appear in the VENONA texts as ALEKSEI.

Chronologically, the first VENONA to mention Elizabeth Bentley was a telegram dated 11 December 1943 from Vasili Zubilin in New York, which was brief because of fragmentation and simply showed her link with Earl Browder: 'CLEVER GIRL has twice seen HELMSMAN [Earl Browder] who [65 groups unrecoverable] more precise picture. We will advise the results.' This was followed the same day by 'On 6th December CLEVER GIRL advised that [69 groups unrecoverable]'.

The next VENONA, a very fragmented text dated 23 February 1944 from New York, established CLEVER GIRL as an important intermediary between the *rezidentura* and the extensive organization led by Nathan Gregory Silvermaster in Washington DC (see Chapter XII):

> In reply to No. 626. The PAL/POLO [Nathan Silvermaster/ William Ludwig Ullman] material goes through CLEVER GIRL. ALBERT [Iskhak Akhmerov] [15 groups unrecovered] SHAH [Konstantin Shabanov]. Most of the material received which has been processed by ALBERT [22 groups unrecoverable] at the end of May compelled to [72 groups unrecovered] [18 groups unrecoverable]

This single text served to confirm Bentley's credentials as an important Soviet spy, and showed that her activities were supervised on the Soviet side by Iskhak Akhmerov, a man she knew simply as 'Bill'. She had been introduced to him over dinner soon after Golos's death by her temporary contact Helen Lowry, whom she knew as 'Catherine', and described him as having 'deep-set eyes like round shoe buttons, his high Slavic cheekbones, his straight dark hair that was only kept from falling over one eye by his hat. Certainly he must have spent plenty of money on that tailor-made suit and matching accessories.' He was fond of caviar and lobster and whenever they met he tended to order the most expensive items on the menu. He was, nevertheless, 'a tough character' with 'an undercurrent of menace in his voice'. In fact Akhmerov was a senior NKVD officer, and was married to Helen Lowry, Earl Browder's niece.

On 29 April 1944 Akhmerov submitted a report to Moscow on Bentley which gives a good indication of how his relations with her had deteriorated since their first meeting six months earlier, and his fear that she wished to monopolize the organization that had been built so carefully by Golos:

> On 27th April CLEVER GIRL reported as follows:
> After SOUND's [Jacob Golos] death, HELMSMAN [Earl Browder] [15 groups unrecovered] on HELMSMAN's instructions, SOUND [41 groups unrecovered]. PAL [Nathan Silvermaster] used to meet HELMSMAN before meeting me. In future if HELMSMAN permits my meeting with PAL [4 groups unrecovered] HELMSMAN. Even SOUND used not to meet PAL more often than once in six months.
> Possibly she is making this up and exaggerating. At least [3 groups unrecovered] exclusive control of the PROBATIONERS [agents] and expressed an unreasoning fear that we will contact them direct. It is essential that either MAXIM [Vasili

Zubilin] or I should see HELMSMAN and come to an agreement that the whole group and CLEVER GIRL [15 groups unrecovered] I recommend asking [45 groups unrecovered] AMT [John Abt] [7 groups unrecovered] group:- [Charles] KRAMER [Victor] PERLO, [Charles] PLATO, [Harold] GLASSER, Edward FITZGERALD and others in a group of 7 or 8 FELLOWCOUNTRYMEN [Party members]. [20 groups unrecovered] AMT and PERLO [29 groups unrecoverable] NEIGHBOURS [GRU]. For more than a year MAXIM and I tried to get in touch with PERLO and PLATO. For some reason or other HELMSMAN did not come to the meeting and has just decided to put CLEVER GIRL in touch with the whole group. If we work with this group it will be necessary to remove her and [2 groups unrecovered]. Recently I met PERLO by chance in ARENA's [Mary Price] flat. For your information I have never met HELMSMAN [7 groups unrecovered]

This particular VENONA was of considerable significance because it appeared to confirm some of the personalities previously identified by Bentley to the FBI as her well-connected Communist agents who worked in the government: John Abt worked in the Congress, as did Charles Kramer who served on Senator Kilgore's committee and had worked in the Office of Price Administration; Victor Perlo was a statistician with the War Production Board, where Edward Fitzgerald and Henry Magdoff worked; Harold Glasser, Solomon Adler and William Taylor were in the Treasury Department; Charles Flato was a senior civil servant; Mary Wolfe Price was a veteran union activist then working for the political journalist Walter Lippmann. A further unidentified covername, STORM, was added to the FBI's inventory of the network from a text dated 13 May 1944 which Akhmerov sent to Moscow:

On HELMSMAN's [Earl Browder] instructions CLEVER GIRL [Elizabeth Bentley] contacted through AMT [John Abt] a new group in CARTHAGE [Washington DC] [53 groups unrecoverable] MAGDORF – KANT [Henry Magdoff]. GOOD GIRL's impressions: They are reliable FELLOWCOUNTRYMEN, politically highly mature; they want to help with information. They said that they had been neglected and no

> one had taken any interest in their potentialities [29 groups unrecoverable] STORM. RAIDER [Victor Perlo], PLUMB [Charles Kramer], TED [Edward Fitzgerald] and KANT will go to TYRE [New York] once every two weeks in turn. PLUMB and TED know PAL [Nathan Silvermaster]. We shall let you have identifying particulars later.

The inclusion of Magdoff was significant only in that this was the sole occasion in which his name appeared in a VENONA text, but it nevertheless tended to support Bentley's recollection that she had collected Party dues from him, and he had been a member of a group of Communist volunteers that had gathered around Perlo.

Control of this group, which had been considered highly productive by Golos, became a matter of contention for Bentley, who was determined to take over her late lover's role as case officer. A VENONA dated 11 July 1944 from New York elaborated on her bitter dispute with her Soviet controller, Iskhak Akhmerov, over his direct access to Nathan Silvermaster, into which Earl Browder had been reluctantly drawn:

> Your number 3038. By post No. 5 of 7th July there was sent to you a detailed communication of ALBERT [Iskhak Akhmerov] about CLEVER GIRL. [Elizabeth Bentley] Here are the contents:
> CLEVER GIRL is very much taking to heart the fact of ALBERT's direct contact with PAL [Nathan Silvermaster], evidently supposing that we do not trust her. She is offended at HELMSMAN [Earl Browder] for having consented to our liaison with PAL. ALBERT assumes CLEVER GIRL [20 groups unrecovered] [55 groups unrecoverable] [87 groups unrecovered]

Later the same month, on 28 July 1944, Stepan Apresyan telegraphed Moscow about a crisis that had arisen with Mary Price, a valued source and CPUSA member of long-standing. Once again, the issue at stake was Bentley's control over a useful source:

> Your No. 3028. Some weeks ago CLEVER GIRL told ALBERT [Iskhak Akhmerov] that HELMSMAN [Earl Browder] as a result of a conversation with DIR [Mary Price] had apparently decided that DIR must be withdrawn completely

from our work in order to employ her fully on FELLOWCOUNTRYMANLY [Party] work. In HELMSMAN's opinion DIR's nerves have been badly shaken and her health is poor, which renders her unsuitable for our work. In ALBERT's opinion it is possible to get HELMSMAN to change his opinion about the advisability of this decision which ALBERT suggests was made under pressure from CLEVER GIRL, who for some reason dislikes DIR. ALBERT has informed CLEVER GIRL that if DIR is really ill she will need rather to be withdrawn for a rest, but afterwards be used on liaison with a conspirative apartment etc. She has been working for a long time and has acquired considerable experience. ALBERT proposes that she should not be employed on active FELLOWCOUNTRYMANLY work. Telegraph your opinion.

Fedosimov's account coincides with what Elizabeth Bentley later told the FBI about Mary Price, for whom she had acted as a courier, collecting extracts from Lippmann's confidential office files from her Georgetown house. 'I would go to Washington once a month to pick up any material she had. She on her part would come up to New York once a month. Our travelling expenses would be paid by the Party. This meant that the information would be coming through every two weeks.' In fact Price could not take the strain, gave up her job in Washington and took an extended holiday in Mexico. Upon her return Bentley had argued that Price, who was turned down for a job by OSS in the autumn of 1943 because of her past Communist connections, should be dropped from the network and allowed to rejoin the Party openly, thereby provoking another furious disagreement. She also asserted that it had been the neurotic Mary Price who had enabled the NKVD to penetrate OSS by recruiting General Donovan's assistant, Major Duncan Lee.

A telegram from Moscow on 20 September 1944 served to confirm Bentley's links to two OSS officers, Donald Wheeler (IZRA) and Maurice Halperin (HARE), and showed the ease with which the Centre could monitor OSS's rather feeble attempts at counter-espionage. At this point Bentley's codename had become MYRNA:

> Reference No. 741. Try through KOCH [Duncan C. Lee] to obtain [8 groups unrecovered] tell MYRNA [Elizabeth

Bentley] temporarily to cease liaison with IZRA [Donald Wheeler] and HARE [Maurice Halperin]. In future liaison may be re-established only with our permission. Give KOCH the task of compiling a report on the Security Division of the HUT [OSS].

A Rhodes Scholar who had worked for General Donovan's law firm in New York before the war, Duncan Lee had been born in China to missionary parents and had joined the CPUSA soon after he had graduated from Yale. As Bentley recalled for the FBI: 'Although I succeeded in getting from him more than Mary [Price], he almost always gave it to me orally and rarely would he give me a document, although under pressure he would hand over scraps of paper on which he had written down important data.' As for Maurice Halperin, a senior figure in OSS's Latin America division, Bentley described him as 'a well-balanced, stable person, with a wife, two lovely children, and a happy home life; I don't believe there was a nerve in his body. Moreover, he had never been openly associated with the Communists.'

Three days later, on 23 September 1944, a text from New York confirmed Bentley's role as Lee's controller:

> No. 764. KOCH [Duncan Lee] advises that RADIO ANNOUNCER [General Donovan] will soon return and decide the question of his trip. The HUT [OSS] intends to send him to INDIA or CHINA for 5–6 months. From what MYRNA [Elizabeth Bentley] says KOCH agrees that we should get in touch with him there. We are giving MYRNA the task of getting exact data on when and where exactly KOCH is going and on what mission.

The last few VENONA texts relevant to Bentley include two of an administrative nature, the first appearing to be an unwise proposal to use World Tourists as a mail drop, which might have compromised her. This was a topic of a telegram sent to Moscow by Fedosimov on 30 November 1944, and copied to Gromov in Washington:

> Allen WARDWELL wrote a letter GRANDFATHER [Evgeni Kiselev] in which he asks for advice about the person in the USSR with whom an agreement should be made regarding the setting up of a parcels office in WASHINGTON, which is

being planned by WARDWELL's friend – John Rothschild. Inasmuch as ROTHSCHILD's plan directly threatens the existence of MYRNA's cover, we think it necessary through GRANDFATHER to advise WARDWELL to approach Comrade MIKOYAN direct (which is what he himself is contemplating doing) and for us to report to Comrade MIKOYAN that [3 groups unrecovered] the setting up of this office. Telegraph your decision. For the time being through GRANDFATHER we are answering WARDWELL that the question is being gone into and we will give an answer in a few days' time.

The final Bentley VENONA, sent from New York on 21 December 1944 and copied to Gromov in Washington DC, also referred to Bentley as MYRNA, and US Service & Shipping Corporation, for whom she worked, as 'MYRNA's firm':

The COMBINE [Foreign Trade Ministry] has already asked the FACTORY [Amtorg] three times about the expediency of continuing the contact with MYRNA's firm and at the same time proposes to recommend to the COMBINE other firms. In particular the COMBINE is interested to know whether one can have dealings with the Amalgamated Bank and the Francis Morris Corporation. In ANTON's line [Amtorg] the answer will be given that it is essential to continue the present contact with MYRNA's firm; however it should be borne in mind that eventual contracts between the COMBINE and other firms may require impossible conditions from MYRNA's firm [20 groups unrecoverable].

In all probability, Bentley had no knowledge of these events, nor played any direct part in the subject of the exchanges between New York and Moscow. Similarly, she was probably not consulted over this fragmented telegram, dated 25 March 1945, in which Moscow directed the New York *rezidentura* about Olga Khlopkova's link with Helen Lowry, which somehow involved two unidentified sources, codenamed ARTEM and BERG, and perhaps some unspecified intervention by the FBI.

Your No. 267. We sanction JULIA's [Olga Khlopkova] acquaintance with ELZA [Helen Lowry]. Conduct their meetings in the future [11 groups unrecovered] MYRNA by the KhATA [FBI] and [1 group unrecovered] intelligence service. To recruit ELZA for [3 groups unrecovered] if ever ARTEM [4 groups unrecovered] meeting with BERG which was set up by JULIA.

This was the last VENONA to mention Bentley, and in total the collection served to verify many of her claims, although of course the FBI was so reluctant to compromise the source that none of those who were the subject of Bentley's allegations was prosecuted for espionage. The sole exception was William W. Remington of the War Production Board who was convicted of perjury. Having graduated from Colombia in economics, Bill Remington joined the CPUSA and was recruited by Golos to provide classified aircraft production data until he joined US Naval Intelligence in September 1944.

> He was one of the most frightened people with whom I have ever had to deal. It was difficult to get him to bring out carbon copies of documents. Usually he would jot the information down on small scraps of paper, giving them to me furtively and with many admonitions about not letting them fall into the wrong hands.

As a consequence of Bentley's allegations, Remington resigned his naval commission in April 1947 and in January 1953 was sentenced to three years' imprisonment, having been convicted on two counts of perjury. Shortly before his release, he was murdered by another prisoner.

Bentley's appearance before the House Un-American Activities Committee prompted the former *Time* journalist Whittaker Chambers, who had confessed to having acted as a courier for a Soviet spy-ring, to give further testimony relating to Harry Dexter White, and to name Alger Hiss as an agent. Naturally, the accusation caused a sensation, and Hiss was eventually convicted of perjury, but the evidence contained in VENONA was never disclosed. It amounted to a single, damning text from Anatoli Gromov in Washington dated 30 March 1945:

> Further to our telegram No. 283. As a result of A's [Akhmerov] chat with ALES the following was being ascertained:

1. ALES had been working with the NEIGHBOURS [GRU] continuously since 1935.
2. For some years past he has been the leader of a small group of the NEIGHBOURS PROBATIONERS [GRU agents], for the most part consisting of his relations.
3. The group and ALES himself work on obtaining military information only. Material on the BANK [US State Department] allegedly interest the NEIGHBOURS very little and he does not produce them regularly.
4. All the last few years ALES has been working with PAUL who also meets other members of the group occasionally.
5. Recently ALES and his whole group were awarded Soviet decorations.
6. After the YALTA conference, when he had gone on to Moscow, a Soviet personage in a very responsible position (ALES gave to understand that it was Comrade VYSHINSKY) allegedly got in touch with ALES and at the behest of the Military NEIGHBOURS passed on to him their gratitude and so on.

As the Assistant Secretary of State who had attended the Yalta Conference as part of the US delegation, Hiss was the only person who fitted Gromov's profile of ALES. If made public, the description of him as a GRU agent of long-standing would have settled a controversy that, on the basis of Hiss's strenuous denials despite a perjury conviction, lasted for years.

Elizabeth Bentley's catalogue of accusations were attacked by almost everyone she named, and she endured a long campaign of personal vilification until her death in January 1963, at the age of fifty-five. Although she had no knowledge of VENONA, nor of its role in supporting her version of events, she did know that the US government had achieved some success in reading Soviet communications. Her original statement to the FBI, dated 30 November 1945, mentioned that she had relayed a message from Lauchlin Currie warning that the codes had been broken, but this passage was omitted from *Out of Bondage*. When, in 1953, Bentley wrote a six-part series of articles for the *New York Daily Mirror*, she included this item, together with the assertion that Silvermaster had been instructed by the NKVD to find out exactly which ciphers had been compromised.

X

SIMA

IN RETROSPECT, given the testimony of Elizabeth Bentley, and the hidden assistance of VENONA, it seems astonishing that more Soviet spies were not prosecuted. The explanation lies in the identity of a supremely well-placed spy, Judith Coplon, codenamed SIMA.

Once the FBI realized SIMA's identity, and the damage she had inflicted on the espionage investigations being conducted in Washington and New York, the decision was taken to arrest her, almost at any cost. What made VENONA's data on SIMA so fascinating was their comprehensive nature; from the moment SIMA had been spotted in New York as a potential recruit by a fellow civil servant working at the State Department, Flora Don Wovschin (ZORA), in December 1944, right through to the guidance given to her to infiltrate the section of the Justice Department in Washington DC which was of most interest to the NKVD.

Wovschin herself came from a strong Communist background, with both her mother, Maria Wicher (codenamed DAShA), and her stepfather, Enos R. Wicher (codenamed KIN), Russian immigrants, having been enrolled by the NKVD. Clearly, both knew about Flora's activities, for this is stated explicitly by Stepan Apresyan in a text dated 5 December 1944: 'DAShA knows about ZORA's work for us.'

There is also evidence that Enos Wicher, then a scientist working in the Wave Propagation Group at Colombia University's Division of War Research, was an active source, for when he was the subject of a routine security inquiry by the New York military authorities in July 1945, delving into his Party connections, it was reported ten days later by Vladimir S. Pravdin, operating under TASS press agency cover, in a two-part message to Moscow:

> At the regular meeting KIN [Enos Wicher] related the following. On 6th July his immediate superior, Professor ATTWOOD of Colombia University, summoned KIN and showed him a letter from the military COMPETITION [intelligence agency] signed by Captain F. W. Russell from District No. 1 [5 groups unrecoverable] Command, Security and Intelligence Division, 39 Whitehall Street [47 groups unrecoverable] KIN to fill out the enclosed questionnaire. In the questionnaire appeared KIN's surname and his supposed pseudonym (aliases) including 'BILL RAIN', KIN's covername when he was a party organizer in the State of WISCONSIN. Continuation follows.

Although this is the only reference to KIN, his stepdaughter was a significant figure who was adept at taking security precautions.

The first link between Wovschin and Coplon appears in the latter paragraph of a text dated 1 October 1944:

> [61 groups unrecoverable] had in all two very brief meetings with ZORA as a consequence of the tailing. Furthermore, fearing unpleasantness on the part of the KhATA [FBI] SIMA [Judith Coplon] is for the time being avoiding meetings with ZORA [Flora Wovschin] [4 groups unrecovered].

Three days later Apresyan asked Moscow for permission to change Wovschin's handler in New York, Viktor Kirilov (codenamed SULLEN), for Ivan Kamenev: 'Sanction ZORA's transfer from SULLEN who is unsuitable to CHEMIST.'

Whether this switch was the cause of Wovschin's disquiet is unknown, and there is nothing to explain why Kirilov was considered unsuitable. By the middle of the following month both Wovschin and Coplon were dissatisfied, and Nikolai Karpekov (URAL) had been appointed to take over as Wovschin's case officer, with a consultation planned with Stepan N. Shundenko (codenamed NAZAR). Apresyan reported to Moscow on 12 November:

> Before putting ZORA [Flora Wovschin] into URAL's hands (the transfer has been delayed because of the unfavourable election atmosphere) telegraph not later than the 15th November agreement to a personal conversation with her by

NAZAR upon my detailed instruction. This conversation I consider absolutely necessary for the following reasons:
1. ZORA's morale is extremely unsatisfactory.
2. Her communication that in her apartment are lying a lot of materials that she is supposed to turn over to us but up to now has not had an opportunity (the reasons she does not indicate).
3. SIMA is quite dissatisfied with the fact that she was promised a personal talk with our men and there has been no talk notwithstanding.
4. ZORA is asking for additional instructions about her and SIMA's conduct in relation to their work and personal connections.

I consider that URAL will not be able to cope with such a task all at once. I shall give ZORA instruction on the basis of a detailed memorandum which she has sent and which I shall send to you by the next regular post.

Poor relations between Wovschin and Coplon during the summer of 1944 may have been the reason for the crisis, for on 21 November Moscow was informed: 'SIMA in August this year [1 group unrecovered] wrote ZORA a penitent note.' In any event, Flora certainly met Shundenko, for Apresyan submitted a lengthy note of what had transpired to Moscow on 5 December 1944:

As a result of two detailed conversations with ZORA [Flora Wovschin] on such questions [4 groups unrecovered] NAZAR [Stepan Shundenko] arrived at the conviction that ZORA, despite her youth, is extremely serious, well developed and understands her tasks. [39 groups unrecoverable] [1 word unrecovered] only rarely meeting her personally. Skilled leadership is all the more important now that through ZORA we are processing and are counting on drawing into active work SIMA and Marion DAVIS (henceforth LOU). To orient ZORA on transferring to the BANK [US State Department], KhUTOR [Economic Administration], HUT [OSS] or another analogous establishment (the RADIO STATION [US Office of War Information], according to what she says is beginning to wind up its work and in half a year will probably cease independent existence). The majority of the materials that

ZORA turned over to us earlier were not of interest because ZORA's subject in the RADIO STATION is poor in opportunities for our line.

3. The time is ripe for signing on SIMA; after careful preparation through NAZAR to entrust the carrying out of it to ZORA. ZORA enjoys the full confidence of SIMA on whose readiness to work if only she is told whither her materials are going ZORA casts no doubt (SIMA guesses whither).

4. To entrust to ZORA after LOU gets work of interest to us (ZORA all the time is aiming LOU at this) the gradual preparation of LOU's signing on.

5. To decide the question of direct liaison between the OFFICE [*rezidentura*] and SIMA and LOU (by-passing ZORA) depending on the outcome of the two signings on.

6. Inasmuch as ZORA's mother (DAShA) [Maria Wicher] and stepfather's [Enos Wicher] reactions to their compulsory isolation from the progressive movement are having a bad effect on ZORA's own mood, to entrust BECK [Sergei Kurnakov] with carrying in a cautious manner a special explanatory conversation with them. DAShA knows about ZORA's work for us.

We have taken measures for the rapid unburdening of ZORA of the materials which have accumulated. In case of emergency arrangements have been made at her request for her to get in touch with the OFFICE herself.

This text, the longest recovered linking Wovschin to Coplon, also showed that the former was acting as a group leader, recruiting both Coplon and Marion Davis Berdecio, codenamed LOU, who worked at the US embassy in Mexico City.

On 31 December 1944 Apresyan had more to report to Moscow:

SIMA has got work in the Registration of Foreign Agents Branch of the War Office Division of the Department of Justice. Further investigation [53 groups unrecoverable] week. It is definitely known that in a few months' time the CABARET [Office of the Co-ordinator of Inter-American Affairs] will be transferred intact to the BANK [US State Department] under the command of the chief it has always had.

On 8 January 1945 Apresyan gave a further update to Moscow, and this was the first telegram in the series that Arlington Hall broke sufficiently to show that the Justice Department had been penetrated by a spy who had been moved to Washington DC early in 1945. Evidently Coplon had been looked over by one of the *rezident*'s subordinates, Vladimir S. Pravdin.

> SERGEI's [Vladimir Pravdin] conversation with SIMA [Judith Coplon] took place on 4 January. SIMA gives the impression of being a serious person who is politically well developed and there is no doubt of her sincere desire to help us. She had no doubts about whom she is working for and said that the nature of the materials in which we are interested pointed to the fact that it was our country that was in question. She was very satisfied that she was dealing with us and said that she deeply appreciated the confidence shown in her and understood the importance of our work.
>
> SIMA's transfer to a new job was made at the insistence of her superiors [64 groups unrecoverable] generalizing materials from all departments. SIMA will probably start work on 15 February.
>
> On the basis of this preliminary information there is reason to assume that in her new job SIMA will be able to carry out very important work for us throwing light on the activities of the KhATA [FBI]. The fruitfulness of her work will be to a considerable extent dependent upon our ability to organize correct and constant direction. It should be remembered that SIMA from an operational point of view is quite undeveloped and she will need time to learn conspiracy and to correctly gain an understanding of the questions which interest us.
>
> A final decision on the question of direction and liaison can be taken only after she has moved to CARTHAGE [Washington DC] when it will be ascertained specifically what her new job consists of.

By 15 January 1945, in a text that was not intercepted, Moscow had demanded more information about Pravdin's rendezvous with Coplon. Apresyan replied on that date:

> Your telegram 138. Telegram no. 22 reported in detail about the results of SERGEI's meeting with SIMA. We will telegraph additional information later.

In the same despatch, Apresyan explained what had happened to Flora's recent successful recruitment of Marion Davis Berdecio, which had been recommended by a highly skilled NKVD officer, Lev Vasilevsky, later the *rezident* in Mexico City, who operated under diplomatic cover as Lev Tarasov:

> LOU [Marion Davis Berdecio] has received orders from the CABARET [Office of the Co-ordinator of Inter-American Affairs] to take up work in CARTHAGE [Washington DC] on 11 January. In connection with this, work out the sending of a letter of recommendation from YURI [Lev Tarasov] or sanction signing on LOU through ZORA. Since LOU is beginning to work it is extremely important to direct her efforts from the very beginning along a line which we need, and for this direct contact and leadership are necessary.

The next VENONA is dated 26 June 1945, by which time Coplon had taken up her new position with the Justice Department in Washington DC. She was still being run by the New York *rezidentura*, and evidently had already supplied her Soviet contact with an analysis of her division's work:

> Your No. 4195. After SIMA's [Judith Coplon] transfer to CARTHAGE [Washington DC], she was instructed to refrain from removing documents until she was quite sure that she was trusted. As you were advised earlier, on the advice of her superiors, SIMA is studying the Russian language with the aim of [1 group unrecovered] a post in the department of the CLUB [Department of Justice] which is investigating the actions of the USSR and the Communists. SIMA was given the task of studying the CLUB, its methods of work, the way in which documents are kept. On this matter SIMA compiled [121 groups unrecoverable]

This was followed by a reply from Moscow on 24 March 1945 in which the Centre suggested Coplon should be handled in future by Nikolai P. Karpekov:

> First. [11 groups unrecovered] Let ZORA [Flora Wovschin] meet [12 groups unrecovered] to ZORA on [27 groups unrecovered]
>
> 2. Since SERGEI's [Vladimir Pravdin] departure for BABYLON [San Francisco] will cause a break in the liaison with SIMA [Judith Coplon], we propose that she be handed over to URAL [Nikolai Karpekov] for technical liaison. Warn URAL about being extremely careful in meeting ZORA. Point out to SIMA that her main task is to consolidate her hold on the new work in the CLUB [Department of Justice]. Therefore at first she should not be active in acquiring new contacts [59 groups unrecovered]

The implications of Pravdin's move to the San Francisco *rezidentura* would be returned to in July, but in the meantime on 28 March Moscow provided the most damning evidence against Wovschin, helpfully summarizing the extent of her betrayal for the FBI, but also disclosing that she had been rebuked for having attempted, in an unwelcome manifestation of zeal, to recruit other sources, thereby placing herself in danger:

> With Post No. 1 were received ZORA's [Flora Wovschin] reports in which there are the following facts which deserve serious attention:
>
> 1. In the report of 2 February 1945 in 2 pages, she, describing the situation concerning the change of working location, names institutions of the COUNTRY [America] by the code designations adopted by us in our telegraphic and written correspondence CLUB, BANK, CABARET.
>
> 2. In the reports of 1 and 3 February ZORA several times mentioned the words BANK, CABARET, HOUSE, CLUB. It is not a question about communications which have been [2 groups unrecovered] in the OFFICE [*rezidentura*] in which you filled in the prearranged designations, but about [1 group unrecovered] written personally by ZORA, nos. 8, 10, 111, 112.
>
> 3. In the report of [1 group unrecovered] January 1945 ZORA in detail sets forth the following story: 'SIMA's chief, WOOLWORTH [Robert Wohlforth] from the Military Department of the CLUB entrusted ZORA with finding out in

SIMA

her [31 groups unrecovered] was such an informer. ZORA gave [19 groups unrecovered] John DUNNING [3 groups unrecovered]. To DUNNING's question, whether she was interested in this information [11 groups unrecovered] the BANK ZORA answered that another institution, whose name she had been forbidden to disclose, was interested in the information and that this other institution would get in touch with him. A member of the Military Department of SIMA's institution Alexander SACKS in a conversation with ZORA [2 groups unrecovered] about the proposal [10 groups unrecovered] by him declined. SACKS gave ZORA the task of trying to get in the RADIO STATION [Office of War Information] materials about Swiss-German financial operations and [38 groups unrecovered]

PART II To ZORA's question to SACKS and WOOLWORTH, why they are not receiving material from the RADIO STATION through an official representative, [2 groups unrecovered] institutions of the COUNTRY including the BANK, WOOLWORTH is trying to seek out [5 groups unrecovered] the CLUB. WOOLWORTH told ZORA that in the HUT [OSS], BANK, RADIO STATION, FARM [4 groups unrecovered] many people who [17 groups unrecovered] by the next post answer:
1. Why [1 group unrecovered] ZORA.
2. Were these reports read [1 group unrecovered] by the liaison man.
3. Did MAY [Stepan Apresyan] and SERGEI [Vladimir Pravdin] see these reports.
4. Who told ZORA [3 groups unrecovered] and then told '[1 group unrecovered]' [13 groups unrecovered] to WOOLWORTH and SACKS.
6. Why did ZORA begin to take [33 groups unrecovered] steps taken to curtail ZORA's dangerous activities.

Without waiting for instructions from us after you reply to the questions which have been raised, immediately and in detail enlighten our liaison man about the serious mistakes he has committed in the work with ZORA. As an ultimatum warn ZORA that if she does not carry out our instructions and if she undertakes steps without our consent, we shall

> immediately terminate all relations with her. Forbid ZORA to recruit all her acquaintances one after the other. Take all steps to see that ZORA's activities do not lead to serious political complications with the COUNTRY. This example clearly illustrates not only the falling off in the *rezidentura*'s work of controlling and educating PROBATIONERS [agents], but also the lack of understanding by our operational workers of the most elementary rules in our work.

Apart from the strong suggestion that Wovschin had written numerous memoranda to the Centre about her highly sensitive work, this particular VENONA proved that the Soviets had realized that some parts of their most secret communications had been compromised, and that the codewords BANK, CABARET, HOUSE and CLUB were known to the Americans. This was disturbing news, for Coplon had never been privy to VENONA, but evidently she had seen something that had enabled her to tip off the NKVD that the codes were being solved, although there was little Moscow could do to rectify retrospectively the breach in the security of their communications. Nevertheless, this VENONA showed conclusively that the Soviets knew at the beginning of February 1945 that some aspects of their most secret code had been broken by the Americans who were using the information in counter-espionage investigations.

A brief fragment of a two-sentence text from Leonid Kvasnikov in New York, dated 5 July 1945, suggested that the handover of Coplon to Karpekov was still the matter of some discussion:

> URAL [Nikolai Karpekov] in liaison with SIMA [Judith Coplon] is not being used but after his transfer [4 groups unrecovered] is necessary further working out.

These VENONA intercepts represent the entirety of the material on Judith Coplon, but they were more than enough to make the FBI realize in 1948, as the text of 8 January 1945 indicated, that a spy had been at work in the Justice Department. As soon as the FBI's Robert Lamphere extracted the vital date of the spy's commencement in her new post, 15 February 1945, on an internal transfer from New York, Judith Coplon was confirmed by FBI inspector Leo Lauchlin in consultation with the Assistant Attorney-General as SIMA, for she was the only person to have switched from the Justice

Department's Economic Warfare section to Washington DC. Preliminary inquiries into her background showed that her parents were living in Brooklyn, and she had graduated in 1943 from Barnard College, where she had been involved briefly with the Young Communist League. The question for the FBI was how she could be caught on a charge of espionage, bearing in mind that her position gave her access to files on the FBI's current investigations, which was doubtless why no prosecutions had resulted from Bentley's allegations. By the time the FBI had gone in pursuit of Nathan Silvermaster's network, there was absolutely no evidence to be found, even in the extensive photographic laboratory discovered in the basement of his suburban home. Quite obviously, Judith Coplon had allowed the NKVD to remain one step ahead of the FBI, tipping off the Soviets each time a new suspect came under the FBI's scrutiny, so the only action to be taken was to remove the suspects from their jobs. This had effectively eliminated the Silvermaster and Perlo rings, but allowed their members to evade prosecution. As Coplon was routinely handling internal security dossiers at her office in the Foreign Agents Registration section of the Justice Department, her hand in their escape was all too obvious. The only advantage to the FBI was to learn which personalities currently under investigation were of interest to the Soviets. It was in this way that suspicion hardened against Joseph Bernstein, whose name appeared on one of the FBI data slips compromised by Coplon.

Coplon was placed under discreet surveillance which revealed that she was having an illicit affair with Harold Shapiro, a Justice Department attorney, and that she made two trips a month to New York to visit her parents. When she was followed to Manhattan on 14 January 1949 she was seen to meet a man for dinner who subsequently was identified as Valentin A. Gubitchev, an employee of the United Nations Secretariat. They were watched at two further meetings, on 18 February and 4 March. At this latter rendezvous both were arrested, and Gubitchev was found to be carrying an envelope containing $125, while Coplon's handbag revealed a wealth of classified data, including some documents that had been prepared by the FBI as a 'barium meal' to test whether Coplon gave them to her Soviet contacts.

At her trial the FBI concealed the exact nature of the 'confidential informant' that had led to the investigation of Coplon and she deployed the defence that her relationship with Gubitchev was entirely romantic, and that the information she was carrying was nothing more than notes she had prepared while writing a novel. The prosecution neatly destroyed the 'innocent liaison' ploy by disclosing details of her affair with Harold Shapiro. Coplon was convicted and received a sentence of between forty months and ten years' imprisonment for conspiring to pass classified secrets to Gubitchev, who was also convicted.

Coplon's conviction was later overturned on appeal, on the technicality that the FBI's telephone intercept had been unlawful. As the clear impression had been given that the FBI had begun its investigation as a consequence of a wiretap on Coplon's office line, all the evidence that flowed from that source was deemed inadmissible. The alternative was to reveal that the FBI had been led to Coplon by VENONA, but that expedient was considered too high a price to pay, so she was freed to marry one of her lawyers, Albert II. Socolov, and settle in Brooklyn where she opened a chain of restaurants.

As well as losing Coplon, the FBI also missed Flora Wovschin, who had been responsible for her recruitment. She too had joined the Communist Youth League at Barnard College, and later had gone to work for the Office of War Information in Washington DC. In 1947 she had resigned from the civil service to marry an Amtorg engineer, but by the time the FBI started to look for her in 1949 she had moved to Moscow. No action was taken against her mother and stepfather, but the FBI did attempt to identify the other members of her network. The fact that Flora had continued to be active after the war was revealed in a text from Moscow dated 11 March 1945, marking Apresyan's appointment as *rezident* in San Francisco, which designated Vladimir Pravdin as her controller, with a *referentura* clerk, Olga V. Khlopkova, responsible for processing her information. In fact Khlopkova was herself a senior NKVD officer, apparently with some direct link to Beria, who occasionally used her own personal cipher:

> [16 groups unrecoverable] in San Francisco the work of ALBERT's [Iskhak Akhmerov] office. The operational direction of ZORA [Flora Wovschin] [6 groups unrecovered] JULIA [Olga Khlopkova] will deal with his documents under SERGEI's [Vladimir Pravdin] direction.

The scale of Flora's activities can be judged by this item, sent from Moscow two days later:

> Your 203. ALAN – Ralph Bowen, works in the BANK [State Department] as assistant [3 groups unrecovered] economics. He and his wife Sue are acquaintances of ZORA and together with the latter were members of the GYMNASTIC organization [Young Communist League]. In so far as ZORA works in the BANK, [5 groups unrecovered] with them the former friendly relations.
>
> DROP – Philip E. MOSELEY. Up to 1943 worked in the Russian Section of the HUT [OSS]. Since 1943 has been in the BANK in the Division of Territorial Studies. In 1932–34 has [2 groups unrecovered] member of the staff of HARVARD University and [42 groups unrecovered] friend of BLERIOT. According to the latter's information is progressively inclined.
>
> DUVER – our PROBATIONER [agent] in VADIM's office.
>
> ROBERT – connected with the NEIGHBOURS.
>
> OSWARD – Benjamin GERIG [6 groups unrecovered] in the BANK. We have no other data on [1 group unrecovered].

Whether Flora remained active until her departure for Moscow is uncertain, but her absence ensured that the FBI made no further progress in its pursuit of her. According to the CIA, Flora participated in anti-American propaganda operations during the Korean War, and died soon afterwards.

XI

The HUT

ONE OF the clearest impressions gained from the study of VENONA is the Soviet preoccupation with hostile intelligence agencies. A large proportion of the texts concern the HUT ('IZBA'), the NKVD's covername for the local intelligence service, which in the Washington–New York–San Francisco circuits during the war meant the Office of Strategic Services. In Russian *izba* is a particular type of log cabin inhabited by peasants, and is quite distinct from *khata*, the Ukrainian thatched cottage.

Obviously, only a small proportion of the total Soviet intelligence traffic was recovered, but as a representative sample of NKVD activities, ENORMOZ and IZBA emerge as top priorities. VENONA also demonstrates the impressive success that both the NKVD and GRU achieved in recruiting sources within the OSS, and the first texts, which date back to 1942, show how Vasili Zubilin responded to an inquiry sent from Moscow on 17 May about OSS's Russian section:

> No. 325 [20 groups unrecovered] of the HUT in the Library of Congress. SOUND [Jacob Golos] became acquainted with [Philip Clin] KEENEY [19 groups unrecovered] [21 groups unrecoverable] [20 groups unrecovered] We are interested in the Russian Section of the HUT. [19 groups unrecovered] [21 groups unrecoverable]

Clearly, Moscow must have been responding to a communication from Jacob Golos about what was then the Co-ordinator of Information's Office, the US intelligence agency that was to become the Office of Strategic Services a month later. Although the message is badly fragmented, the reference to Philip Keeney, then in the Foreign Economic Administration, was of interest, as he was to be a spy suspect. Whatever the exact content, Zubilin replied on 22 May:

The HUT

In reply to No. 325

In the opinion of the East European Section of the HUT, the US Military Intelligence here is incapable of the admitted mandate [14 groups unrecovered] military intelligence [1 group unrecovered] not [1 group unidentified] and is based on premature evaluation by the agents entrusted with [11 groups unrecovered] section of the HUT treats with contempt Military Intelligence, although it is subordinate to it.

In the section work two well-known experts: the Consultant on the Balkan question – Professor John Moseley of Cornell University and the Chief of the Russian Section Joshua STARR. Employed by the section are:

1. Dr John Sheldon CURTISS – assistant librarian of the ROOSEVELT Library at Hyde Park, author of the book 'Church and State in Russia'. Sympathizes with the USSR and this year completed a piece of research on the Protocols of the Elders of Zion, which is meant for publication.

2. Samuel BLOOMFIELD – junior researcher, who worked some time for [8 groups unrecovered] manager of the 'Progressive Bookshop' in Washington (check him and let us know the results).

3. Thomas P. WHITNEY [11 groups unrecovered] then [3 groups unrecovered] Columbia University. In 1941 he took the post of [14 groups unrecovered] Russian history.

4. Thomas HALL – researcher in Russian history

5. John Scott NEARING – consultant on Soviet industry. This year he sent a mass of materials on the Soviet war industry. The materials have not yet been worked over (our source IVANOV).

6. Professor LORIMER of the American University – consultant in population problems.

7. I. G. RUDD – Jewish emigrant from Russia who used to work [1 group unrecovered] Wall Street. Graduated from Harvard University.

8. Professor WUORINEN – lecturer in Finnish history at Columbia University, consultant on the Finnish question.

We will report on the other employees when we receive [1 group unrecovered].

Strategic surveys finished by the section include surveys on the Northern Caucasus, Transcaucasia, and Finland. HALL and FRYE [7 groups unrecovered].

(PART II) [153 groups unrecovered] and a number of other sections of the HUT [22 groups unrecovered] Price Administration and the Office of [26 groups unrecoverable] parallel appraisal of general American opinion [153 groups unrecovered] population. Foreign minorities, including [21 groups unrecovered] study in schools. The need of translators.

(PART III) 6. [20 groups unrecovered] relationship to the USA.
7. [5 groups unrecovered] relation of the USA to the mandate. [128 groups unrecovered] from organs [70 groups unrecovered] one of the small political parties and opposition [21 groups unrecovered]
8. Relationship of the government to [5 groups unrecovered]. The Military Intelligence of the USA [108 groups unrecovered]

(PART IV) [48 groups unrecovered, 98 groups unrecoverable]
11. BIR ... [48 groups unrecovered].

Although the text is very disjointed, Zubilin had obviously supplied Moscow with the information demanded with extraordinary speed, correctly naming nine members of the East European section, one in the Social Sciences section of the Research and Analysis Branch, and one in the Baltic section, demonstrating that even the embryonic OSS was comprehensively penetrated by the NKVD. To have taken just five days to identify correctly the key personalities in the Russian section was a remarkable achievement. The text also served to implicate John Scott Nearing codenamed IVANOV, and Professor John H. Wuorinen.

A month later, on 18 June 1942, Zubilin had more to say about OSS:

'[1 group unrecovered] GEL' reports that '[8 groups unrecovered] [translation deleted] [2 groups unrecovered] department of the HUT and [translation deleted] from the Board of Economic Warfare, in WASHINGTON [7 groups unrecovered], that military and government circles are

The HUT

reacting somehow to [14 groups unrecovered] [8 groups unrecoverable] JUKES [8 groups unrecovered]. Documentary materials and [4 groups unrecovered] a report on meteorological units in Soviet ports, aircraft instruments, [3 groups unrecovered]. [1 group unrecovered] that [14 groups unrecovered].

This VENONA text is remarkable because it is the first of the OSS series to have names deleted, the second person identified in the accompanying footnote only as having served on the Board of Economic Warfare from December 1941 until December 1943.

The first definite Soviet source to be identified within OSS was Duncan Lee, codenamed KOCH, and the first VENONA report attributed to him occurred on 26 May 1943 in a message from Zubilin to Moscow:

KOCH [Duncan Lee] reports that at the CAPTAIN [President Roosevelt]–BOAR [Winston Churchill] conference [1 group garbled] [16 groups unrecovered] known. The HUT has no [40 groups unrecoverable] information from ISTANBUL [8 groups unrecovered] known to the Romanian ambassador but in the situation after [53 groups unrecovered] thousand dollars in support of an underground diversion and espionage group in France.

In the middle of June KOCH is going [2 groups unrecovered] month to CHUNGKING to acquaint himself there with the work of the HUT group. With him will go an American army colonel [1 group unrecovered] at CHUNGKING [1 group unrecovered] espionage group. If it is considered necessary to establish [6 groups unrecovered] with him there, we will arrange a password.

We discussed with KOCH the question of his removing documents for photographing. KOCH said that in some cases he agrees to do this, but as a rule he considers it inexpedient. He promised to think [6 groups unrecovered]

This was to be the first of five texts referring to Lee, clearly a key NKVD spy close to the top of the OSS hierarchy who at this early stage had not been drawn completely into Zubilin's network. This text alone must have provided sufficient collateral for the FBI to pinpoint Lee, but in any event he was denounced by Elizabeth Bentley in November 1945. Having handled his information, Bentley gave a comprehensive account of his activities and mentioned his trip to China. Although the VENONA described his departure as being in the middle of June, he actually left the USA on 29 June, on a fact-finding tour of OSS's bases in Asia for General Donovan, and was not to return until 3 October. In the event he reached China, but nearly failed to return when he and his two companions, Jack S. Service of the US embassy in Chungking, and the war correspondent Eric Severeid, en route from Kunming in a C-46, were forced to parachute into the Naga Hills and make an epic journey across the Burmese forest to India. Not only did the three passengers complete their journey safely, but no sooner had they bailed out of their stricken aircraft than the engines recovered and the pilot landed safely at Chabua.

The next VENONA to mention Lee, dated 8 June 1943, showed that he was not acting alone, and implicated Maurice Halperin, code-named HARE, J. Julius Joseph (CAUTIOUS), and Carl Marzani (COL-LEAGUE):

> [20 groups unrecovered] about the HUT and RADIO STATION [Office of War Information] [24 groups unrecovered] PROBATIONERS [agents] HARE [Maurice Halperin], KOCH [Duncan Lee], CAUTIOUS [J. Julius Joseph] (he works in the Far Eastern Section of the HUT on the question of the maritime resources of JAPAN. COLLEAGUE [Carl Marzani] (he works in the Photographic Section PICTORIAL DIVISION, RUFF [Franz L. Neumann] and UCN/19 [9 groups unrecovered] COMPETITORS [intelligence service] [49 groups unrecovered] with which we are now occupying ourselves. On receipt of full information about the people [1 group unrecovered]

Halperin, who was to appear a record sixty-eight times in VENONA, was to become chief of the Latin American section in OSS's Research and Analysis Branch, and had been one of Bentley's contacts. Born in Boston to Jewish immigrants from the Ukraine, and educated at Harvard, Halperin had taken his master's degree in modern languages at Oklahoma University, and obtained a doctorate from the Sorbonne. Coincidentally, he had attended St John's College, Annapolis, with Samuel Chew, the cryptographer who worked on some of his traffic, and who became convinced that he had once spotted Halperin at Arlington Hall. Halperin returned to teach Spanish at Oklahoma University and became close to the CPUSA, as well as an acknowledged expert on Latin America and Mexico. In December 1941, instead of taking a teaching post in Haiti for the State Department, he was recruited to join the Co-ordinator of Intelligence to advise on Latin America. His first task was to write a report on Mexico, and this was the basis of a report from William Donovan to President Roosevelt dated 23 December 1941 which was highly critical of the local embassy's preparations for war. This document established Halperin's reputation and started his climb in what was to become OSS.

According to Bentley, Halperin 'not only had access to the OSS secret cable room and the reports from their undercover men abroad, but because of an exchange agreement he was also able to secure confidential State Department cables and reports. These were of great interest to the NKVD.' In her statement to the FBI she added rather more detail, naming Willard Park as a co-conspirator (a name omitted entirely from her book), and recalled that Halperin

> had come to Washington DC after some trouble at Oklahoma University and, together with a former colleague of his at Oklahoma University, WILLARD PARK, who taught anthropology there, had indicated to BRUCE MINTON of 'New Masses' that they desired to be placed in contact with some Communists in the East. I also learned that during his stay in Oklahoma, HALPERIN had been a Communist Party member but upon his arrival in Washington had apparently temporarily lost contact. HALPERIN was employed by OSS in the Latin American Division of the Research and Analysis branch and PARK was in the Political Section of the Office of the Coordinator of Inter-American Affairs. MINTON apparently communicated to GOLOS the desire of HALPERIN and PARK to make a Communist contact in this section and my subsequent meeting with them was a result of the arrangements made by GOLOS. My first meeting with HALPERIN was in Washington DC at PARK's residence, which I recall was over the District line in Maryland and on that occasion I discussed with them the work they were

> doing ... PARK was not a Party member although I know he did occasionally make contributions to the Party.

In the VENONA text above (dated 8 June 1943), only UCN/19 remains unidentified, as RUFF was Franz L. Neumann, a German refugee who had read economics at London University before emigrating to the US in 1936. An expert on the Reich's economy, he had joined OSS in February 1942. Elizabeth Bentley was able to fill in the gaps on the others. J. Julius Joseph was a veteran Communist from Allentown, Pennsylvania, who was recruited by Golos in 1942. He had worked in the War Manpower Commission until he was drafted into the US Army in 1943, but after three weeks of basic training he used his influence to obtain a transfer into OSS's Japanese section where, according to Bentley,

> he was of invaluable use to us, not only because he knew in advance of the Americans' plans concerning Japan, but because for a period he worked in the Library of Congress next door to the confidential Russian division, whose people trustingly gave him all the information that was of interest to us. Joe, incidentally, for all his zeal, never seemed to learn the correct underground procedure. He was continually getting into difficulties that had us alternately worried and amused. One famous occasion, having been told either to burn documents or flush them down the toilet, he crammed a mass of flaming papers into the toilet, with the result that the seat was set on fire. His puzzled landlord, surveying the damage, finally walked out of the apartment muttering to himself, 'I don't see how that could possibly have happened.'

In her 1945 statement to the FBI, Bentley had given further details of Joseph's espionage, which became really effective after he had been screened and given a complete security clearance by Army Counter-Intelligence and the FBI:

> he was able to supply me with considerable material relating to the work of the Japanese and Russian divisions of OSS. It is my recollection that he made available to me written reports which I believe were carbon copies of the actual reports but I am unable to state positively if there

The HUT

were any labels on such reports indicating they were confidential, restricted or secret; nor do I recall the contents specifically of such reports except that some of them dealt with the administrative organization of those two divisions of OSS. My association with JOSEPH continued until December 1944 and up until that time he continued to supply me with this same type of material.

On 9 June 1943 Pavel P. Klarin, under vice-consular cover in New York, reported more from Halperin and Lee:

> HARE [Maurice Halperin] reports that according to information of a branch of the HUT [73 groups unrecovered] in Italy. Also Italian workers are returning from GERMANY. 2. KOCH [Duncan Lee] reports that the HUT has received from its branch in SIDON [London] two confidential reports on [3 groups unrecovered]. One of them from 30 April says that EDEN is inclined to side with the Poles but BOAR [Winston Churchill] takes a more moderate position proposing to cede Byelorussia and the UKRAINE to the USSR and Eastern Prussia to POLAND [13 groups unrecovered] Poles and the chances for [18 groups unrecovered] HUT from [30 groups unrecoverable] PILET-GOLZ [Swiss Foreign Minister] [13 groups unrecovered] diplomatic relations of the USSR.

On the same day, Stepan Apresyan supplied more from Lee, this time about information he had extracted from Dewitt Poole.

> KOCH reports that Dewitt POOLE, head of the Nationalities Branch of the HUT, compiled a report on the activities of the Roman Catholic priest ORLEMANSKIJ. In February of this year ORLEMANSKIJ met him and communicated his desire to go to MOSCOW with a view to ascertaining the position of the USSR in the religious question and trying to clarify the relations between the two countries. On returning to the COUNTRY [America] he handed over all the documents he had brought to the representative of the VATICAN who thanked him and sent the documents to the Pope. Recently ORLEMANSKIJ had a talk with POOLE, relating that he had discussed with our Government the question of the future of Poland and had told Comrade STALIN that it was impossible

to have dealings with any of the members of the existing Polish Government in SIDON [London]. Comrade STALIN is alleged to have objected, stating that only two members are totally unacceptable and that the future Polish Government must consist of members of the present government, the new Polish group in SMYRNA [Moscow] and representatives of the American Poles according to the mutual choice of the CAPTAIN [President Roosevelt] and ORLEMANSKIJ. In the talk with POOLE, ORLEMANSKIJ stated that he considers the participation of the Poles in the COUNTRY inexpedient. With regard to the frontiers of Poland ORLEMANSKIJ expressed himself vaguely but said, however, that allegedly according to a statement of Comrade STALIN the decision about the CURZON line was 'thrust' upon him by the TEHERAN Conference. POOLE considers ORLEMANSKIJ a simple and honourable man who made the journey entirely on his personal initiative. POOLE asked Bishop [Fulton J.] SHEEN about the reasons for the imposition upon ORLEMANSKIJ of a disciplinary penalty. SHEEN allegedly answered that although ORLEMANSKIJ was given punishment for drawing the Catholic church together with the USSR [6 groups unrecovered] to dissuade other priests who want to act independently of the Catholic leadership.

A few days ago GRANDPAPA [Evgeni D. Kiselev] was in the presence of SHAH [Konstantin A. Shabanov] and met ORLEMANSKIJ who recounted his talks in SMYRNA almost the same as to POOLE. This confirms our previous conclusion about the garrulity and unreliability of ORLEMANSKIJ.

Certainly Halperin enjoyed wide access to OSS's secrets, and his messages were not restricted to Latin American topics, as the first part of the following text, which deals with the failed 20 July assassination plot against Hitler, dated 25 August 1944, from Stepan Apresyan, indicates:

HARE reports:
1. According to the BANK [State Department] information [2 groups unrecovered] in CARTHAGE [Washington DC] have applied to the BANK with a request to send to [5 groups unrecovered]. The boss of the BANK [4 groups unrecovered],

The HUT

as they are a thorn in the flesh and it is best to get rid of them.
2. According to the information of the representative of the COUNTRY [America] in the Vatican, the first secretary of the German embassy in the Vatican, KESSEL, with his ambassador's permission has had an interview with an Allied officer. He said that the aim of the recent coup d'état was to set up a government which would try to obtain a peace with the Allies including the USSR consisting of 50 per cent conservatives and 50 per cent social-democrats. The coup d'état was originally scheduled for after STALINGRAD and there was the Allies' decision about unconditional surrender. KESSEL said that the proposals for dismembering Germany were damping the ardour for anti-Hitler of his group which would prefer [1 group unrecovered] Germany completely occupied even by Soviet troops than dismembered. The letter [4 groups unrecovered] suspicious of the Allies and the USSR.
3. The Vatican has proposed to the ambassador of the COUNTRY that an inter-Allied administration should be set up to administer the Baltic States with a view to establishing freedom of religion and so on.
4. According to the information of the representatives of the COUNTRY in TANGIER, the Spanish Ambassador in ALGIERS SAN GRONIZ [23 groups unrecoverable] under DECREE [Lend-Lease] after the defeat of Germany and supply only those countries which can be used against Japan.

Duncan Lee was also credited as the author of this text from Stepan Apresyan, dated 15 September 1944, about an OSS investigation into Communist infiltration which had named Halperin as a suspected Soviet source:

> According to KOCH's advice, a list of 'reds' has been compiled by the Security Division of the HUT. The list contains 4 surnames of persons who are supplying information to the Russians. One of them sounds like JIMENEZ. The list is divided into two categories:
> 1. Open FELLOWCOUNTRYMEN [Party members]
> 2. Sympathizers, left-wing liberals, etc. (among them HARE). KOCH is trying to get the list.

Maurice Halperin (HARE) was undeterred by the OSS security inquiry, as is demonstrated by this text from New York sent the following month and dated 10 October 1944:

> HARE communicates [1 group unrecovered] the BANK [State Department] a telegram from BARI of 25 September, in which is discussed the introduction by TITO of strict regulations about the movements and activity of the military missions of the COUNTRY [America] and the ISLAND [Britain]. In the telegram it is communicated that the ISLAND has replied by the termination of supplies to the partisans and the evacuation of the wounded. The probable cause of the introduction of strict measures this year he considers to be the intention of TITO to conceal from the missions the existing control over the country that he exercises.
>
> RADIO ANNOUNCER [General Donovan] has appointed KOCH [Duncan Lee] chief of the Japanese Section of the secret department of the COMPETITION [intelligence service].
>
> KOCH advises that his section has men in CHINA working with a little group of Japanese FELLOWCOUNTRYMEN [Communists] in FELLOWCOUNTRYMAN territory on the problem of despatching people to JAPAN. The plan consists in the use of Korean FELLOWCOUNTRYMEN and of the situation that JAPAN is importing Korean manpower. Details are being ascertained.
>
> According to a communication of KOCH the HUT [OSS] is very much concerned about the fate of its people in territories occupied by the Red Army particularly in Germany where the concentration of the HUT's people is higher than in other countries. The HUT fears that its people will be shot and [5 groups unrecovered] in [2 groups unrecovered] requirement of regulating the question with the Russians. [3 groups unrecovered]

Halperin had been an active agent since at least 8 June 1943, the date of the first VENONA text to mention him, the content of which had an obvious link with OSS's Latin America branch:

The HUT

Your 2143

HARE has handed over material on [5 groups unrecovered] by a responsible official of the HUT on 7 June. The contents are as follows: [1 group unidentified] revolution in RIO [Buenos Aires] [13 groups unrecovered] 5 June. On 6 June the junta dissolved the congress, suppressed the communist newspaper 'LA NORA', and prohibited meetings of any political organizations attended by more than three persons. [1 group unidentified], that [48 groups unrecoverable] views that do not differ from the conservative policies of CASTILLO's government. CASTILLO's overthrow was accomplished by the joint efforts of two groups which recognized the necessity of avoiding a popular uprising: 1) General RAMIREZ's group, which wishes to [3 groups unrecovered] and foreign policy of CASTILLO [3 groups unrecovered] that [14 groups unrecoverable] RAWSON [4 groups unrecovered]

PART II CASTILLO's conservative internal policy [62 groups unrecovered] of military equipment from the COUNTRY [America] [11 groups unrecovered] RAWSON [22 groups unrecovered] ARMOUR in charge of the work of the organization. [4 groups unrecovered] which had been proclaimed was scared off by the simultaneous [17 groups unrecoverable] and at the head of the government was General RAMIREZ. The latter's position remains unclear, as he has not got a firm base for running the country. In view of the ease with which the preceding government was overthrown, in the near future it is possible that [2 groups unrecovered] popular uprising. SECOND. Telegrams from ARMOUR, ambassador of the COUNTRY, to the BANK [State Department] 1) In a series of [1 group unidentified] telegrams ARMOUR optimistic that the situation in RIO [5 groups unrecovered] 2) On 2 June he reported what 'a certain radical representative' gave him on the first of June concerning preparations for a revolution. ARMOUR concluded that the official [1 group unrecovered] by RAMIREZ of rumours concerning preparations for a revolution represented an attempt to conceal the publication of plans. 3) On 4 June ARMOUR [2 groups unrecovered] 'revolutionary movement' organized by RAMIREZ, [39 groups unrecovered] ARMOUR visited Captain Karlos MARTINEZ, whom ARMOUR 'knew well', and transmitted a personal letter from RAWSON indicating that the 'revolutionary movement', although [2 groups unrecovered] armed forces, will follow democratic principles.'

PART III 5) In his next telegram, of 4 June, ARMOUR indicated that he [6 groups unrecovered] (information from HARE his reports to the BANK was also confused, as was ([43 groups unrecovered] measure, this prevents the COUNTRY from recognizing the new government in RIO. One of the important motives of the leaders of the revolt was an effort to get arms, which they can get in their opinion only by breaking relations with the Axis. 8) In the last telegram, of 6 June, ARMOUR reported that events were developing very unfavourably. 9) On 7 June ARMOUR [15 groups unrecoverable] [25 groups unrecovered]

The next text with information attributed to Halperin was sent by Klarin on 17 June 1943, and demonstrated what Bentley had claimed about his access to State Department cables:

HARE reported that the first matter was the gist of information from the Algerian office of the HUT.
1. General GEORGES arrived in Algiers on 6th May from FRANCE, accompanied by Colonel DUVAL. From there he will go to the ISLAND [England] where he is to head the French Military Mission. Before he left FRANCE, GEORGES was offered the leadership of the Secret Anti-Fascist Army, but he refused because of the lack of arms and radio equipment. According to DUVAL, the Germans removed all weapons from FRANCE. 'FRANC-TIREUR' and the British maintain contact with the Secret Army but other organizations refused because of the [24 groups unrecovered] FRANC-TIREUR and the 'liberation groups' [4 groups unrecovered] anti-Fascist groups in FRANCE. RAS [General de Gaulle] chose his general for North AFRICA and GIRAUD chose his for the South. Both [6 groups unrecovered] orders, money and weapons.
2. [4 groups unrecovered] [24 groups unrecoverable] to Hitler the time [58 groups unrecovered] to RAS.

The HUT

The second matter was information from correspondence between the BANK [State Department] and ambassadors:
1. On 7th June the Embassy of the COUNTRY [America] in TURKEY reported that the Turkish Ambassador to ROMANIA who had arrived on leave, had given the following clarification of the situation in ROMANIA – In view of the heavy losses of the army, the people's morale is low. The Germans fear complete demoralization. The Romanians consider that the Allies will win the war. Propaganda about the 'Soviet menace' is continuing but the press and radio are becoming more and more friendly towards the Allies.

PART II There are no longer any objections about the 'New Order in Europe'. The King is trying to force a coalition government headed by the Ministry of Justice. In GALATZ a crowd of people shouted out 'Down with ANTONESCU'. [25 groups unrecovered]

2. MIDSHIPMAN informed the BANK that the proposal about [53 groups unrecovered] military operations against [7 groups unrecoverable].

4. The Embassy of the COUNTRY in CHINA transmitted the gist of ACHESON's report on the situation in CHINA which states that CHIANG KAI-CHEK and his supporters consider that the military and economic situation is unlikely to improve unless immediate steps are taken; the morale of the troops is sinking; in many areas an armed truce between the Japanese and the Chinese troops exists which helps [13 groups unrecoverable] 10 per cent; great agrarian unrest is taking place; in CHANSI province General SUN TIEN YING with 30,000 troops has gone over to the puppet government. Information from HARE [20 groups unrecovered] and adversaries of SIKORSKI, [38 groups unrecovered]

On 24 June 1943 Klarin reported on another batch of Halperin's State Department cables:

HARE reports that the Ambassador of the COUNTRY [America] in SPAIN, HAYES, on instructions from the BANK is systematically protesting against a series of actions by the Spanish Government. The Spanish Minister for Foreign Affairs, JORDANA, told HAYES that the COUNTRY was obliged [6 groups unrecovered] the Spanish Government since it [1 group unrecovered] a gradual break with the Falange and the establishment of a more democratic regime.

The Ambassador of the COUNTRY in SPANISH MOROCCO, CHILDS, told the BANK about [4 groups unrecovered] of the Commander of the Spanish troops in MOROCCO, ORGAZ, which was made by him [1 group unrecovered] their joint meeting with [10 groups unrecovered]

The following month, on 8 July 1943, Klarin reported that Halperin had supplied more State Department cables:

HARE handed over the following telegrams, dated 9th June, from the Ambassador of the COUNTRY [America] in STOCKHOLM, JOHNSON, to the BANK:

'During his recent visit to STOCKHOLM the Chargé d'Affaires of the COUNTRY'S Embassy in FINLAND, MCCLINTOCK, was invited to the Soviet Legation and when questioned by the Soviet representatives as to what was known about the rumours of poison gas being sent to FINLAND by the Germans for use on the Eastern Front, he replied that he knew nothing. He said that the Finns were not prepared for gas warfare and therefore [22 groups unrecovered] [45 groups unrecoverable] the attempt by the Germans to form a 'Russian Army' from Soviet prisoners of war has failed. In May of this year the 'Army of VLASOV [4 groups unrecovered] only 300 men.

Just over a week later, on 17 July 1943, Klarin had heard more from Halperin, including details of a plot to assassinate Hitler, which seemed almost calculated to infuriate the NKVD:

HARE has handed over a copy of a HUT [OSS] document, marked [2 groups unrecovered], which was a report about [5 groups unrecovered] of 25th June 1943 '[2 groups unrecovered] [42 groups unrecoverable] from a SIDON [London] source dated 18th June:

'A highly placed officer [1 group unrecovered] whose information has so far been correct, points out that four officers of the German Army have arrived in the ISLAND via SWITZERLAND with a proposal of the following [1 group

The HUT

unrecovered]: officers of the German Army will either assassinate HITLER or get rid of him by other [20 groups unrecoverable] Allies can even partially occupy GERMANY on condition that they break with RUSSIA.'

2. A report from another SIDON source, dated 12th June:

[50 groups unrecoverable] the military 'dispose of [4 groups unrecovered] and they will take on themselves [14 groups unrecovered] [33 groups unrecoverable] authority over the German people [24 groups unrecovered] propose to the COUNTRY [11 groups unrecovered] between the German and Russian fronts. The German troops should fall back to their 1939 frontiers. The proposal goes on to state that the occupation of POLAND, the Baltic States, BESSARABIA, YUGOSLAVIA and CZECHOSLOVAKIA by COUNTRY-ISLAND troops and then the withdrawal of German troops [6 groups unrecovered] bloodshed [45 groups unrecovered] arrested and several persons were executed. The number of conspirators [46 groups unrecovered] against [1 group unidentified] DER. Please telegraph immediately your evaluation of this report.

No response to this communication is recorded in VENONA, and the next despatch from Halperin was reported from New York on 21 July:

According to information sent to the BANK [State Department] by DREYFUS, the COUNTRY's [America] Ambassador in IRAN, and received by us from HARE [Halperin], RICKENBACKER in a conversation on the way to the USSR with the Turkish and British Ambassadors [33 groups unrecovered] reliable sources it is known that CAPTAIN [President Roosevelt] is greatly angered by RICKENBACKER's trip to the USSR which was not cleared with him, as he considers it inexpedient.

PAL [Nathan Silvermaster] reports that the head of the BANK is very angry that CAPTAIN is by-passing him by deciding important questions of foreign policy and is not letting him read his correspondence with BOAR [Winston Churchill] [11 groups unrecovered] with the Allies in advantageous [1 group unrecovered] agreement.

There then followed a gap in the texts concerning Halperin for more than fifteen months, until 11 October 1944 when he reported his posting to London had been postponed to the New Year:

> According to advice from HARE [Halperin] RADIO ANNOUNCER [General Donovan] has finished a project for the organization of a branch of the HUT [OSS] for obtaining strategic information in Europe in the postwar period. The despatch of HUT people to SIDON [London] for this purpose is expected shortly. HARE expects to be sent temporarily to SIDON in January. The HUT refused to organize an information centre in the PROVINCES [Latin America] at this time therefore HARE's trip there fell through.

A week later, on 19 October 1944, Apresyan sent a brief telegram of a political nature from New York, presumably extracted by Halperin from the OSS cable room described by Bentley:

> According to information of HARE:
> 1. In telegrams to the BANK [State Department] dated 26th and 27th August [Robert] MURPHY passed on a request by King MICHAEL of Romania for the depatch of troops to Romania of troops of the COUNTRY [America] and the ISLAND [Britain] 'for moral support [1 group unrecovered].'
> 2. The military division of the COUNTRY in IRAN will be left there until 1st March 1945. It has been decided that this is the date on which its stay will end.

On 20 September 1944 Halperin and Lee were linked again, for the last time, in a VENONA text from Moscow to New York:

> Reference No. 741. Try through KOCH [Duncan Lee] to obtain [8 groups unrecovered] tell MYRNA [Elizabeth Bentley] temporarily to cease liaison with the HUT [OSS] and HARE [Halperin]. In future liaison may be re-established only with our permission. Give KOCH the task of compiling a report on the Security Division of the HUT.

This directive regarding Elizabeth Bentley's sources inside OSS must have exacerbated her conflict with the New York *rezidentura*, and when she defected in November 1945 the NKVD must have assumed the worst about her contacts. In any event, this text represents the last time Lee was mentioned. After the war he gave evidence to the House Un-American Activities Committee and, although he corroborated much of Bentley's testimony, he denied any involvement with espionage. Instead of suing Bentley, he went into a private law practice in Washington DC. The FBI kept him under discreet surveillance and recommended his dismissal from the US Army Reserve, in which he held the rank of lieutenant colonel. Lee lost his appeal, and then left the country to live in South America.

As for J. Julius Joseph, he was to be mentioned in just one further text, despatched to Moscow by Stepan Apresyan on 13 October 1944:

> According to a report from CAUTIOUS [J. Julius Joseph] the HUT has developed and accepted a project [49 groups unrecovered] the COUNTRY [America] against the USSR [12 groups unrecoverable] anti-Soviet position proceeding from [3 groups unrecovered] the USSR and the COUNTRY is in future unavoidable. Ina TELBERG, an employee of the Planning Division of the HUT who has pro-Soviet leanings, reported to CAUTIOUS that the new people being accepted for responsible posts in [14 groups unrecovered] TELBERG [26 groups unrecovered] CAUTIOUS has been promoted Second Lieutenant. At present [3 groups unrecovered] Economic Sub-Division of the Far East Division [37 groups unrecovered]

The very next day, 14 October 1944, Apresyan announced that Joseph's sister Emma, who also worked for OSS, had been recruited:

> [5 groups unrecovered] sister of CAUTIOUS (henceforth 'IVY') about whom a report has already been made, has been accepted for work in the Department of Foreign Posts of the HUT [OSS]. In about a month's time she will be sent to a HUT post in CEYLON for a tour of one and a half to two years. Her work will consist in [2 groups unrecovered] arriving at the post.
>
> IVY is a FELLOWCOUNTRYWOMAN [Communist] who is highly spoken of by MYRNA [Elizabeth Bentley]. If we wish to establish liaison with her in CEYLON, MYRNA will make up the password. Telegraph instructions.

No action was taken against either J. Julius Joseph or Halperin, and in the context it must have seemed unlikely that Ina Telberg, who was then an analyst in OSS's Far East Division, was a spy.

Concern about the scale of Soviet penetration of OSS is clear from this text dated 1 June 1943 from Pavel Klarin:

> [118 groups unrecovered] HABSBURG [12 groups unrecovered] VANBERY, SFORZA, STURDZA, DAVILA, DEUTSCH and CZERNIN – [75 groups unrecovered] after which they will apply officially to CAPTAIN [President Roosevelt] and PRESS. The Chief of the Nationalities branch of the HUT DEWITT POOLE learned about this matter and [14 groups unrecovered] SPORZA and [87 groups unrecovered]

There was no clue to the source of this highly fragmented text, but four days later another telegram from Klarin referred to Carl August Wittfogel, whose name had been excised from the initial VENONA release, suggesting that a sensitive name had been identified:

> Reference No. 2384
> MERI on his own initiative that his known to your friend VITFOGEL [Carl August Wittfogel], who supports [19 groups unrecovered], told MERI [31 groups unrecoverable] ... CEN explained that this is [13 groups unrecovered] also on the fact that MERI's information confirm OSIPOV's [Nikolai V. Orlov] information [2 groups unrecovered]. RUFF indicates that according to rumours in circulation among workers in the HUT [OSS] [17 groups unrecovered]

On 8 June 1943 Klarin reported to Moscow, and referred to Milton Felson, who served with OSS between 1942 and 1945:

> UCN/6's wife received [5 groups unrecovered] description of his stay in the town of ALGIERS. From the letter one can gather that the HUT's [OSS] group now [15 groups unrecovered] [Milton] FELSON a former Spanish veteran [51 groups unrecovered] made the acquaintance in ALGIERS of the husband and [3 groups unrecovered] to the wife but could not because of [20 groups unrecovered] and leisure hours spend much time in the Red Cross building park 2–3 [32 groups unrecovered]

On 15 June, Klarin mentioned three unidentified sources, GARD, ARTHUR and RACHEL:

The HUT

1. GARD confirms there are 6 [1 group unidentified] [63 groups unrecoverable]

2. GARD sent a film containing codes and letters prepared in LONDON for each of these [1 group unrecovered] with a Swedish seaman. The letters are signed by GARD. The seaman was to pass the film to ARTHUR, whom he knew personally. ARTHUR was to pass it to the man in the LOT [unidentified] Department whence the codes and letters [7 groups unrecovered]. The arrangements for passing them on were to be made with the help of the man from the LOT Department or his assistants.

3. Since the man from the LOT Department is in Switzerland, the delivery of the codes, according to GARD [118 groups unrecovered] [1 group garbled] with ARTHUR.

4. [1 group unrecovered] in Brussels [1 group unrecovered] RACHEL's people; in ANTWERP GARD's people. GARD sent [1 group unrecovered] RACHEL [1 group unrecovered] and the letters by ordinary post from LISBON. The codes and instructions are to be delivered by ARTHUR.

5. GARD states that [11 groups unrecoverable] arrival in [1 group unrecovered] GARD avoided passing on to us the address and password for liaison in Switzerland with the LOT Department man on the grounds that the latter is connected in Switzerland with the HUT [OSS] and with a group of French refugees [8 groups unrecovered], will then at the right time be [1 group unrecovered] to this group [23 groups unrecoverable] from the HUT that the LOT Department man fled to Switzerland because the Germans had found out about his activities. The flight was organized by the Americans as if [14 groups unrecovered] no grounds for detaining him. [14 groups unrecovered] How was the account reported [8 groups unrecovered]

On 7 July 1943 Zubilin introduced some of his new sources inside OSS, including OFFICER, about whom there must have been sufficient collateral for him to be identified:

SERGEI [Vladimir Pravdin] reported through a contact man he had met OFFICER with whom [3 groups unrecovered] good personal relations. OFFICER [1 group unrecovered]

stated that on several occasions he had let it be understood
[5 groups unrecovered]. It is known that he spent 18 years in
JAPAN where he maintained contact through [8 groups
unrecovered] for the INSTITUTE [8 groups unrecovered] . . .
DER who at the moment [2 groups unrecovered] works in
the Japanese Section of the local COMPETITORS [intelligence
agency] and is looking for a good successor. OFFICER can
maintain contact with the suggested local
counter-intelligence officer in his capacity [13 groups
unrecovered] in FRANCE in 1941, there he [30 groups
unrecoverable] in the HUT and the RADIO ANNOUNCER
[General Donovan]. From there he got documents on the
USSR which were potentially of great interest. Not being in
touch with us here, he could not photograph them but sent
short extracts to SIDON [London] to be passed on to us. [3
groups unrecovered] got other information from the
successor and passed on a little [20 groups unrecovered] our
task. He reported that the local COMPETITORS were seeking
all kinds of information relating to us. [36 groups
unrecovered] Apparently to the local COMPETITORS
[1 group unrecovered] that OFFICER [1 group unrecovered]
the internal political [1 group unrecovered] military
position.

PART II The COMPETITORS approached OFFICER with
information about the USSR. He only gave general
information. Specifically they are seeking [11 groups
unrecovered] OFFICER [1 group unrecovered]. OFFICER [8
groups unrecovered] 'the American generals flatly refused to
undertake military operations in Europe this year [10 groups
unrecoverable] [1 group unrecovered] According to
OFFICER's information the Americans are at present sending
to AFRICA [1 group unrecovered] in LIBYA [75 groups
unrecovered]. They parted as [1 group unrecovered].
SERGEI's impression that OFFICER is sincere and wishes to
afford us material [12 groups unrecovered] from JAPAN the
verification of OFFICER and [5 groups unrecovered] JAPAN.
[9 groups unrecovered] for sending his wife to ALBANIA [38
groups unrecovered]

The HUT

On 20 July 1943 the first VENONA text regarding OSS to mention Nathan Gregory Silvermaster's network was sent to Moscow, and seemed to identify Emile Despres as an NKVD source inside OSS, recently returned from London:

> PAL [Nathan G. Silvermaster] reports that a number of government [1 group unrecovered] of the COUNTRY [America] [65 groups unrecoverable] influence [59 groups unrecovered] absence [9 groups unrecoverable] if in the country there were a special food-stuff [8 groups unrecovered]. The food-stuff [25 groups unrecovered] national [27 groups unrecoverable] food-stuff [69 groups unrecovered]. The advantageous position held by the British in [68 groups unrecoverable]
>
> PART II [10 groups unrecovered]. On [2 groups unrecovered] '[1 group unrecovered] D' [180 groups unrecovered]. Furthermore the government of the ISLAND [Britain] had begun in recent times to take a more friendly attitude to [12 groups unrecoverable] [19 groups unrecovered]. Among the officers of the army of the COUNTRY there is observable [28 groups unrecovered] [1 group unrecovered] of NABOB [Henry Morgenthau] [27 groups unrecovered]
>
> PART III The contents of a report of the HUT worker [Emile] DESPRES who has just returned from the ISLAND: No [53 groups unrecoverable] [39 groups unrecovered]. A united organization SALAD [Board of Economic Warfare] – HUT [remainder unrecovered]

On 9 September 1943 the New York *rezidentura* introduced yet another unidentified OSS source, codenamed KhAZAR, apparently well-informed about events in Serbia:

> The HUT [OSS] suggested to KhAZAR that he should go to Yugoslavia illegally [23 groups unrecovered] TITO and the HUT [56 groups unrecovered] KhAZAR [27 groups unrecovered]. We consider KhAZAR a PROBATIONER [agent] who is devoted to us [10 groups unrecoverable] NEDIC showed him a letter from his friend who is working in the BANK [State Department] in [5 groups unrecovered] General

NEDIC who promised [1 group unidentified] with the Americans [60 groups unrecovered] [20 groups unrecoverable]

On 13 October 1943 Klarin telegraphed Moscow about a source codenamed MIRAGE, and information from MIRAGE's wife about John Scott Nearing Jr, *Time*'s correspondent in Stockholm, and Edmund W. Stevens, who represented the *Christian Science Monitor* in Riga and then Moscow. Evidently, Nearing had been invited to work for OSS:

> MIRAGE's wife reports that IVANOV [John Scott Nearing] has left for STOCKHOLM on behalf of 'Time' magazine. Work in the HUT which [7 groups unrecovered] he rejected. STEVENSON [11 groups unrecovered] in the USSR as a correspondent for 'The Christian Science Monitor'.

'Stevenson' was most likely an error for Edmund Stevens, a graduate of Columbia University who moved to Moscow in 1934, married a Soviet named Nina the following year, and thereafter spent much of his life representing British newspapers and magazines in Russia. A secret CPUSA member, Stevens had previously been married to a Hungarian, Edith Emery, who was another Party activist, and she later married a member of the Central Committee's politburo, Roy B. Hudson. In August 1942 Stevens was appointed to General Russell Maxwell's staff as an adviser and accompanied Ambassador W. Averell Harriman to Moscow. In 1945 he wrote *Russia is No Riddle*, in praise of Stalin, and died in Moscow in 1992, still working as a foreign correspondent and insisting that he had never joined the Party. The fact that he had been granted the almost exclusive privilege of owning his own mansion in Moscow, and that Nina experienced no difficulty in sending underground art for exhibition and sale in New York, strongly suggested a degree of KGB cooperation.

The totality of the OSS VENONA intercepts show deep and prolonged Soviet penetration of the organization, but what is truly astonishing is the fact that OSS's Security Division was aware of the situation as early as September 1944, when a text from New York listed twenty internal suspects. According to Elizabeth Bentley, much the same information had been provided to her by Duncan Lee who had given her 'a slip of paper on which he had written down the names of people that the OSS considered dangerous risks, divided into three categories – "known Soviet agents," "known Communists," and "Communist sympathizers". In the first group were three names – none of whom I knew; in the second was an active member of the Perlo group, and in the third, Maurice Halperin.' The VENONA list dated 22 September 1944 made no distinction, and its provenance is difficult to judge:

> Further to No. 741. On the Security Division of the HUT's list of FELLOWCOUNTRYMEN [Communists] are the following: [9 names deleted] Donald WHEELER [10 names deleted] Both the [deleted] and [deleted] are included in a list of persons 'concerning whom it is known that they give information [10 groups unrecoverable] such persons and a proposal [6 groups unrecovered] dismissal.

The US authorities have deleted nineteen of the names on the list, leaving only Donald Wheeler, doubtless in respect of the Privacy Act, and it is only by scrutinizing the remaining VENONA traffic that one can guess who was included in the original version. The excised footnotes strongly suggest that virtually everyone has been identified.

IZRA was the codename assigned to Donald N. Wheeler, a veteran CPUSA member, mentioned in this brief text from New York, dated 1 October 1944, from Apresyan, which was added to a much longer, two-part message on another subject:

> Materials about the conspiracy and the COMPETITORS [intelligence service] of the ISLAND [England], as it turns out, have to be obtained through IZRA [Donald Wheeler] and so I am passing the task on to VADIM [Anatoli Gromov].

In another VENONA text, dated 15 January 1945, Stepan Apresyan showed that Nathan Silvermaster, now codenamed ROBERT, still enjoyed easy access to OSS's secrets:

> ROBERT reports that: the Research Section of the HUT has compiled information about the ability of Hungary to pay reparations. According to the information the national income of Hungary will total 60–65 million dollars the first year following the conclusion of military operations with a

drop in hostilities in the future. Hungary can pay in petroleum products, bauxite and agricultural products. She can export 16 million dollars' worth of petroleum products a year.

While the above telegram may not have been of much significance, a partially fragmented text, dated 10 February 1945 from Silvermaster, listing some of OSS's more socially prominent personnel based in Germany, did excite some interest in Moscow:

> From ROBERT has been received a memorandum [16 groups unrecovered] in the memorandum it says: '[13 groups unrecovered] DAVID BRUCE, PAUL MELLON, JUNIUS MORGAN, HENRY MORGAN, SUYDAM CUTTING, JOHN AUCHINCLOSS, GORDON AUCHINCLOSS, LESTER ARMOUR, ALFRED DUPONT, RAYMOND GUEST, WILLIAM VAN ALAN, [2 groups unrecovered], HAROLD COOLIDGE, E. BIGELOW, ALLAN DULLES, LLOYD CABOT BRIDGES [7 groups unrecoverable]

This prompted a request from Moscow dated 22 February 1945:

> Your 137
> Try to obtain through ROBERT [Nathan Silvermaster] more detailed information on the workers of the HUT, who you list, [6 groups unrecovered]

Another VENONA, dated 27 June 1945 from Washington DC, proved Moscow was continuing to receive information about the Balkans from inside OSS, although on this occasion the text was too fragmented to implicate the source:

> [75 groups unrecoverable] American [12 groups unrecovered] he arrived with [2 groups unrecovered] HUT a day before the arrival [18 groups unrecovered] English and American governments. Detailed announcements [38 groups unrecovered] Robert WOLFF, who is working in the Balkan Section of the Branch of Research [166 groups unrecoverable] mentioned the president of a large [1 group unrecovered] firm [4 groups unrecovered] (or like this) as a business participant. His participants on [4 groups unrecovered] do not know the Russian language. The manager [7 groups unrecovered]

Paul Neff, one of the TICOM/3 team at Schloss Bergsheidegen, receiving an award.

Cater W. Clarke (right) headed the Special Branch of US military intelligence and was responsible for setting up the VENONA project.

Left William Weisband, the Russian-born Signals Intelligence expert who gained access to the BRIDE project as a linguist but turned out to be an experienced Soviet spy. He certainly betrayed many details of the progress made by the AFSA cryptographers, but was never convicted of espionage because VENONA was considered too secret to reveal in court. Instead he was prosecuted for contempt, having refused to answer questions about his prewar membership of the CPUSA.

Below Frank Rowlett was the first head of the CIA's specialist unit known as 'Staff D', which was dedicated to researching leads provided by VENONA.

Meredith Gardner (left), the linguistic genius at work on 'the Russian problem' at Arlington Hall in 1946, surrounded by the women clerks who undertook much of the painstakingly difficult cryptanalysis before the introduction of computers.

Arlington Hall, Virginia, America's equivalent of Bletchley Park where early success on Japanese ciphers and German one-time pads encouraged the cryptographers to concentrate on the Soviet traffic.

Gene Grabeel, the former schoolteacher who was a member of the very first BRIDE team in 1943, and who achieved the original breaks into the Soviet trade traffic.

FBI Special Agent Robert Lamphere who in October 1948 was appointed a permanent liaison officer for the VENONA material and supervised many of the early investigations into clues that led to the arrests of Klaus Fuchs and the Rosenbergs.

Above Originally the FBI's liaison officer with US military intelligence, S. Wesley Reynolds was the first Special Agent to be indoctrinated into VENONA in September 1947, and participated in many of the subsequent molehunts.

Above Stephan Apresyan, the NKVD *rezident* in New York who appears in dozens of VENONA texts as MAY. He was responsible for handling dozens of agents and was transferred to San Francisco in March 1945.

Below Oliver Kirby, a Bletchley Park veteran, was an inspired cryptographer who led a TICOM team in Schleswig that recovered valuable cryptographic data from the Nazis. He was to be one of the principals dealing with 'the Russian problem' between 1946 and 1952.

Above Leonid Kvasnikov, head of a separate *rezidentura* in New York devoted to coordinating Operation ENORMOZ, the collection of intelligence about the atomic bomb. Codenamed ANTON, Kvasnikov was one of the few NKVD officers with a technical background and was officially accredited in the US as an engineer attached to Amtorg.

The Arlington Hall bowling team, whose members were all working on VENONA (with the exception of Louise Derthick); left to right, back row: Cecil Phillips, William Lutwiniak (later the NSA's top cryptographer), Paul Derthick (deputy manager of all Soviet manual systems in the 1950s). Front row: Frank Lewis, Louise Derthick.

Mildred Hayes spent 28 years on the VENONA project and was responsible for finally closing it down.

Joan Malone Callahan was the first US liaison officer to GCHQ at Eastcote, and remained in England for three years. A skilled Russian linguist and a brilliant 'depth reader', she made a vital contribution to VENONA's success and acted as VENONA's liaison officer with the CIA.

Gloria Forbes managed the processing of all the diplomatic messages between 1943 and 1950 and proved herself to be an exceptional traffic analyst.

Ivor Montagu. The third son of Lord Swaythling, Montagu was an ardent Communist throughout his life and used his position as a war correspondent for the *Daily Worker* to visit military sites at the height of the Blitz and submit reports to his GRU controller, Colonel Sklyarov. MI5 never suspected he had been a spy or realised he had run a network known as the X GROUP until VENONA's London traffic was cracked in the 1960s and he was identified as the source appropriately codenamed NOBILITY.

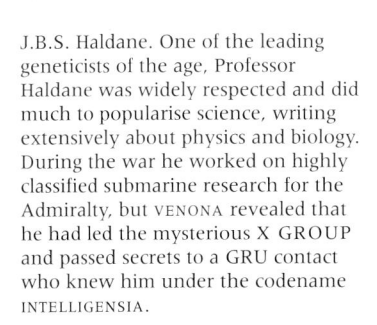

J.B.S. Haldane. One of the leading geneticists of the age, Professor Haldane was widely respected and did much to popularise science, writing extensively about physics and biology. During the war he worked on highly classified submarine research for the Admiralty, but VENONA revealed that he had led the mysterious X GROUP and passed secrets to a GRU contact who knew him under the codename INTELLIGENSIA.

The HUT

On 29 June there followed an equally unrewarding text from Washington DC about a source abbreviated as 'I':

> To the 8th Department
> I's materials. We are transmitting a telegram of a representative of the HUT in Belgrade Lieutenant [Robert G.] MINOR [22 groups unrecovered], in the capacity of leader of the legitimate government. [82 groups unrecovered] [Yugoslav Foreign Minister Josip] SMODLAKA [7 groups unrecovered] [30 groups unrecovered]

Such abbreviations were not unusual, and often were used by Soviet handlers as a shorthand for regular and reliable agents. Most likely, the 'I' is a reference to IZRA, the NKVD's Washington source, Donald Wheeler. As for Smodlaka, the context is difficult to interpret. A Croat from Dalmatia, he was a pre-1918 Yugoslav patriot and a member of the home rule assembly in Zagreb. Having campaigned against Austro-Hungarian rule, Smodlaka had retired from politics in 1918, but Tito appointed him his Foreign Minister, and installed him in a villa outside Bari in 1944, although in reality the Partisan leader retained control over Yugoslav foreign policy for himself.

Wheeler's identification had been based on an important text from New York, dated 30 May 1944 from MAY, (Stepan Apresyan), which had neatly summarized the membership of a new network:

> The PROBATIONERS [agents] of the new group have given the following personal histories of themselves:
> 1. TED [Edward J. Fitzgerald], an old FELLOWCOUNTRYMAN [Communist], capable, reliable, works in the Civilian Allocation Division of the DEPOT [War Production Board]
> 2. KANT [Henry S. Magdoff] became a FELLOWCOUNTRYMAN a long time ago, being [8 groups unrecovered], works in the Machine Tool Division of the DEPOT.
> 3. RAIDER [Victor Perlo], an old FELLOWCOUNTRYMAN, reliable, capable, works in the Aeroplane Allocation Division of the DEPOT [4 groups unrecovered] ARENA [Mary Price] through [8 groups unrecovered] STORM.
> 4. PLUMB [Charles Kramer], an old FELLOWCOUNTRYMAN, reliable, works on the KILGORE Committee [62 groups

unrecoverable] ARENA's apartment. [46 groups unrecovered] Donald Wheeler 'IZRA', has been a FELLOWCOUNTRYMAN for several years, a Trade Union official, capable, works in the Labor Division, Research & Analysis Branch of the HUT [6 groups unrecovered] PART II [31 groups unrecovered] he did not maintain contact with [53 groups unrecovered] about this group from SOUND [Jacob Golos] [3 groups unrecovered] material on them). CHAR ... [39 groups unrecoverable]. (He is everywhere in [14 groups unrecovered] For this purpose the Trade Unions [8 groups unrecovered] Trade Unions, working class and progressive contacts of the local FELLOWCOUNTRYMEN. [9 groups unrecovered] He maintains a close relationship with MUSE and has repeatedly tried to marry her. He is a close friend of SLANG [Jane Foster Zlavotski] [3 groups unrecoverable] and often comes to TYRE [New York] with her (SLANG has spoken very well of him). Harold GLASSER, an old FELLOWCOUNTRYMAN. Temporarily abroad (evidently STORM knew him well). Concerning the remaining members of the group we will advise later.

This text was especially helpful to the counter-intelligence analysts seeking to trace the old NKVD spies in OSS, one of whom was MUSE, a woman who had been credited as a key source inside OSS in a telegram from Apresyan to the 8th Department, dated 4 July 1944:

MUSE reports:
1. According to information from the Head of the 'Secret Funds' department of the HUT, Emerson BIGELOW, the ISLANDERS [British], without the knowledge of the TOWNSMEN [Americans] have purchased several million Portuguese escudos to help the Polish government in exile. BIGELOW declares that he got this information from the Polish COMPETITORS [intelligence service].
2. The North European Department of the Secret Intelligence Branch of the HUT closely watches the movement of our money in Europe. On instructions of the BANK [State Department] the HUT is trying to ascertain whether NEGRIN is receiving money from SMYRNA [Moscow]. The BANK

The HUT

considers that the position as stated by NEGRIN with regard to the Spanish Junta serves only as cover for a different kind of activity on the instructions of SMYRNA. An agent of the HUT, Colonel GIL, who has deeply infiltrated into Spanish emigré circles, reported to his superiors that NEGRIN receives from SMYRNA a considerable sum of money. According to another report which has reached the HUT, CASADA is supported by a woman working for the COMPETITORS of the ISLAND [Britain].

3. According to the opinion of a worker of the Romanian Section of the HUT the Romanian Government is preparing for peace talks with SMYRNA which apparently [8 groups unrecoverable] stopped the issue to Germans of exit visas with the exception of diplomatic ones.

According to the information of the same worker the Romanians are receiving gas masks from the Germans in exchange for other commodities. In his opinion this fact confirms the Germans' intention to use gas against the Red Army. For some time sealed railway cars have been leaving from Romania with a directive forbidding them to be opened until HITLER's personal instructions are received.

MUSE was active again, according to a text from New York dated 23 September 1944:

> A report from MUSE. The Chief of the Bulgarian Section of the Secret Branch of the HUT [OSS] COMPETITION [intelligence service] is HALLAS. Of the Romanian Section is BONCESCU, an anti-Soviet, anti-Semite, from a wealthy Romanian family. In the Turkish Section work GURNEY and Gordon LOUD.
>
> [55 groups unrecoverable] the Philippines, middle of 1945 – the Continent. The plan does not foresee the possibility [4 groups unrecovered]

Although MUSE has not been identified in the VENONA footnotes, the best candidate remains Helen Tenney, who was a young, attractive, wealthy Iberian analyst for OSS, whom Bentley said was

> a Communist of long standing, who had been very active in Spanish organizations during the Civil War . . . She had

worked in New York for an organization set up by the Office of Strategic Services for the purpose of finding people of all nationalities who could be trained in sabotage and intelligence and then sent abroad to carry on undercover work. Helen had been quite valuable in that position. She had brought to Yasha [Jacob Golos] the dossiers of all the prospective candidates so that we would know what type of people they were employing.

She was doing excellent work in the OSS bringing us stacks of ditto-machined confidential reports from their undercover operatives in places as far away as Persia and Kurdistan.

When the FBI closed in on Helen Tenney, her chauffeur tipped her off to their interest, and when she was required to give evidence to Congress she pleaded the Fifth Amendment and remained silent. She was fired by the War Department and later, after a suicide attempt, she was detained as a mental patient in the Whitney Payne Clinic where she was visited by Bentley in 1947 at the FBI's request. Her passport was revoked and she died insane, insisting that she 'had never talked'. Linked to MUSE by the man who hoped to marry her was SLANG, who apparently had spoken well of him. She was Jane Foster, a fiery Party member from San Francisco who had graduated from Mills College in 1935 before travelling to Moscow, Berlin and Paris. She got married in Java. Returning to the USA in 1940, she became active in the New York Party, and the following year was invited to join the Board of Economic Warfare as an expert on Indonesia, where she worked alongside Charles Flato. In September 1943 she was recruited by OSS's Morale Operations branch and assigned to the South-East Asia division, and early the following year, having married a fellow Party member, George Zlatovski, was transferred to Ceylon (Sri Lanka). When she finally returned to the USA in 1946 her husband was in Germany, and she renewed her friendship with Alfred and Martha Stern, who introduced her to Jack Soble. According to her own account, *An Unamerican Lady*, she gave him a classified report she had written about Indonesia, and recognized much of it in a speech given to the United Nations by the Ukrainian delegate, Dmitri Manuilsky: 'Although OSS had labeled my Indonesian report "Top Secret", I did not attach any importance to that fact. After all, it only contained my own experiences and observations, and items that Sukarno and other Indonesian officials had wanted me to make public.'

Jane Zlatovski later went to join her husband in Salzburg, where he worked for military intelligence, and she was employed by the local US Information Service radio station. They eventually settled in Paris, and in January 1957 were taken in for interrogation by the French DST when Jack and Myra Soble were arrested. They refused to return to the USA to give evidence against the Sobles, and were indicted on espionage charges. The French authorities declined to extradite them, so they remained in Paris where Jane Zlatovski died in September 1979.

The FBI's interest in Jane Zlatovski had originated with Boris Morros, but there was also some VENONA evidence against her, albeit slim, but enough to identify her as SLANG, credited in the third and final part of a text from Iskhak Akhmerov in New York, dated 30 June 1943, about the Vice-President, Henry Wallace, who headed the Board of Economic Warfare:

> PART III 6. SLANG [Jane Foster] told [1 group unrecovered] the following: 'The President sent BOATSWAIN [Henry Wallace], the head of the WAREHOUSE [Board of Economic Warfare] a plan for setting up a committee for [19 groups unrecovered] The committee is subordinate to the BANK [State Department] and CAPTAIN [President Roosevelt]. The head of the BANK has been appointed chairman of the committee which [50 groups unrecovered] MURPHY [64 groups unrecovered]

As well as being an important target for the NKVD, OSS was the subject of much interest from the GRU, although only five VENONA texts survive. The first, dated 12 July 1943 from Pavel P. Mikhailov of the Soviet consulate-general in New York, revealed the existence of a source codenamed SMITH, who was later identified as Leonard E. Mins who had worked for OSS as a Russian interpreter since April 1942. Elizabeth Bentley recalled that Bella Joseph, who was employed to make confidential films for the General Staff in OSS's Movie Division, once encountered Mins at headquarters and had 'fled in panic'. Years before, she had known him quite well, 'remembering that he was an open Communist, she was terrified of being seen with him'. Clearly Bella, who was married to J. Julius Joseph, codenamed CAUTIOUS by the NKVD, had no idea that Mins was an active GRU spy:

> SMITH [Leonard Mins] has passed the following information:
> 1. He has had a talk with [John A.] MORRISON (deputy chief of the Russian section of OSS). The latter stated:
>
> (a) At the War Department there is a group of officers known now under the name of 'the twelve apostles'. The latter consists mainly of officers of the Intelligence Division (G2).
>
> (b) SMITH has identified through MORRISON only three of the members of this group: TRUMAN, MACGUIRE, CLAYTON (all from G2).
>
> (c) In this group there is being propagated the idea of war with the USSR [26 groups unrecoverable] MORRISON considers the preparation for war with the USSR was recently begun; that the direct aim is to pave the way for the maintainance in the USA after the war of a large army, which in turn will permit the higher officers to keep their ranks, high rates of pay, etc.
>
> (d) In MORRISON's opinion this idea constitutes also one of the measures of the military clique in paving the way for the establishment of a military dictatorship in the country. '[I group garbled] that friction within the ROOSEVELT Administration and between that Administration and Congress [5 groups unrecovered] in the conduct of the war and the post-war transition of power into the hands of the military'.
>
> 2. Later SMITH had a talk (together with MORRISON) with Stuart HAYDEN (an employee of the bureau for working out plans for the administration of liberated countries, a prominent CHICAGO correspondent). He also spoke of the present tendency towards a military dictatorship which is supported by a section of the big industrialists.
>
> 3. Herbert WOLLNER an employee of the Department of Finance also spoke to SMITH on this same subject. He called this tendency 'a striving for a dictatorship of the Fascist type'.
>
> 4. At one of the universities a group of 81 army officers has

The HUT

completed training in Russian. It is intended for the formation of a General Staff special Cryptographic [69 groups unrecoverable] [54 groups unrecovered]

The next month, on 16 August, Mikhailov had more to say about OSS's Russian section, also attributed to Mins, and a report about China, from three hitherto unknown sources, Joseph M. Bernstein, codenamed MARQUIS, Thomas A. Bisson, codenamed ARTHUR, and RHODES:

1. Information of MARQUIS [Joseph Bernstein].
(a) After unsuccessful conversations with the Communist Party about the role of the 8th Army, CHIANG KAI-SHEK sent an extra five divisions to strengthen the army blockading the SHENSI–KANSU–NINGSIA areas (ARTHUR's [Thomas Bisson] information).
(b) For a while in government circles the question of sending their representatives for direct contact with the government of the areas indicated was urgently discussed. This situation is explained by the desire of the American command to establish air bases on the territory of these regions.
(c) In the Lend-Lease Division of the War Department among the commissioned personnel there is an increasing resistance to fulfilling shipments for the USSR (particularly in connection with the Red Army line). The most vehement advocate of the curtailing shipments is Major A. PEABODY. (Information of RHODES, an employee of the Division and an old acquaintance of FARLEY).
(d) Military circles are also resisting Lend-Lease consignments to the Chinese government, insisting along with this on increasing consignments to General STILWELL. (The same source).
Information of SMITH [Leonard Mins]. Beginning on 13th August the Russian Division of the OSS has been working day and night on the compilation of some kind of urgent report (SMITH could not find out the details – he supposes the report is being prepared for ROOSEVELT's conference with CHURCHILL).

RHODES in this case was most likely Peter C. Rhodes, a well-known journalist and writer, originally from the Philippines. According to Elizabeth Bentley, Rhodes had experienced some difficulty over his US citizenship because his father had been German, and apparently his mother, a British intelligence agent, had killed him during the First World War. Whatever the truth, both Rhodes and his Belgian wife were CPUSA members, and he was to be sent to the Mediterranean to broadcast from a propaganda station in Egypt, which meant the Soviets could maintain contact only with his wife.

The next day, 17 August, Mikhailov had more to report from Mins, who had been suspended from OSS because of his Communist links:

> 1. On 16th August 1943 the hearing of SMITH's [Leonard Mins] case took place before the Appeals Board of the Civil Service organization. Six colleagues in OSS came forward in his defence, including the Chief of the Russian Section, ROBINSON. The latter insists upon SMITH's return to work in OSS. The result will be made known at the end of August. At the moment SMITH has gone away for a two weeks' holiday.
> 2. An acquaintance of SMITH, an artist and technical illustrator, ISADORE STEINBERG, has been taken on for work in the War Department as a member of the publications bureau and expert on military publications matters attached to the Adjutant-General's office. STEINBERG is a CORPORANT [Communist] and owner of the firm PRODUCTION ILLUSTRATION in NEW YORK at 155 West 20th Street. SMITH strongly recommends him, he has known him for 15 years. OPPEN is also well acquainted with him. As SMITH is still at the stage of being checked he has been directed for the time being to refrain from meeting STEINBERG. We consider that the latter will be useful to us both as a source for secret publications of the War Department and for general military and political information. It would be best to recruit him through OPPEN.
> 3. In CAIRO [1 group unrecovered] a branch of OSS. The complement of staff is being recruited.
> 4. In reply to your No. 11312. The people recommended by [Thomas] BABIN who have finished the radio course have

been sent to England with radio units. The question of their being developed by us falls to the ground.

5. The other names of the woman who gave SIMON [information] about talks with the President is Josephine Treslow [Adams].

In connection with METEOR's transfer to CAPITAL [Washington DC] the Trade Representative must [1 groups unrecovered] our man. It is desirable that it should be to an administrative post – Director of Transport Accounts Division or Deputy Director of the Publications Section.

Although the identities of OPPEN and METEOR remain unknown, Josephine Truslow Adams was to become notorious as a wholly unreliable informant for Earl Browder who was misled into thinking she had direct access to the White House. In fact the art teacher from Brooklyn had painted Eleanor Roosevelt after they had met when the first lady visited Swarthmore College in 1941. Thereafter Truslow Adams fantasized a close relationship with the Roosevelts and even manufactured some bogus correspondence. When she was introduced to Browder in July 1942, he believed her. She gradually became more delusional, and little is known about the latter part of her life which was spent in psychiatric institutions.

Much more is known about MARQUIS and ARTHUR. Joseph Bernstein (MARQUIS) was of particular interest to the FBI as he had long been an espionage suspect. A gifted linguist, born in Connecticut, he had been educated at Yale and the Sorbonne before working as a newspaper reporter in Bucharest. Upon his return to the USA in 1938 he had worked with Julio Alvarez del Vayo, formerly Spain's leftist Foreign Minister in the republican government, and then for Otto Katz, the Czech journalist who wrote, *J'Accuse* about the fall of France in 1940 under the pseudonym André Simone. Katz, of course, was a well-known Communist who was to return to Prague after the Communists seized power, and later became the editor of the Party's daily paper, *Rude Pravo*. In 1940 Bernstein had been refused a civil service appointment after he had been found to have lied on his application about his European travels. He had omitted all reference to his prewar job in Romania, and had concealed some unexplained journeys between Switzerland and Turkey. A civil service commission inquiry had judged him unsuitable for government employment, lacking 'loyalty or morality', but he had not come under suspicion as a Soviet spy until March 1946 when he had been logged meeting another spy suspect, Mary Jane Keeney, then a member of the Allied Committee on Reparations. Her husband, Philip C. Keeney, had appeared in a May 1942 VENONA as one of Jake Golos's contacts.

The material in the VENONA text of 16 August attributed to MARQUIS was of compelling interest to the FBI because of its likely provenance. Obviously Bernstein had no direct access to information about Chiang Kai-Shek and General Stilwell in China, so where had he obtained it? The most likely source was, as mentioned, Thomas Bisson, codenamed ARTHUR, the organizer of the Institute of Pacific Relations and a member of the editorial board of the pro-Communist periodical *China Today*. Bisson appeared on the journal's masthead under the pseudonym 'Lawrence Hearn', alongside Philip Jaffe who called himself 'John W. Phillips'. He was also a founder of *China Today*'s controversial successor, *Amerasia*, which in January 1945 was to publish classified data from OSS in an article and lead to a major espionage investigation.

The *Amerasia* case collapsed before the six defendants could be prosecuted because the FBI's evidence was based on an OSS investigation that had depended on illegal wiretaps and warrantless searches. The offending *Amerasia* article had come from an OSS report written by Kenneth Wells who had drawn extensively on a British intelligence assessment of postwar policy in South-east Asia, concentrating on Thailand. Tipped off by the British, and encouraged by Wells, OSS's security section conducted its own surveillance on *Amerasia*'s editorial offices at 225 Fifth Avenue, New York and one Sunday evening in March made an illicit search of Philip Jaffe's suite and darkroom. Inside were hundreds of classified official documents from virtually every branch of government, including the Office of Naval Intelligence (ONI), War Department, State Department. Office of Postal and Telegraph Censorship, and OSS. Further surveillance implicated Jaffe, three of his editorial staff, and his main contacts: Andrew Roth of the Office of Naval Intelligence, Jack Service of the State Department, and Emmanuel Larsen, who had left the ONI in 1944 to join the State Department. Altogether seven suspects were arrested in June, and a mass of secret documents were seized, but all the charges were later dropped because the prosecution case was so dependent on inadmissible evidence. Surprisingly, none of the seven was willing to plea bargain and testify against a co-defendant, which left the FBI with vast quantities of collateral material, particularly about Mary Keeney and Joseph Bernstein, that did not begin to make sense until years later, when VENONA became available. For example, Philip Jaffe was monitored by the FBI as he attempted to deal with an approach from Bernstein who had asked, on behalf of the Soviets, for copies of Jaffe's accumulated collection of secret State Department documents. Far from being dismayed by the request, Jaffe's principal concern had been to avoid entrapment by OSS *agents provocateur*, and he had sought advice from Earl Browder, among others, about establishing Bernstein's credentials as a bonafide Soviet spy. The technical and physical surveillance had been inconclusive, but VENONA showed that MARQUIS was indeed a valuable NKVD source, as was ARTHUR. However, no public statement about MARQUIS was ever made, and although Bernstein was subpoenaed to give evidence to a Grand Jury investigation of Soviet espionage in New York in 1953, he escaped prosecution and continued to contribute articles to CPUSA journals until his death in 1975. The FBI's interest in him as a Soviet spy kept his name on the Security Index until 1966.

Similarly, although Jack Service had been implicated as one of those who had leaked information to Jaffe, there was no firm evidence that any of his material had reached the Soviets, except of course for what had appeared in *Amerasia* itself. Accordingly, Service had kept his job as a diplomat until his dismissal in 1951 on a Loyalty Board recommendation, serving in administrative roles, without a security clearance, in the New Delhi embassy and the US consulate in Liverpool, his previously promising career effectively terminated by his involvement with Jaffe. In 1962 he resigned, aged fifty-three, to study at the University of California at Berkeley, and in 1971 published a defence of his position in *The Amerasia Papers*.

Others implicated in the *Amerasia* affair were John C. Vincent and John P. Davies, both officials in the State Department's China section. Vincent, who had spent nineteen years in the consular service in China, had been one of those on the State Department's distribution list for the Wells report on Thailand. He had worked briefly under Lauchlin Currie at the Foreign Economic Administration when he first returned to Washington from Chungking in May 1943, and was considered a leftist sympathizer. His State Department career finally ended when he was dismissed after a Loyalty Board review of his case in December 1951. His colleague, John Davies, had grown up in China with Jack Service, and his employment was terminated by the Loyalty Board in 1954. Also fired from the State Department was Jimmy Larsen, from whose apartment 700 government documents had been recovered at the time of his arrest. He subsequently tried to find work as a journalist, but died in 1988, having spent the previous twenty-five years on the reception desk of a hotel in Washington DC.

Finally, Andrew Roth, the ONI intelligence officer indicted by the Grand Jury in August 1945 on charges of conspiring to steal government property, moved abroad as a correspondent for *The Nation* and remained in England when his passport expired as the compiler and publisher of *Parliamentary Profiles*, an annually updated digest of British Members of Parliament.

On 23 August 1943 Mikhailov reported to Moscow with more OSS material from Leonard Mins:

> SMITH [Leonard Mins] has made the acquaintance of Lt Col. William GAYLE [9 groups unrecovered] FORT DIX NEW JERSEY (This division at the end of August will be redeployed to Camp PICKET, near LYNCHBURG VIRGINIA, 160 miles South-West of WASHINGTON), Not [87 groups unrecovered] that attitude of the majority of the senior army officers, [14 groups unrecovered] PATTON, who is at the moment with the Army in SICILY, [19 groups unrecovered] of the Chair of Economics of the university in NASHVILLE (TENNESSEE) a CORPORANT [Communist] whom SMITH also knows. If it is possible, check. SMITH has been instructed to refrain for the moment from private meetings [2 groups unrecovered] proposals [24 groups unrecovered]

Two days later, Mikhailov mentioned No. 16, PHIL, and No. 22, identified as Captain Hogman of OSS:

> PHIL has been getting the Intelligence Bulletins through No. 16 from Captain HOGMAN (Covername No. 12), who works in OSS. [12 groups unrecovered] PHIL, [2 groups unrecovered], [1 group unrecovered] No. 65). PHIL has been

given the task of obtaining all the issues for this year; this was not done earlier since according to [1 group unrecovered] of RUAN [Ilya M. Saraev], he used to get them regularly out of the War Department.

Finally, on 8 September, Mikhailov sent this comprehensive report to Moscow:

[24 groups unrecovered] KLARK is not a CORPORANT [Communist]. SMITH discussed this subject with him cautiously, not being a close acquaintance of his. KLARK has avoided meeting MAX. The one remaining chance is for MAX to try once more to see KLARK.

(b) SMITH [Leonard Mins] would not establish who gave the lecture to the General Staff on the war with USSR.

(c) Your instructions on the recruitment of DONALD were given to NICK [Irving C. Nelson] in good time. The latter has not yet succeeded in arranging his meeting with him.

(d) RUDI has not so far come to a meeting, on the grounds that [1 group unrecovered] increased shadowing. It is evidently for the same reason that JACK will not agree to a meeting with me either.

(e) Control of NICK has been transferred from METEOR to DEIGHTON and control of MAX has been transferred to MASTERCRAFTSMAN.

(f) The balance of cash on 1st September 1943 (taking into account the balance of the purchasing fund and after repayment of 1,247 American dollars to fund No. 2 is 10,640 American dollars.

3. Your additional task has been given to RUDOLF. It will be given also to SOURCE 13. The latter, after being asked repeatedly, through PHIL to inform us personally on military-political questions, has given his first piece of information. (It is about the talk with the British major.) We are using this to make him increase his activity.

MATVEJ [Milton Schwartz] has applied for a loan of 1,200 dollars: he requires this because of personal financial difficulties. NICK supports the request but [30 groups unrecoverable] MOK [Vladimir V. Gavriluk] should be approaching VLADIVOSTOCK. Make sure that instructions are given about landing and about the provision of papers, a ticket and money for the journey.

That the Soviets were always anxious to extend their reach into OSS is obvious from several VENONA texts with a continuing theme of manoeuvring sources into General Donovan's organization. This was true of Elizabeth Bentley's friend Mary Price, who was turned down by OSS because of her 'past Communist associations', and Helen Scott-Keenan, codenamed SPRUCE. As late as 22 June 1945 part of a VENONA text from Washington DC mentioned that

> SPRUCE [Helen Scott-Keenan] wants a transfer to the BANK [State Department] of the HUT [OSS] and she began to do something or other in this respect. A few days ago it became known to SPRUCE that there is a requirement on the staff of the COUNTRY's [America] representative on the commission on war criminals, officially called 'The Office of the US Chief of Counsel for the Prosecution of Axis War Criminals,' for a technical worker [2 groups unrecoverable] this staff to the number of 17 is being selected and will be co-ordinated with the HUT. In the person of the special assistant to the 'Director' – Ferdinand L. MAYER and all its members will be considered employees of the HUT. With our sanction SPRUCE applied to the HUT. She reports that a detachment will [11 groups unrecovered] chief representative of the COUNTRY on the Commission on [71 groups unrecoverable]

At the end of the war many of those who were to be compromised by VENONA left government service, but when OSS was disbanded by Harry Truman's Executive Order of September 1945, the Research and Analysis Branch was absorbed into the State Department. Maurice Halperin was one of those who made the transition but his overtly pro-Soviet views were widely known, and early in February 1946 the FBI Director J. Edgar Hoover informed the State Department that Halperin had been named as a Soviet spy by Elizabeth Bentley. At this point Halperin resigned and moved to Brooklyn to work as a lobbyist at the United Nations for the American Jewish Congress, before joining Boston University. However, in March 1953 he was subpoenaed to appear before a Senate Internal Security Subcommittee to answer Elizabeth Bentley's accusations, and he pleaded the Fifth Amendment, the right not to incriminate himself. The university suspended him pending an investigation, and Halperin promptly fled to Mexico with his wife, leaving their son David with his parents. He was appointed an adjunct professor at the National University in Mexico City, and the Halperins acquainted themselves with other expatriate Communists, including Alfred and Martha Stern. In 1958 the Halperins visited Prague and the Soviet Union, and took a job with the Latin American section of the Institute of World Economics and International Affairs. After three years in the Soviet capital, where they became friendly with the British defector Donald Maclean, the Halperins moved to Havana. Maurice then took a teaching post at the Simon Fraser University in Vancouver in September 1968. He retired a decade later and, following the death of his wife in 1988, ventured only occasionally over the border before he died two years later.

In his retirement Halperin continued to deny any involvement in espionage, and has no explanation for why Elizabeth Bentley named him as a spy, nor why Nathaniel Weyl testified before Congress that when he had been a CPUSA functionary he had known Halperin as the CPUSA's representative to the Mexican Party. All he admitted was that while in Washington DC he had gossiped to journalists about the friction between OSS and the FBI:

> we chatted about some of the jurisdictional scuttlebutt floating around, but mainly about Latin America. I was very careful not to reveal classified information, though naturally my views and opinions were enriched by my knowledge of classified material. But this was being done and there was no, what shall I say – it didn't contravene the rules. I want to again emphasize that there was a line I never crossed – out of prudence, perhaps, I mean, I did have some prudence at time.

Unfortunately, Halperin died before he could be confronted with the damning evidence against him contained in VENONA, and there can be no doubt that he spied for the NKVD. There remains a suspicion that he may not have acted alone. Perhaps significantly, his assistant in both OSS and the State Department, Irving Goldman, was also a CPUSA member. In 1953, after Goldman had left the State Department's Office of Intelligence and Research to become a professor at Sarah Lawrence College, he gave evidence to Congress in which he acknowledged his CPUSA membership.

The question remaining is how many other OSS officers spied. Official Comintern archive documents recently released in Moscow give some additional clues and suggest that the NKVD expressed an interest in the CPUSA backgrounds of Lillian Hoell in September 1944, and two months later in Lillian S. Traugott, who had joined the Party in 1937 and had worked for OSS in New York, London and Stockholm. Since the NKVD invariably inquired into the Party connections for potential recruits, it is likely that both were recruited or at least approached.

Of course OSS occasionally recruited Communists precisely because of their political backgrounds. Milton Wolff, for example, who was the last commander of the Abraham Lincoln Brigade in the Spanish Civil War, worked for Colonel S. W. (Bill) Bailey of British Special Operations Executive and OSS nominating veterans of the International Brigade, mainly Czechs, Yugoslavs and Greeks, for commando training prior to being dropped into Nazi-occupied Europe, and himself worked in northern Italy. Before Bailey was dropped into Yugoslavia in December 1942 he had undertaken a recruitment tour across Canada, interviewing candidates suggested by Wolff. Similarly, the Lincoln Brigade veterans Irving Goff, Vincent Lossowki and Irving Fajans served with OSS in Italy. Goff ran a radio station broadcasting to Communist partisans, won the Legion of Merit and after the war became a senior CPUSA organizer in Louisiana and then New York. When General Donovan was challenged about Irving Goff being 'on the honour roll of the Young Communist League' he replied: 'I don't know if he's on the Communist honour roll, but for the job he did in Africa and Italy, he's on the honour roll of OSS.'

Other CPUSA members who worked for OSS included the cartographer Leo M. Drozdoff, who switched from OSS to the State Department but pleaded the Fifth Amendment in 1952 when asked if he had acted as a Party organizer under the name Michael Zorn; Jack S. Harris; Professor John K. Fairbank of Harvard; Paul V. Martineau; David Zablodowski who became head of the Publications Division of the UN Secretariat; and George Wuchinich, who had fought with the Lincoln battalion, served in China and with Tito in Yugoslavia.

XII

The Silvermaster Group

ALTHOUGH Elizabeth Bentley was the first to alert the FBI to the scale of the Soviet network operating in Washington DC, it was VENONA that served to put flesh on the bones. Bentley's disadvantage was that she had no documentary evidence to support her charges, and she had never met any of the spies she denounced. Her veracity was to be challenged constantly, but she was never told that most of her accusations had been corroborated by VENONA.

Bentley's main target was Nathan Gregory Silvermaster, unquestionably one of the NKVD's most important spies, who was responsible for organizing an extensive network in Washington DC. Silvermaster's career had been extraordinary. Born in the Ukraine, his family had fled to China to escape the pogroms, and emigrated to California just after the First World War. He was granted American citizenship, obtained a doctorate in economics at the University of California, and played a key role in the 1933 general strike in San Francisco. After his graduation he taught at a Roman Catholic school and then worked for the State Labor Department before moving to Washington DC to join the Farm Security Administration in the Department of Agriculture. Never an open member of the CPUSA, he was one of Jacob Golos's best contacts, as was his wife Helen, the daughter of Baron Witte, the socialist aristocrat from the Baltic region sometimes known as the Red Baron. Silvermaster operated under the codename PAL and ROBERT, and Helen was to be known as DORA, although she appears to have been drawn into active support work by William Ludwig Ullman slightly later in 1944.

The scope of Silvermaster's organization was usefully revealed in a VENONA text dated 31 August from Vladimir Pravdin in New York:

Your No. 3686. Your proposal about using AILERON [Abraham G. Silverman] as a group leader cannot be realized for the time being, as the management has decided on the transfer of AILERON's and DONALD's [William L. Ullman] branch to a provincial town which will make it all but impossible to use them. In order to stay in CARTHAGE [Washington DC], AILERON proposes to resign and get from ROBERT [Nathan Silvermaster] a situation in his establishment. Although PAGE [Lauchlin B. Currie], who is practically the master of the establishment, is in strained relations with AILERON and will evidently be against taking him on, ROBERT hopes to influence PAGE through PEAK [Virginius Frank Coe]. ROBERT admits that the concentration of people in one establishment is inadvisable, but thinks that this is the only thing to do. For DONALD who is on military service, postponement is impossible. He and AILERON are making an attempt to stay in the old institution but to transfer to another branch that is remaining in CARTHAGE, but hopes for success [21 groups unrecoverable] about 'MIKHAILOV' no communication was made. The workers of the OFFICE [*rezidentura*] do not know about the MIKHAILOV you mention. Please be more specific.

This text confirms Silverman, Ullman, Coe and Currie as members of Silvermaster's ring, and shows how each used his influence to help the other climb into a position of even greater influence within the US administration. In this instance the beneficiary was Abraham Silverman, formerly a statistician with the Railroad Retirement Board, but later employed as a civilian by the Air Corps at the Pentagon. According to Bentley:

> he had access during most of the war to many military secrets. He was a tall, broad-shouldered, heavy man with thick glasses and untidy hair who was regarded by most of his associates as being an expert in his field but slightly odd ... [He was] frightened of his own shadow. He saw FBI men behind every bush, and he would arrive at an appointment dripping with cold sweat, yet somehow – I could never figure out now – he kept on going. Periodically he would threaten to resign, and wearily the Silvermasters

would invite him over for a meal of his favourite broiled lobster. Then, when he was well fed and at peace with the world, they would argue him into continuing.

Silvermaster's ploy succeeded, and Silverman continued to supply him with huge quantities of classified documents from the Pentagon, as exemplified by this message from New York, dated 3 July 1943, containing highly secret details of the US Army Air Force:

> PART I according to information of the administration of the Army Air Forces of the COUNTRY [America] of 21 April this year which was received from AILERON [Abraham Silverman] through PAL [Nathan Silvermaster] [3 groups unrecovered]: Numerical strength of the Army Air Force of the COUNTRY (the first figure in the COUNTRY, the second abroad):
> 1. Commissioned personnel including warrant officers (the senior non-commissioned rank):
> Pilots 39,096; 12 [2 groups unrecoverable]
> Bombardiers 5,742; 1,882
> Navigators 4,690; 2,168
> Observers 410; 165
> Those responsible for armament: 987; 3,613
> Bombardiers 1,214; 910
> Meteorologists 669; 434
> [1 group unidentified] 1,94; 877
> [1 group unidentified] 487; 162
> [41 groups unrecovered]
> ... gunnery 3,021; 0.
> [9 groups unrecovered] Total officers and warrant [15 groups unrecoverable]
> Aviation school 11 [2 groups unrecovered]; 0.
> 2. Enlisted personnel:
> Pilots 609; [2 groups unrecovered]
> Radio operators 42,306; 502
> Flight [36 groups unrecoverable]
> PART II Armourers trained in gunnery 10,025; 4,136
> Armourers untrained in gunnery 24,104; 8,581
> Radio operators untrained in gunnery 25,803; 8,599
> [3 groups unrecovered] 1,900; 83,945

Persons undergoing government training 32,102; 3.
[51 groups unrecoverable]
... chief [1 group unidentified] 445; 0.
Office of Coast Artillery 64; 0.
Engineer Corps 3,246; 1,332
Chaplains 866; 0.
Office of Chemical Warfare 1,274; 72
Financial Department [25 groups unrecoverable]
Medical Corps 19,138; 183.
Veterinary Corps
Military Police
Armament department
Quartermaster
Communications Corps
Women's Army Corps
Others
Total officers 35,944; 7,682
PART III Enlisted personnel
Coastal artillery 841; 0.
Engineer Corps 45,527; 32,713
Office of Chemical Warfare 4,580; 1,972
Financial department 5,675; 79.
Medical Corps 60,921; 1,439
Veterinary Corps 701; 0.
Military Police 30,247; 2,905
Armament department 40,404; 10,256
Quartermaster 70,580; 5,190
Communications Corps 71,528; 31,819
Women's Army Corps 2,496; 0.
Others 114,462; 15,007
Total enlisted personnel of the Air Forces 463,662

Silverman's statistics must have been of enormous importance to Moscow, first as a means of verifying information received through official liaison, and second as a method of building up a complete American order-of-battle. On 6 July 1943 New York transmitted more figures he had collated:

PAL [Nathan Silvermaster] passed me [3 groups unrecovered] information [64 groups unrecoverable] 00; workers of the

HUT [OSS] 7,000 (including officers 2,000; other ranks 5,000). Total 7,686,000

According to material of the statistical department on the size of the Air Force of the COUNTRY [America] received from POLO and AILERON [Abraham Silverman], the COUNTRY intends to complete by March of 1944 [1 groups unrecovered] Air Force in [4 groups unrecovered] (first figure is the number of groups; second – total number of airplanes):

1. For [1 group unrecovered] military [65 groups unrecoverable] 2. [1 group unrecovered] 10 1/2; 504. Special [3 groups unrecovered] 5; group unrecovered] 0. Military transport 22 1/2; 117.

2. For non- [1 group unrecovered] military theatres: Heavy bombers 9 1/4; 444. Medium bombers 3 1/3; 213. Light bombers 1/4; 16. Light dive bombers 1/4; 24. Fighters 13; 1,300. [60 groups unrecoverable] ning [4 groups unrecovered] 0; 28,777.

Silverman's senior position also allowed him to exert influence on behalf of others in the group, such as retaining William Ullman in Washington DC, a coup pulled off with help from Lauchlin Currie, who worked on the White House staff with the rank of deputy administrator to the President, as one of his six principal aides, and the CPUSA member Virginius Frank Coe. Born in Richmond, Virginia, Coe had taken his doctorate at the University of Chicago and then taught at the University of Toronto. In 1939 he joined the Federal Security Administration and the National Advisory Defense Council and then worked in the Treasury's Division of Monetary Research under Harry Dexter White, succeeding him when White was appointed Assistant Secretary of the Treasury. When questioned by the Senate Internal Security Subcommittee in 1952 about Bentley's allegations – having also been named as a spy (together with his brother Charles) by Whittaker Chambers – Coe initially invoked the Fifth Amendment and remained silent, but then later denied her charges. By November 1952 he was the administrative head of the International Monetary Fund. Similarly, Ullman, who resigned from the Treasury's Division of Monetary Research in March 1947, took the Fifth Amendment in 1953 while under cross-examination about espionage but told the FBI that 'both he and the Silvermasters considered Bentley a hysterical, highly emotional nuisance'.

As for Currie, the Scottish-born Keynesian economist, regarded by many as a brilliant theoretician with an unrivalled grasp of international monetary policy, VENONA made his connection to Abraham Silverman explicit. Having lectured at Harvard, and obtained his professor's chair at the Fletcher School of Law and Diplomacy, he was very influential within Roosevelt's White House, and had been the architect of the Chinese version of Lend-Lease, a scheme he had created after his visit to Chungking in the summer of 1941. His complicity with Silvermaster was evident in the very first sentence of a long text dated 10 August 1943, most of which resisted the cryptographers:

> PAGE [Lauchlin Currie] turned over to AILERON [Abraham G. Silverman] a memorandum about the political situation of the USA which was [1 group unrecovered] for the BANK [State Department] [354 groups unrecoverable]

When Nathan Silvermaster came under FBI investigation in the summer of 1943, Currie was one of those interviewed, as the New York *rezidentura* reported on 2 September 1943:

> SOUND [Jacob Golos] has reported that the KhATA [FBI] has resumed investigation of the case of PAL [Nathan G. Silvermaster]. A few days ago two representatives of the KhATA visited PAGE [Lauchlin Currie] and began to [1 group unrecovered] about PAL in particular is he a FELLOWCOUNTRYMAN [Communist]. PAGE apparently replied that he knows PAL [3 groups unrecovered] FELLOWCOUNTRYMAN organizations he does not [3 groups unrecovered] of PAGE, what [3 groups unrecovered] the representatives of the KhATA replied that [13 groups unrecovered] PAL's information: [1 group unrecovered] FARM SECURITY ADMINISTRATION BALDWIN has had to give in his resignation as the personal [1 group unrecovered] insistence of CAPTAIN [President Roosevelt]. BALDWIN is known to PAL as a liberal and [11 groups unrecovered] reactionary elements in the Ministry of Agriculture. Now BALDWIN has been appointed assistant chief of AMGOT

The Silvermaster Group

> [American Military Government of Occupied Territories] in ITALY. In PAL's words [1 group unrecovered] BALDWIN [7 groups unrecovered] impression that CAPTAIN [21 groups unrecovered] of CARTHAGE [Washington DC] there exists the opinion that [6 groups unrecovered] because he proved [31 groups unrecovered] of the Supreme Secretariat [35 groups unrecovered] signifies a change in the policy of the BANK [State Department] in future.

The FBI concluded that Silvermaster was a Communist and had recommended that he be dismissed from his post on the Board of Economic Warfare, which he had gained, according to Elizabeth Bentley, through the discreet intervention of Currie and Harry Dexter White. The Russians had

> decided that Silvermaster's valuable talents were being wasted in a nonproductive agency and he was encouraged to move into a more strategic part of the government. With the aid of Lauchlin Currie (administrative assistant to President Roosevelt) and Harry White, he became head of the Middle East Division of the Board of Economic Warfare (on loan from the Farm Security Administration).

Silvermaster rallied his friends to his defence and after further pressure from Currie and White, Silvermaster's dismissal notice was withdrawn and he was allowed to resign quietly and return to the Department of Agriculture, where he continued to run his network undisturbed. Currie also escaped unscathed, and when Bentley's testimony was made public he denied all charges of espionage. He left the country for Bogota, on an assignment for the International Bank of Reconstruction and Development, and in the middle of 1949 took up an appointment with the Colombian government. He was divorced in 1953 to marry a Colombian, and five years later took up Colombian citizenship. He died in 1993, having returned to the USA only briefly, always denying any involvement in espionage.

As for Ullman, he was a quiet, unassuming Treasury official who came from a wealthy background in Springfield, Missouri. He graduated from Harvard, and had been befriended by Nathan (Greg) and Helen Silvermaster in Washington DC. The trio shared a house together and he was instructed to abandon his CPUSA membership because, according to Elizabeth Bentley, he had 'become a member of the Silvermaster group. Under Greg's training he became one of the best agents we ever had. His only weakness was that he was unable to operate under his own steam for any period of time, and so he continually needed encouragement and guidance.' Ullman stayed in the Treasury Department for much of the war, and after he had been drafted into the Air Corps, he used his influence to get a senior position in the Pentagon. From there, as PILOT, he supplied a mass of data, as Apresyan reported to Moscow on 29 December 1944:

> PILOT advised on December 21st:
> 1. On the Western front the English are doing nothing. They have already withdrawn their troops into winter quarters.
> 2. Colonel of the Air Force of the COUNTRY [America] ROSENBLAT saw in China caves and concrete buildings where they keep cargoes which have arrived from the COUNTRY in the course of the last few years but which have not been used. In his words the whole army of the COUNTRY in China is disgusted with CHIANG KAI-CHEK and with the fact that while not waging war on the Japanese he is nevertheless taking and stockpiling materials from the COUNTRY. [General] STILWELL in conversations with CHIANG KAI-CHEK has constantly requested a reply to the question when CHIANG KAI-CHEK is to begin fulfilling the obligation undertaken in 1941.
> 3. One of the strongest and most evil of the COUNTRY's forces in China is the HUT [OSS] which is closely connected with the secret police of the DILI. The HUT supplies DILI with arms stores and instructs them in the methods of the secret police of the COUNTRY. The HUT proposed to the Central Government [6 groups unrecovered] agents of the DILI led by the HUT [5 groups unrecovered] Supporters of the Northern [3 groups unrecovered] Army of the COUNTRY's attitude to [3 groups unrecovered] North [33 groups unrecoverable] Please advise on what questions about China we should send you information by telegraph.

The debate about supervision continued until October when two further telegrams gave differing advice. On 1 October 1944 Fedosimov

The Silvermaster Group

revealed tensions between Silvermaster and the *rezidentura* over how his group should be run, attributing Silvermaster's determination to supervise every aspect of his network to the kind of bad habits that Jacob Golos had given Elizabeth Bentley:

> Your telegram No. 4270. On the question of the possibility of splitting ROBERT's [Nathan Silvermaster] group into smaller units ALBERT [Iskhak Akhmerov] gave the following answer: KOLTSOV's [unidentified] meeting with RICHARD [Harry Dexter White] and KOLTSOV's attempt to obtain answers to a number of questions of an international character produced an unfavourable impression on ROBERT. ROBERT was surprised at our decision to have recourse to the aid of a special man for raising with RICHARD which ROBERT himself as leader of the group, in his own words, is working ceaselessly. Why did we decide to ask RICHARD [25 groups unrecoverable] in other words this step of ours is taken as a mark of insufficient confidence in his business abilities. It is true the latter expressed regret at having reacted touchily [6 groups unrecovered] in ALBERT's opinion shows that ROBERT is jealous about encroachments [15 groups unrecovered] not to agree to our measures circulated to 'by-pass' ROBERT. ALBERT is convinced that an attempt to 'remove' members of the group, however circumspectly, will be received [1 group unrecovered] unfavourably by ROBERT. I said that in that case he could in the meantime have a chat with ROBERT about the possibility of breaking the group into three sub-groups for greater secrecy and more effective organization of the work, leaving however the overall direction in ROBERT's hands.
>
> PART II ALBERT warned me that for the time being the question can only be put in this form and that he will discuss it with ROBERT when occasion offers. At the same time he observed that his relations with ROBERT were very good and that the latter would consent to a meeting between ALBERT himself or FIRTREE [Helen Scott-Keenan] and any member of the group. Possibly in ROBERT's tendency not to 'relinquish' anyone, SOUND's [Jacob Golos] education is making itself felt.

2. Your points 3, 4, 5, 6 and 7 have been passed on to ALBERT in detail.

3. ALBERT promised to write specially on your point 1. For the time being he told me the following:

ROBERT is not restricting himself to receiving material from the PROBATIONERS [agents], but is giving them tasks in consultation with ALBERT. The instruction not to impersonalize the group's materials will be borne in mind (it is already being carried out). PILOT [William L. Ullman] is bringing ROBERT's wife (he is not married himself) into the processing of materials. She is not only in the know about her husband's work, but actively helps him in the processing.

There is no information about the KhATA's [FBI] inquiry being finished. ROBERT is no less interested in a favourable outcome than we are and is trying to keep abreast of developments. If they have not dismissed him from his present work it means that there is no concrete information about his work for us but only suspicions connected with his FELLOWCOUNTRYMANLY [Communist Party] membership. His wife is not free from suspicion [21 groups unrecoverable] questions raised in your letter No. 3 and which have in the meantime remained unanswered we will remind ALBERT.

The materials on the conspiracy and the COMPETITORS [intelligence service] of the ISLAND [Britain], as it turns out, have to be obtained through IZRA [Donald Wheeler] and so I am passing the task on to VADIM [Anatoli Gromov].

Although only KOLTSOV remains unidentified, for he was not a member of the New York *rezidentura* but sent from Moscow on a special assignment, his contact with Harry Dexter White is the first VENONA reference to White. Certainly contact had been established with White by Iskhak Akhmerov, whom he knew as 'Bill Greynke', for in May 1941 Vitali Pavlov had held a rendezvous with White in a Washington DC restaurant, in an operation he described in his autobiography, *Operation SNOW* (1998). Then the relatively inexperienced deputy head of the NKVD's American department, Pavlov had travelled by ship to New York accompanied by Mikhail Korneyev. Posing as diplomatic couriers, they made their delivery of mail to the consulate general and then went to Washington for the

The Silvermaster Group

sole purpose of re-establishing contact with White. Having taken elaborate counter-surveillance measures, Pavlov met White over lunch and asked for his intervention regarding American policy in the Far East. Pavlov claims this inspired two memoranda to Henry Morgenthau, in June and November 1941, that in turn led to a hardening of attitudes towards the Japanese, culminating in President Roosevelt's historic ultimatum of 26 November. According to Pavlov, there was a direct link between his conversation with White and the Secretary of the Treasury's briefs addressed to the Secretary of State Cordell Hull and the President. At the conclusion of the encounter Pavlov resumed his journey back to Moscow via San Francisco, Hawaii, Japan and Vladivostock.

In later months White was to be mentioned on many occasions, making the importance of his role unmistakable. The VENONA evidence is significant because he vehemently denied all charges of espionage to Congress, shortly before he succumbed to a heart attack. Elizabeth Bentley admitted that she had never met him, so her testimony did not have the authority of an eye-witness, first-hand account, although her recollection of him as 'one of the most important members of the group' was compelling. She remembered him as

> Under Secretary of the United States Treasury and right-hand man of Secretary Morgenthau. He was in a position not only to give valuable information but also to influence United States policy in a pro-Soviet direction. According to Greg [Nathan Silvermaster], he had been tied up with the revolutionary movement for many years, although no one seemed to know whether or not he had ever been a Communist Party member. He had been giving information to the Russians during the thirties but had ceased abruptly when his contact, who was later identified as Whittaker Chambers, turned 'sour' in 1938.

Whatever the decision about breaking up Silvermaster's group, the *rezidentura* continued to deal with the membership collectively, as is demonstrated by a fragmented final part of a much longer, unrecovered telegram dated 14 October 1944:

> PAGE [Lauchlin B. Currie] told this to AILERON [Abraham G. Silverman], ALBERT [Iskhak Akhmerov] and ROBERT

[Nathan G. Silvermaster]. ROBERT personally [1 group unrecovered] [56 groups unrecoverable] this purpose to curtail the group's work for us for a few months. ALBERT agreed and [64 groups unrecoverable] in CARTHAGE [Washington DC] or nearby. In his note ALBERT tells about ROBERT's business proposition. Telegraph instructions.

By 21 November Silvermaster prompts two messages from Apresyan, the first indicates that he is as active as ever, while the second marks his reward for dedication:

ROBERT [Nathan Silvermaster] reports:
1. During his visit to the Chinese 8th Army [US Ambassador Patrick J.] HURLEY asseverated his friendship. CHOU EN-LAI should be warned that HURLEY cannot be trusted. He thinks HURLEY is a CHIA HUO-U [unidentified] stooge of CHIANG KAI-CHEK. Even the BANK [State Department] considers HURLEY's views to be in contradiction to the BANK's policy.
2. The HUT [OSS] has passed on to the Army a list of 20,000 'reliable Germans' with whom the HUT considers it safe to have dealings. It is impossible to obtain the list here at the moment. Perhaps it could be procured in SIDON [London]. An analogous list of Austrians has been compiled by the ISLANDERS [British].

No. 913
1. ALBERT [Iskhak Akhmerov] asks for word to be passed to you that ELZA [Mrs Akhmerov] and he profoundly [20 groups unrecoverable]
2. ROBERT is sincerely overjoyed and profoundly satisfied with the award given him in accordance with your instructions. As he says his work for us is the one good thing he has done in his life. He emphasized that he did not take this only as a personal honour, but also as an honour to his group. He wants to see the reward and the book.
3. DORA [Helen Silvermaster] is very uneasy about the fate of her relations and again asks news of their whereabouts.

How the *rezidentura* resolved the question of overall control over the Silvermaster group is unknown, but a text dated 15 January

The Silvermaster Group

1945 implies that Moscow was keen to deal with Lauchlin Currie without an intermediary:

> Find out from ALBERT [Iskhak Akhmerov] and ROBERT [Nathan Silvermaster] whether it would be possible for us to approach PAGE [Lauchlin Currie] direct. State what you know, [. . . groups unrecovered]

The scale of Silvermaster's productivity is evident from the following text from Stepan Apresyan on 17 October 1944 which identifies several British secret reports from the Ministry of Economic Warfare that had been photographed, as well as a clutch of routine State Department cables:

> Today we received from ROBERT [Nathan G. Silvermaster] 56 undeveloped films including the following materials:
> 1. Reviews by the Ministry of Economic Warfare on the Far East according to information on the economic COMPETITION.
> 2. A review by the Ministry of Economic Warfare on the economic situation of GERMANY.
> 3. A memorandum from CAPTAIN [President Roosevelt] on DECREE [Lend-Lease] to the French.
> 4. A review by the Ministry of Economic Warfare about [22 groups unrecoverable] negotiations of the COUNTRY [America] and the ISLAND [Britain] about DECREE.
> 7. Reports of the embassy of the COUNTRY in SIDON [London] about [1 group unrecovered] GREECE.
> 8. Measures taken [6 groups unrecovered] in Sweden.
> 9. Negotiations on DECREE with FRANCE.
> 10. [8 groups unrecovered] about the situation in ITALY.
> 11. A report of the Embassy with the COUNTRY in MADRID about German assets in Spain.
> 12. The economic scale of defence.
> 13. A memorandum [3 groups unrecovered] from CAPTAIN on the question of DECREE for [1 group unrecovered]
> 14. A telegram to the BANK [State Department] from the Embassy of the COUNTRY on [2 groups unrecovered]
> 15. A memorandum on the executive committee on [19 groups unrecovered]

16. [5 groups unrecovered] international cartels.
17. Instructions on the dissolution of the National Socialist Parties of GERMANY and affiliated organizations.
18. The situation on economics control of [10 groups unrecovered]
20. A general review [4 groups unrecovered] crises of the COUNTRY. The materials are recent. [15 groups unrecovered] at once the undeveloped films.

The next day, 18 October, Moscow was informed about Churchill's summit with Roosevelt:

> ROBERT [Nathan G. Silvermaster] advises that by the end of one of their meetings in the LAND [Canada] CAPTAIN [President Roosevelt] and BOAR [Winston Churchill] reached the following agreement with regard to GERMANY:
> 'It will be necessary to take political and economic measures and at the same time as military disarmament to ensure that GERMANY will no longer pose a threat to general peace. As part of such a programme the RUHR should be wrested from GERMANY and handed over to the control of some international council. Chemical, metallurgical and electrical industries must be transported out of GERMANY. The aim must consist [35 groups unrecoverable]

On 13 December Apresyan reported from New York:

> ROBERT [Nathan G. Silvermaster] has passed on to us a secret document 'The Post-War Troop Basis' drawn up by division G-3 on the 19th August [tabular summary of the document follows]
> PART III To the document is attached an explanation of the same date in which it is said in particular that the document replaces a provisional document drawn up on the 24th of June. The document was sent to you by post on the 8th December. [5 groups unrecovered] Telegraph whether the contents of the British Ministry of Foreign Affairs' commentary of the 3rd July on the 'Handbook of Civilian Affairs in Germany' should be telegraphed. The document was sent to you by the same post.

The Silvermaster Group

This particular text proved to be a milestone for Meredith Gardner's cryptanalytical attack, for it was one of the very first messages to be read anything like completely. When Gardner had accomplished this, by May 1947, it represented proof that the Soviets had been running a well-informed spy in the US War Department's General Staff in 1944, and this news was to encourage him and others to pursue VENONA for further leads.

On 13 December 1944 Apresyan sent two despatches to Moscow from Silvermaster:

> ROBERT [Nathan G. Silvermaster] handed over a Top Secret telegram of the COUNTRY's [America's] legation in Switzerland of 10th November drawn up on the basis of information from the German Aviation industrialists:
>
> 'Disposition of German fighter aircraft strength: Balkans 500, Strategic reserve 3,000 of which 2,000 on the Eastern Front and 1,000 on the Western Front and in Germany. (Legation note: no evidence here of existence of strategic reserve. Possibly this in other words means aircraft of a scarcely usable nature). Eastern Front 2,000, Western and Germany 2,200. In October the number of bombers on hand all active aircraft 6,100.
>
> In comparison with Anglo-American, the majority of German aircraft is obsolete.
>
> Full effort of the industry could produce monthly about 900 machines of all types mostly underground but it is hoped that [19 groups unrecoverable] Messerschmidt. For carrying and launching flying bombs [3 groups unrecovered]
>
> Heinkel 111. Production of Mark 52s drastically curtailed.
>
> Dornier factory at Friedrichshafen again operating in spite of air attacks and furthermore is producing new types of fighter.
>
> MET-210 (Twin engine fighter) in increasingly used. The most powerful of German fighter planes is the Heinkel 177. Again there is no lack of ground and air crews. In industrial and military aviation circles the attitude towards the position of the German Air Force is pessimistic. This information relates to October.

No. 968. ROBERT [Nathan G. Silvermaster] handed over a secret telegram of worker of the COUNTRY HOUSE [US embassy in Moscow] [Ambassador George] KENNAN to the BANK [State Department] of 17th November:

'Yesterday I had a frank conversation with some highly placed persons about speeding things up. According to local [15 groups unrecoverable] representatives and departments. In addition there were two special causes of delay not connected with us, which I shall communicate . . . have never been so bored and cold as now when for days and weeks on end I have had to be idle but shall of course stick it to the end.' Note: [5 groups unrecovered] but we hope it is of interest.

On 19 December Apersyan reported:

According to ROBERT's [Nathan G. Silvermaster] information the COUNTRY's [America] adviser in CASERTA considers that Romania will be able to pay reparations of 300 million dollars and that she will [3 groups unrecovered] 55 per cent of her export surpluses to the Soviet Union in the course of six years.

In the following long telegram, dated 4 January 1945, Pavel Fedosimov set out the slightly tangled relationship between Silvermaster and Akhmerov, drawing attention to ROBERT's hope to enter into an unwise partnership and buy a farm outside Washington DC with his fellow conspirator who worked in the Treasury, William Ludwig Ullman, codenamed PILOT:

In a special letter of 2 January ALBERT [Iskhak Akhmerov] reports, while intimating to ROBERT [Nathan G. Silvermaster] for a long time the advisability of setting up a separate group of two or three persons whose technical work (the delivery, filming and safekeeping of materials) would not be concentrated in ROBERT's apartment. ALBERT explained that we are not proposing to deprive him of the direction of the people but we want to create the most secure possible conditions for the processing and safekeeping of materials, since, judging by well-known facts, the KhATA [FBI] is probably interested in ROBERT's activities, and there

The Silvermaster Group

is no guarantee that, as a result of some accident, materials he may have at his place when it happens will not fall into the hands of the KhATA, and that our sources would not be compromised in this way since at the moment everything is concentrated in one place. After many friendly conversations on this subject ROBERT agreed in principle with our opinion.

It is possible ROBERT thought we wanted to take away some of his people counting on getting better results and concluded from this that we were not altogether satisfied with his achievements. In ALBERT's opinion he succeeded in convincing ROBERT that our sole aim was organizational security. It must be said that on the basis of our workers' information ROBERT has been inclined to be critical and dubious of our ability to deal with the PROBATIONERS [agents]. Especially indicative from this point of view is the incident with KOLTSOV [36 groups unrecoverable] AILERON [Abraham G. Silverman] our worker. If ALBERT proposed this ROBERT would undoubtedly reject it. Therefore ALBERT is trying to convince him of the necessity of setting up a small group whose technical work would be concentrated outside ROBERT's apartment, ROBERT retaining the general direction of it.

PART II It has been decided to train ZhOLUD [Bela Gold] for the processing of materials in their own apartment. The couple are conscientious, capable and fairly well disciplined. Notwithstanding, however, their devotion to the FELLOWCOUNTRYMEN [Communist Party] and personally to ROBERT, the latter has from time to time complained of their caprices. Thus a few weeks ago DORA [Helen Silvermaster] told FIRTREE [Helen Scott-Keenan] in ROBERT's and PILOT's [William L. Ullman] presence that the couple were trying to get themselves free of us. ALBERT does not regard this seriously but he no longer doubts that it costs ROBERT great pains to keep the couple and the other PROBATIONERS in check and to get good work out of them. Being their leader in the FELLOWCOUNTRYMANLY line ROBERT has the opportunity to give them orders.

In ALBERT's opinion our workers would hardly manage to work with the same success under the

FELLOWCOUNTRYMANLY flag. We may possibly set up direct liaison with ACORN, AILERON and the rest, but it is doubtful whether we could secure from them the same results as ROBERT, who, constantly dealing with them, has many advantages over us. The whole group of ROBERT's [54 groups unrecoverable]

PART III ROBERT reacted very unfavourably saying that before ALBERT's time somebody else tried to part him and PILOT, that he did not believe in our orthodox methods and so on. As he said, it would not be hard to separate PILOT from him, but he [32 groups unrecoverable] PILOT will not cool off towards our work. It goes without saying that PILOT is not so deeply devoted to us as ROBERT and DORA are, for he comes from a well-to-do family of western Americans. In ALBERT's opinion, for PILOT's successful work we are in large measure indebted to ROBERT and DORA, and treat PILOT very solicitously, and in the near future we shall gain nothing at the cost of separating PILOT from ROBERT. ALBERT is trying not to permit a joint business like a farm or an aerodrome and has advised ROBERT to let PILOT work out this project himself if the latter is sure of success saying that in case of need we should render PILOT some financial support. In ALBERT's opinion the project is unrealizable and later they will drop it. ROBERT is displeased by our interference in his personal affairs, which is what he considers the farm to be. In his words, all these years he and the others have worked at high pressure and they want to acquire a farm rather for relaxation than as a cover. For a long time PILOT and DORA have been drawing up all kinds of plans relative to the farm.

PART IV In PILOT's opinion the farm will be a good pretext for his absence in CARTHAGE [Washington DC] in case of dismissal, for having been dismissed he could hardly remain in CARTHAGE even temporarily without legal income. Seeing how much they were carried away by the idea ALBERT did not consider it wise to insist [29 groups unrecoverable] leadership of this new group will have to be left to ROBERT.

This has been expounded but does not mean that the

The Silvermaster Group

mutual relations of ALBERT with ROBERT are strained or that ROBERT does not want to obey us. ROBERT esteems ALBERT highly and would not [2 groups unrecovered] any request of ours if ALBERT requested, for organizationally ALBERT has become very close to us.

ALBERT emphasizes the soundness and timeliness of the award and gift to ROBERT, who is pleased at our high evaluation of him.

Note by the OFFICE [*rezidentura*]. In the same letter ALBERT adduces short biographical data on ACORN and ZhENYa [Sonia Gold] which we shall send by post.

ACORN has not been identified positively but ZhOLUD was Bela Gold, Sonia's husband, who worked in the Foreign Economic Administration. While he gave Silvermaster documents from his office, Sonia (ZhENYA) worked as a secretary in the Treasury Department between August 1943 and August 1947, in a post arranged by Harry Dexter White. Accordingly, Silvermaster's network had increased by two, with ACORN to follow. Being one of the few cryptonyms unaccounted for (along with BERG and ELSA), much speculation centres on ACORN's identity, the principal candidate being William H. Taylor, named by Bentley in her Congressional evidence as a Soviet spy who had been placed in the Treasury by Harry White in January 1941. Originally from Canada, Taylor had known Silvermaster since his days at the University of California, and was posted to China in May 1941. He returned in September 1942, having spent nine months as a prisoner of the Japanese, and served in London from May 1944. In 1946 he was appointed assistant director of the International Monetary Fund's Middle East Department, where he resisted the US government's demand for his dismissal. He consistently denied Bentley's charges, and devoted much of the rest of his life to picking holes in her witness statements.

Akhmerov's complaints about the way the *rezidentura* had handled Silvermaster were taken seriously in Moscow. On 17 January Moscow responded:

1. The letter which I transmitted to you ALBERT [Iskhak Akhmerov] wrote before receipt of your latest instructions about ROBERT [Nathan G. Silvermaster] and PILOT [William

L. Ullman]. I consider it useful to advise you for orientation of ALBERT's concrete views against the *rezidentura*.
2. I will reply by the next post to the letter which was transmitted.

The admission of Sonia Gold (née Steinman) into the Silvermaster group was a useful addition, for she was for a period a typist for Harold Glasser, then the director of the Treasury's Division of Monetary Research, who was himself another Soviet source, codenamed ROUBLE and a member of the parallel network run by Victor Perlo (see Chapter XIII). This text was followed later the same day from New York with more about Akhmerov:

> Your number 6218. I am bearing in mind your reminder about the line of conduct in respect of the leadership of the FELLOWCOUNTRYMAN's [i.e. Party] organization. However, as ALBERT [Iskhak Akhmerov] has already firmly promised ROBERT [Nathan G. Silvermaster] and SACHS to pass on to HELMSMAN [Earl Browder] certain materials (in particular concerning the Chinese FELLOWCOUNTRYMEN [Communists] and it is hard for him to go back on his word, please permit by way of exception the passing on of these materials to HELMSMAN through VADIM [Anatoli Gromov] or ECHO [Bernard Schuster], at the same time warning ALBERT that this is the last time. ALBERT emphasized that SACH's attitude to this question was very jealous and he gave him to understand that he would not hand certain materials over to us without a guarantee that they would be handed over to HELMSMAN too and, should we refuse, he might try to establish liaison with HELMSMAN over our heads.

In a text dated 18 January 1945, attributed to Apresyan, the *rezident* again shows how Silvermaster routinely acquired classified appreciations from OSS:

> ROBERT [Nathan G. Silvermaster] reports that: the Research Section of the HUT [OSS] has compiled information about the ability of Hungary to pay reparations. According to the information the national income of Hungary will total 60–65 million dollars for the first year following the conclusion of military operations with a drop in hostilities in the future.

The Silvermaster Group

Hungary can pay in petroleum products, bauxite and agricultural products. She can export 16 million dollars' worth of petroleum products a year.

As well as receiving huge quantities of information from OSS, Silvermaster had supervised the most comprehensive penetration of the US Treasury through Harry Dexter White and Sonia Gold but, as this telegram dated 18 January 1945 proved, was anxious not to surrender control of this part of his network:

> According to ROBERT's [Nathan G. Silvermaster] report, he may be presented with an opportunity of obtaining from RICHARD [Harry Dexter White] ROUBLE's [Harold Glasser] appointment to RICHARD's post, as the latter will soon be appointed assistant secretary. MAY's [Stepan Apresyan] note: It is possible that this is a slip of the pen, for RICHARD and others are already assistants if [1 group unrecovered] NABOB's [Henry Morgenthau Jr] department, where he obviously can be promoted to the post of deputy. ROBERT has repeatedly suggested that ROUBLE be turned over to him. According to our information he could get better results from ROUBLE than our line. He suspects that ROUBLE is connected with us through other channels. ALBERT [Iskhak Akhmerov] emphasizes that ROUBLE was passive in the RAIDER [Victor Perlo] group although he was able to give us valuable material. Some months ago ROBERT complained that ROUBLE was hiding important documents from ZhENYa [Sonia Gold] (his secretary). If we are convinced of ROUBLE's good faith toward the FELLOWCOUNTRYMEN [Party] ROBERT would like to take him into his group. ROBERT has always been against appointing two of our groups to one department and instead asks that our PROBATIONERS [agents] from RICHARD's department be under his direction to avoid misunderstandings. In ALBERT's opinion, if ROUBLE is reliable from our point of view he ought to be turned over to ROBERT. ROBERT does not want to promote ROUBLE to RICHARD's post unless he takes him into his group; on the other hand he is not quite sure that he will be able to get ROUBLE into this post, as it is possible that somebody else is already earmarked for it. Wire your decision by priority

telegram not later than 21 January indicating the method of establishing contract between ALBERT and ROUBLE if you agree to include ROUBLE in ROBERT's group.

Of all Silvermaster's sources, Harry Dexter White was undoubtedly the most significant, and VENONA made clear the extent of his co-operation. On 4–5 August 1944 Stepan Apresyan reported from New York on a conversation with White when he was codenamed JURIST:

> KOLTSOV advises: 'On 4th August I arrived in TYRE [New York]. I have not seen MAXIM [Vasili Zubilin] since Monday. I pass on the contents of a conversation with JURIST on 31st July at his apartment. To my questions JURIST replied as follows:
> 1. [1 group unrecovered] without attempting [3 groups unrecovered]: a) DECREE [Lend-Lease] [15 groups unrecovered] interest and so on. Definitive decisions were not arrived at possible [26 groups unrecovered] obtaining the document extremely risky. [10 groups unrecovered] 5 to 10 years [28 groups unrecovered] family of nations.' On the technique of control over Germany while reparations are being paid there is for the time being no definite opinion. JURIST thinks that a definite amount of reparations should be set in marks and this amount should be subsequently retrieved and reduced if Germany fulfils her obligations; if she does not, Germany should be reoccupied [12 groups unrecovered] JURIST's opinion the letter [13 groups unrecovered] with NABOB [Henry Morgenthau] or CAPTAIN [Franklin Roosevelt].
>
> PART III (c) the trade policy of the COUNTRY [America] [1 group unrecovered] which will be put into effect by means of bilateral agreements with individual states covering 2–3 years. There will be one set of conditions or removal of tariff barriers.
>
> (d) Loans. In this sphere the only concrete thing that is being done is the preparation of a credit for us of 10 milliards [13 groups unrecoverable] . . . The credit will be repaid by the export of our raw material to the COUNTRY [2 groups unrecovered] be caused by NABOB's not being able to get conversations on this business with CAPTAIN.

2. NABOB and JURIST's trip to SMYRNA [Moscow] is being delayed for an indefinite period and may take place after the elections. On 5th August both are leaving for NORMANDY and SIDON [London] where [7 groups unrecovered] suppose that the ISLAND [England] will [1 group unrecovered] with them about DECREE payments. The fact is that the ISLAND's dollar balances have risen as a result of the transport work and the expenditure made by the army of the COUNTRY in Europe; therefore the COUNTRY is demanding partial repayment of the DECREE loan [51 groups unrecovered] use of amphibians.

4. The programme of the oil conference [5 groups unrecovered, 58 groups unrecoverable]

5. The role [16 groups unrecovered] there will be achieved a compromise agreement to exclude from the Polish Government the most hostile elements [3 groups unrecovered] Committee of Liberation in the COUNTRY. [31 groups unrecoverable] MIKOLAJCZYK.

7. Finland has lost the sympathy of the people in the COUNTRY, therefore the restoration of the 1940 frontier will not arouse objections from the COUNTRY.

8. As regards the Baltic Countries the COUNTRY thinks that we seized them, but the restoration of the pre-war situation will not arouse any protest in the COUNTRY.

9. JURIST is convinced that CAPTAIN will win the elections if [1 group unrecovered] not [3 groups unrecovered] severe military disaster. TRUMAN's nomination is calculated to ensure the votes of the conservative wing of the party. As regards the technique of further work with us JURIST said that his wife was ready for any self-sacrifice; he himself did not think about his personal security, but a compromise would lead to a political scandal and the discredit of all supporters of the New Deal, therefore he would have to be very cautious. He asked whether he should [5 groups unrecovered] his work with us. I replied that he should refrain. JURIST has no suitable apartment for a permanent meeting place; all his friends are family people. Meetings could be held at their houses in such a way that one meeting devolved on each every 4–5 months. He proposes infrequent

conversations lasting up to half an hour while driving in his automobile.

JURIST has fixed the next meeting for 17th–19th August and arranged appropriate conditions for it. He returns to CARTHAGE [Washington DC] about the 17th August. I leave for CARTHAGE on the 8th of August and from there for SMYRNA on the 12th of August. Telegraph the date of receipt of this telegram.

As well as disclosing information about the administration's attitude towards the structure of postwar Europe, White was occasionally consulted about American negotiating positions on loans, as is evident from this fragmented VENONA text from New York dated 18 January 1945:

> According to ROBERT's [Nathan G. Silvermaster] information CAPITALIST [Averell Harriman] advised the BANK [US State Department] that we had requested a loan of 6 billion dollars [1 group unrecovered] years at 2–2 ½ per cent annually. In RICHARD's [Harry Dexter White] words we could get a loan under much more favourable conditions. [24 groups unrecoverable] [1 group unrecovered] strategic materials [17 groups unrecovered] [38 groups unrecoverable]

On 19 March 1945 Moscow seems to have authorized KOLTSOV to approach Harry Dexter White direct, for the Centre asked Apresyan and Akhmerov in New York:

> [3 groups unrecovered] In sending KOLTSOV to meet RICHARD [Harry Dexter White] we were guided by [34 groups unrecovered] with KOLTSOV [37 groups unrecovered] [41 groups unrecoverable] [1 group unrecovered] first part of the telegram gives [4 groups unrecovered] worker'. Neither ALBERT [Iskhak Akhmerov] nor ROBERT [Nathan G. Silvermaster] it seems understood the point of our measures on this matter. In a conversation with KOLTSOV [135 groups unrecovered]

Moscow followed this on 21 March 1945 with this directive to Apresyan and Akhmerov:

> The proposal of ALBERT [Iskhak Akhmerov] and ROBERT [Nathan G. Silvermaster] [53 groups unrecovered] ALBERT [3 groups unrecovered] ROBERT with P. [41 groups unrecovered]. We consider that in this case ALBERT and ROBERT have displayed excessive hastiness. Entrust to ROBERT the leadership [2 groups unrecovered] P. ROBERT should trust [12 groups unrecovered] P. trusts ROBERT, informs him not only orally, but also by handing over documents. Up to now PAGE's [Lauchlin B. Currie] relations with ROBERT were expressed, from our point of view, only in common feelings and personal sympathies. [6 groups unrecovered] question of more profound relations and an understanding by PAGE of ROBERT's role. If ROBERT does not get P.'s transfer to our worker, than he [7 groups unrecovered] raising with PAGE the question of P.'s closer complicity with ROBERT.

Moscow's continuing concerns about protecting White and Silvermaster are evident in this next highly fragmented VENONA text sent to New York on 29 March 1945 about possible leakage through the CPUSA:

> We have already informed you in number 1160 of the fact that the composition of ROBERT's [Nathan G. Silvermaster] group is known to many FELLOWCOUNTRYMEN [Party members] in CARTHAGE [Washington DC]. It has been ascertained further that there is known also RICHARD's [Harry Dexter White] connection [43 groups unrecoverable] [16 groups unrecovered] ROBERT with ALBERT [Iskhak Akhmerov] [14 groups unrecovered] ALBERT [6 groups unrecovered] ROBERT [15 groups unrecovered] details of the work of the group. Pass on to ALBERT [23 groups unrecovered]

White was considered so valuable a source that, wherever he went, Moscow demanded on 6 April 1945 that contact was maintained:

> Tell ALBERT [Iskhak Akhmerov] to make arrangements with ROBERT [Nathan G. Silvermaster] about maintaining contact with RICHARD [Harry Dexter White] and PILOT [William L. Ullman] in BABYLON [San Francisco] [9 groups unrecovered]

Nor was Silvermaster's information limited to purely financial matters. He was exceptionally well-informed about the Treasury but had his tentacles in every part of Washington's political life and, as indicated in this text dated 8 April 1945, Moscow regarded him as well informed on many issues relating to postwar reconstruction:

> [14 groups unrecovered] on the opposition movement in GERMANY. His information [1 group unrecovered] GOERDELER, LEUSCHNER, HAU [1 group unrecovered] [KhAU [1 group unrecovered] [1 group unrecovered] and MIRENDORF has been confirmed by a number of other items of agent material. The NEWS [Novosti Press Agency] also gave valuable information with a sketch of the Catholic movement in GERMANY and a list of well disposed and [4 groups unrecovered]. The information received from ROBERT about [11 groups unrecovered] opposition movement in GERMANY we are interested in the following questions:
> 1. The illegal opposition organizations existing at present in GERMANY, their personnel, programmes and activities.
> 2. The fate and political views of the German generals who were dismissed from the direction of work: General Field-Marshals MANSTEIN, KLUGE, BRAUSCHITSCH, KUECHLER; Colonel-Generals – former Chief of General Staff HALDER and ZEITLER. Former Commander of the Reserve Army FROMM, former Commander of the Northern group [76 groups unrecovered], VON [39 groups unrecovered] former Minister of Finance of the Prussian cabinet [2 groups unrecovered] POPITZ, former Staats-Sekretr of the Ministry of Internal Economy LANDF [31 groups unrecovered]

On the same day Moscow, under Beria's signature, issued instructions about the Silvermaster group that confirmed Akhmerov's status as its controller:

> According to information we have received from VADIM [Anatoli Gromov] the COMPETITORS [counter-intelligence agency] of the COUNTRY [America] and the ISLAND [England] have worked out joint measures for strengthening work [71 groups unrecovered] transmission of information by telegraph. Give tasks [15 groups unrecovered] ELSA [29

The Silvermaster Group

groups unrecovered] and people devoted to us. In the work with ALBERT's [Iskhak Akhmerov] group it is essential to adhere to the following:

1. JULIA's [Olga V. Khlopkova] meeting with ART [Aleksandr Koral] or BERG [unidentified] should not be more than 3 times a month.
2. [13 groups unrecovered]
3. ROBERT's [Nathan G. Silvermaster] materials should be conveyed to TYRE [New York] only on film and in small batches.
4. ELSA, BERG and ART, who are to be co-opted by ALBERT for the purpose, are to take turns in making the trip to CARTHAGE [Washington DC] for ROBERT's materials. With the PROBATIONERS [agents] [3 groups unrecovered] ROBERT and his wife DORA [Helen Silvermaster].
5. As regards the work with the PROBATIONERS in TYRE, follow the same principles. Organize the work of your [50 groups unrecovered]

Despite the VENONA evidence, Harry Dexter White remained a powerful figure in Washington DC long after the war, even though he had been denounced as a Soviet spy by Whittaker Chambers as early as 1942, and the discreet investigation that was conducted as a result of Bentley's charges showed that he had used his influence to help both Nathan Silvermaster and other members of his network to obtain sensitive posts inside the federal government. When eventually Harry Dexter White's name was made public, as a result of Elizabeth Bentley's testimony to Congress in July 1948, his denials went unchallenged because, a week after he had given his evidence, he succumbed to a heart attack.

As well as White, Silvermaster's sources within the Treasury included Bela Gold and his wife Sonia, but all Bentley's claims were rejected by Silvermaster, who labelled her a neurotic. A combination of physical security and VENONA gradually allowed the FBI to reconstruct most of his spy-ring. For example, Silvermaster was spotted meeting Aleksandr Koral on 1 December 1945, and he was later matched to the cryptonym ART, assigned to one of the couriers moving documents and exposed films between Washington DC and New York. When interviewed in 1947, Koral conceded that he had received his instructions from a man he knew as Frank, whom he identified from the FBI's photo collection as Semyon M. Semyonov, an Amtorg engineer and member of Leonid Kvasnikov's *rezidentura*, later to be identified by Harry Gold as one of his principal controllers.

Born in England, Koral had moved to the US in 1900, aged thirteen, and in 1922 had been employed by the Board of Education in New York as an assistant engineer in the bureau of construction. Under the FBI's interrogation Koral admitted having worked as Semyonov's courier, servicing a dozen of his contacts in New York, initially because he needed the money to pay for his sick son's hospital bills. Koral also confirmed that in October 1945 he had been sent to Washington DC to collect material, probably government contract data, from the Silvermasters.

Silvermaster himself escaped prosecution, as he and his wife took the Fifth Amendment when required to give evidence to Congress, but the expedient of allowing him to return to the Department of Agriculture had ensured that he had been denied further direct access to classified information. Similarly, some of his colleagues in the department who fell under suspicion, including Lee Pressman, Nathan Witt and Harold H. Collins, were isolated so they could do no damage. By the time his home was raided by the FBI, the photographic laboratory in his basement had been sanitized of anything incriminating, having been warned through Judith Coplon by the Russians of the imminent danger. It is only with the release of VENONA that the immense scale of his network's espionage has been judged by anyone outside the intelligence community.

XIII

The RAIDER

As important as the Silvermaster group, according to Elizabeth Bentley, was the network run by Victor Perlo, a Communist of long-standing who worked as a statistician for the War Production Board. Although she publicly named only Charles Kramer as a member of Perlo's organization, she described the others she met in March 1944 in the Central Park West apartment of John Abt:

> 'one worked also in the War Production Board and could furnish data on planes, tanks and guns. The second was headed for the Department of Commerce, but as he was not a well man, it was doubtful whether he could be of great value. Besides those four, there were others who worked variously in the research department of the OSS, the Treasury, the Foreign Economic Agency and with the UNRRA.

Bentley recalled that Perlo had somehow discovered that Abraham Silverman was in touch with the Russians and had made a thorough pest of himself by volunteering his help, to the extent that the Silvermaster group had felt threatened by his indiscretion. Eventually Perlo had been recruited by Jacob Golos. After Golos's death Bentley had adopted the role of courier, servicing Perlo and Silvermaster simultaneously, but separately.

Independent testimony to support Bentley's allegations of espionage came from Whittaker Chambers, the disaffected *Time* magazine journalist, and the former CPUSA activist Nathaniel Weyl. Then the FBI received an anonymous letter from a well-informed source who turned out to be Perlo's ex-wife Katherine. Linking all this evidence was VENONA, which eloquently demonstrated Victor Perlo's activities as RAIDER. Among the first references to him was this indication, in the second part of a longer text from Stepan Apresyan in New York, that he had clashed with William Batt of the War Production Board:

> 1. In the COUNTRY [America] it is proposed to begin cutting down the strength of the army on 1st October in accordance with the demobilization plan.
> According to a report from DONALD [William L. Ullman] the boss of the COUNTRY HOUSE [US embassy in Moscow] is trying to get BATT sent to SMYRNA [Moscow] in connection with postwar trade relations. NABOB [Henry Morgenthau] objects to BATT being sent. In DONALD's opinion BATT's reputation is such that his trip will not be allowed under any circumstances. We have already given you in number 561 RAIDER's [Victor Perlo] information about BATT's anti-Soviet feelings.

This long, almost complete text dated 10 March 1945 sheds light on, among other topics, the military establishment's opposition to the construction of what was eventually to become La Guardia Airport on Long Island:

> To the 8th department. Information from RAIDER [Victor Perlo]. As a result of observations on the job in his agency and participation in various official conferences RAIDER has told our man about some changes in the mutual relations between civilian and military agencies.
> 1. In December and January, when various war industries were sharply increased the DEPOT [War Production Board] and the War Manpower Commission gave them strong support. BYRNES, director of War Mobilization, issued various directives curtailing civilian production. The DEPOT sharply curtailed programmes that had been approved by its branches locally permitting the output of small quantities of products for civilian requirements in small plants, reduced the civilian programme for [2 groups unrecovered] railroad equipment, decreased the allotment of materials to non-military programmes, and so forth. The War Manpower Commission tightened the limitation on manpower utilization and forced certain transfers of workers for carrying

out special programmes for filling military orders. The military departments during this time not only increased their orders for war materials, but also sharply increased the programmes for articles of civilian need, namely [2 groups unrecovered], screen cloth, textiles.

2. In recent weeks a marked shift in the conduct of civilian organizations has been noted. The DEPOT, [3 groups unrecovered] carried out by the War Manpower Commission, now maintain that the military departments are placing unjustifiably large orders, particularly for non-combat items, which are also needed for the civilian economy, that the production of a minimum quantity of goods for civilians must be permitted [1 group unrecovered] manpower which the military really don't need, [14 groups unrecoverable] which could be indirectly used in the war, that the military should be limited to a certain extent in their procurements. The military departments, on the other hand, have not retreated from their position of resistance to any production or activity for which they actually do not feel a direct need.

PART II 3. Perhaps the most striking expression of this new line of the DEPOT's was a statement made by Hiland BATCHELLER, Deputy Chairman of the DEPOT (at that time Acting Chairman, as KRUG was then absent), at a meeting of the Production Executive Committee on 12 March. From information received from a leading person who was present at the meeting it is known that BATCHELLER stated fairly openly [3 groups unrecovered + 273 not yet available]

PART III [150 groups not yet available + 5 unrecovered] at Philadelphia. It is also hard to believe that this position is connected in any way with the movement among reactionary congressmen to restrict export [1 group unrecovered] [44 groups unrecoverable] is not directed against war production, but in many respects amounts to support of it, especially in cases where a firm stand by the military may impede production. On the other hand, in the conduct of the heads of the military departments it has been possible for a long time to see traces of political pressure exerted on them. For example, the proposal to build an additional airport at NEW YORK in order to relieve the growing pressure of military and ordinary civilian air transport on the overloaded main field has been shelved and [1 group unrecovered] by the military departments. Mayor LA GUARDIA and others have visited WASHINGTON and written sharp letters of protest to KRUG. On 15 March this question was under discussion in the production review committee, where the vote was 9 to 5 on construction of the airport. The 5 votes cast against it were those of the military members. They made a protest against this decision in the Production Executive Committee, which [5 groups unrecovered] would support the opinion of the Production Review Committee.

There followed a highly secret assessment of the introduction of jet engines, from Anatoli Gromov in Washington DC, dated 29 June 1945:

To the 8th department. Information of RAIDER [Victor Perlo]
Colonel BANKER of the American Army Air Forces, on 8th June this year at a meeting in the DEPOT [War Production Board] on the work of the aviation industry, told me:
1. The motor of the new propellerless planes of which the most important is the 'P-80' is still [3 groups unrecovered] perfected at this time. In the factory they operate only 25 hours. [1 group unrecovered] in the Pacific Ocean theatre, at present, mainly are being used the fighters 'P-47' and 'P-51 MUSTANG'. The P-51 is the standard fighter but the P-47 is considered especially valuable for spotting targets with support, taking into account its flight and analogous work at low altitudes. The production of P-47 planes, possibly, will be considered in [12 groups unrecoverable] [5 groups unrecovered] ISLAND [England] used high-grade fuel '115–145' [1 group unrecovered], in the Pacific Ocean theatre fuel '100–130' is still being used. Fuel '115–145' will be introduced there only after 1 January 1946, when in the Pacific Ocean will be [13 groups unrecovered] fuel, changes are needed in the cooling systems of the motors. [12 groups unrecovered]

Later the same day Gromov sent a further, longer message to Moscow, headed identically 'To the 8th Department. Material from

The RAIDER

RAIDER' in which he prefaced two pages of statistics: 'I am sending information extracted from the secret programme of the JOINT AIRCRAFT COMMITTEE of the DEPOT [War Production Board] of 25 May of this year concerning aircraft construction planned for 1945–46. In the first column is given the figure for the aircraft construction planned for April–December 1945; in the second column is the analogous figure for the whole of 1946.'

One name omitted from Bentley's *Out of Bondage*, was that of Harold Glasser, one of the key figures in the Perlo group who, according to VENONA, was active throughout 1945. The first example of his espionage occurred in a text from Gromov in Washington DC dated 28 March 1945:

> At the very beginning of April there will be sent from here to MOSCOW an American delegation, headed by Isador LUBIN to take part in the work of the Reparations Commission. From NABOB's [Henry Morgenthau] establishment [US Treasury] [2 groups unrecovered], in the capacity of a member, a young lawyer, an American of French extraction, Josiah Ellis DuBOIS, born 21 October 1910, in the town of CAMDEN, NEW JERSEY, married, graduated from PENNSYLVANIA University Law School, working now [1 group unrecovered] of NABOB [3 groups unrecovered] senior consultant). DuBOIS is an intimate friend of ROUBLE [Harold Glasser] and we recently [30 groups unrecovered] works with NABOB. ROUBLE maintains the most friendly relations with him and asserts that DuBOIS [2 groups unrecovered] to us and by his views is a FELLOWCOUNTRYMAN [Communist]. He has never been a member of any FELLOWCOUNTRYMAN organizations whatsoever. At one time, soon after arrival in [6 groups unrecovered] used to express his leftist views, but later under the influence of ROUBLE he became more discreet. NABOB had talks with him about his trip to MOSCOW on 22 and 23 March and on 24 March the BANK [State Department] had already inquired of us about a visa for him. In conversation with ROUBLE on the subject of his trip to the SOVIET UNION DuBOIS repeatedly expressed his [50 groups unrecovered] and a senior worker of the KhATA [FBI] SAM [50 groups unrecoverable] but ROUBLE refused

321

having warned him to wait. ROUBLE considers [9 groups unrecovered] He indicates that on the strength of the relations existing between him and DuBOIS he can normally obtain by asking [5 groups unrecovered] and [3 groups unrecovered] what it is all about. I request instructions.

Glasser's reach extended to access of State Department cables, as Gromov reported on 21 June 1943:

ROUBLE's [Harold Glasser] material: We transmit a telegram of the Ambassador of the COUNTRY [America] in SMYRNA [Moscow] number 1818 of 30 May 1945 addressed to the BANK [State Department]. 'According to an article by L. VOLODARSKIJ [38 groups unrecoverable] of VOLODARSKIJ does not give any more specific details or a more precise determination of this estimate. [8 groups unrecovered] figure of 250 milliard gold roubles (roughly about 50 milliard dollars).

The fact that the Russians' estimate of their war losses will of course be astronomical (see Embassy telegram number 1230 of 18 April 1945), is merely confirmed by the figure of 100 milliard dollars quoted above. It is very likely that the total national wealth of the Soviet Union in the pre-war period was valued at a sum less than the 100 milliard dollars indicated in this article as being the losses in the Ukraine alone.'

On 21 June 1945 the *rezidentura* in Washington DC gave news of another delivery from Glasser, consisting of a report on Nazi banking transactions in Switzerland, attributed to the OSS chief in Berne:

To the 8th Department
ROUBLE [Harold Glasser] material:
  Here are the contents of a letter of an employee of the Counter-espionage Division of the HUT [OSS] in SIDON [London], Gerstle MACK of 8th March this year, to the representative of NABOB's [Henry Morgenthau] department [US Treasury].
1. The head of the German Section has requested us to transmit to you the following information, dated 26th

February this year and received from our representative in BERNE, SWITZERLAND.

2. [2 groups unrecovered] reliable informant stated that Nazi funds are being sent abroad not through ordinary banking channels but with the aid of individuals working in [2 groups unrecovered] banks or connected with them. In particular, it is reported that the following persons, who enjoy the confidence of the Nazi Party, [4 groups unrecovered]: a) PILGER from the DRESDNER BANK. b) SCHMOLL from the FROMBEG BANK in BERLIN [67 groups unrecoverable] WEHRLI BANK. f) VON KLIM from the Ministry of Foreign Affairs. g) LIKUS from the Ministry of Foreign Affairs or RIBBENTROP's Bureau.

3. We believe that this list may [19 groups unrecoverable]

Two days later Glasser handed over another State Department cable to a Soviet contact:

To the 8th Department. Material from ROUBLE [Harold Glasser]. I am transmitting the contents of a telegram from a representative of the BANK [State Department] in Helsinki telegram #265 of 29 May addressed to the BANK:

'The following communication was sent to London under number 16, to Berne under number 2 and to Stockholm under number 73. According to information received from a source of uncertain reliability, the Germans, WILLI DAUGS (a known agent) and Otto ENRICH, protected their assets in Finland, by a bogus transfer in November 1944, of about one million dollars, to an American living in Zurich E. V. DWIGHT Jnr. DWIGHT until 1941 worked for Henry MANN, formerly living in Berlin but now is in New York, at 64 Wall Street. ENRICH and DAUGS, it is confirmed, were owners of the firms ERGOSSCO and GIKKANGSKI, makers of machine guns. The firm TIKKAKOSKI is on the Proclaimed List. DAUGS and ENRICH since the first half of 1944 have been living in Stockholm and at present are wanted by the Finnish police for smuggling securities out of Finland.

It is reported that the Finnish embassy in Washington has the sum of 323 thousand American dollars kept in the dossier on Suomi machine guns. This money was placed

there for TIKKAKOSKI by Irjosaa STAMOINEN, who visited
the USA in 1940 on a diplomatic visa, as a minister on a
special mission. The money was to finance the production of
Suomi machine guns in the USA, however the project was
not accomplished. Inasmuch as DAUGS cannot use this
money himself, he transferred his rights to it to DWIGHT.
Under an agreement between DWIGHT and ERGO of 24
November 1944, based on judgment of the Magistrates Court
letters number 145 and 146, the Bank of Finland apparently
told GATES to pay on 30 June 210 thousand American
dollars in Argentine currency in Buenos Aires or in Brazilian
currency in Rio. Under armistice agreements Finland
undertook not to permit export of German property, without
preliminary consent of the Allied Control Commission, but if
steps are not taken immediately, the above indicated sum
will be exported as property of an American citizen. An
unofficial memorandum was delivered to the Foreign Office
with the request for an investigation and suspension of
action until [4 groups unrecovered] [37 groups
unrecoverable]

While Glasser's data may not have had any strategic significance, they must have been received well in Moscow. His final despatch, as revealed by VENONA, is dated 28 June 1945:

To the 8th Department.
ROUBLE's [Harold Glasser] material. In addition to our #815.
We transmit an excerpt from the internal memorandum of
the worker of the institution of NABOB [US Treasury] J. B.
FRIEDMAN from 18 June of this year: 'This morning major
WHEELER GREY was [5 groups unrecovered] raised the
following questions in connection with our discussion of 14
June. At our suggestion, the War Department agreed to
include in the definition of war crimes the third category,
namely: 'Invasions of other countries and initiation of wars
of aggression in violation of international law or treaties.'
According to GREY, this interpretation was discussed with the
workers of JACKSON [46 groups unrecoverable] objection, if
we insisted upon it. I have said that the Treasury Department
will insist upon the inclusion of this addition, in so much as

our purpose is to guarantee such a situation, in which all top leaders in industry, business and finance would be included in this directive. GREY [5 groups unrecovered] fear lest this directive would be interpreted in the field as an instruction to pick up even the members of the Nazi Youth Organization who gathered old paper [3 groups unrecovered] interpretation will be highly funny, for 1 fear that the workers in the field will arrest only as few criminals as possible [141 groups unrecoverable]

Elizabeth Bentley testified that at one point she had acted as a courier for Glasser, but the VENONA texts attributed to him date from between March and June 1945, when he was being supervised by the *rezidentura* in Washington DC. She said Glasser had been a member of the network run by Victor Perlo, but later had left the group to be handled, with one or two other agents, by an American employed by a US government agency. She remembered that this individual's identity had been known to Charles Kramer, who had named him as Alger Hiss, from the State Department, and that Hiss had passed Glasser on to a Russian.

The only other member of the Perlo group identified by Elizabeth Bentley in *Out of Bondage* is Mildred Price, whom she accused of providing an apartment in which the cell could meet. Married to Harold Coy, about whom nothing more is known, her sister was Mary Price, and she was the executive head of the China Aid Council, a Communist front. Bentley said that at first she had 'regarded Mildred merely as an intermediary with Mary, but soon we discovered she would be a valuable adjunct to our apparatus in her own right'. She was:

> the organizer of the Communist unit which functioned in the Institute of Pacific Relations – a foundation for Far Eastern studies which had originally been set up by well-meaning philanthropists but which had long since fallen under the domination of the Communists. The organization, because of its respectable past and high-sounding title, had been able to enroll in its ranks a vast number of 'innocents', among them professors and businessmen who were interested in Pacific affairs. Hence it had become the centre of all Communist activity in the Far Eastern field,

offering a protective covering to a number of smaller, more obviously pro-Communist enterprises that clustered around it. Among these were the China Aid Council, of which Mildred was executive secretary, and their magazines *China Today* and *Amerasia*.

Mildred Price used the IPR as a pool from which suitable prospects could be talent-spotted, but apart from Duncan Lee, Bentley could only recall her rejecting Philip Jaffe, *Amerasia*'s editor, as a candidate because he was too well-known as 'a red'. Another contact was Michael Greenberg, a CPGB member and graduate of Trinity College, Cambridge, who was awarded a PhD from Harvard in 1941, and worked as Lauchlin Currie's administrative assistant at the Foreign Economic Administration before he succeeded Owen Lattimore as chairman of the IPR. Also named by Bentley was Solomon Leshinsky of the United Nations Relief and Rehabilitation Administration, Norman Burster of the Justice Department, Irving Kaplan of the War Production Board, and Allan Rosenberg of the Foreign Economic Administration.

Of these, only Philip Jaffe was pursued by the FBI as an espionage suspect following a leak of classified OSS material to the journal. Originally he had been placed under surveillance as a key figure in the *Amerasia* case (see Chapter XI), and although indicted in August 1948 with Andrew Roth and Emmanuel S. Larsen, the charges were dropped because the FBI's copious evidence had come from illegal wiretaps and searches which could not be used in court. He was later cited for contempt, having pleaded the Fifth Amendment more than a hundred times before Senator Millard Tydings Committee in the Senate, which had been set up to look into Joseph McCarthy's allegations of spies in the State Department, but was acquitted in April 1951, and thereafter sought an immunity from prosecution, apparently anxious to avoid prosecution for wartime espionage, for which the Statute of Limitations did not apply. Following his acquittal the FBI conducted four lengthy interviews with Jaffe, which remain classified, but he did implicate Joseph M. Bernstein as a courier and the latter was to emerge in VENONA under the covername MARQUIS (see Chapter XI).

Postscript

VENONA inflicted irreparable damage on Soviet espionage, but also took its toll on the men and women cryptographers who wrestled with it over thirty-five years. Some worked on the material for a relatively short period, Cecil Phillips having moved on in 1950 to a career in automation and management; others, such as Gene Grabeel, devoted their entire careers to breaking out just a few groups at a time, teaching and inspiring successive generations of VENONA cryptographers. Mildred Hayes, who spent twenty-eight years on VENONA at the NSA, was given the painful task of closing the operation down and consigning the messages and worksheets to the archives. Others did not survive so well, a few developing muscular difficulties in their hands because of the repetitive nature of the work, sliding pieces of paper up and down lists of unrecovered codegroups. Nervous breakdowns occurred, a linguistic genius took to the bottle, another committed suicide and one woman became so obsessed that she abandoned personal hygiene.

The work, nevertheless, was hugely rewarding, and not unlike a perpetual mystery, the cryptanalysts playing the role of detectives searching for concealed clues that might reveal a hitherto unsuspected Soviet spy, or provide the proof needed to corner a known agent, or destroy or even enhance a well-known reputation. It was possible for their work to have an impact far beyond the realm of espionage. Those privy to VENONA's secrets maintained their oaths of loyalty and discretion, even though the material they handled included items with potentially profound political implications. If Richard Nixon had known that his early postwar allegations of widespread Communist penetration could be confirmed by just a handful of VENONA texts, his electoral chances and career would have been greatly improved years before he became President.

Digging deep into VENONA offered tantalizing glimpses of the NKVD's machinations. Just one tiny fragment, dated 31 August 1943, from Pavel Klarin to Moscow, illustrates the possibilities: '[75 groups unrecoverable] "Paul HAGEN. [1 group unidentified] is close to the wife of KAPITAN. [9 groups unrecovered].'

Who was Paul Hagen, and why was his proximity to Eleanor Roosevelt of interest to the Soviets? In fact, his real name was Karl Frank, and he was a Communist refugee who had fled his native Germany. After his arrival in the United States, which had been assisted by Lauchlin Currie who had supported his visa application, he had led the 'New Beginning' group, an organization that was actually a Communist front. He was also connected with another Soviet agent, Alfred Stern, whom he had met on an earlier visit to the United States in 1937. What Currie's motives were for helping Frank, or perhaps for facilitating his access to the President's wife, can only be guessed at, but the few words that were solved, combined with a knowledge of the personalities concerned, suggested the remainder was well worth pursuing.

Another well-known person to be spotted was Isadore F. Stone, codenamed PANCAKE, then the Washington editor of *The Nation*, who was to achieve considerable recognition as a journalist and historian. Although, as the author of the controversial six-volume series *A Nonconformist History of Our Times*, his leftist credentials were scarcely a secret, his contact with the NKVD most definitely was. He was alluded to in three VENONAs to Moscow. The first, dated 13 September 1944 from Apresyan, reporting on the TASS correspondent's efforts to cultivate Stone, was hardly incriminating:

> Your number 4247. SERGEI [Vladimir Pravdin] has three times attempted to effect liaison with PANCAKE [Isadore Stone] in CARTHAGE [Washington DC] in the line of cover but each time PANCAKE declined on the grounds of being busy with trips. IDE [Samuel Krafsur] has carefully attempted to sound him but PANCAKE did not react. PANCAKE occupies a very prominent position in the journalistic world and has vast connections. To determine precisely his relations to us we will commission ECHO [Bernard Schuster] to make a check.

This was followed on 23 October by a fuller account:

> SERGEI [Vladimir Pravdin] in CARTHAGE [Washington DC] has made the acquaintance of PANCAKE [Isadore Stone[.

Postscript

Earlier SERGEI had several times tried to contact him personally and also through IDE [Samuel Krafsur] but the impression has been created that PANCAKE was avoiding a meeting. At the first conversation SERGEI told him that he had very much desired to make his acquaintance since he greatly valued his work as a correspondent and had likewise heard flattering [23 groups unrecoverable] PANCAKE to give us information. PANCAKE said that he had noticed our attempts to contact him, particularly the attempts of IDE and a couple of the TRUST [Soviet embassy in Washington DC], but he had reacted negatively fearing the consequences. At the same time he implied that the attempts at rapprochement had been made with insufficient caution and by people who were insufficiently responsible. To SERGEI's reply that naturally we did not want to subject him to unpleasant complications, PANCAKE gave him to understand that he was not refusing his aid but one should consider that he had three children and did not want to attract the attention of the HUT [FBI]. To SERGEI's question how he considered it advisable to maintain liaison PANCAKE replied that he would be glad to meet but he rarely visited TYRE [New York] where he usually spent [54 groups unrecoverable] His fear is primarily explained by his unwillingness to spoil his career. Materially he is well secured. He earns as much as 1,500 dollars a month but it seems, he would not be averse to having a supplementary income. For the establishment of business contact with him we are insisting on [1 group unrecovered] reciprocity. For the work is needed a qualified [2 groups unrecovered] CARTHAGE. Telegraph your opinion.

The third VENONA to mention I. F. Stone, dated 23 December, gives a little more away about how his relationship with the NKVD developed:

Correspondents who have contacts with the military leaders, BUMBLEBEE, SWING, PANCAKE [Isadore Stone] and CHEF in a conversation with SERGEI [Vladimir Pravdin] maintained that the General Staff of the COUNTRY [America] is very much alarmed at the German offensive which may delay for several months the renewal of the American general offensive which is calculated to crush Germany in concert with us. BUMBLEBEE had a chat with the head of the ARSENAL [War Department] who told him that if the Germans seize LIEGE and the adjacent areas on the front it will take a further 3–4 months to reorganize the American offensive and longer to make good the stocks of artillery equipment now concentrated in this area. BUMBLEBEE was recently in France for a month and there concluded from a chat with EISENHOWER that the American plan provides for a breakthrough into the left bank of the RHINE in the middle of January. At this period the Americans were counting on our offensive in Poland, primarily in the direction of CRACOW.

The NSA successfully identified SWING as a radio commentator, but neither he nor Stone could be said on the basis of the texts to have actively engaged in espionage. Rather, it would appear that both collaborated to the extent of relaying remarks made by the Secretary of State for War, Henry Stimson, and General Eisenhower. However, that evaluation was to change, years later, when the KGB's General Oleg Kalugin disclosed that one of his first tasks in the United States had been to re-establish contact with Stone, who had been considered a valuable source. Kalugin had joined the Washington DC *rezidentura* in July 1965 under press attaché cover, and had met Stone for lunch every couple of months until August 1968, when Stone angrily denounced the Soviet invasion of Czechoslovakia and refused all further contact.

At GCHQ, interest in VENONA continued to the very last moment, in part a reflection of the British preoccupation with Soviet penetration. In the 'wilderness of mirrors' which so baffles counter-intelligence specialists, VENONA remained an irrefutable resource, far more reliable than the mercurial recollections of KGB defectors and the dubious conclusions drawn by paranoid analysts mesmerized by Machiavellian plots. The attraction of VENONA is easy to grasp: it represented a completely authentic window into the KGB's operations, without any of the blurring associated with other intelligence sources. Of course the unrecoverable groups made tantalizing gaps in the text, but occasionally almost complete documents were recovered, and many of these allowed those indoctrinated into VENONA's secrets to share in Moscow's deliberations. The classic example is that of a lengthy report sent by the Naval GRU in Washington in December 1942 concerning an illegal agent, codenamed the AUSTRALIAN WOMAN, who was later identified by the FBI as Francia Mitynia, alias Edna Patterson, and addressed to 'Name No. 42' in Moscow, who was probably Captain A. I. Egorichev:

> Herewith material on the despatch and legalization of the AUSTRALIAN WOMAN.
> PART I
> [16 groups unrecovered] Chiefly [36 groups unrecoverable] and demanded [52 groups unrecovered] for a month or two it is possible to [3 groups unrecovered] documents. In [4 groups unrecovered] the AUSTRALIAN WOMAN [32 groups unrecovered] establishments [104 groups unrecovered] [6 groups unrecoverable] presentation of documents, three referees and the completion of a detailed questionnaire including such questions as the names and addresses of obvious employers, places of residence, particulars of parents, relations, etc, after which all the papers go to the FBI (counter-intelligence) for checking. It is impossible at present for the AUSTRALIAN WOMAN to get work in these establishments.
> 2. The basic document which gives proof of American citizenship is the birth certificate. The birth certificate does not, as a rule, serve as an everyday means of identification. The ordinary, everyday documents are the driver's licence, the draft registration card (for men) and various passes and identity papers issued by establishments, businesses, companies and firms. The NEIGHBOURS [GRU] are of the opinion that birth certificates were formerly issued by the churches. Now they are issued by hospitals. Archives of birth records are carefully preserved by the Americans and checking a copy of a birth certificate does not cause the FBI any great difficulty. The driver's licence [2 groups unrecoverable] each adult. As the name and address of the holder are recorded on it, it also serves as an ordinary, everyday means of identification. Licences are issued by the transport department of the City Police (Traffic Department).

To obtain them one has to fill up a short questionnaire giving basic biographical details and present a licence from another state or pass a written examination on the traffic regulations of the city in question and a driving test. An American needs no other papers. The NEIGHBOUR [NKVD *rezident*] who promised to draw up a birth certificate said the other day that, in view of the postponement of his appointment to CANADA, his opportunities in this respect had come to naught. [13 groups unrecovered] posting to CANADA for this purpose. In his opinion it is possible in the last resort to forgo a birth certificate at home or simply to do without papers at first.

PART III

[29 groups unrecoverable] The prospects of a new system of documentation being instituted in the USA are uncertain. The FBI insists on registration and on taking [38 groups unrecoverable] about 20 million persons have been fingerprinted. These are mainly: aliens (all aliens are fingerprinted), merchant seamen and crews of ships coming here, servicemen, employees and workers in defence plants and government establishments. The issue of fingerprint identifications to [2 groups unrecovered] is becoming popular. A number of TAYLOR's people had their fingerprints taken in order to get passes into the ports.

PART IV

4. The landing of an illegal from our ships requires careful organization. The GREENS [counter-espionage agency] keep a watchful eye on our ships and people. During the period from September to December 1942 there were two cases of attempts to inspect two ships for a second time. The following cases are known:

    (a) During the inspection of a ship, the passengers and crew were checked a second time on a trivial pretext.
    (b) There was a personal search of numbers of a crew going into the city 'in order to discover smuggled letters'.
[2 groups unrecovered] to search [41 groups unrecoverable] naval intelligence [3 groups unrecovered] with the object of recruitment. There are repeated cases of our sailors not returning to their ships. Individual

Postscript

members of crews are questioned as to whether there are any outsiders on board.

PART V

Contrary to the previous arrangements, the Americans only admit the crews of our ships into the city if they show their passes. They are permanent passes and are kept by the captain. They are issued to each sailor arriving in the USA for the first time after his fingerprints have been taken. The information on the pass is checked on departure from the port and on return. The number of checkpoints varies. Crews of ships [45 groups unrecoverable] in principle remains as before. All objects brought here which are being taken away, packages and letters are inspected.

4. In clothing and appearance, our women serving on ships are clearly distinguishable from the local women. This is because of their stockings, their berets (American women wear hats), their handbags and their untidiness. They do not take any trouble over their hair or their make-up. Suits or overcoats of medium quality differ little from the American ones.

PART VI

5. The possible landing ports are SAN FRANCISCO and PORTLAND. Up to 15 of our ships arrive in Portland each month. 6 to 7 arrive in SAN FRANCISCO.

SAN FRANCISCO

Advantages:

(a) A large city in which it is easy to disappear.
(b) Easier to get a hotel room or a furnished room if necessary.
(c) Easier to buy a train ticket.
(d) Less danger of the AUSTRALIAN WOMAN's meeting [60 groups unrecoverable]

PORTLAND

Advantages:

(a) DAVIS can be relied upon. His work is such that he sees personally to the ships and is in the port practically all the time.

(b) If necessary DAVIS can avail himself of the help of our other people there.
Disadvantages:
(a) The city is small. It would be harder to disappear in it. It is necessary to [2 groups unrecovered] on the day of landing.
(b) It is harder to get a hotel room and practically impossible to take a furnished room. Our people have been watched and are well known. It would be more difficult to pass the time until the departure of the train.
(c) DAVIS is overburdened with his own work.

PART VII
6. Sleeper tickets on long distance trains may be bought at the ticket office two or three days in advance. Names and addresses are required when making a reservation. Two or three trains a day leave for NEW YORK. The trip takes up to five days and one must change in CHICAGO. The southern route through NEW ORLEANS should be rejected. [35 groups unrecoverable] The press reports that the checking of cars is in force along the west coast, especially around LOS ANGELES and to the south. To combat desertion, the military police took the papers of enlisted men in trains at PORTLAND and SAN FRANCISCO. Civilians are not liable to have their papers checked. Carriages on long distance trains consist of common sleepers and separate compartments – there are compartments for one person (roomettes) and for two or three persons (compartments) and special class compartments (drawing-rooms). In this instance a roomette would be the most suitable. One boards the train 20 to 30 minutes in advance. One can eat in the restaurant car or order in the compartment.

PART VII
7. Money. The FBI keeps a strict check on all the numbers and series of banknotes. My expenditure is also subjected to checking through the bank. Money received in the homeland by our citizens who come here [15 groups unrecoverable] series. End of part one.

As well as demonstrating Moscow's relative ignorance about conditions in the United States, this remarkable text shows the reluc-

Postscript

tance of the Centre to delegate any responsibility to *rezidenturas* or, for that matter, to individual GRU officers. Clearly the reporting officer was under an obligation to explain every detail, even if this required passing derogatory comments about Soviet womanhood. Quite how far Edna Patterson got as an illegal in the United States has not been disclosed, but the VENONA footnotes suggest that the FBI identified her without too much difficulty, and she later appeared in the traffic codenamed SALLY.

It was insights such as these into the way the NKVD and GRU operated that made the VENONA texts so absorbing for the counter-intelligence experts assigned to follow up the leads they contained. The messages revealed a breathtaking bureaucracy with massive direct control exercised by personnel many thousands of miles away from the scene. It was this tendency to centralize and supervise every aspect of an operation that led some to hope that the messages might contain significant clues to some of the unresolved mysteries that had dogged Western security agencies for decades.

One such investigation, conducted mainly in England before it spilled over to the United States, concerned Sir Roger Hollis, formerly the Director-General of the Security Service who retired in 1965. When suspicion was cast on his loyalty, a new effort was made to find clues in VENONA that might shed light on undiscovered Soviet spies. As far as Hollis was concerned, the exercise proved fruitless, but there was good reason to suppose that there might have been evidence relevant to him.

For *aficionados* of crossword puzzles and other conundrums, VENONA represents the ultimate challenge, offering the possibility of exposing dozens of spies and traitors around the world. When the project was finally abandoned, there were a few who advocated total declassification and release, partly because VENONA represented an ideal opportunity to set the historical record straight, particularly on such controversial cases as that of the Rosenbergs whose innocence was persistently proclaimed by a few leftist apologists and conspiracy theorists.

One of those keen to disclose the VENONA texts was James Angleton, the legendary chief of the CIA's counter-intelligence staff, who regarded the decrypts as a kind of holy grail, irrefutable proof of Soviet espionage at a high level and on a grand scale. Doubtless his motive was not just to educate the public and their politicians, but to allow scholars and amateur sleuths, unconstrained by government regulation, to track down more clues and identify more miscreants.

VENONA's very existence remained a closely-guarded secret until 1980, for although Kim Philby had published his memoirs *My Silent War* in 1968, and made many references to a joint Anglo-American counter-espionage operation that led to the arrest of Klaus Fuchs and was in pursuit of a leak codenamed HOMER [Donald Maclean] from inside the British embassy in wartime Washington DC, he made no mention of BRIDE. This was a strange omission, but it is likely that he wanted to avoid drawing attention to material that he must have feared, even from the safety of Moscow, could contain compelling proof not just of his own duplicity, but also provide hot leads to the treachery of so many others. In fact it was not until 1980 that the *Newsweek* journalist David C. Martin gave an account in *Wilderness of Mirrors* of Angleton's career, and that of Bill Harvey (also of the CIA). He described a massive cryptological undertaking that had originated with the capture of a Soviet codebook in Finland, only to be betrayed by a spy inside the AFSA named William Weisband. Martin admits that Angleton had encouraged his 'first thoughts of writing a book about Harvey', but the two men fell out as Martin became increasingly critical of the CIA's counter-intelligence culture in which supposition and conjecture became blurred with reality.

Despite Martin's revelations, the VENONA cat remained firmly within the bag, as is demonstrated by James Bamford's *The Puzzle Palace*, the very first detailed history of the NSA, published in 1982, which contains no reference to BRIDE or VENONA. The relative dearth of information was, of course, quite deliberate, for almost all those who had been indoctrinated into the operation hoped that at some future moment a breakthrough would be achieved that would reveal more of the unrecovered groups. Peter Wright, the MI5 officer who broke ranks to write *Spycatcher* in 1987, revealed the extent to which the molehunters had relied on VENONA and hoped for a counter-intelligence bonanza but, to their amazement, the principal enemy, Soviet totalitarianism, simply collapsed, and that astonishing development more than any other has allowed the Cold War to be brought to a close, and its greatest secret to be revealed.

APPENDICES

I   OSS Personnel Identified in VENONA as CPUSA Members

II   Cryptonyms in 1940/41 London GRU Traffic

III   The GRU *rezidentura* in London

IV   The VENONA Releases

All VENONA texts may be downloaded from:
http://www.nsa.gov:8080/docs/venona.htm

APPENDIX I

OSS Personnel Identified in VENONA as CPUSA Members

Name	Cryptonym	VENONA
Thomas Babin		12 August 1943
Joseph M. Bernstein	MARQUIS	16 August 1943
Emerson Bigelow		4 June 1944
Thomas A. Bisson	ARTHUR	16 August 1943
Michael J. Burd	TENOR	24 June 1943
Emile Despres		20 July 1943
Jane Foster	SLANG	30 June 1943
Maurice Halperin	HARE	8 June 1943
Betty Johnstone	UCN/22	18 June 1942
Emma Joseph	IVY	14 October 1944
J. Julius Joseph	CAUTIOUS	8 June 1943
Mrs Ray Gertrude Kahn	DINA	9 June 1943
Duncan C. Lee	KOCH	9 June 1943
Carl Marzani	COLLEAGUE	8 June 1943
Leonard Mins	SMITH	16 August 1943
Philip E. Moseley	DROP	13 March 1945
Franz L. Neumann	RUFF	
Peter C. Rhodes		16 August 1943
John Scott	IVANOV	13 October 1943
Helen Scott-Keenan	SPRUCE	22 June 1945
Gregory Silvermaster	PAL	6 July 1943
Edmund Stevens		13 October 1943
Ina Telberg		13 October 1944
Helen Tenney	MUSE	23 September 1944
Rifat Tirana		18 June 1942

APPENDIX II

Cryptonyms in 1940/41 London GRU Traffic

Covername	Date	Content/identity	VENONA Page
AIDA	5 June 1941	Connected with PORTER	206
ARTHUR	24 July 1941	Fragmented report	228
	31 July 1941	Reports on German panzers	238
	5 August 1941	British order-of-battle	239
BARON	18 March 1941	Czech railway data	187
	3 April 1941	Troop movements from Prague	190
	3 April 1941	Reference to ENIGMA	192
	17 May 1941	DICK discusses intercepts	202
	17 June 1941	Report from source of huts	215
	24 June 1941	Czech troop movements	219
	25 June 1941	Fragmented report of troops	221
	29 July 1941	Reports Czech rail traffic	230
	12 August 1941	Connected to NOBILITY	251
	14 August 1941	Reports Czech troop movements	254

Appendix II

Covername	Date	Content/identity	VENONA Page
BAUER	16 August 1940	Lieut. Hein has volunteered	70
	7 September 1940	To collect documents	117
	11 September 1940	Czech, based at Malpas	124
	16 September 1940	To be paid for documents	129
	3 October 1940	Meets NARK in Chester	151
BOB	11 July 1941	Recent marriage	225
BOND	2 June 1941	Reports radio DF data	259
BORN	6 March 1941	Describes establishment	185
	31 July 1941	Typist in intelligence section	232
BROWN	22 July 1940	Wireless operator in flat	28
	13 August 1940	To move to his old flat	58
	4 September 1940	Asdic source at Henry Hughes	109
BUSINESSMAN	14 August 1940	Nazi parachutists in Newbury	63
	17 July 1941	Fragmented report of comrades	227
CAMILLE	24 June 1941	Fragmented text	217
CARPENTER	26 July 1940	Radio operator/London	39
	29 August 1940	Reports air raids in London	98
	2 September 1940	Reports air raid on docks	104
	7 September 1940	To recruit five military sources	117
	13 November 1940	Fragmented text	177

Covername	Date	Content/identity	VENONA Page
	29 April 1941	Reports tank production	197
	5 June 1941	Reports bombing in Stepney	208
	6 August 1941	Met MARK on 4 August	240
	9 August 1941	Fragmented text	246
DUBOIS	5 June 1941	Fragmented text	210
	11 July 1941	Relays report from BOB	225
FUKS	10 August 1941	Klaus Fuchs meets Kremer	247
INTELLIGENTSIA	25 July 1940	J. B. S. Haldane, head of X Group	36
	6 September 1940	Lives in the provinces	112
	2 October 1940	Source warns of codebreak	148
	11 October 1940	Bomb disposal technique	161
	15 October 1940	Air Ministry source	163
	4 November 1940	Serviceman friend in Wales	173
IRIS	1 August 1940	Reports visit to Liverpool	48
	20 September 1940	Kremer to decide her work	137
	31 July 1941	Meets SONIA	236
JEAN	5 June 1941	Fragmented text	21
JOHN	31 July 1941	Leon (Len) Beurton	236
KARL	3 September 1940	Failed to make rendezvous	106

Appendix II

Covername	Date	Content/identity	VENONA Page
	21 September 1940	Necessity to meet him	137
LEOPOLD	21 September 1941	Failed to meet at agreed place	139
LYONMAN	12 June 1941	Fragmented text	213
MARK	16 August 1940	To be in contact with MARTHA	70
	3 October 1940	Reports meeting with BAUER	151
	6 August 1941	Gives radio to CARPENTER	240
MARTHA	8 July 1940	Alta Lecoutre, secretary to Labarthe	8
MARY	11 July 1940	Given small assignment to star	9
	24 July 1940	Rendezvous in London	34
	13 August 1940	May leave for home	57
	16 August 1940	Has departed	70
	21 September 1940	To be paid £30 a month	137
MASTER	29 April 1941	Reports work on Halifax bomber	197
	5 June 1941	Reports damage in Birmingham	208
MINISTER	15 July 1940	Reports air raids in South Wales	4
	22 July 1940	To be put in touch with BROWN	27
	28 August 1940	Reports air raids in London	98
	2 September 1940	Reports air raid on Kingston	104

Covername	Date	Content/identity	VENONA Page
	4 September 1940	In contact with BROWN/London	28
	7 September 1940	To recruit two military staff	117
	20 December 1940	Suitable for work	179
	31 July 1941	Meets NICK	232
MUSE	15 July 1940	Woman wireless operator	15
	26 July 1940	Radio reception difficulties	39
	10 August 1940	Working on radio	55
	13 August 1940	Transmits from Soviet embassy	58
	27 August 1940	Transmission heard on schedule	93
	27 August 1940	To listen on Thursdays	97
	30 August 1940	Radio instructions	103
	5 September 1940	Radio instructions	110
	18 September 1940	Signal not received	134
	20 September 1940	Signal received well	136
	26 September 1940	Complaint signal not taken	146
	25 November 1940	Ready to listen for signals	178
	31 July 1941	Meets SERGEANT's wife	234
NOBILITY	6 September 1940	Ivor Montagu in London	112
	17 September 1940	Reports six destroyers in Thames	132
	16 October 1940	Reports German beam on Bristol	165
	30 October 1940	Newspaper correspondent	171
	20 December 1940	Passed material through X Group	179

Appendix II

Covername	Date	Content/identity	VENONA Page
	12 August 1941	Link to BARON	251
PORTER	5 June 1941	Connected with AIDA	206
POULTRY DEALER	13 August 1940	Reports CPGB contact	58
	14 August 1940	Contact with Tom Wintringham	63
	4 October 1940	Reports bombing of Hounslow	154
	9 October 1940	Reports bombing of Hounslow	158
RESERVIST	6 September 1940	British Army colonel	113
	18 October 1940	Gunner, wounded in France	167
		Tank expert, Ministry of Supply	
	25 April 1941	Meeting not held	196
SERGEANT	31 July 1941	His wife in contact with MUSE	234
	6 August 1941	Reports on aerial photography	240
SONIA	31 July 1941	Ursula Beurton, meets IRIS	236
STANLEY	22 July 1940	Canadian, in poor health	28
	26 July 1940	Wireless operator	39
	3 August 1940	Receiving difficulties	51
	27 August 1940	Request for readiness report	93
	5 September 1940	To begin transmitting	110
	13 June 1941	Fragmented text	214
	31 July 1941	Moves house	232
	13 August 1940	Stops work to move flat	55

Covername	Date	Content/identity	VENONA Page
TECHNICIAN	20 December 1940	Not in contact with X Group	179
THERAPUTIST	14 August 1940	Airman at Prestwich	63
	17 August 1940	Air raid on his aerodrome	74
	24 August 1940	Reports RAF losses	86
	7 September 1940	Reports air raid on Swansea	115
	7 September 1940	Instructed to supply documents	117
	3 October 1940	Demand for fighter training data	151
VIKER	6 August 1941		240
WRITER	14 August 1940	Seaman arrived from Glasgow	60, 90
	15 August 1940	Air raid on the *Malines*	68
	20 August 1940	Urges move to new job	77
	26 August 1940	Reports on Harwich defences	89
	5 September 1940	Requests check	110
	3 October 1940	Evacuated from France	151

APPENDIX III

The GRU *rezidentura* in London

Name	Cover	Dates in London
Nikolai V. Aptekar	chauffeur	March 1937–April 1944
Boris Dikiy	Cherny's secretary, ass. air attaché	January 1940–
Ivan M. Kozlov	secretary	April 1941–November 1945
Simon Kremer	secretary	February 1937–1946
Maj. Anatoli Lebedev	ass. military attaché, army	April 1941–November 1943
Mikhail I. Mikhailov	attaché at consulate	December 1939–July 1943
Fedor I. Moskvichev	military attaché's clerk	December 1939–January 1943
Maj. Boris Shvetsov	ass. military attaché, air	October 1940–April 1942
Col. Ivan A. Sklyarov	military attaché	October 1940–March 1946
Nikolai M. Timofeev	chauffeur	September 1939–June 1943

APPENDIX IV

The VENONA Releases

[Release] No.	Circuit	Type	Date of Traffic	Pages
1	New York–Moscow	NKVD	June 1944–October 1945	80
2	New York–Moscow	NKVD	November 1941–December 1943	433
3 v.1	New York–Moscow	NKVD	January 1944–July 1944	337
3 v.2	New York–Moscow	NKVD	August 1944–December 1944	348
3 v.3	New York–Moscow	NKVD	January 1945–July 1945	93
	Moscow–New York	NKVD	January 1945–July 1945	93
	Washington–Moscow	NKVD	March 1945–November 1946	67
4 v.1	Washington–Moscow	GRU	April 1943–May 1944	56
	Moscow–Washington	GRU	February 1943–April 1944	35
	New York–Moscow	GRU	May 1941–September 1943	84
4 v.2	Washington–Moscow	Naval GRU	April 1943–November 1943	258

Appendix IV

No.	Circuit	Type	Date	Pages
	Moscow–Washington	Naval GRU	January 1943–July 1943	120
4 v.3	Mexico City–Moscow	NKVD	December 1943–November 1944	157
	Moscow–Mexico City	NKVD	February 1944–May 1946	175
5 v.1	Moscow–Washington	Diplomatic	June 1942–August 1946	28
	Washington–Moscow	Diplomatic	June 1943–February 1946	14
	Circulars	Diplomatic	June 1945–May 1947	12
	Moscow–San Francisco	Diplomatic	February 1946–November 1946	20
	New York–Moscow	Diplomatic	May 1944–September 1945	6
	Moscow–New York	Diplomatic	May 1944–September 1944	4
	Stockholm–Moscow	Diplomatic	November 1942–October 1944	12
	Moscow–Stockholm	Diplomatic	September 1944–October 1944	4
	Ottawa–Moscow	Diplomatic	August 1944	3
	Ankara–Moscow	Diplomatic	March 1944	1
	Harbin–Moscow	Diplomatic	November 1943	2
	Tokyo–Moscow	Diplomatic	September 1943	1
	Moscow–Havana	Diplomatic	September 1944–July 1945	6
	Moscow–Harbin	Diplomatic	March 1944–July 1945	4
	Moscow–Bogota	Diplomatic	February 1945–October 1945	4
	Moscow–Montevideo	Diplomatic	October 1944–May 1945	10
	Moscow–Meshed	Diplomatic	January 1946	1
	Moscow–Capetown	Diplomatic	July 1946	1
	Moscow–Kazvin	Diplomatic	May 1945	1
	Moscow–Addis Ababa	Diplomatic	December 1944	1

VENONA

No.	Circuit	Type	Date	Pages
	Moscow–Tokyo	Diplomatic	November 1943–December 1944	1
	Moscow–Meshed	Diplomatic	January 1946	1
	Moscow–Tokyo	Diplomatic	November 1943–December 1944	4
	Harbin–Moscow	Diplomatic	November 1943–March 1944	3
	Stockholm–Moscow	Diplomatic	October 1944	1
	Buenos Aires–New York	Diplomatic	July 1941–December 1942	4
	New York–Buenos Aires	Diplomatic	November 1941–September 1943	4
	Moscow–Washington	Trade	December 1942–December 1943	2
	New York–Moscow	Trade	April 1944	1
	Fairbanks–Moscow	Trade	April 1944	1
	Montreal–Moscow	Trade	September 1944	4
	Washington–Moscow	Trade	December 1942–May 1943	17
	New York–Moscow	Trade	January 1945	1
	Portland–Moscow	Trade	June 1943	3
	Washington–Moscow	Trade	January 1943	1
	Moscow–Ottawa	Trade	November 1944	2
	London–Moscow	Trade	March 1942	1
	Ottawa–Moscow	Trade	January 1944–January 1945	6
	Moscow–Ottawa	Trade	November 1944–December 1944	4
	Moscow–Portland	Trade	May 1944	1
	Portland–Washington	Trade	January 1945	2
5 v.2	Moscow–Montevideo	NKVD	May 1944–January 1945	105
	Bogota–Moscow	NKVD	May 1944–January 1945	61
	Moscow–Bogota	NKVD	May 1944–January 1945	17
	Moscow–Havana	NKVD	February 1947	2

Appendix IV

No.	Circuit	Type	Date	Pages
	Moscow–Ottawa	NKVD	March 1944–November 1944	7
	Moscow–Berlin	NKVD	June 1947	1
	Moscow–Sofia	NKVD	September 1945–March 1947	36
	Moscow–Berlin	NKVD	June 1947	1
	Moscow–The Hague	NKVD	December 1945	2
	London–Moscow	NKVD	September 1941–November 1946	40
	Istanbul–Moscow	NKVD	June 1944–January 1945	40
5 v.3	Moscow–Canberra	NKVD	August 1943–June 1948	329
5 v.4	Moscow–London	GRU	March 1940–April 1942	95
5 v.5	Moscow–London	GRU	September 1945–March 1947	194
	Moscow–Sofia	GRU	June 1940–March 1942	4
	Moscow–Prague	GRU	March 1940–April 1940	2
	Moscow–Paris	GRU	April 1940	3
	Mexico City–Moscow	GRU	February 1947–December 1947	7
	Ottawa–Moscow	GRU	January 1944	11
5 v.6	Stockholm–Moscow	NKVD	September 1941–April 1946	298
5 v.7	Stockholm–Moscow	GRU	April 1940–November 1944	255
	Stockholm–Moscow	Naval GRU	February 1941–October 1944	190
	London–Stockholm	Naval GRU	October 1945	2
6 v.1	New York–Moscow	NKVD	June 1943–February 1945	51
	Moscow–New York	NKVD	May 1945	2

Glossary of Soviet Covernames

Covernames	Identity
19	Eduard Beneš
ABRAM	Jack Soble, later CZECH
ACORN	William H. Taylor
ADAM	Mikhail F. Shiskin
AIDA	Esther Trabach Rand, later KLO
AIDA	Unidentified agent in London GRU traffic
AILERON	Abraham G. Silverman
AKHMED	Unidentified spy, formerly THRUSH, in New York traffic
AKIM	Sergei G. Lukianov
ALAN	Unidentified member of London *rezidentura*
ALAN	Ralph Bowen
ALBERT	Iskhak Akhmerov
ALEK	Allan Nunn May
ALEKSANDR	Unidentified member of New York *rezidentura*
ALEKSEI	Anatoli Yakovlev, member of the XY *rezidentura*, New York
ALES	Alger Hiss
ALEXANDER	Simon Kremer, GRU *rezident* in London formerly BARCh
AMT	John Abt
ANITA	Unidentified spy in London GRU traffic
ANT	Kristel Fuchs
ANTENNA	Julius Rosenberg, later LIBERAL
ANTON	Leonid R. Kvasnikov, XY *rezident*
ARENA	Mary Wolfe Price, later DIR
ARMOUR	Spy in Republic Aviation, identity protected, formerly STAMP
ARNO	Harry Gold
ARNOLD	Unidentified spy, later FAKIR
ARSENIJ	Andrei I. Shevchenko

Covernames	Identity
ART	Helen Koral, formerly MIRANDA
ARTEK	Leonid B. Abramov
ARTHUR	Thomas A. Bisson
ARTHUR	Unidentified spy in London GRU traffic
ARTISTE	Herbert W. Tattersell
ARTUR	Unidentified spy in London GRU traffic
AUSTRALIAN WOMAN	Francia Mitynia, alias Edna Patterson, an illegal, later SALLY
AUTHOR	Vladimir B. Morkovin
BARCh	Simon Kremer, later ALEXANDER
BARON	Karel Sedlacek
BASS	Michael J. Burd
BAUER	Lieutenant Hein of the Czech Army
BEAR	US Republican
BECK	Sergei N. Kurnakov, formerly CAVALRYMAN, member of New York *rezidentura*
BEER	Unidentified spy, formerly L, in New York traffic
BEN	Sgt Alfred T. Hughes
BERG	Unidentified spy, formerly SENOR, in New York traffic
BIBI	Unidentified source in New York NKVD traffic
BILL OF EXCHANGE	Robert Oppenheimer
BLACK	Thomas L. Black, later PETER
BLOCK	Unidentified spy, formerly OSPREY, in New York traffic
BOAR	Winston Churchill
BOATSWAIN	Vice-President Henry Wallace, also DEPUTY
BOB	Boris Krotov, member of NKVD *rezidentura* in London
BORIS	Aleksandr Saprygin, cipher-clerk in New York *rezidentura*
BRION	Boris Shvetsov
BROTHER	Unidentified spy, later THOMAS, in New York traffic
BROWN	Unidentified spy in London GRU traffic
BUMBLEBEE	David Greenglass, later CALIBRE
BUSINESSMAN	Unidentified spy in London GRU traffic

Glossary of Soviet Covernames

Covernames	Identity
CALIBRE	David Greenglass, formerly BUMBLEBEE
CALISTRATUS	Aleksandr Feklisov, member of New York *rezidentura*
CAMILLE	Unidentified spy in London GRU traffic
CAPITALIST	Averell Harriman
CAPTAIN	President Roosevelt
CAUTIOUS	J. Julius Joseph
CAVALRYMAN	Sergei N. Kurnakov, later BECK, member of the New York *rezidentura*
CHARLES	Klaus Fuchs, formerly REST
CHARON	Grigori M. Kheifets, NKVD *resident* in San Francisco
CHEMIST	Ivan Kamenev
CLARK	Igor Gouzenko
CLAUDE	Walter S. Clayton
CLEMENCE	Unidentified spy, later LEE, in New York traffic
CLEMENS	Unidentified agent in New York NKVD traffic
CLEVER GIRL	Elizabeth Bentley, later MYRNA
COLLEAGUE	Carl Marzani
CONSTRUCTOR	Abraham Brothman, later EXPERT
CORK	William Pinsly
CRUCIAN	Anton S. Ivancic
CUPID	Unidentified spy, formerly JEANETTE, in New York traffic
CZECH	Jack Soble, formerly ABRAM
CZECH	Robert O. Menaker
DAEDALUS	Pierre Cot
DAN	Unidentified spy in London NKVD traffic
DANDY	Unidentified spy in London NKVD traffic
DASHA	Maria Wicher
DAVIS	Unidentified spy, formerly LONG, in New York traffic
DEIGHTON	Contact for Irving Nelson
DEPUTY	Vice-President Henry Wallace, also BOATSWAIN
DICK	Member of London GRU *rezidentura*
DIK	Unidentified GRU case officer in London
DINA	Mrs Ray Gertrude Kahn
DIR	Mary Wolfe Price, formerly ARENA

Covernames	Identity
DONALD	William L. Ullman, also PILOT and POLO
DORA	Helen Silvermaster
DOUGLAS	Joseph Katz, also X and INFORMER
DROP	Philip E. Moseley
DUBOIS	Unidentified spy in London GRU traffic
DUVER	Unidentified member of New York *rezidentura*
ECHO	Bernard Schuster
EDWARD	Unidentified source in London NKVD traffic
EFIM	Semen I. Makarov, NKVD *rezident* in Canberra
ELLEN	Unidentified GRU spy in London
ELSA	Unidentified spy in New York traffic
ELZA	Helen Lowry (Mrs Akhmerov)
EMILYA	Unidentified spy, formerly STELLA, in New York traffic
EMULSION	Unidentified spy, later SIGNAL, in New York traffic
ERIC	Leona O. Franey, formerly ZERO
ERIE	Unidentified atom spy, later GEORGES
ERNEST	Spy in Manhattan Project, formerly HURON
EXPERT	Abraham Brothman, formerly CONSTRUCTOR
EXPRESS MESSENGER	Ricardo Setaro, later JEAN, KARL, RAY
FAKIR	Unidentified spy, formerly ARNOLD
FERRO	Ric Throssell
FERRO	Aleksandr N. Petroff, formerly FIN
FIN	Aleksandr N. Petroff, later FERRO
FIRTREE	Helen Scott-Keenan, OSS, also SPRUCE
FISHERMAN	Unidentified spy in New York traffic
FRED	Fred Rose, MP in Canada
FROST	Boris Morros
GARD	Unidentified spy in Europe
GAVR	Identity protected
GEORGES	Unidentified atom spy, formerly ERIE
GIFT	Grigori Kasparov, NKVD *rezident* in San Francisco
GIRLFRIEND	Unidentified woman agent in Canberra traffic
GLORY	Unidentified woman agent in Canberra traffic

Glossary of Soviet Covernames

Covernames	Identity
GNAT	Victor Kravchenko
GNOME	William Perl, later YaKOV
GOOSE	Harry Gold, later ARNO
GRANDFATHER	Evgeni D. Kiselev
GRANDPAPA	Evgeni D. Kiselev
GRANDSON	Unidentified codename in Canberra traffic
GROWTH	Unidentified spy, formerly ODESSITE
HARE	Maurice Halperin
HARRIER	Cordell Hull
HARRY	Jacob Epstein
HAVRE	Identity protected
HELMSMAN	Earl Browder
HENRY	William M. Malisoff, later TALENT
HICKS	Guy Burgess
HOMER	Donald Maclean
HUDSON	Unidentified spy, later JOHN
HUGHES	Alfred Sarant
HURON	Spy in Manhattan Project, later codenamed ERNEST
IDE	Samuel Krafsur
INFORMER	Joseph Katz, also DOUGLAS and X
INTELLIGENSIA	Prof. J. B. S. Haldane
IRIS	SONIA's GRU case officer in London
IVANOV	John Scott Nearing
IVY	Emma Joseph
IZRA	Donald Wheeler
JACK	Unidentified agent in London NKVD traffic
JACK	Unidentified spy in OSS
JANE	Unidentified GRU spy in London
JEAN	Ricardo Setaro, formerly EXPRESS MESSENGER, also RAY, KARL
JEANNE	Christina Krotkova or Sara Veksler, formerly OLA
JEANNETTE	Unidentified spy, later CUPID, in New York traffic
JEROME	André Labarthe

Covernames	Identity
JOHN	Len Beurton
JOHN	Unidentified spy, formerly HUDSON
JOHN	Unidentified spy in London GRU traffic
JOHNSON	Anthony Blunt
JUAN	Juan Gaytan Gody
JULIA	Olga V. Khlopkova, member of the San Francisco *rezidentura*
JUPITER	Unidentified spy, later ODD FELLOW, in New York traffic
JURIST	Harry Dexter White, later RICHARD and LAWYER
KANT	Henry Magdoff
KANT	Mark Zborowski, formerly TULIP
KARL	Ricardo Setaro, also EXPRESS MESSENGER, JEAN, RAY
KARL	Unidentified spy in London GRU traffic
KARLOS	Christian Cananova Subercaseaux
KEEN	Unidentified spy, formerly OSPREY, in New York traffic
KHAZAR	Unidentified OSS spy in New York traffic
KIN	Boris N. Yartsev, married to Stockholm *resident*
KIN	Enos Wicher
KINSMAN	Unidentified spy, formerly SOLID, in New York traffic
KLARK	Unidentified GRU case officer in London
KLIM	Unidentified spy in New York traffic
KLO	Esther Trabach Rand, formerly AIDA
KOCH	Duncan C. Lee
KOLO	Sava S. Kosanovic
KULAK	Thomas Dewey
KURT	Unidentified spy, formerly PLUCKY
L	Unidentified spy, later BEER, in New York traffic
LAWYER	Harry Dexter White, also JURIST and RICHARD
LEAF	Unidentified agent in NKVD London traffic
LEE	Unidentified spy, formerly CLEMENCE in New York traffic

Glossary of Soviet Covernames

Covernames	Identity
LENS	Michael Sidorovich
LESLEY	Lona Cohen
LIBERAL	Julius Rosenberg, formerly ANTENNA
LIGHT	Aleksandr Raev, member of New York *rezidentura*
LINA	Zoya Semenovna Myakotina, member of New York *rezidentura*
LINK	William Weisband
LONG	Unidentified spy, later DAVIS, in New York traffic
LOU	Marion Davis
LOUIS	Alfred K. Stern
LUCY	Rudolf Rosessler
LUKA	Pavel Klarin, TASS correspondent in New York
LYONMAN	Unidentified spy in London GRU traffic
MAK	Member of New York NKVD *rezidentura*
MARGO	Margarita Neklen Hansberger de Paul
MARK	Unidentified GRU case officer in London
MARQUIS	Joseph H. Bernstein
MARS	Vasili Sukhomlin
MARTHA	Alta Lecoutre
MARY	Unidentified spy in London GRU traffic
MASTER	Unidentified spy in London GRU traffic
MASTERCRAFTSMAN	Wilbur N. Christiansen
MASTERCRAFTSMAN	Charles B. Sheppard
MATVEJ	Milton Schwartz
MAX	Unidentified source in New York traffic
MAXIM	Vasili Zubilin Zarubin, NKVD *rezident* in New York, then Washington DC
MAY	Stepan Apresyan, NKVD *rezident* in New York
MERI	Unidentified agent in New York NKVD traffic
METEOR	Unidentified member of the New York *rezidentura*
METER	Joel Barr, formerly SCOUT
MIDSHIPMAN	Unidentified spy in New York NKVD traffic
MIM	Mikhail I. Mikhailov, member of NKVD *rezidentura* in New York
MINISTER	Unidentified spy in London GRU traffic

Covernames	Identity
MIRAGE	Unidentified spy in New York NKVD traffic
MIRANDA	Helen Koral, later ART
MOK	Vladimir V. Gavriluk
MUSE	Helen Tenney
MYRNA	Elizabeth Bentley, formerly CLEVER GIRL
NABOB	Henry Morgenthau
NAZAR	Stepan N. Shundenko
NEEDLE	Jones Orin York
NICK	Irving C. Nelson
NICK	Amadeo Sabatini
NIK	Unidentified GRU case officer in London
NIL	Unidentified member of the Rosenberg network
NOBILITY	The Hon. Ivor Montagu
NOISE	Identity protected, formerly SPLINE
NYNA	Unidentified agent in New York traffic
OAK	Unidentified agent in New York NKVD traffic
ODD FELLOW	Unidentified spy, formerly JUPITER, in New York traffic
ODESSITE	Unidentified spy, later GROWTH
OFFICER	Jan Fierlinger
OLA	Christina Krotkova or Sara Veksler, later JEANNE
OLD	Saville S. Sax
OPPEN	Unidentified agent in New York NKVD traffic
OSIPOV	Prince Nikolai Orlov
OSPREY	Unidentified spy, later BLOCK, in New York traffic
OSPREY	Unidentified spy, later KEEN, in New York traffic
OSWARD	Benjamin Gerig
OTTO	Unidentified source in London NKVD traffic
PAGE	Lauchlin B. Currie
PAL	Nathan Gregory Silvermaster, later ROBERT
PALM	Boris L. Lvovich, French consul-general
PANCAKE	Isadore Stone

Glossary of Soviet Covernames

Covernames	Identity
PAUL	Unidentified member of the New York *rezidentura*
PEAK	Virginius Frank Coe
PERS	Unidentified spy in Manhattan Project, formerly VOGEL
PETER	Thomas L. Black, previously BLACK
PETROV	Lavrenti Beria
PHIL	Unidentified spy in OSS
PHLOX	Rose Olsen
PILOT	William L. Ullman, also DONALD and POLO
PLUCKY	Unidentified spy, later KURT
PLUMB	Charles Kramer
POLO	William L. Ullman, also DONALD and PILOT
PORTER	Unidentified spy in London GRU traffic
POULTRY DEALER	Unidentified spy in London GRU traffic
PRINCE	Laurance Duggan, formerly SHERWOOD
PROFESSOR	Frederick Rose, Australia
QUANTUM	Unidentified atom spy
RACHEL	Unidentified spy in Europe
RADIO ANNOUNCER	General William Donovan
RAIDER	Victor Perlo
RAS	General de Gaulle
RAY	Ricardo Setaro, also EXPRESS MESSENGER, JEAN, KARL
RAY	Identity deleted
REDAKTOR	Konstantin A. Umansky
RICHARD	Harry Dexter White, formerly JURIST and LAWYER
RELAY	Doubtful identification of Morton Sobell, later SERB
RESERVIST	Territorial colonel in the Ministry of Supply, London
REST	Klaus Fuchs, later CHARLES
ROBERT	Unidentified agent in New York NKVD traffic
ROBERT	Nathan Gregory Silvermaster, formerly PAL
ROMAN	Robert Soble
ROMAN	Professor's name protected

Covernames	Identity
ROSA	Unidentified agent in London NKVD traffic
ROUBLE	Harold Glasser
RUAN	Ilya M. Saraev
RUDOLF	Unidentified member of New York *rezidentura*
RUFF	Unidentified spy in OSS
RUPPERT	Franz L. Neumann
S-1	Herman R. Jacobson
SALLY	Francia Mitynia, alias Edna Patterson, an illegal, formerly AUSTRALIAN WOMAN
SANTO	Unidentified codename in Canberra traffic
SCORPION	Prof. Sergei J. Paramonov
SCOUT	Joel Barr, later METER
SEAL	Unidentified agent in New York NKVD traffic
SEAMAN	Unidentified agent in New York NKVD traffic
SEAMAN	Vladimir Petrov in Stockholm traffic
SENOR	Unidentified spy, later BERG, in New York traffic
SERB	Doubtful identification of Morton Sobell, formerly RELAY
SERES	Dr Ivan Subasic
SERGEANT	Unidentified spy in London GRU traffic
SERGEI	Vladimir Pravdin, TASS correspondent in New York
SHAH	Konstantin A. Shabanov
SHERWOOD	Laurance Duggan, later PRINCE
SIGNAL	Unidentified spy, previously EMULSION, in New York traffic
SIMA	Judith Coplon
SIMON	Unidentified member of New York *rezidentura*
SISKIN	Unidentified member of New York NKVD *rezidentura*
SISTER	Frances Burnie
SKRIB	Unidentified agent in New York NKVD traffic
SLANG	Jane Foster Zlatovski
SMART	Unidentified atom spy
SMITH	Leonard E. Mins
SOLID	Unidentified spy, later KINSMAN, in New York traffic

Glossary of Soviet Covernames

Covernames	Identity
SONIA	Ursula Kuczynsky
SOUND	Jacob Golos
SOURCE 13	Unidentified spy in New York NKVD traffic
SPIRITED	Unidentified codename in Canberra traffic
SPLINE	Identity protected, later NOISE
SPRUCE	Helen Scott-Keenan, OSS, also FIRTREE
STAFFMAN	Unidentified member of the New York *rezidentura*
STAMP	Spy in Republic Aviation, identity protected, later ARMOUR
STANLEY	Kim Philby
STANLEY	Unidentified GRU source in London
STELLA	Unidentified spy, later EMILYA, in New York traffic
STEPAN	Pavel Fedosimov
STOCK	Mikhail A. Shalyapin, clerk in New York *rezidentura*
STORM	Unidentified agent in Washington DC traffic
SUK	Unidentified agent
SULLEN	Viktor Kirilov
TALENT	William M. Malisoff, formerly HENRY
TECHNICIAN	Fedor A. Nosov, TASS correspondent in Sydney
TECHNICIAN	Unidentified spy in London GRU traffic
TED	Edward Fitzgerald
THERAPUTIST	Fighter pilot in London GRU traffic
THOMAS	Unidentified spy, previously BROTHER, in New York traffic
THRUSH	Unidentified spy, later AKHMED, in New York traffic
TINA	Unidentified atom spy
TOURIST	James Hill
TULIP	Mark Zborowski, later KANT
TWAIN	Semyon N. Semyonov, member of XY *rezidentura* in New York
UCN/6	Unidentified covername
UCN/9	Cedric Belfrage

Covernames	Identity
UCN/19	Unidentified covername in Washington DC traffic
UCN/22	Betty Johnstone
UCN/41	Unidentified covername in New York traffic
URAL	Nikolai Karpekov
VADIM	Anatoli Gromov, NKVD *rezident* in Washington DC
VARDO	Elizaveta Zarubina
VIKER	Unidentified spy in London GRU traffic
VIKTOR	Pavel M. Fitin
VOGEL	Unidentified spy in Manhattan Project, later PERS
VOLUNTEER	Morris Cohen
WASP	Ludmilla N. Alexeef
WASP	Ruth Greenglass
WEST	Unidentified agent in London NKVD traffic
WOOLWORTH	Robert Wohlforth
WRITER	Seaman on the SS *Malines*
X	Joseph Katz, also DOUGLAS and INFORMER
YaKOV	William Perl, formerly GNOME
YOUNG	Dr Theodore Hall
YURI	Lev Tarasov (Vasilevsky)
ZERO	Leona O. Franey, later ERIC
ZhENYa	Sonia Gold
ZhOLUD	Bela Gold
ZONE	Unidentified spy in New York NKVD traffic
ZORA	Flora Don Wovschin
ZOYA	Aleksandra Zarubina

Glossary of Soviet Cryptonyms

Cryptonyms	Identity
ACADEMICIAN	Communist Party Member
ADMINISTRATOR	Chief of GRU's Western Europe Department
ARSENAL	US War Department
BABYLON	San Francisco
BANK	US State Department
BALLOON	Atom bomb
BAR	British Intelligence
CABARET	Office of the Co-ordinator of Inter-American Affairs (CIAA)
CAMP-2	Los Alamos
CARTHAGE	Washington DC
CLUB	US Department of Justice
COLONISTS	British
COLONY	Britain
COMBINE	Soviet Ministry of Foreign Trade
COMPETITOR	Local counter-intelligence agency
COMPETITION	Military intelligence
CORPORANT	Communist Party member
CORPORATION	Communist Party
COUNTRY	United States
COUNTRY HOUSE	US embassy in Moscow
COUNTRYSIDE	Mexico
DECREE	Lend-Lease
DEPOT	War Production Board
DIREKTOR	Chief of GRU
ENORMOZ	Atomic bomb development programme

Cryptonyms	Identity
EUREKA	Young Communist League
FACTORY	Amtorg
FELLOWCOUNTRYMAN	Communist Party member
FRATERNAL	Communist Party
FUNICULAR	Atomic bomb
GASTRONOMIA	France
GREENS	Hostile or local counter-intelligence agency
GYMNAST	Young Communist League member
HUT	Office of Strategic Services (OSS)
ISLAND	Great Britain
ISLANDERS	British
KhATA	Federal Bureau of Investigation
KhUTOR	Economic Administration
LAND	Canada
LEAGUE	US government
LESOVIA	Canada
LOT Department	Unidentified
MUSIC	Radio
NAVAL NEIGHBOURS	Naval GRU
NEIGHBOUR	NKVD *rezident*
NEIGHBOURS	GRU
NEWS	Novosti Press Agency
NOOK	Foreign Ministry, Australia
OFFICE	*Rezidentura*
PERIPHERY	Countryside
PLANT	Soviet consulate-general in New York
POLECATS	Trotskyites
POOL	British Embassy in Washington DC
PRESERVE	Argonne Radiation Laboratory, Chicago

Glossary of Soviet Cryptonyms

Cryptonyms	Identity
PROBATIONERS	Agents
PROVINCES	Latin America
RADIO STATION	Office of War Information
RATS	Jews
RIO	Buenos Aires
ROOF	Legal cover
SALAD	US Board of Economic Welfare
SASHA	United States
SAUSAGE-DEALERS	Germans
SHELTER	United Nations Relief and Rehabilitation Administration (UNRRA)
SIDON	London
SMYRNA	Moscow
STORE	Soviet Government Purchasing Commission
TOWNSMEN	Americans
TRUST	Soviet embassy
TYRE	New York
WAREHOUSE	US Board of Economic Warfare
X GROUP	GRU Network in London

Notes

CHAPTER I: Breakthrough!

1. For further details of Captain Kowalewski's mission, see David Kahns', *The Codebreakers* (1966), pp. 357, 579.
2. After the war the consulate building was rebuilt and opened as a hotel.
3. Rex Bosley, Stockholm, November 1946, PRO file FO 511/121
4. Ibid.
5. The Schloss Burgscheidungen was surrendered to the Russians by the American occupiers in April 1945. Later it was used as an educational establishment by the East German Communist Party, and in 1990 was sold into private hands. The four surviving daughters of the original owner, Graf Adelberg von der Schulenburg, who was divorced in 1927 and died in 1951, now live in Germany.
6. For details on Onodera's purchases, see his widow's account, *At the North Sea* (in Japanese and German).

CHAPTER II: Compromised

1. Yuri Modin's version of these events, in *My Five Cambridge Friends* (1995), is wholly unreliable. For example, SIS was not informed of VENONA by William Weisband; Philby met Meredith Gardner only once; Maclean was in Washington DC for four-and-a-half years, not three, and returned to London only three times during that period.
2. When Rudolf Abel was arrested he told his lawyer James Donovan that the only person likely to be implicated was a young pseudo-intellectual, Alan Winston, whom he had met when Winston was at graduate school. Details of Winston's military service were found in his possession. See James B. Donovan, *Strangers on a Bridge* (1964), p. 81. When Louise Bernikow wrote about the case in *Abel* (1970), she gave Winston the pseudonym 'Paul Owen', p. 19. According to Abel's version, the two men had met by chance in Central Park; presumably this was an attempt to protect Lona Cohen who had probably introduced them since she knew them both. When questioned by the FBI, Alan Winston denied Abel (whom he had known as an Englishman named 'Martin Collins') had tried to recruit him.
3. For a detailed account of Port Radium, see 'Nuclear Winter' by Stuart Wavell in the *Sunday Times* magazine, 26 April 1998.

CHAPTER III: The GRU's London Network

1. For May's cross examination, see Royal Commission Report (Canada, 1946), p. 395.
2. Colonel Zabotin's fate is unknown. He fled Canada for New York in December 1945, was seen to board the SS *Alexander Suvorov*, and reportedly either died aboard or soon after his arrival in Russia.
3. For slightly differing accounts of Dr

369

May's confession, see Iain Adamson, *The Great Detective* (1966), and Leonard Burt, *Commander Burt of Scotland Yard* (1959).
4. Ivor Montagu, *The Youngest Son* (1970).
5. According to Peter Wright (*Spycatcher* [1987] p. 375) HASP showed that Ursula Kuczynsky 'was already running a string of agents' in 1941. In fact the only relevant VENONA, dated 31 July 1941, refers only to her husband.

CHAPTER IV: The Canberra VENONA

1. Zaitsev was discovered to have been identified in Japanese wartime records as the GRU's principal contact in Tokyo for the Soviet spy Richard Sorge. Zaitsev had held the post of Second Secretary at the embassy until his hasty withdrawal in 1941, following Sorge's arrest.
2. According to Ian Milner's declassified Ministry of Interior file in Prague, mentioned by Phillip Deery in 'Cold War Victim or Rhodes Scholar Spy?' (*Overland*, no. 147, Winter 1997), the tip was received from 'our agent in the American counter-intelligence agency'. The file dated 29 November 1960 reveals that Milner reported on his university students throughout the 1950s.

CHAPTER V: The Cambridge Ring

1. See Peter Wright, *Spycatcher*, p. 183. Wright refers to 'David and Rosa' but in the VENONA text it is 'Jack and Rosa'.

CHAPTER VI: Operation ENORMOZ

1. Sergei Kurnakov (BECK) returned to Moscow after the Second World War and died in July 1949.
2. Aleksandr Fomin was identified as Aleksandr Feklisov, a senior KGB officer who was to be appointed *rezident* in Washington DC, and played a key role in the 1962 Cuban missile crisis.
3. The misinterpretation of PERS as PERCY has created a myth. For example, Philip Knightley, in his autobiography *The Hack's Progress* (1997), refers to PERCY, whereas the name does not appear in any VENONA text.

CHAPTER VII: The Émigrés

1. Victor Kravchenko, *I Chose Freedom* (1947).
2. David Dallin, *Soviet Espionage* (1955).

CHAPTER VIII: British Security Coordination

1. See William Stephenson *British Security Co-ordination 1941–45* (1998).

Bibliography

Adamson, Iain, *The Great Detective* (Frederick Muller, 1966)
Albright, Joseph, and Kunstel, Marcia, *Bombshell* (Random House, 1997)
Ball, Desmond and Horner, David, *Breaking the Codes* (Allen & Unwin, 1998)
Bamford, James, *The Puzzle Palace* (Houghton, Mifflin, 1982)
Belfrage, Cedric, *The Frightened Giant* (Secker and Warburg, 1957)
Belfrage, Cedric, *Something to Guard* (Columbia University Press, 1978)
Belfrage, Cedric, *The American Inquisition* (Bobbs-Merrill, 1973)
Benson, Robert Louis and Warner, Michael, *Venona: Soviet Espionage and the American Response 1939–1957* (National Security Agency, 1996)
Bentley, Elizabeth, *Out of Bondage* (Devin-Adair, 1951)
Bernikow, Louise, *Abel* (Trident, 1970)
Bly, Herman O., *Communism: The Cold War and the FBI Connection* (Huntingdon House, 1998)
Bohm, David, *Infinite Potential*
Burt, Leonard, *Commander Burt of Scotland Yard* (Heinemann, 1959)
Carpozi, George, *Red Spies in Washington* (Trident Press, 1965)
Clark, Ronald, *J.B.S.* (Quality Books, 1968)
Clubb, Edmund O., *The Witness and I* (Columbia University Press, 1974)
Dallin, David, *Soviet Espionage* (Yale University Press, 1955)
Donovan, James B., *Strangers on a Bridge* (Atheneum, 1964)
Foote, Alexander, *Handbook for Spies* (Museum Press, 1964)
Gamow, George, *My World Line* (Viking, 1970)
Haldane, Charlotte, *Truth Will Out* (Vanguard Press, 1950)
Haldane, J. B. S., *The Inequality of Man*
Heiskanen, Raimo, *Stella Polaris* (Keururu, Helsinki, 1994)
Huss, Pierre J. and Carpozi, George, *Red Spies in the UN* (Coward-McCann, 1965)
Jordan, George Racey, *From Major Jordan's Diaries* (Harcourt Brace & Company, 1952)
Kahn, David, *The Codebreakers* (Weidenfeld & Nicolson, 1966)
Kalugin, Greg, *The First Directorate* (St Martin's Press, 1994)
Kirschner, Don S., *Cold War Exile* (University of Missouri Press, 1995)
Klehr, Harvey, *The Secret World of American Communism* (Yale University Press, 1995)
Klehr, Harvey and Radosh, Ronald, *The Amerasia Spy Case* (University of North Carolina Press, 1996)

Knightley, Philip, *The Hack's Progress* (Jonathan Cape, 1997)
Kravchenko, Viktor, *I Chose Freedom* (Robert Hale, 1947)
Kravchenko, *I Chose Justice* (Scribner's, 1950)
Kuczynski, Ruth, *Sonia's Report* (Chatto & Windus, 1991)
Lamphere, Robert, *The CIA–KGB War* (Random House, 1986)
Martin, David C., *Wilderness of Mirrors* (Harper & Row, 1980)
Modin, Yuri, *My Five Cambridge Friends* (Hodder Headline, 1995)
Montagu, Ivor, *The Youngest Son* (Lawrence & Wishart, 1970)
Moorehead, Alan, *The Traitors* (Harper & Row, 1952)
Morros, Boris, *My Ten Years as a Counterspy* (Werner Laurie, 1959)
Moynihan, Daniel Patrick, *Secrecy* (Yale University Press, 1998)
Pale, Erkii, *Totuus Stella Polariksesta* (Ahtokari, Helsinki, 1994)
Pale, Erkii, *Suomen Radiotiedustelu 1927–1944* (Hakapaino, Oy, 1998)
Peake, Hayden, *OSS and the Venona Decrypts* (Intelligence & National Security, Vol. 12, No. 3)
Peat, David F., *Infinite Potential* (Helix Books, 1996)
Peierls, Rudolf, *Bird of Passage* (Princeton University Press, 1985)
Philby, Kim, *My Silent War* (MacGibbon & Kee, 1968)
Radosh, Ronald and Milton, Joyce, *The Rosenberg File* (Holt, Rinehart & Winston, 1983)
Rees, David, *Harry Dexter White* (Coward, McCann & Geoghegan, 1973)
Report of the Royal Commission (Canada, 1946)
Report of the Royal Commission (Australia, 1956)
Smyth, Henry D., *Atomic Energy for Military Purposes* (Princeton University Press, 1945)
Stephenson, William, *British Security Coordination 1941–45* (St Ermin's Press, 1998)
Stone, I. F., *The Hidden History of the Korean War 1950–51* (Little, Brown, 1952)
Stone, I. F., *The War Years, 1939–45* (Little, Brown, 1988)
Sudoplatov, Pavel, *Special Tasks* (Little, Brown & Company, 1994)
Weinstein, Allen and Vassiliev, Alexander, *The Haunted Wood* (Random House, 1998)
Whitaker, Paul and Kruh, Louis, *From Bletchley Park to Berchtesgaden* (Cryptologia, Vol. XI, No. 3)
Wright, Peter, *Spycatcher* (Viking Penguin, 1987)

Index

Abt, John (AMT) 229, 317
Abwehr 66
Adamic, Louis 225
Adams, Arthur A. 176–8
Adams, Josephine Truslow 281
Adler, Solomon 229
AFSA (Armed Forces Security Agency) 34
aircraft construction 321
Akhmedov, Colonel Ismail 98, 145, 176–7
Akhmerov, Iskhak (ALBERT) 121, 211, 277, 309, 312; appearance and character 228; and Bentley 228–9, 230; and Silvermaster group 297, 304–7, 308, 314–15; and White 298
Albam, Jacob 214
Aleksandrov, Aleksandr M. 97–8
Alexander, Hugh 29
Alexeef, Ludmilla N. (WASP) 202
Amerasia case 282–4, 326
American Army Cipher Bureau (MI-8) 1
Amtorg (FACTORY) 11
Angelov, Lieutenant Pavel N. 72, 73
Angleton, James 35, 335–6
Antonov, Viktor 117
Appel, Sam 210
Apreysan, Aleksandra xvi
Apresyan, Stepan (MAY) xvi, 36, 172–3, 230–1, 302, 310–11; appointment as *rezident* in San Francisco 246; change in codenames telegram 171–2; and Coplon 239–40, 241; and Cot 91–2; and Fuchs 148, 149; and Kravchenko 200, 204–5, 205–6; and Lukianov 48–9; and Maclean 132; and Morros 211–12; report sent on Allied plan for invasion of France's Mediterranean coast 122–4; reports and telegrams sent to Moscow 19, 20, 124–7, 157, 195–6, 201–3, 255–6; and Rosenberg ring 157–8, 159, 160, 161–2, 165–6, 167; and Silvermaster 271–2, 300, 302–4; and Wovschin 237–8, 238–9; and York 43
Aptekar, Nikolai V. 53
Armed Forces Security Agency (AFSA) 34

Army Air Forces (US) personnel 291–2, 292–3
army, British; organizational structure 70
Arnot, Robin Page 62
ARTHUR (unidentified spy) 266–7
ASIO (Australian Security and Intelligence Organization) 35, 102; adoption of aggressive counter-intelligence approach 113; attempt at finding out identities of codenames 112–13; creation 98, 99; and defection of Petrov 116; interview of Burnie 111–12; and Throssell 109
Association of Scientific Workers of Australia 112
atomic weapons *see* Manhattan Project
Atomic Weapons Research Establishment 139
Australia (Canberra VENONA) 27, 29, 95–120; and ASIO *see* ASIO; and Clayton network 101–3, 107–10; composition of *rezidentura* 117; and Curtis memorandum 96–7, 99, 103; naivety over espionage matters 97–8; organization of Security Service 99–101; recruitment of Milner and Hill by Makarov 104–5; requirement of organization to counter Soviet espionage 95–6, 98; turmoil within Soviet colony in Canberra 114–15
Australian Security and Intelligence Organization *see* ASIO

Babin, Tomo 93
Bailey, Colonel S.W. 288
Baldwin 294–5
Balkans 272
Baltenko, Colonel 26
Baltics 311
Bamford, James 336
Barkovsky, Vladimir B. 144
Barmine, Alexander 207–8
Barr, Joel (METER, formerly SCOUT) 160, 161, 168–9, 171, 173, 191
Batcheller, Hiland 319
Batt, William 318

373

VENONA

BCRA (Bureau Centrale de Renseignement et d'Action) 91
Belfrage, Cedric (UCN/9) 217, 218, 219–20, 221–2
Beneš, Eduard (19) 122
Bentley, Elizabeth (CLEVER GIRL, later MYRNA) xvi, 223–35, 289; and Akhmerov 228–9, 230; background 224; ; and Belfrage 221–2; and Brothman 154, 155; and Browder 227, 228, 229, 230 ; codename in VENONA 226–7; conflict with New York *rezidentura* 264; defection 223, 225, 226, 264; disaffection with NKVD 225, 226; and Glasser 325; and Golos 223, 224–5; and Halperin 252, 253–4, 286, 231, 232; and Helen Tenney 275–6; information provided to FBI 226; and Joseph 254–5; and Katz 164; and Kheiffets 185; and Lee 252, 270–1; and Mary Price 230, 231; memoirs *Out of Bondage* 225, 321, 325; and Mildrid Price 325–6; and Mins 277–8; and Perlo group 317, 325; personal vilification against after allegations 235; and Rhodes 280; and Silvermaster group 230, 235, 289, 290–1, 295, 296; testimony 170, 307; VENONA texts mentioning 227–8, 229–30, 231–2, 232–4; and White 299, 315
Berdecio, Marion Davis 239, 241
BERG (unidentified spy) 315
Beria, Lavrenti (PETROV) 52, 116, 200, 201
Bernstein, Joseph M. (MARQUIS) 245, 279, 281–2, 283, 326
Bethe, Hans 21, 194
Beurton, Len (JOHN) 54, 57–8, 86
Beurton, Ursula *see* Kuczynsky, Ursula
Bialoguski, Dr Michael 116
Bicher, Colonel 30
Bigelow, Emerson 274
Bisson, Thomas A. (ARTHUR) 279, 282
Black, Thomas L. (BLACK, later PETER) 164, 172, 173, 179–80
Bloomfield, Samuel 249
Blunt, Anthony (JOHNSON) 37–8, 94, 136, 137, 138, 139, 140
Bly, Herman O. 192
Bodsworth, Wilfred 28, 134–5
Bohm, David 182, 183
Bohr, Niels 21, 184
Bonde, Count Carl 8
Bosley, Rex 8–9
Bowen, Ralph (ALAN) 247
Boyer, Professor 179
Branigan, William 192
Bransten, Louise 184–5

Breit, Gregori 179, 181
BRIDE 24, 29, 34, 37–8, 134, 336
British Security Coordination *see* BSC
Bross, Major Alarich 10
Brotherus, Heikki 7
Brothman, Abraham (CONSTRUCTOR, later EXPERT) 154–5, 172
Browder, Earl (HELMSMAN) 21, 22, 196, 220, 283, 308; and Adams 281; and Belfrage 222; and Bentley 227, 228, 229, 230; imprisonment for forgery 223–4
BSC (British Security Coordination) 216–22; and Belfrage 221–2; creation 216; liaison with FBI 216; and ONA 220; tasks 216
Buckley, Edward J. 226
Budenz, Louis 225
Buenos Aires (RIO) 259–60
Bundy, William 30, 31
Burd, Michael J. (BASS) 162
Bureau Centrale de Renseignement et d'Action (BCRA) 91
Burgess, Guy (HICKS) 135, 137, 139, 140
Burgscheidungen 30–3
Burhop, Eric 106–7
Burnie, Frances (SISTER) 109–12, 116
'Buro Cellarius' 10
Burster, Norman 326

Cable 906, 1, 2, 4, 10
Cairncross, John 37
Cambridge Ring 121–40; *see also* Blunt, Anthony; Burgess, Guy; Cairncross, John; Maclean, Donald; Philby, Kim
Campaigne, Howard 32
Campbell, Lucille 16, 17
Canada (LAND, also LESOVIA) 136
Canberra (VENONA) *see* Australia
Carr, Sam 73
Castillo 259
CAZAB 35
Chabanov, Konstantin 24
Chadwick, Sir James 74
Chalet, Marcel 89
Chambers, Whittaker xvi, 234, 299, 315, 317
Chapin, John H. 177, 178
Cherny, Ivan 66
Chevalier, Haakon 186–7
Chew, Dr Samuel P. 30, 252–3
Chiang Kai-Chek 261, 279, 296
Chichayev, Ivan A. 66, 67
Chifley, Ben 98, 99
Chilton, Brigadier Frederick 98
China 261, 279, 296
Christiansen, Wilbur N. (MASTERCRAFTSMAN) 105

374

Index

Churchill, Winston (BOAR) 121, 123, 124, 125, 127, 217, 255, 302
CIA (Central Intelligence Agency) 34–5
CIAA (Coordinator of Inter-American Affairs) (CABARET) 225
Clark, David 60–1
Clark Kerr, Sir Archie 127, 128, 129, 131
Clark, Ronald 83
Clarke, Colonel Carter W. 11, 24
Clayton, Walter (Wally) S. (CLAUDE) 96, 97, 101–3, 107–10, 116, 120
Clegg, Hugh 153
Cockburn, Claud 104
Coe, Virginius Frank (PEAK) 290, 293
Cohen, Lona (LESLEY) 146, 163–4, 189, 191, 194
Cohen, Morris (VOLUNTEER) 42, 163, 164, 191, 194
Collins, Harold H. 316
Colville, Sir Jock 59
Commonwealth Investigation Branch 95, 99
Communist Party of Australia *see* CPA
Compton, Professor Arthur 21, 141
Coplon, Judith (SIMA) 236–47, 316; arrest and trial 245–6; background 245; handling of 237, 241–2, 244; imprisonment and overturning of conviction 246; in Justice Department 241; relations with Wovschin 236, 238–9; surveillance and discovery of as spy by FBI 244–5; tipping off of Moscow on solving of codes 244; work for Soviets 240
Corderman, General 11
Cot, Madame 92
Cot, Pierre (DAEDALUS) 59, 90–2
Coudert, Captain Ferdinand 11–12
CPA (Communist Party of Australia) 101, 103
CPUSA; infiltration of by FBI 197
Cripps, Sir Stafford 56
Cunningham 202
Currie, Lauchlin B. (PAGE) 225, 290, 293, 294–5, 299, 301, 313, 328
Curtis memorandum 96–7, 99, 103
Curtiss, Dr John Sheldon 249

Dallet, Joseph 182
Dallin, David J. 200, 205, 206
Dallin, Lydia *see* Estrina, Lydia
Dalziel, Allan 109, 111, 114
DAN (unidentified spy) 139–40
Daugs, Willi 323, 324
Davies, John P. 283, 284
Davis, Robert R. 183
DAVIS (unidentified spy) 333–4
de Gaulle, General (RAS) 88, 91, 260

de Paul, Margarita Neklen Hansberger (MARGO) 20
Deane, General John 33
Deprez, Joseph 91
Deriabin, Piotr 226
Despres, Emile 269
Dewavrin, André 91
Dewey, Thomas (KULAK) 20
Dikiy, Boris 53
'Document J' 117
Dodd, Martha *see* Stern, Martha
Dolgov 47
Donovan, General William (RADIO ANNOUNCER) 33, 258, 288
Doyle, Bernadette 183
Driberg, Tom 104
Drozdoff, Leo M. 288
Dubois, Josiah Ellis 321, 322
Duggan, Laurance (PRINCE, formerly SHERWOOD) xvi, 172
Dunning, John 243
Dunning, Mary Jo 16–17
Duval, Colonel 260
Dwight, E.V. 323, 324
Dwyer, Peter 46, 134

Eastman, Max 205
Eden, Anthony 128–9
Egorichev, Captain A.I. 331
Ehrensvard, Major-General C.A. 6, 8
Elitcher, Max 165–6
Elliott, Nicholas 138
Elmquist, Lieutenant Karl 16
Eltenton, Dolly 187
Eltenton, George C. 187
Emery, Edith 270
ENORMOZ Operation 22, 50, 141–97, 248; disclosing of information by Hall 142–4, 145–7; and Fuchs 85, 147–53, 191; and Greenglass 155–7; GRU and NKVD cooperation 196; and Kvasnikov 'XY' *rezidentura* 144–5; line of communications with Los Alamos 189–90; and Nunn May 74–5, 141, 191; and Oppenheimer 181–9; penetration of university centres of atomic research 141–2; recruitment from CPUSA members 194–6, 197; Rosenberg's network 157–69; scientist list telegram 20–2, 141, 142; unresolved identities of spies 170–5, 190–1, 197; *see also* Manhattan Project
Enrich, Otto 323
Epstein, Jacob (HARRY) 20
ERIE (unidentified spy) 171, 172, 175, 180, 191
ERNEST *see* HURON
Estrina, Lydia (Dallin) 200, 203, 204, 205

Evans, Geoffrey 30, 31
Evatt, Dr 117-18
Ewart, William 192

Fairbank, Professor John K. 288
Fajans, Irving 288
FBI (Federal Bureau of Investigation) (KHATA) 134; compilation of Soviet codenames 23-4; illicit entries against Eastern bloc diplomatic premises 24-5; infiltration of CPUSA 197; liaison with BSC 216; and Manhattan Project 192-4, 197; and Markov letter 45-6; monitoring of Soviet activities 94; recruitment of double agents 46-7; and registration 332
Fedosimov, Pavel I. (STEPAN) 36, 132, 232-3, 296-7
Fedotov, Petr V. 108
Feinstein, Genevieve 14, 17
Feklisov, Aleksandr S. (CALISTRATUS) 144, 160-1
Felson, Milton 266
Fermi, Enrico 181, 185, 186, 190
Fierlinger, Captain Jan (OFFICER) 219, 267-8
Finland 262, 311, 323, 324; collaboration with Sweden 5-6; cooperation with Japanese in work on Soviet ciphers 3-4; and Operation STELLA POLARIS 5-10
Fischer, Louis 205
Fitin, General Pavel M. (VIKTOR) 19, 33, 104
Fitzgerald, Edward J. (TED) 230, 273
Flato, Charles 229, 276
Floud, Bernard 104
Folkoff, Isaac 184
Fomichev, Sergei 50
Foote, Allan 58, 78, 86-7
Foster, Jane see Zlatovski, Jane
FRA (Swedish National Defence Radio Institute) 5-6, 7, 120
France (GASTRONOMIA) 260
Franey, Joseph J. 47, 168
Franey, Leona O. (ERIC, formerly ZERO) 47, 168, 172
Frank, Karl 328
Franken, Charlotte 78-9
Friedman, William 2
Fuchs, Klaus (CHARLES, formerly REST) 82, 84, 134, 147-53, 170-1, 172, 188, 194; arrest and interrogation 29, 46, 58, 187; confession 153; and Haldane 84; imprisonment xvi; investigation of 152-3; link with Halperin 151-2; and Manhattan Project 85, 147-53, 191; and Peierls 174; and Ursula Kuczynski 54, 58-9, 86, 87-8;

value of information given to Moscow 151

G-2 branch 22
Gamow, George 188-9
GARD (unidentified spy) 266-7
Gardner, Meredith 11, 13-14, 18-19, 27, 29, 39, 40, 45; discovery of atomic scientist list 20-1, 141; first message read completely 303; identification of codenames for Rosenbergs 169; linguistic background 22-3
Gavriluk, Vladimir V. (MOK) 285
Gayle, Lt Col William 284
GCHQ (Government Communications Headquarters) 2, 29, 37, 68, 138-9, 330
Georges, General 260
Germany 314; British and Allied policy on post-war structure 124-7, 302; claim of involvement of intelligence service in; Operation (STELLA POLARIS) 9-10; Nazi banking transactions in Switzerland 322-3; reparations issue 310
Gibson, Harold 66
Glading, Percy 76
Glasser, Harold (ROUBLE) 229, 308, 309, 310, 321-5
Gluck, Max 111
Gody, Juan Gaytan (JUAN) 20
Goff, Irving 288
Gold, Bela (ZHOLUD) 305, 307, 315
Gold, Harry (GOOSE, later ARNO) 153-5, 160, 164, 170, 172, 189, 194; and Brothman 154-5; confession 153, 155; and Fuchs 153, 171; and Greenglass 155; release from prison 191
Gold, Sonia (née Steinman) (ZHENYA) 307, 308, 309, 315
Goldman, Irving 287-8
Goldsmith, Hyman 181
Golos, Jacob (SOUND) 185, 219-20, 248; background and career 223; and Belfrage 222; and Bentley 223, 224-5; and Brothman 154; heart failure 225; network of agents 221, 225, 254; and Perlo 317
Gorsky, Anatoli see Gromov, Anatoli
Gould, Joseph 56-7
Gouzenko, Igor (CLARK) 15, 50, 98, 116, 118, 151, 178; contribution to VENONA programme 26-7; defection 11, 25, 26, 50; description of GRU cipher procedures 25-6; effect of defection on Moscow 25, 50, 135-7, 138; and Nunn May 71, 72, 73, 141
Grabeel, Gene 11, 14, 18, 327

Index

Grabski, M. 133
Grafpen, Grigori B. 52
Greece 123
Green, Oliver C. 53–4
Greenberg, Michael 326
Greene, Graham 104
Greenglass, David (BUMBLEBEE, later CALIBRE) 155–7, 160, 164, 167, 170, 194, 330
Greenglass, Ruth (WASP) 155, 156–7, 160, 170
Greg, Nathan 295, 296
Gregg, Joseph 225
Grey, Nigel de 37
Griazanova, Iya 115
Grierson, Helen 60–1
Grigulevich, Joseph 189–90
Gromov, Anatoli (Gorsky) (VADIM) 36, 52, 122, 129–31, 214, 226, 234–5, 320–1
Gromyko, Andrei 33
GRU (Soviet Military Intelligence Service) (NEIGHBOURS) 11, 52, 196; cipher operations 25–6; effect of Gouzenko's defection 25; London network (X-GROUP) 52–94
    and Cot 90–2; Green's network 53–4; and Haldane see Haldane, Professor J.B.S.; and Labarthe 88–90; and Nunn May 71–5; officers 53; organization 81; ring centred on Springhall 60–1; Ursula Kuczynsky's network 54–9; Weiss's network 59–60; X-GROUP 61–71, 75, 81; operation of illegals 331–5; and OSS 277
Gubitchev, Valentin 245, 246

Haas, Loren G. 47, 168
Haldane, Charlotte 78–9, 82–3, 84–5
Haldane, Lord 77
Haldane, Professor J.B.S. (INTELLIGENSIA) 69, 71–5, 82; abilities 77; air-raid precautions expert 80; background 76–8; commitment to Communist Party 76, 78, 83; connection with Montagu 76, 79–80; contribution to war effort projects 85–6; death 86; and Fuchs 84–5; and Kahle 85; post-war activities 86; sources of 75–6; and Spanish Civil War 78; submarine work 80–1, 85; uncertainty about extent of; treachery 84
Halifax, Lord 127, 129–30, 132
Hall, Dr Theodore (YOUNG) 22, 142–4, 145–7, 160, 163, 197
Hall, Thomas 249
Hallamaa, Colonel Reino 5, 6, 8, 34

Hallock, Lieutenant Richard 14, 15, 16
Halperin, Maurice (HARE) 252–4, 255, 265, 271; access to OSS confidential reports and cables 253, 256, 260–2; background 252–3; and Bentley 231, 232, 252, 253–4, 286; denial of espionage 287; and Fuchs 151–2; information provided by 258–60, 262–3; and OSS security inquiry 257–8; post-war career 286–7
Halpern, Aleksandr 218–19
Harriman, Averell (CAPITALIST) 133, 134
Harris, Jack S. 288
Harrison, Richard 182
Hartikainen, Lieutenant Pentti 7, 8
Harvey, Bill 34, 336
HASP material 114, 120
Hausamann, Major Hans 65
HAVRE 219
Hawkins, David 197
Hayashi, Colonel 2
Hayden, Stuart 278
Hayes, Colonel 22, 39, 40
Hayes, Mildrid 327
Hearn, Warren R. 192
Heilmann, Horst 4
Hein, Lieutenant (BAUER) 60
Heineman, Kristel and Robert 153
Heinrichs, General Erik 5, 6
Heisenberg, Werner 21
Hemblys-Scales, Robert 98
Henschke, Erich 56
Hill, James F. (TOURIST) 104, 105–6, 116
Hilton, John 80
Hirose, Major 2
Hiskey, Clarence F. 175–6, 177
Hiskey, Marcia (née Sand) 175–6
Hiss, Alger (ALES) xvi, 234–5, 325
Hitler, Adolf
    plot to assassinate 256–7, 262–3
Hoell, Lillian 288
Hogman, Captain 284–5
Hollis, Sir Roger 98, 104, 335
Hoover, Calvin 33
Hoover, J. Edgar 46, 192, 193, 194, 216, 286
Howse, Philip 27, 29
Hughes, Alfred T. (BEN) 100, 101, 113, 120
Hull, Cordell (HARRIER) 125
Hungary 271–2, 308–9
Hurley, Patrick J. 300
HURON (later ERNEST) 171, 172, 173, 175, 177, 179–80, 181, 188, 190–1
Hyde, Douglas 78

Ilyichov, General Leonid 52
Institute of Pacific Relations (IPR) 325, 326

IRIS 54, 55–6
Ivancic, Anton S. (CRUCIAN) 93, 218
Ivanov, Piotr 183, 184

JACK (unidentified spy) 140
Jacobson, Herman R. (S-1) 162
JADE 14, 17–18, 19–20, 22, 29
Jaffe, Philip 282, 283, 326
Japan 258, 299; cooperation with Finland in work on Soviet ciphers 3–4; decryption of diplomatic traffic 1–3
Jardine, Don 47, 48
jet engines, introduction of 320
Joseph, Bella 277–8
Joseph, Emma (IVY) 265
Joseph, J. Julius (CAUTIOUS) 252, 254–5, 265, 278
Joys, Alice 18

Kahle, Colonel Hans 84–5
Käkönen, Colonel Uljas 8
Kallman, Dr Heinz 59
Kalugin, General Oleg 330
Kamen, Dr Martin 184
Kamenev, Ivan (CHEMIST) 237
Kaplan, Irving 326
Karpckov, Nikolai (URAL) 237, 241–2
Kasparov, Grigori P. (GIFT) 36, 184
Katyn woods massacre (1939) 36, 46
Katz, Joseph (DOUGLAS, INFORMER, later X) 42, 164, 171, 179, 225–6
Katz, Otto 281
Keeney, Mary Jane 282, 283
Kenney, Philip C. 248, 282
Kessel 257
KGB 44, 45
Kharkovetz, Georgi 117
KHAZAR (unidentified spy) 269–70
Kheiffets, Grigori M. (CHARON) 36, 41–3, 46, 50, 184, 184–5, 187, 190
Khlopkova, Olga V. (JULIA) 228, 233, 246, 315
Kirby, Lieutenant Oliver 12, 32–3, 37
Kirilov, Viktor (SULLEN) 237
Kiselev, Evgeni D. (GRANDFATHER, also GRANDPAPA) 24–5, 256
Kislytsin, Filipp 117
Kistiakowski, Dr George 21, 156
Klarin, Pavel P. (LUKA) 19, 20, 41, 46, 91, 213, 255, 327–8; background 41; and BSC 218–19; and Halperin 255, 260, 261, 262; and OSS 266–7; withdrawal 50
KLARK (unidentified GRU case officer) 285
Klein, Caroline 224
KNICKEBEIN (night navigation system) 64–5, 76

KOLTSOV (unidentified) 297, 298, 312
Koral, Aleksandr 315–16
Koral, Helen (ART, formerly MIRANDA) 172
Korneyev, Mikhail 298–9
Kosanovic, Sava S. (KOLO) 93
Kossarev, Grigori 50
Kovalenok, Evgeni 115
Kovaliev, Nikolai 117
Kowalewski, Captain 3
Kozlov, Ivan M. 53
Krafsur, Samuel (IDE) 328, 329
Kramer, Charles (PLUMB) 229, 230, 273–4, 317, 325
Kravchenko, Victor (GNAT) 198–207; background and career 198–9; book written by 199, 203; death 207; defection 23, 50; evidence before House Committee on Un-American Activities 199; litigation against Paris magazine 199; monitoring of by NKVD 200–7
Kremer, Simon (ALEXANDER) 53, 58, 62, 69, 88–9, 152
Krivitsky, Walter 23, 98, 164, 204
Krotkova, Christina (OLA, later JEANNE) 172, 204, 206
Krotov, Boris (BOB) 136, 137, 138, 140
Kuczynsky, Jurgen 54, 56, 58, 84
Kuczynsky, Professor Robert 54
Kuczynsky, Ursula (Beurton) (SONIA) 86–7; and Fuchs 54, 58–9, 86, 87–8; and Kahle 84; network of 54–9
Kullback, Colonel Solomon 16
Kurnakov, Sergei N. (BECK, formerly CAVALRYMAN) 21, 22, 142–3, 146, 171
Kutrzeba, Professor 133
Kuznetsov, Colonel Fedor F. 52
Kuznetsov, Pavel S. 215
Kvasnikov, Leonid R. (ANTON) 22, 46, 48, 244; and ENORMOZ Operation 143–5, 147, 155–6, 159, 163, 165, 169, 195, 196; establishment of New York; *rezidentura* 36
Kylmänoja, Lieutenant Tauno 8
Kyrre, Thoralf 10

La Guardia Airport 318, 319–20
Labarthe, André (JEROME) 59, 88–90
Labour Party (Australia) 117–18
Lambert, Rudolph C. 181, 182
Lamphere, Robert J. 23, 24, 37, 151, 152, 153, 244
Landau, Jacob 220, 221
Larsen, Emannuel S. 282, 326
Larsen, Jimmy 284
Lauchlin, Leo 244
Lautkari, Major Emil 7–8
Lawrence, Dr Ernest 21, 142, 147, 191

Index

LEAF (unidentified agent) 139, 140
Lebedev, Major Anatoli 53
Lecoutre, Alta (MARTHA) 59, 88, 89
Lee, Major Duncan (KOCH) 225, 231, 264, 326; background 232; and Bentley 252, 270–1; information passed on 251–2, 255–6, 257–8; post-war career 265
Lend-Lease (DECREE) 279
Leshinsky, Solomon 326
Lettres Français, Les 199
Levin, Don 204
Lewis, Frank 16
Lifanov, Ambassador 115
Linton, Freda 178
loans, US 310–11, 312
Lockwood, Rupert 106, 117
Lomanitz, Giovanni Rossi 182, 183
London (SIDON); GRU network see GRU; KGB apparatus in 52
Long, Leo 37
Lorimer, Professor 249
Los Alamos (CAMP-2) 21, 22, 44, 141, 189–90, 194
Lossowki, Vincent 288
Lowry, Helen (ELZA) 228, 233
Lubszynski, Hans 59
Luftwaffe 64
Lukianov, Sergei G. (AKIM) 46, 48–50
Lvovich, Boris (PALM) 113

Macartney, William 76
McCarthy, Joseph 326
McDonald, Katie 18, 22
Mackenzie, Sir Robert 46
Maclean, Donald (HOMER) 39, 46, 82, 139; defection xvi, 133, 135, 140; identification of as a spy 134–5; information sent to Moscow 122, 124–30, 132, 133–4
Maclean, Melinda (wife) 132
Magdoff, Henry S. (KANT) 229, 230, 273
magnetic mines 81
Makarov, Semen I. (EFIM) 95, 97; and Burnie 109–11; and Clayton 102–3; departure 114; information sent on Security Service in Canberra 99–101; and Throssell 107–8; unpopularity and criticism of by Moscow 104–5, 114–15
Malisoff, William M. (HENRY, later TALENT) 172
Malone, Joan 28
Manhattan Project 36; and FBI 192–4, 197; inter-allied relations 148; scientist list 20–2, 141, 142; secrecy of 191–2; sites 141–2; Soviet infiltration of 74–5, 142; see also ENORMOZ Operation
Mannerheim, Field Marshal Gustaf 4, 5, 6
Manning, Edward T. 177, 178

Marini, Ferruccio 224
Markov, Colonel (alias Mironov) 47, 50, 51
Markov letter 45–6, 49
Martin, David C. 336
Martineau, Paul V. 288
Martola, Anneli 8
Marzani, Carl (COLLEAGUE) 252
Massing, Herde xvi
MAX (unidentified) 285
Medvedeva, Nadezhda Ivanovna 204
Menaker, Robert Owen (CZECH) 164, 214
Menzies, Sir Robert 117
Menzies, Stewart 216
Meredith, Frederick 59
METEOR (unidentified) 281
Meyer, Marie 18
MI5 87, 88; and Haldane 77, 83–4, 86; and Nunn May 72, 73, 74, 75; protection of VENONA 83, 86; security lapses 94
Michael, Jerome 181
Mikhailov, Mikhail I. (MIM) 53
Mikhailov, Pavel P. 176, 178, 277, 279, 280–1, 284, 285–6
Mikolajczck, M. 133
Mikoyan 233
Miller, Floyd C. 164
Miller, Robert T. 225
Milner, Dr Ian 103–4, 104–5, 106, 116
Milsky, Mikhail 50
Milstein, General Solomon 50
Mins, Leonard E. (SMITH) 277–8, 279, 280, 284, 285
Minton, Bruce 185, 253
MIRAGE (unidentified spy) 270
Mironov, Colonel *see* Markov, Colonel
Mitchell, Graham 138–9
Mitynia, Francia *see* Patterson, Edna
Modin, Yuri 45
Molotov 128, 131, 133, 134
Montagu, Ewan 62
Montagu, Ivor (NOBILITY) 61–3, 76, 79–80, 82, 83
Moorehead, Alan 71, 87–8
Moravec, General Frantisek 65–7
Morgenthau, Henry (NABOB) 125, 126–7, 299, 309, 318, 321
Morkovin, Vladimir B. (AUTHOR) 162
Morrison, John A. 278
Morrison, Philip 194
Morros, Boris (FROST) 46, 108, 207, 211–12, 277; cancer 215; memoirs 214
and Zubilin 193, 208–9
Moseley, Philip E. (DROP) 247
Moseley, Professor John 249
Moskvichev, Fedor I. 53
Moss, Tom 29

379

Motinov, Colonel 72
Myakotina, Zoya Semenovna (LINA) 214

Napoli, Nichola 22
National Security Agency (was AFSA); see NSA
NATO (North Atlantic Treaty Organization) 97
Nearing Jr, John Scott (IVANOV) 249, 250, 270
Neff, Colonel Paul 30, 31, 32
Nelson, Irving C. (DEIGHTON) 285
Nelson, Steve 182, 183, 187, 192, 193
Neumann, John von 21
Night Interception Committee 64
night navigation system (KNICKEBEIN) 64–5, 76
Nixon, Richard 327
NKVD (Soviet Intelligence Service) (NEIGHBOUR) 11; change in cyper procedure 38; and CPUSA 196–7; deciphering traffic 29–30; effect of Gouzenko's defection 25; monitoring of Kravchenko 200–7; preoccupation with émigrés 198; suspension of activities in London 52–3
Northbury, Jeffrey, 28, 134
Nosov, Fedor A. (TECHNICIAN) 101, 103, 113–14
(NSA) (National Security Agency) 34, 35
Nunn May, Allan (ALEK) 71–5, 87, 197; background 71; contact and recruitment by (GRU) 72, 73–4; conviction and imprisonment 50, 73, 141; and Manhattan Project 74–5, 141, 191; MI5 surveillance of 75

Office of Strategic Services see OSS
Öhquist, Lieutenant-General Harald 7
Oldfield, Maurice 45
Olsen, Rose (PHLOX) 195, 196
ONA (Overseas News Agency) 220, 221
Onodera, Lieutenant-General Makoto 6, 34
OP-20-G 1, 2
OPPEN (unidentified agent) 280, 281
Oppenheimer, Dr J. Robert (BILL OF EXCHANGE) 181–9
Oppenheimer, Frank 181, 182
Oppenheimer, Kitty 181, 182
Orlemanskij 255, 256
Orlov, Alexander 163, 200
Orlov, Andrei R. 180
Orlov, Nikolai V. (OSIPOV) 266
(OSS) (Office of Strategic Services) (HUT) 33, 34, 231, 248–88; and *Amerasia* case 282–4, 326; awareness of Soviet penetration by Security Division of 270–1; disbanded 286; and GRU 277; investigation into Communist infiltration of 257–8; recruitment of Communists 288; and Silvermaster's network 269, 271–2; Soviet sources within 248, 251, 266–8, 269–70, 273–6, 281–2 *see also* Halperin, Maurice; Lee, Major Duncan; Mins, Leonard E. Zubilin's reports on 248–50, 250–1
OTPs (one-time pads) 12, 13, 14, 15, 22, 118, 119
Ovakimian, Gaik 23
Overseas News Agency see ONA

Paasonen, Colonel Aladar 5, 8, 34
Påhlson, Major Svente 8
Pakhomov, Ivan 114, 115, 117
Pale, Bror Erkki Sten 6, 7, 9
Palme Dutt, Rojani 106
Panfilov, Alexsandr P. 52
Paramonov, Professor Sergei J. (SCORPION) 112
Park, Willard 253, 254
Park, William Z. 225
Paterson, Geoffrey 46, 134
Patterson, Edna (Francia Mitynia) (AUSTRALIAN WOMAN, later SALLY) 331–2, 335
Paulio, Lieutenant-Captain Heikki 6
Pavlides, Mari 207
Pavlov, Vitali G. 50, 298–9
Peierls, Alfred 174
Peierls, Eugenia 174, 175
Peierls, Sir Rudolf 85, 174–5, 181, 189, 194
Perelman, Morris 180
Perl, William (GNOME, later YAKOV) 165, 167, 171
Perlo, Katherine 317
Perlo, Victor (RAIDER) 225, 229, 230, 273, 308; and Bentley 317, 325; information sent 318–21; network of 308, 317–26 *see also* Glasser, Harold; Kramer, Charles; Price, Mildred
PERS (unidentified spy) 173–4, 175
Petersén, Major Carl 5, 6
Petrov, Evdokia 114, 116, 118
Petrov, Vladimir (SEAMAN) 51, 115–16; defection 106, 109, 116–18, 135; falling out with Lifanov 115; information given on cipher; methodology 15, 118–19
Petsamo codebooks 3–4, 13, 30, 32, 33, 34
PHIL (unidentified spy) 284–5
Philby, Kim (STANLEY) 37–8, 134, 135, 136–7, 139; defection 139, 140; identification of as spy 138; and

Index

Sedlacek 68; and VENONA 44–6, 51, 336
Phillips, Cecil 14, 15, 16, 17, 27, 29, 37, 38, 327
Pinsky, Paul 178–9
Pinsly, William (CORK) 162
Plaitkais, Janis 117
Poland 311; Commission 129, 130–1, 133–4; future of 127–8, 255–6
Pollitt, Harry 83
Pontecorvo, Bruno 185, 190, 191
Poole, Dewitt 255, 256
Portland 333–4
Pravdin, Olga B. 92
Pravdin, Vladimir S. (SERGEI) 90, 92–3, 93–4, 219, 236, 246, 267; and Coplon 240; and Maclean 132; move to San Francisco 242; and Stone 328–9
Prenant, Professor Marcel 59
Pressman, Lee 316
Price, Mary Wolfe (ARENA, later DIR) 229, 230–1, 286, 325
Price, Mildred 325–6
Prichard, Katharine 107
Pugachev, Colonel Grigori P. 53
PURPLE cypher 2

QUANTUM (unidentified spy) 170–1, 189

RACHEL (unidentified spy) 266–7
Raev, Alexsandr (LIGHT) 160–1
Ramirez, General 259–60
Ramsey, Norman F. 194–5, 196
Rastvorov, Yuri 226
Rathman, George 183
Razin, Vasili F. 114
Redmont, Bernard 225
Reed, Sir Geoffrey 99
Rees, Goronwy 104
Reiss, Ignace 200–1
Remington, William W. 234
RESERVIST 69–70, 71
Reynolds, S. Wesley 24, 27
Rhodes, Peter C. 279, 280
Richards, Ron 111
Rickenbacker 263
Rockefeller, Nelson 225
Roessler, Rudolf (LUCY) 65, 68
Romania 129, 130, 261, 264, 275, 304
Roosevelt, Eleanor 328
Roosevelt, President (CAPTAIN) 18, 20, 121, 123, 124, 125, 127, 263, 299, 302
ROSA (unidentified agent) 140
Rose, Fred (FRED) 178
Rosen, Lieutenant Leo 2
Rosenberg, Allan 326
Rosenberg, Ethel xvi, 161, 169–70, 191, 335
Rosenberg, Julius (ANTENNA, later LIBERAL) 169–70, 194, 335; death by electric chair xvi, 191; identification of as a spy 169–70; network of 157–69
Rossby, Captain Ake 6
Rossi, Bruno 21
Rotblat, Joseph 75
Roth, Andrew 282, 284, 326
Rothschild, John 233
Rothschild, Victor and Tess 140
Routon, Kenneth R. 192
Rowlett, Colonel Frank B. 2, 16, 34
Royal Commission on Soviet Espionage (1946) 95
Rudd, I.G. 249

Sabatini, Amadeo (NICK) 42, 43, 164
Sacks, Alexander 243
Sadovnikov, Valentin 114, 115
SAM project 176
San Francisco (BABYLON) 333, 334; *rezidentura* in 36, 42
Saprygin, Aleksandr P. (BORIS) 25, 93–4, 136
Sarant, Al (HUGHES) 158, 160, 161, 168, 169, 191, 194
Sax, Saville S. (OLD) 143, 146
Schulenburg, Graf von der 31, 32
Schulze-Boysen, Harro and Libertas 4
Schuster, Bernard (ECHO) 143, 157, 196, 1954
Schwartz, Milton (MATVEJ) 285
Scott-Keenan, Helen (FIRTREE, also SPRUCE) 286, 297
Sedlacek, Karel (BARON) 65, 67–9
Sedov, Leon 200
Semyonov, Semyon (TWAIN) 19, 20, 46, 48, 144, 154, 162, 196, 316
Service, Jack 282, 283
Setaro, Ricardo (EXPRESS MESSENGER, later JEAN, KARL, RAY) 172
Shabanov, Konstantin A. (SHAH) 228, 256
Shalyapin, Mikhail A. (STOCK) 19, 20, 210, 214
Shapiro, Harold 245, 246
Shaplen, Joseph 201, 202, 203
Shedden, Sir Frederick 98
Sheehan, Olive 60
Sheppard, Charles B. (MASTERCRAFTSMAN) 162
Shevchenko, Andrei I. (ARSENIJ) 46–7, 162, 168
ships, demagnetizing of 81–2
Shishkin, Mikhail F. (ADAM) 137
Shumovsky, Stanislav 43
Shundenko, Stepan N. (NAZAR) 213, 214, 237, 238

381

Shvetsov, Major Boris (BRION) 53, 54, 67
Sidorovich, Ann 164, 165
Sidorovich, Michael (LENS) 160, 164–5
Signals Intelligence Service *see* SIS
Signals Security Agency *see* SSA
Sillitoe, Sir Percy 87, 95, 97, 98
Silverman, Abraham G. (AILERON) 290–3, 299, 305
Silvermaster, Helen (DORA) 225, 289, 298, 300, 305, 306
Silvermaster, Nathan Gregory (ROBERT, formerly PAL) 225, 228; access to OSS secrets 271–2; background and career 289; and Bentley 230, 235; denial of espionage 295; escapes prosecution 316; FBI investigation of 294–5, 298; information sent on OSS 308–9; penetration of US Treasury 309–10; productivity and information sent 301–2, 303–4, 314; plan to buy farm with Ullman 304, 306–7
Silvermaster network 227, 245, 269, 289–316; and Akhmerov 297, 304–7, 308, 314–15; and Bentley 289, 290–1, 295, 296; and the Golds 307, 308, 309; relations with *rezidentura* 297–8, 299–300, 300–1, 304–7, 307–8; scope of 289–90; sources within US Treasury 315; *see also* Coe, Virginius Frank; Currie, Lauchlin B.; Silverman, Abraham G.; Ullman, William; White, Harry Dexter
SIMA *see* Coplon, Judith
SIS (Signals Intelligence Service) 1–2, 45
Skardon, Jim 87, 88, 106, 153
Sklyarov, Colonel Ivan 52, 53, 62, 63–4, 69–70, 152
SKRIB (unidentified agent) 211
Skryagin, Nikolai A. 202
SMART (unidentified spy) 171
Smith, Ben 147, 148
Smith, Captain William B.S. 12
Smodlaka 273
Smyrna 275
Smyth, Professor Henry D. 180
Sobell, Morton (possibly RELAY, later SERB) 161–3, 166
Soble, Dr Robert A. (ROMAN) 210, 213
Soble, Jack (ABRAM, later CZECH) 207, 209–11, 213–14; arrest 214; background 209–10; committing of suicide 215; and Zlatovskis 209, 211, 276, 277
Soble, Myra 210, 277
SOE (Special Operations Executive) 216
Sokolov, Major 72
SOLID (unidentified spy) 170, 171
Sonderkommando Nord 10

Soustelle, Jacques 59
Sovio, Colonel Jussi 6
Spain 261–2, 275
Springhall, Douglas 60–1, 76
SSA (Signals Security Agency); deciphering of Soviet intercepts 10–17
Stalin 3, 255–6
STANLEY (unidentified GRU source) 60
Starr, Joshua 249
Staub, Hans 21
Steinberg, Isadore 280
STELLA POLARIS Operation 5–10
Stephenson, Sir William 216, 217, 218
Stern, Alfred K. (LOUIS) 209, 211, 212, 215, 328
Stern, Martha (née Dodd) 209, 215, 276
Stettinius, Edward 33
Stevens, Edmund W. 270
Stewen, Colonel 6
Stilwell, General 279, 296
Stimson, Henry L. 1
Stone, Isadore F. (PANCAKE) 328–30
Strang, Sir William 126
Strassman, Fritz 21
Stupenkov, Aleksei A. 201, 202, 203
Subercaseaux, Christian Cananova (KARLOS) 20
submarines; deployment of sonar systems to detect 81; Haldane's work on 80–1, 85
Sudoplatov, General Pavel 46, 66, 163, 185, 186, 188, 189, 190
Swartz, Captain Pehr 8
Sweden; collaboration with Finland in Operation STELLA POLARIS 5–10
Swedish National Defence Radio Institute *see* FRA
Swift, Carlton 34–5
Switzerland 267, 303; Nazi banking transactions 322–3
Szilard, Leo 186, 190

Tarasov, Lev (YURI) 46, 48
Target Identification Committee *see* TICOM
Tartakow, Jerome 194
Tatlock, Jean 181
Tattersell, Herbert W. (ARTISTE) 109
Taylor, A.J.P. 104
Taylor, Sir Geoffrey 21
Taylor, William H. (ACORN) 229, 307
Telberg, Ina 265–6
Teller, Edward 21
Tenney, Helen (MUSE) 274–6
THERAPUTIST 60
Thistlethwaite, Dick 134
Thorn, Commander Torgil 5, 6, 7
Throssell, Ric (FERRO) 107–9, 120
Thummel, Paul 66

Index

TICOM (Target Identification Committee) 30-2, 33
Tikander, Wilho 33
Tiltman, Brigadier John 14
Timofeev, Nikolai M. 53
TINA (unidentified spy) 174-5, 191
Tisler, Frantisek 25
Tito 216, 258, 269, 273
Tournelle, Guy de la 91
Toynbee, Phillip 104
Traugott, Lillian S. 288
Treuil, Raymond 91
Trotsky 200, 206
Truman 311
TUBE ALLOYS project 71

UCN/9 see Belfrage, Cedric
Ullman, William Ludwig (DONALD, also (PILOT and POLO) 171, 289, 290, 298, 313, 318; background 295-6; denial of espionage 293-4; plan to buy farm with Silvermaster 304, 306-7
Umansky, Konstantin A. (REDAKTOR) 220, 221
Uren, Captain Ormond 60
Urey, Dr Harold 21, 142, 176
US Treasury 309
Ustinov, Klop 75

Van Loon, Ernie 151, 153
Vasilevsky, Lev 48, 190, 241
Vavilov, Professor Nicolai 78
Veall, Norman 73-4
Veksler, Sara 201, 202, 203-4
VENONA; abandonment of 335; attraction of 330-1; breakthroughs in deciphering 18-19, 20-1, 30; and Burgscheidungen discoveries 30-3; and Cable 906, 1, 2, 4, 10; and CAZAB 35; and CIA 34-5; compiling of Soviet codenames by FBI 23-4; doubt about devoting resources to 36-7; duplication of OTP pages discovery 14-17, 18, 22, 118-19; early attempts at deciphering and breaking code 10-14; effect of involvement on cryptographers 327; and FBI 23-4; Gouzenko's contribution to 26-7; and Petsamo codebooks 3-4, 13, 30, 32, 33, 34; secrecy of 34, 336; served as proof of GRU activities in London 82; Soviet knowledge of some aspects of; secret code being broken 244; translation efforts 27-9; value as counter-espionage instrument 50
Vernon, Major Wilfred 59, 76
Vincent, John C. 283-4
Virkkunen, Lieutenant Veikko 6
Wagner, Buro 6

Wagoner, T.A. (Tom) 14
Wake, Robert F.B. 112-13
Walden, General Rudolf 7
Wallace, Henry (BOATSWAIN, also DEPUTY) 121, 277
Wanat, Frank 16
War Manpower Commission 318-19
War Production Board (DEPOT) 318, 319, 321
Warburg, Felix 220
Weinberg, Joseph W. 182-3
Weinberg, Muriel 183
Weisband, Mabel 43
Weisband, William (LINK) 38, 39-41, 119; background 39-40; compromising of VENONA 44-5, 51, 336; death 41; FBI's lead to and denial of espionage 41, 44, 45, 46
Weiss, Ernest D. 59
Wells, Kenneth 282
Werner 43
West, Audrey 28
Weyl, Nathaniel 287, 317
Wheeler, Donald (IZRA) 231, 232, 271, 273-4
White, Harry Dexter (JURIST, later RICHARD and LAWYER) xvi, 127, 171, 297, 309; and Bentley 299, 315; and Chambers testimony 234; denial of espionage 299, 315; heart attack 299, 315; information sent 310-12; and Silvermaster group 225, 295, 307, 309, 315; Soviet contact with 298-9; and US Treasury 293; value of to Soviets 299, 313-14
Whitney, Thomas P. 249
Whitrod, Ray 113
Wicher, Enos R. (KIN) 236-7, 239
Wicher, Maria (DASHA) 236, 239
Willsher, Kay 178
Witt, Nathan 316
Wittfogel, Carl August 266
Wolff, Milton 288
Wollner, Herbert 278
Wolston, Arnold 210
Woody, Mabel 40, 44
World Tourists 223-4, 232
Wovschin, Flora Don (ZORA) 236, 237-9, 242-4, 246-7
Wright, Peter 140, 336
WRITER 59-60
Wuchinich, George 288
Wuorinen, Professor John H. 249, 250

X GROUP 61-71, 75, 81

Yakovlev, Anatoli A. (Yatskov) (ALEKSAI) 93, 144, 149, 163; Bentley on 227; and

Yakovlev, Anatoli A. – *cont.*
  Gold 154–5; and PERS 175; rebuke from Moscow 145; and Rosenberg ring 158; tension between Kurnakov and 143
Yartsev, Boris N. (KIN) 117
Yartseva, Mrs 114
Yatskov, Anatoli A. *see* Yakovlev, Anatoli A.
Yerzin, Pavel D. 144
York, Jones Orin (NEEDLE) 42–3
Young, Courtney 87, 98–9, 112
Younger, Mark 113–14
Yugoslavia 217, 269, 273

Zablodowski, David 288
Zabotin, Colonel Nikolai 26, 51, 72, 73, 74, 178
Zaitsev, Colonel Viktor S. 95
Zarubina, Elizaveta *see* Zubilina, Elizaveta
Zarubin, Major-General Vasili M. *see* Zubilin, Vasili
Zborowski, Mark (KANT, formerly TULIP) 171, 200–1, 203, 204–5, 205–7
Zenzinov, Vladimir 205
Zindle, Harold 183
Zlatovski, George 211, 276, 277
Zlatovski, Jane (Foster) (SLANG) 209, 211, 274, 276–7
Zubilina, Elizaveta (VARDO) 35–6, 46, 185–6, 188–9, 193
Zubilin, Vasili (MAXIM) 35, 90, 91, 196, 210, 227; appearance 193; background 36; and Belfrage 217, 219–20; investigation into by Moscow 143; and Markov letter 47, 48, 49; and Nelson 183, 192; and Morros 193, 208–9; reports on OSS 248–50, 250–1
Zubko, Lieutenant Leonard M. 11